IP NETWORK DESIGN

IP Network Design

Cormac Long

Osborne/**McGraw-Hill**
New York   Chicago   San Francisco
Lisbon   London   Madrid   Mexico City
Milan   New Delhi   San Juan   Seoul   Singapore
Sydney   Toronto

Osborne/**McGraw-Hill**
2600 Tenth Street
Berkeley, California 94710
U.S.A.

To arrange bulk purchase discounts for sales promotions, premiums, or fund-raisers, please contact Osborne/**McGraw-Hill** at the above address. For information on translations or book distributors outside the U.S.A., please see the International Contact Information page immediately following the index of this book.

IP Network Design

1234567890 DOC DOC 01987654321

ISBN 0-07-212999-9

Publisher
Brandon A. Nordin

**Vice President &
Associate Publisher**
Scott Rogers

Acquisitions Editor
Francis Kelly

Acquisitions Coordinator
Alex Corona

Project Manager
Dave Nash

Technical Editors
Amit Shah, CCDA
Henry Benjamin, CCIE

Cover Design
William Chan

Production
MacAllister Publishing
Services, LLC

To Sarah, for her love and understanding.

CONTENTS

Preface   xvi

Acknowledgments   xviii

Chapter 1   Principles of Network Design   1

       Design Objectives   2

          Performance   2

          Redundancy and Resilience   4

          Accommodating Growth and Change   5

          Management and Manageability   6

          Security   7

          Disaster Recovery   7

          Cost   7

       Understanding the Networking Environment   8

          Network Applications   9

          The Cost of Downtime   10

       Achieving the Design Goals   10

       The Importance of Being Predictable   12

       Fundamental Design Principles   13

Chapter 2   Designing the Wide Area Network (WAN)   17

       Designing a Wide Area Network (WAN) Topology   18

       Flat Versus Hierarchical   18

       Flat WAN Topology   20

          Advantages of a Flat WAN Structure   23

       Limitations of a Flat Design   25

          Routing Protocol Limitations   25

       Conclusion   31

       Hierarchical   31

       PVC and Leased Line Aggregation   32

          Cost-effective Bandwidth Deployment   33

          Shorter Leased Line Distances   34

          Reduced Core Router Ports or Interfaces   35

          Less Routing Protocol Neighbors   35

          Route Summarization   35

       Broadcast Control in the WAN   37

       Disaster Recovery   37

       Issues with a Hierarchical Design   37

WAN Costs	37
Additional Router Hops	38
Conclusion	41
The Hierarchical Layers	41
The Tier-3 Layer	41
The Tier-2 Layer	44
The Backbone: Tier-1	47
WAN Design Parameters	52
Cost	52
Availability and Performance	53
Redundancy and Resilience	55
How Real Is the Resilience?	57
Chapter 3 Choosing the WAN Technology	59
Design Considerations for Serial Links	60
Designing IP over Frame Relay	64
Broadcasting over Frame Relay	64
Using Sub-Interfaces in an IP Environment	65
PVC Meshing and IP Redundancy	68
Dynamic Routing over Frame Relay	72
Frame Relay Traffic Management	76
Private Frame Relay	78
ISDN Design Issues with IP	79
IP Routing over ISDN	79
Using ISDN for Redundancy	82
PPP and Multilink PPP	86
Designing IP over ATM	87
Benefits of ATM	88
ATM Design Issues	89
Private ATM	97
Voice and Data Integration	98
Chapter 4 Fundamental IP Routing Design	107
Designing an IP Addressing Plan	108
Choice of Major Network Addresses	108
Subnet Planning	109
VLSM	111
Planning for Route Summarization	114
Categorizing IP Routing Protocols	122
Distance Vector and Link State Protocols	122

Classful and Classless Routing   123
Classful Route Advertisements and Summarization   124
Choosing a Routing Protocol   125
Scalability   126
Routing Updates   126
Routing Protocol Stability   127
Speed of Convergence   130
Routing Metric   133
Support of VLSM   135
Discontiguous Networks   135
Route Summarization   136
Understanding Load Balancing   141
Security   142
When To Use Static Routes   143
Routing Information Protocol   145
RIP Version 1   145
RIP Version 2   146
RIP Convergence   147

Chapter 5 Scalable IP Routing I-OSPF   151

Open Shortest Path First (OSPF)   152
Why Use OSPF?   152
How OSPF Operates   154
Link State Advertisements (LSAs)   155
Neighbor and Adjacency Formation   159
SPF Algorithm   161
OSPF Convergence   163
OSPF Network Types   164
Broadcast Networks and Designated Routers   165
Point-to-Point Networks   168
Non-broadcast Networks   168
Point-to-Multipoint Networks   171
Designing Within the Hierarchical Structure   172
Rules for the OSPF Area Structure   174
Scaling Limitations for OSPF Areas   179
OSPF Routers   181
Stub Areas   188
Totally Stubby Areas   190
Not-So-Stubby Areas (NSSA)   190
Virtual Links   193

Variable-Length Subnet Masking (VLSM)	197
Route Summarization in OSPF	198
How OSPF Summarizes	199
OSPF and ISDN	202
OSPF Demand Circuit	202
Conclusion	205

Chapter 6 Scalable IP Routing II- EIGRP and Protocol Redistribution   207

EIGRP Operational Characteristics	208
Protocol Overview	208
EIGRP Concepts and Operation	210
EIGRP Convergence	218
Convergence and DUAL	218
Convergence Problems with EIGRP	219
Load Balancing with EIGRP	225
VLSM	227
Route Summarization	228
The Automatic Summarization Myth	229
The Power of Manual Route Summarization	230
EIGRP over NBMA Networks	233
PVC Bandwidth Allocation	234
EIGRP in a Multiprotocol Environment	236
Protocol Redistribution	236
Preventing Routing Loops	238
Route Determination	239
Migrating from IGRP	243
Migration Strategy	244
Issues Worth Noting	245
A Case Study in EIGRP Migration	246
EIGRP and OSPF: Comparison Summary	248
Complexity of Operation	248
Design Restrictions	248
Ease of Configuration	249
Scalability	249
Convergence	249
Route Summarization	250
VLSM	250
Proprietary	250
Misconceptions in the Marketplace	251
Conclusion	252

Chapter 7   BGP and Internet Routing   253

BGP Operation and Characteristics   254
   BGP Overview   254
   Fundamental Internet Architecture   256
   When Is BGP the Correct Option?   257
   EBGP and IBGP   259
   Synchronization   261
   BGP Stability - Problems and Solutions   263
   IGP Redistribution into BGP   265
   BGP Redistribution into IGP   266
BGP Path Selection and Manipulation   270
   BGP Attributes   270
   BGP Route Selection   278
   BGP Filtering   278
   Attribute Manipulation and Policy-Based Routing   281
   Policy Based Routing Examples   282
BGP Resilience and Redundancy   285
   Default Routes to Each ISP   285
   Default Routes in Tandem with BGP   287
   Receiving Full BGP Routes   289
Scalable AS Routing   290
   Route Aggregation   290
   Route Reflectors   292
   Route Reflector Design and Migration Issues   296
   BGP Confederations and Private AS   297
   Peer Groups Within BGP   299

Chapter 8   Designing the LAN I-The Campus   301

Campus Network Design Goals   302
   Performance Parameters   302
   Diversity of Applications and QOS   303
   Effective Resilience   304
   Scalability   309
Understanding the Campus Network   310
   Client-Server Traffic Flow   310
   To Switch or Not To Switch?   310
Designing a LAN Topology   321
   Segmentation Using Routing   321
   Segmentation Using Switching   325
   The Importance of Layer 3 Switching   330

Campus Hierarchical Design 335

 Access Layer 336

 Intermediate Layer 337

 Campus Backbone 343

 Collapsed Backbone versus Distributed 348

 Routed Backbone versus Switched 350

 Sample Campus Topology 358

Chapter 9 Designing the LAN II - VLANs, Multicasting, and QoS 361

VLAN Planning 362

 Why Implement VLANs? 362

 The Physical Scope of VLANs 365

 VLAN Management 367

 VLAN Trunking 368

VLAN Gateways and Resilience 370

Spanning Tree Protocol (STP) 378

 Spanning Tree Refresher 378

 Fundamental Design Issues 383

 Optimizing STP 390

 STP and Port Aggregation 394

IP Multicasting 396

 The Significance of Multicasting 396

 An Overview of IP Multicasting 399

QoS and RSVP 422

 RSVP Overview 423

 RSVP Operation 424

 Design and Implementation Considerations 431

Chapter 10 Network Security 435

Developing a Security Strategy 436

 Productivity Versus Protection 436

 Elements of Information Protection 437

 Risk and Vulnerability Assessment 438

 Developing a Security Policy 440

Security Tools 441

 Packet Filtering 442

 Encryption 449

 Virtual Private Networks (VPNs) 453

 Intrusion Detection Systems (IDSs) 454

Contents

Password Management   456
Security Servers   457
IPv6 and IPSec   458
Firewalls   461
Firewall Functions   461
Firewall Architecture   464
Firewall Policies   467
Security Design and Implementation   476
Device Security   476
Network Security   477
Protection Against Common IP Threats   479

PREFACE

A good design is the foundation upon which any network must be built. As networks grow in scale and complexity, the importance of a solid network design becomes increasingly evident. This book focuses on the design of IP networks, due to the increasing prevalence of IP as the leading desktop protocol within the industry.

Network design requires a significant depth of technical, logical, and organizational skills. It is a goal and intention of this book to address each of these skills. The greater part of the book aims to impart a good understanding of the technical issues involved with the different IP-based technologies. To work in network design, an engineer requires extensive practical experience combined with a theoretical understanding of the technologies and how they relate to one another. This book certainly does not claim to replace the need for experience, far from it. Instead, it is intended to complement networking experience.

The primary focus is on state of the art IP internetworking technology and how the principles of network design can be applied to it. I have deliberately aimed to concentrate on the technology itself rather than technological features. The features employed on networking devices change incessantly and this information can easily be accessed in any case. Understanding the principles of design and mastering the application of the technology is a greater challenge. These principles that are outlined in Chapter 1 provide a recurring theme throughout the text.

The list of principles that I compile in the first chapter is based entirely on my own experience. To adequately design any network, a logical process must be followed, culminating in the formation of a design plan for the network. The elements of this procedure will be explained. One of these elements is the technical expertise necessary to design the network. It may sound obvious, but no matter how good the design process is in theory, a network cannot be designed without the necessary technical skills. The level of these skills is certainly not to be underestimated. The design engineer must have a sound understanding of all the relevant internetworking theory coupled with extensive practical experience in support, configuration and troubleshooting. In some organizations the design department is regarded with higher status and importance than the network support group. This reflects the importance of network design as a basis for successful network implementation. However, the perceived higher 'status' of the design department is something that must be earned. Engineers who work in design must be adequately prepared for the task. This preparation entails gaining the necessary theoretical understanding of the technology coupled with ample practical experience in its implementation. Design is not a role that engineers should enter without first gaining experience in support and network implementation. Networks cannot be designed competently by people who have never installed or supported the technology. In other words, you cannot design a network that is typically based on a complex mix of technology without clearly understanding the technology from both a theoretical and practical standpoint. Network support could, at the very least, be regarded as an apprenticeship that must be served prior to graduating to network design. This analogy can be used to make the point. However, I personally dislike it, as there is an implicit undermining of the important network support function.

The use of a coherent design process and the availability of suitably qualified technical staff are the first prerequisites to a satisfactory network design. These elements enable the formulation and initial implementation of a design plan. In order to gain lasting benefit, it must be ensured that the initial design is followed and not compromised over the lifetime of the network. The whole point of designing a network methodically rather than simply "patching it together" is to provide predictability. A well-designed network is characterized by predictability in performance, resilience, and scalability. If the original design is compromised repeatedly, it will become eroded into non-existence. The net result of this is that predictability is lost. The network may be characterized by erratic performance. Tasks such as fault resolution and the addition of new nodes can become minor projects in themselves. This highlights the final challenge in the network design cycle and that is to avoid compromising the original design plan for the sake of "quick fixes." The design is there for a reason and it should accommodate growth and change in the vast majority of cases without having to be radically altered.

In terms of technical content, the early chapters emphasize the importance of the WAN infrastructure. The employment of technologies such as HDLC, Frame Relay, ISDN, and ATM are examined in detail.

Chapter 4 studies the issues encountered with IP networks as they scale. The more rudimentary routing techniques such as static routing and distance-vector IP routing are described in terms of their application and limitations. Concepts such as route summarization and *variable-length subnet masking* (VLSM) are described. This chapter sets up the next three chapters, which deal with specific IP routing protocols suitable for large networks.

Chapters 5 to 7 describe three scalable IP routing protocols. A detailed technological description of *Open Shortest Path First* (OSPF) is provided in chapter five. The complexities of OSPF are studied along with the design issues that are encountered with that protocol. Cisco's *Enhanced Interior Gateway Routing Protocol* (EIGRP) is studied due to the large penetration of that vendor within the enterprise networking market.

The focus moves from the enterprise network to routing in the Internet in Chapter 7, which deals with *Border Gateway Protocol* (BGP). Due to the complexity of BGP, its operation is first described in detail prior to an examination of the design issues that must be resolved on BGP networks.

Chapters 8 and 9 relate to the design of large-scale campus LANs. Technologies such as switched ethernet, the spanning tree protocol, and *virtual LANs* (VLANs) are discussed from an operational and design perspective.

There is an increasing industry trend towards heterogeneous networks that incorporate traditional data applications with real-time applications such as voice, video, and multimedia. For this reason I have included a section on IP multicasting and *Quality of Service* (QOS) provision.

The final chapter studies the security of IP networks. A methodology for ensuring a high level of network security is first described. The tools and techniques that can be used to help achieve the security goals on an IP network are then discussed.

This is a book about design rather than configuration. Device configuration and the exact nature of the software features are constantly changing for every vendor within the industry. This is one of the reasons that I mainly do not engage in detailed vendor-specific discussions on configuration. The book deals with the different elements of state of the art IP networks rather than vendor-specific implementations. The technology is mostly dealt with in a vendor-independent manner, although throughout the book, there are examples of specific vendor implementations as appropriate.

The different approaches to network design are always likely to stimulate debate. If you as a reader would like to provide me with feedback on this text you can do so by e-mailing me through my Web site at http://www.cormaclong.com. This site also provides a variety of internetworking technical support information. I hope you find the book informative and enjoyable.

CORMAC LONG

http://www.cormaclong.com

ACKNOWLEDGMENTS

This book required an enormous effort for more than 6 months and its completion would not have been possible without the input of a number of parties.

I would like to thank McGraw-Hill for once again believing in my work. The input and support of Steve Elliot ensured that the book got published in a timely manner. Alex Corona also provided administrative support. Beth Brown of MacAllister Publishing Services helped see me through the final production stages.

I particularly want to thank my wife Sarah for several reasons. Not only did she provide tremendous support and understanding during the difficult months of this project, but she also managed to help with the proofreading!

ABOUT THE AUTHOR

Cormac Long, CCSI™, M.Eng.Sc. has more than 15 years of engineering experience in local and wide area internetworking. As an IP Internetworking consultant he has provided design, installation and troubleshooting services for several Fortune 500 clients in the United States and Europe. He is founder of ArdRi Communications, an IP network consulting company that also provides training support for Global Knowledge Network. He is the author of Cisco Internetworking & Troubleshooting. His Web site, `http://www.cormaclong.com`, can be visited for IP internetworking technology information relating to this text and beyond.

ABOUT THE REVIEWER

Henry Benjamin is a Cisco Certified Internetwok Engineer, CCIE, 4695, under the Cisco Systems CCIE program. Henry is an IT Engineer for Cisco Systems based in Sydney, Australia. He has more than 9 years experience in Cisco networks including large IP networks and internal Cisco IT design solutions. Henry holds a Bachelor of aeronautical engineering degree from Sydney University. Henry has authored himself and been involved with many other Cisco certification titles. *"This review is dedicated to the loving memory of my mum, Anna Benjamin."*

Principles of
Network
Design

It could be argued that this is the most important chapter of this book. It is certainly the only one with contents that will never become obsolete. The subject matter and principles that are discussed in this chapter are at the heart of most major network problems in the industry, due to lack of observance.

Before designing any network, there must be at least a broad blueprint denoting what the designer is hoping to achieve. The first section of the chapter outlines the broad objectives that characterize a satisfactory network design. This describes the parameters against which a network specification is developed. The key issues and driving forces that must be understood in order to design a network to specification are then described.

Finally and very importantly, the key principles that should be followed in order to achieve the design goals are outlined. These principles apply both to general and specific network design issues. The list of principles that has been compiled is based entirely on experience. Some of the principles may just seem like common sense, but they are rarely followed in practice. It is the lack of observance of these relatively simple principles that is the fundamental reason behind most bad network designs and implementations.

Design Objectives

Before commencing any network design project, it is important to clarify what constitutes a satisfactory network design. What are the goals of the network designer? What are they trying to achieve? A starting blueprint is required that outlines the performance parameters against which the quality of the network design and operation can be measured. When developing a network specification, the first issue is to identify the parameters that are to be specified. These parameters, which are about to be described, are extremely important. They provide a level of focus for the design engineer at the outset of the project and at all times during the design process.

Performance

The parameters against which the performance of the network will be judged must first be ascertained. The performance parameters that are now about to be discussed pertain to most networks. Target values should be set for these parameters as dictated by application requirements and budgetary constraints:

- *Application response time*: The application drives the design. There is no point in having a fast response time across the network if users of the network applications do not experience this response. The response time is particularly relevant for delay-sensitive or real-time applications like multimedia and *Voice over IP* (VoIP). Many traditional legacy applications such as a *Systems Network Architecture* (SNA) or LAT are also very time-sensitive.

  The target set for application response time determines the packet latency or delay that can be tolerated in the network. This could, for example, be used as a blueprint to determine if the latency associated with additional router hops can be tolerated when assessing a design option.

- *Application co-existence*: The IP network is becoming a heterogeneous melting pot for a multitude of applications that are becoming increasingly diverse in nature. Traditional data applications that are sensitive to packet loss are being integrated on the same network as delay-sensitive and real-time applications such as voice, video, and multimedia. This poses additional challenges for the design engineer. Not only must multiple applications be supported on the same network, but also ones that have significantly different characteristics and requirements. All networks must be designed to adequately meet the requirements in terms of delay and packet loss for each application without impairing the performance of other applications. This leads into the area of *Quality of Service* (QoS), which is studied towards the end of this book.

- *Availability*: The availability requirements of network applications dictate the application downtime that can be tolerated. This downtime can occur due to a failure on the application itself or a failure on the network. The network and applications should be designed in order to minimize this downtime.

  Even with a resilient design, downtime can occur on the application while either the network or application is availing of a backup path or device. This is termed the *convergence time* and can result in the loss of sessions with time-sensitive applications.

  Apart from the outright loss of service due to the failure of a network link or device, a degraded service can occur due to congestion on the network or devices. For sensitive applications, this sometimes effectively amounts to a loss of service.

  The application's availability requirements can also translate themselves into pure network performance parameters such as the percentage of dropped packets on the network devices.

Redundancy and Resilience

The need for network resilience is driven by the application availability requirements. After ascertaining the availability requirements of each application, a plan must be put in place to ensure that this availability can be provided. A resilient design must provide full resilience along the client-to-server data path. This entails achieving the following:

- Resilient network access for the client
- Backup links in the data path from client to server
- Backup network devices in the path from client to server
- Resilient network access for the servers
- Resilience in the application

Most network designs are characterized by a tradeoff between cost and availability. Providing a truly resilient design for all aspects of the network in many cases will cause the network budget to be exceeded. It is then a question of prioritizing and defining the exact level of resilience that will be provided for each application and on each part of the network.

It is also important to define what you mean by resilience. Resilience on paper does not always represent dynamic failover in the event of a problem. The classic example is the question of resilience in the local loop. There is not much point in having one leased line as backup for another if they are both in the same local loop cable to the central office.

Another issue is how resilience against degraded service or congestion is incorporated into the network. This again relates to the application availability requirements and the sensitivity to delay and packet loss.

The speed of convergence is another key issue that determines whether the failover to backup paths or devices results in any lost sessions. The specification for convergence speed could, for example, determine the choice of IP routing protocol.

NOTE: *Network designs are typically characterized by a tradeoff between availability and cost.*

Accommodating Growth and Change

The fundamental platform of the network should be designed once. This design must incorporate scalability to cater for growth in applications, users, or the number of sites on the network. The network should only be redesigned if an event fundamentally changes the character of the network, such as a new application that is radically more bandwidth-intensive than any existing application. Another example might be connections to new business partners that require various policies and configurations. The latter is an example of a mini-design project that may change the characteristics of the network.

In order to plan for growth and change, an estimate of the network's life expectancy should be established. Be realistic about this figure. You can only look so far into the future in this field of endeavor. It should not be more than 10 years. If it is expected to be in place for this length of duration, however, then think back 10 years to how different the network was in terms of networking technology, applications, and user requirement and expectations. You will then clearly realize that all networks must be capable of supporting change and evolution.

Network design should be able to incorporate likely future changes without requiring a significant or radical redesign. Growth in the number of users and the implementation of new applications should be provided for. Although accurate estimates on growth or change in these areas might not be realistic, it is important to gain at least a qualitative estimate. With this in place, the network should be able to scale to these requirements by growing rather than being completely overhauled.

Of course, instances will occur where an unforeseen event does require a radical redesign. The company's business strategy might alter and this might affect the networking requirements. The enterprise might merge with another company. In these situations, it may well be a case of "back to the drawing board" for the design engineers.

The fundamental network design is only a starting point, but it is a starting point that rarely should be deviated from in a fundamental manner. Some industry commentators underestimate the importance of network design and choose to bunch it in with network support as an ongoing process. Network design is an ongoing process but should be a process of refinement and modification rather than continuous redesign. Nobody can predict the future with precise accuracy, but it is the first function of the designer to incorporate an educated prediction into the design. To use an analogy, consider a person planning his or her retirement fund. Many unpredictable variables will change before retirement, but that does not mean that he or she cannot have a plan or that the plan must persistently and radically change every time a blip occurs in the stock market.

Scalability is a key issue that will be discussed in each of the upcoming chapters. It will be examined in relation to *wide area network* (WAN) technologies, IP routing protocols, and device deployment and network topology.

Management and Manageability

Network management should be incorporated into the design. It is not sufficient to treat it as an afterthought. Support is usually the second greatest single cost of ownership on a network. It can be minimized through well-planned network management.

Each of the traditional elements of network management should be considered as part of the initial design process:

- *Fault management*: The way in which faults will be dealt with in order to minimize downtime should be decided at the design stage. For example, the simple act of formulating a clear site and device-naming convention can improve the efficiency with which troubleshooting is performed.

- *Configuration management*: A secure and efficient policy for altering configurations and performing changes on the network should be decided prior to rollout.

- *Accounting*: The importance of accounting should be clarified at the outset. Some networking devices support their own accounting features and if accounting is a priority, then this may influence the choice of devices and technology.

- *Performance management*: On any medium to large network, the performance parameters should be monitored on a proactive basis. The old adage "what gets measured improves," while clichéd, is certainly relevant here. Some networks may only require the periodic monitoring of performance statistics.

  The designer should be clear about the type and level of performance management required and feasible within budgetary constraints. This must be incorporated into the design as it influences the features that need to be supported on the network devices.

- *Security*: The issue of security management is discussed separately in the next section.

Security

The final chapter of this book, "Network Security" examines the security of IP networks. In the chapter, the requirement to incorporate the company's security policy into the network design is made apparent. Security risks and vulnerabilities must be addressed at the network design stage. The tools and procedures used to secure a network are also integral to its design.

Disaster Recovery

A disaster recovery plan should be developed in conjunction with any significant network design or redesign. A disaster is a precisely defined term that has a different meaning for different companies and their networks. The complete and outright failure of all core resources is an example of a disaster scenario. This is not to be confused with the design of a network that is resilient against common failures on a communications link or a central router.

   If disaster recovery is not incorporated into the original design, then it may turn out that the eventual disaster recovery solution is excessively expensive to implement or has a very limited scope of recovery. The following questions should at least be answered during the network design phase:

- What defines a network disaster?
- What resources must be recovered during a disaster? In other words, what is the required scope of network recovery?
- To what specification must these resources be recovered? For example, what recovery time is required? What level of degraded service can be tolerated during a disaster period?
- What is the budget for disaster recovery?
- How can the network design support the disaster recovery requirements?

Cost

No matter what anybody says, cost is always a fundamental driving force behind network design. As stated earlier, the design is often characterized by a tradeoff between cost and availability. It is important to accurately quantify the cost associated with each element of the network design prior to advancing too far with any design proposal. The following are some of the major cost contributors to a corporate network:

- *WAN*: The cost of the wide area technology and bandwidth is usually the greatest single contributor to the cost of the network. The issue of WAN costing is discussed in detail in the upcoming two chapters.

- *Support*: Support is usually the second greatest cost component to owning a network. The problem with support cost is that, unlike the WAN cost, it is notoriously difficult to quantify. Stringent management information systems are required to quantify support costs and indeed if they are not measured, then they can easily spiral out of control. Next time you are at a meeting relating to a persistent network problem, look around the room and ask the following questions: How long has the meeting lasted? How many people are here? What is their average salary? How many such meetings have you attended? These meetings represent the adding up of network support costs.

  The cost of support can have a paramount influence on the network topology, technology, and how it is implemented. For example, it may be decided to have a private *Asynchronous Transfer Mode* (ATM) implementation in order to reduce WAN costs. A private ATM network requires access to a highly skilled support staff that is expensive to hire and retain. Without a highly skilled staff, the support cost due to incompetent staff is likely to be even greater. Either way the support costs for a private ATM network must be carefully quantified in order to assess its cost-effectiveness.

- *Investment protection*: When products such as networking devices near the end of their life cycle, do all devices need to be completely replaced? It is important to quantify the level of investment protection offered by vendors when devices require an upgrade or replacement.

Understanding the Networking Environment

The nature of the networking environment must be adequately understood prior to the initial design phase. The key elements that should be evaluated are the nature and requirements of the applications, since the network downtime should also be quantified to serve as a basis for making cost versus availability tradeoffs.

Network Applications

The applications drive the entire design requirement. Designing from the top down is the cliché frequently associated with this principle.

The network design engineer should understand the behavior, characteristics, and requirements of the applications to a reasonable level of detail. The physical and logical location of all servers as well as the distribution of clients should be documented. This is important in order to predict client-to-server traffic flows.

The bandwidth requirements of each application must be quantified in order to assess throughput requirements on the network. The sensitivity of each application to delay or packet loss should also be noted. Time-critical applications such as SNA and LAT are still around and are likely to stay for the foreseeable future. Therefore, they must be accommodated along with new delay-sensitive multimedia applications.

The scope for the addition of future applications should be estimated with the help of management. This is necessary to provide a benchmark for the scalability requirements of the network.

Methods for improving the networking efficiency and bandwidth consumption of applications also should be explored. This is a big issue that is often overlooked. It can fall through the cracks because it is not evidently the responsibility of the network engineer or the applications engineer.

For example, WAN traffic can be dramatically reduced in a Windows NT environment by placing a local *backup domain controller* (BDC) at certain strategic sites. The use of local acknowledgement for *Logical Link Control* (LLC), proxy explorers, and RIF caching can improve performance in an SNA over IP environment.

Networking Protocols   It is important to clearly understand which protocols are used by each application and how these protocols operate. By understanding these technologies, the perceived network requirements can be reduced and performance improved.

Particular issues may occur in multiprotocol environments. These may include, for example, the possible use of IP to transport other protocols such as SNA, Novell, AppleTalk, and voice traffic. The differing nature of each protocol must be understood, such as the bandwidth consumption associated with the protocol's operation, its use of broadcasts and multicasts, its sensitivity to delay and delay variation, and its sensitivity to dropped packets. It is imperative to understand how well features such as QoS techniques and protocol prioritization work in practice. This whole area is dealt with in detail in Chapter 9, "Designing the LAN II—VLANs, Multicasting, and QoS."

The Cost of Downtime

The cost of an hour's downtime can vary from zero to hundreds of thousands of dollars depending on the nature of the corporation's business. It is critical that all personnel associated with the design and support of your network has a clear picture of the cost of network downtime.

The classic tradeoff between cost and availability when performing network design underscores the importance of quantifying the cost of downtime. Without an estimate of the cost of downtime, such a tradeoff analysis cannot be accurately performed.

Achieving the Design Goals

Network design requires extensive practical experience combined with a theoretical understanding of the technologies and how they relate to one another. Hands-on experience is particularly critical and this is often overlooked. An engineer who does not have extensive network support experience is, in my view, not yet equipped to work in design.

The tools that enable you to achieve the design goals are encompassed in the technology itself. You need to have a good knowledge and understanding of topics like scalable routing protocols, cost-effective WAN transport technology, and network management.

Network design models should not be trusted. No network design tool or model on the market is realistically applicable to anything beyond a simple network regardless of what the sales engineers for the various vendors tell you. For this reason, it is recommended that you do laboratory work and perform some proof of concept tests. Designs must be performed in a lab rather than as a theoretical paper exercise. The multitude and interaction of so much technology is simply too complex to verify in anything other than a real-life test bed.

Figure 1-1 displays a network design flowchart that provides an approximate guideline that could be used to approach the basic steps to be followed during the design process:

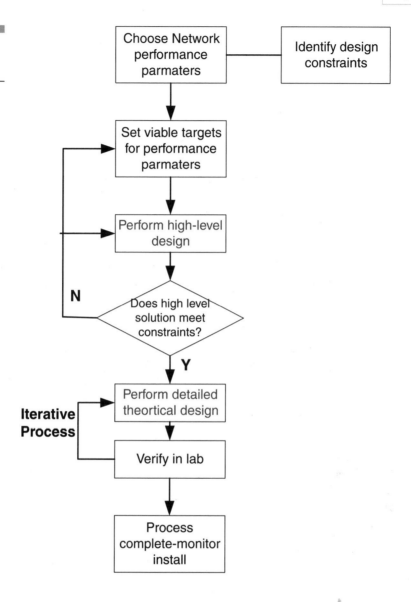

Figure 1-1
Flowchart for the
design process

1. Determine the performance parameters that best specify each of the
   design goals such as the application response time, the packet loss
   percentage, latency, and application availability.
2. Identify any design constraints. The most obvious constraint is budget.
   Other constraints may include the implementation timescale, the

support of legacy equipment, and the incorporation of specialized departments that require unique network specification and policy.

3. After considering the constraints, set targets for the relevant network performance parameters.

4. Commence a high-level design. This is intended to resolve major issues such as the choice of WAN technology, the degree to which routing is used instead of switching, and so on.

5. Then, this high-level design should be compared to the constraints. If the constraints are not met, an iterative step backwards is required. In the event of the constraints being met, the design process can proceed.

6. A specific network design plan can now begin to be formulated. This addresses all technical details and alternatives for the design.

7. Each major aspect of the technical solution should be lab tested. The application response and availability characteristics should also be tested in a lab. This facilitates an iterative refinement of the technical solution.

8. The design is complete when the technical design is fully refined. In some cases, the final lab tests may indicate that the fundamental performance targets or constraints are unrealistic and may have to be revised and compromised. It is, however, an aspiration to tentatively finalize these parameters at the high-level design stage.

The Importance of Being Predictable

Predictability is the difference between a well-designed network and one that is simply patched together. A well-designed network exhibits predictability in the following areas:

- *Performance*: The performance parameters are met with a high degree of consistency.

- *Resilience*: The failure of a link or device will not result in excessive application downtime.

- *Scalability*: The addition of new sites, users, or even new applications should result in a predictable response in terms of network operation. In other words, there should be no requirement for a radical redesign in order to restore performance. Scaling a well-designed network should be like adding building blocks to a pre-existing structure.

Consistency and predictability should be the hallmark of a well-designed and implemented network. It often happens that this is the case when the network is initially installed. However, gradually over time the original design rules are compromised for the sake of a quick fix.

If the design rules are compromised to any significant degree more than once or twice, then the entire design is compromised and effectively no design exists. The result of having no network design is that all predictability is lost. Predictability in performance, resilience, and scalability will no longer be a characteristic of the network. This, of course, is the whole point of planning a network design in the first place.

Consider the case where static routes and access filters are added on various parts of the network in order to facilitate quick fixes. If subsequent changes are to be made, such as the addition of a new server, the entire network must be reassessed due to the effect of the earlier ad hoc changes. The filters and static routes may have to be modified in order to render the server operational. Hence, instead of commissioning a new server and having the predictability that it will work, the task turns into a mini-design project. This leads to the choice of what can be called "designing a network once or designing it a hundred times." If a network is not designed properly at the outset or if that design is compromised, then everyday events such as troubleshooting and adding devices to the network become design projects in themselves.

NOTE: *A well-designed network is characterized by predictability in performance, resilience, and scalability. Once the design is severely compromised, it ceases to exist and predictability is lost. Thus, you can design a network once or design it a hundred times.*

Fundamental Design Principles

This introductory chapter will be concluded by summarizing some fundamental design principles. A number of these principles have already been alluded to in this chapter and will continually be referred to during the course of this book. Sometimes when lost in the details of a design project, the design engineers should refocus on some of these principles:

- *Understand the environment, including all of the design objectives.* You must first be clear on what has to be achieved before attempting to achieve it.

- *The application drives the design requirements.* The network is the structure that facilitates the application. Without understanding the application characteristics and its requirements, the network cannot be designed.

- *Experience is required, both theoretical and practical.* Network design requires extensive practical experience combined with a theoretical understanding of the technologies and how they relate to one another. Hands-on experience is particularly critical and this is often overlooked. An engineer who does not have extensive network support experience is, in my view, not yet equipped to work in design.

  Extensive practical experience should be thought of as a necessary prerequisite to a design role. You cannot design a network without a reasonable understanding of how it works. In certain companies, design engineers look down on support staff, which is confusing, especially since the level of proficiency is often higher in support, where incompetent staff cannot hide so easily.

- *Don't trust network design models.* Internetworking entails a multitude of complex technologies that must successfully interact with each other. The design of large or complex networks cannot be reliably modeled in my view. Such modeling is only appropriate for high-level design. When resolving specific technical details, a lab is required.

- *Design is done in the lab rather than on the whiteboard.* For the same reason that network-modeling techniques should be distrusted, a lab is the single most important design tool. Given the complexity of the more advanced internetwork designs, a design is not valid until it has been verified in the lab.

  Also, do not trust device performance statistics. Vendor tests are often unrealistic. Test the routers, switches, and servers yourself in a test bed. Vary parameters such as the packet size, and measure delay and throughput.

- *Network design usually involves a number of tradeoffs.* Cost versus performance and availability is usually the fundamental design tradeoff.

- *Don't underestimate support cost.* This is the single biggest cost after the WAN costs. Its significance is often minimized because it can be more difficult to quantify. The support cost can be minimized through good design. Do not underestimate the cost of maintaining competent support personnel.

- *Don't try to mirror the corporate structure.* The network design and topology can often mirror the corporate structure of the organization. Although attempting to mirror this structure is not to be discouraged necessarily, the network designer should certainly never become enslaved by it. Such an approach can result in fundamentally flawed designs. Remember, the design objectives are the only essential driving force behind the design.

- *Vendor independence.* Avoid proprietary solutions as far as possible and as far as is prudent. A design should not tie an oranization to a single vendor when there are other viable alternatives. Balanced against this, a proprietary solution should not be discounted as a matter of course. A proprietary solution may represent the best short-term and long-term solution. There are also situations where a vendor represents a virtual monopoly in terms of providing the only viable solution.

- *Don't introduce complexity without a clear benefit.* This principle is true of both network design and device configuration. Additional complexity is likely to increase the support cost and may make the network more difficult to manage. Also, each time a needlessly complex solution is employed, it is possible that an additional piece of software is being used that may have bugs in it. The simplest viable solution should always be implemented. Increased complexity is only justifiable if the outcome is a resulting benefit or requirement.

- *Design every network on its own merits.* Do not work to a set of rigid and possibly over-generalized design rules. Consider every network on its own merits.

- *Take the direct route unless . . .* Traffic should always take the shortest path between source and destination where possible. What exactly constitutes the shortest path depends on the technology employed.

- *Avoid the bleeding edge.* Only use mature and well-tested software and hardware for all devices on the network. Any violation of this principle requires a business justification case and risk assessment.

- *Do not compromise the fundamental design plan.* The design may have to show some degree of flexibility and evolve with the network. This relates to the requirement for a scalable design. However, it must not be compromised at a fundamental level. For example, if you are implementing a three-layered WAN hierarchy, do not compromise this by adding another layer. This could happen if new small routers are added below the access layer or are alternatively directly connecting to the backbone. This comprises and invalidates the original design by either adding another layer or by mixing and matching layers. In such a case, the original design is no longer relevant and you can sometimes go as far as to say that at this point a network design is no longer in place. A network design is merely an academic exercise if it is not fully and precisely implemented as per the original design plan. No changes should be made to the original design without the endorsement of the engineers who formulated that design.

■ *Predictability is the hallmark of a good design.* Predictability in performance, resilience, and scalability is a characteristic of a well-designed network.

■ *Design it once or design it a hundred times!* If a network is not designed properly at the outset or if that design is compromised, then everyday tasks such as troubleshooting and adding new devices to the network become design projects in themselves. This is because without a valid design that has been followed, basic network changes do not form a part of any plan. Thus, they must be treated as isolated projects. The effect of any changes on the network must always be independently assessed if the design plan has been deviated from. This is what is called "designing a network a hundred times," although in actual fact, it may turn out to be more than one hundred mini-design projects!

■ *Don't design by committee or by dictator.* No one person, no matter how skilled or experienced, should be the single and absolute authority in designing the network. Anyone who has ever designed even a moderately substantial network will already know why. Designing a network involves balancing priorities, performing tradeoffs, and addressing a broad range of technical issues at both a general and detailed level. It is essential for anyone to engage in a regular discourse with colleagues in order to keep all of these technical and non-technical issues in appropriate perspective. For example, certain people can go too far down a blind alley or engage in tunneled thinking. A fresh perspective is always needed, as well as people with a different focus.

Okay, so not only should you not appoint a single design dictator (even a talented one), but you should be even more opposed to the "design by committee" approach. Only a small group of people should have the final say and input into the design. Networks should be designed by a small number of competent engineers, not by committees.

Designing the Wide Area Network (WAN)

Designing a Wide Area Network (WAN) Topology

The term topology can be defined in many ways. When I speak of the *Wide Area Network* (WAN) topology, I am referring to the manner and architecture with which the different sites on the network are connected. This is distinct from the actual technology employed in the WAN, such as *Asynchronous Transfer Mode* (ATM), Frame Relay, *Integrated Services Digital Network* (ISDN), and so on. The issue of WAN technologies will be discussed in the next chapter.

In this chapter, we will focus on the fundamental issue of WAN topology, which is not to be confused with the choice of WAN technology. In terms of topology, the fundamental questions to be addressed include the following:

■ Will each site connect to all other sites or to just a single site?

■ Will some form of hierarchy exist in the way that inter-site connectivity is achieved?

■ What is the driving force behind the making of such decisions?

■ What additional functionality is required of each site on the network beyond merely providing network connectivity?

These issues need to be understood before the details of the technological alternatives for the WAN are explored, which is the purpose of this chapter.

Flat Versus Hierarchical

On a large network, one of the most fundamental designs decision to be made in relation to the WAN infrastructure is whether it should take the form of a flat or hierarchical topology.

The basic topology for a flat network is one in which all of the remote or regional sites connect into the same main site. An example of this is shown in Figure 2-1. Variations may be made on this in order to provide resilience. For example, two main offices may exist so that all remote sites connect to each one. An example of this type of flat structure is shown in Figure 2-2. A flat structure can also be thought of as having just two layers or tiers in the WAN topology—the main site(s) is often referred to as Tier-1 and the remote sites are commonly referred to as Tier-2 sites.

Figure 2-1
Flat hub and spoke topology

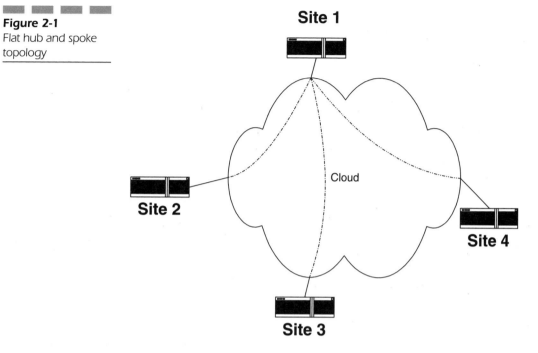

Figure 2-2
Dual-homed flat topology

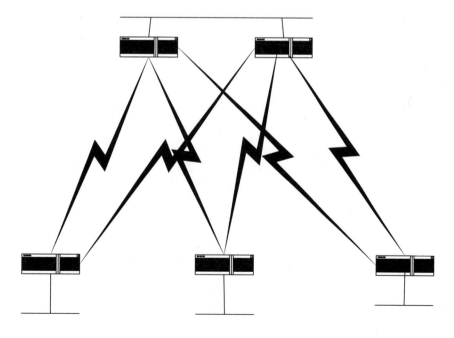

Most networks tend to centralize a large portion if not all of the resources, such as applications servers. This is indicative of a trend within the industry to move toward sharing more applications across the corporation, including Web-based computing, e-mail, and teleconferencing for example. Although it is possible to have networks in which an any-to-any communication requirement exists for major resources, this is unusual. The any-to-any communication requirement can be easily satisfied; however, it is usually for small levels of exceptional traffic rather than bulk traffic. If each site exchanges regular and substantial amounts of network traffic, then anything other than a flat WAN structure would be difficult to implement.

Because most networks do have one or more main sites, you can refer to a topology that has two layers as being flat.

A hierarchical WAN topology involves the introduction of a third layer between the main site(s) and the remote sites. Figure 2-4 provides an example of a hierarchical WAN structure. The remote sites are now termed Tier-3 sites and they connect to the main site via Tier-2 sites. In this type of hierarchy, Tier-3 sites never attach directly to the main site or Tier-1. One exception to this is when an alternate technology such as ISDN is used to backup the primary wide area links, which may, be leased lines or Frame Relay, for example. In this case, the failure of a WAN link at a Tier-3 site would cause the Tier-3 router to dial directly to the main site. It is also possible to design the network so that the Tier-3 router would dial a particular Tier-2 site. A schematic representation of this type of ISDN backup is shown in Figure 2-5. When discussing the issue of network resilience in more detail in subsequent sections, you will see that a number of different methods are available for achieving this important network design goal.

Flat WAN Topology

On a smaller network, the choice between a flat or hierarchical topology tends to be less of an issue, because a flat structure is usually sufficient to ensure good network performance. WANs with less than 10 sites can be considered small, but that rule of thumb can be stretched to 20 sites In general, such networks have one, or possibly two, central sites, and all other sites termed remote or regional sites connect directly to the central site(s).

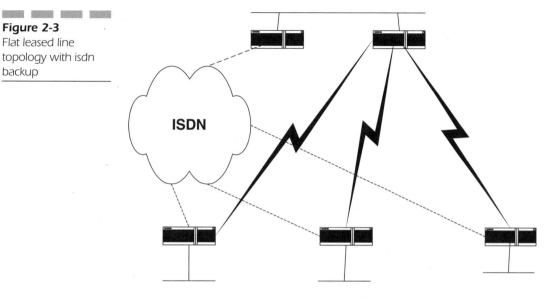

Figure 2-3
Flat leased line
topology with isdn
backup

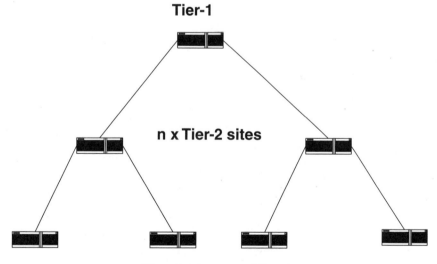

Figure 2-4
Three-tiered
hierarchical topology

Figure 2-5
Hierarchical topology
with dial backup

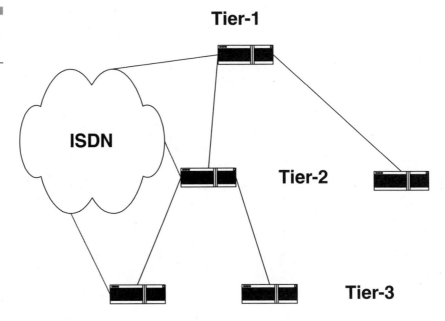

Figures 2-1 and 2-2 show typical sample topologies. In Figure 2-1, all remote sites connect into one central main site. This can be the case when all or most of the network resources, such as applications servers, reside at this central site. Modern networking environments show a strong trend toward centralized resources due to the changing nature of applications. Some examples are Internet-based services that use a central Web server, e-mail, and video conferencing. This trend is only likely to accelerate, as more companies centralize common shared resources, which are often termed *enterprise services,* because they are shared by the entire corporate enterprise.

In Figure 2-2, the centralized resources are shared between two central sites for resilience, which is achieved by dual-homing the remote site to each central site in this example. Dual-homing simply means connecting each remote site to each of the central sites, and a resilient connection from the remote sites can also be achieved through the use of another technology, such as ISDN. For the network in Figure 2-3, the central site is connected to ISDN if the link from a remote site fails. In this example, one central site exists; however, the ISDN dials a different router at the main office. Thus, protection is provided against a failure on the main WAN link from each remote site, and also resilience protects against a failure on the main router at the central site. No fallback is available, however, in an event such as a serious and prolonged power outage at the central site.

Some resources may also reside at remote sites. These resources will usually serve clients at that particular site; hence, the traffic does not have to cross the WAN. Particular instances may occur in which a server at one remote site has to be accessed by clients at another remote site. For example, when referring to Figure 2-1, clients at Site 2 need to login to a server at Site 4. The connectivity for such a session is provided via the central site because no direct WAN link exists between Site 2 and Site 4. Although scenarios like this do happen in practice, it is more common on smaller networks not to have a requirement for direct communication between the remote sites. Usually, the resources that clients need are available either locally or at the central site. A network like this is said to have a flat wide area topology, meaning that all sites connect back to one or more central sites. This can also be described as a hub and spoke topology with the central site being the hub.

Another piece of jargon that is also used in this context is that the network is collapsed back to the central site. On a reasonably small network, introducing another tier between the remote sites and central site is usually unnecessary. After all, getting back to the fundamental design principles that were discussed in Chapter 1, "Principles of Network Design," why introduce added complexity and cost without a clear need and benefit?

Advantages of a Flat WAN Structure

I will now summarize the main advantages and motivations for employing a flat WAN structure.

Simplicity   A flat structure is the simplest type of WAN topology. One of this book's recurring themes is that designs should remain as simple as possible. Simplicity is an advantage that should certainly not be underestimated, and solutions should only be as complex as is necessary. However, as you will see, when networks grow in size, the justification for the greater complexity of a hierarchical design increases.

Less Router Hops   Each router hop on a network introduces the latency associated with a routing table lookup. Therefore, when designing a routed IP network, it is important to ensure that the minimum number of router hops are incurred between any source and any destination within the network. With a simple two-layered flat structure, the number of router hops from remote sites to the main site(s) is minimized.

Less PVCs and Less Subnets   A flat structure uses the minimum number of leased lines or virtual circuit links used to connect the remote sites to the central site.

For packet or cell switched technologies such as Frame Relay or ATM, this can reduce the number of IP subnets being used, if point-to-point Frame Relay or ATM is being implemented. If the multipoint form of these technologies is being used, then no savings in IP subnet address space takes place, as the whole WAN cloud is then a single multipoint IP subnet. Minimizing the number of IP subnets used in the WAN is not necessarily a major goal of a network designer, but it can provide the following benefits:

- It reduces pressure on the IP addressing plan, particularly if subnet address space is at a premium.
- Less IP subnets in the WAN helps reduce the size of the routing tables, which in turn has a number of advantages. The latency associated with routing table lookup is reduced as the size of the table decreases. Also, with smaller tables, less network bandwidth is consumed with routing updates. Finally, for certain IP routing protocols, excessively large routing tables can place pressure on router memory requirements.

IP subnet address space can also be conserved using *variable length subnet masking* (VLSM). Routing tables sizes can also be minimized using route summarization, and these features will be in subsequent chapters.

Regardless of whether you are using leased lines or a point-to-point or point-to-multipoint WAN technology, it is true that a flat topology reduces the number of leased lines or *permanent virtual circuits* (PVCs). At first sight, this might seem like a clear cost saving, but this is not always the case, particularly in the context of leased lines. Two factors usually drive the cost of leased lines: bandwidth and the physical distance between the connected sites. It may happen that a flat structure means that many leased lines connect geographically dispersed remote sites to the central site. The long distances entailed increase the cost of these serial links. Also, having a direct connection between each remote site and the central site might not be the most cost-effective deployment of WAN bandwidth. For example, if a large number of remote sites each had a 56k connection to the central site and many of these sites had a relatively low-bandwidth utilization on these links, it would make better sense to connect a number of such sites to a single geographically local site and connect this designated site over a T-1 back to the main site. The site used for aggregation would therefore introduce another layer into the hierarchy. Refer to Figure 2-4 for an example of this type of aggregated structure.

However, it is very important to note that the cost of the WAN connections depends on a number of factors such as the technology employed (Frame Relay or leased line), bandwidth requirements, and physical distance. The pricing structure can vary dramatically, depending on the wide area carrier, site locations, and bandwidth requirements. It is imperative to finalize all of this in a very precise manner with the telecommunications carrier prior to making any cost-related decisions. In the real world, these companies, just like any vendor in this business, have slick sales people who work on a commission basis. From my experience, it's definitely a case of buyer beware. The pricing structure should be very precisely defined in writing before making a decision as to what carrier to use or the type of WAN solution.

Remember:
- Buyer Beware! Carefully finalize all pricing plans with the carrier prior to making any cost-based decisions in relation to the WAN technology.

Limitations of a Flat Design

Now consider the case where over 50 remote sites are connecting directly into a central site. Assume that the network is also projected to grow eventually to approximately 100 sites. Let's examine some of the issues that may be created with a simple flat design.

Routing Protocol Limitations

As any network grows, the scalability of the routing protocol can become an issue. This is a subject that is examined in great detail in subsequent chapters. For now, the potential limiting factors surrounding the IP routing protocol will be summarized.

Non-scalable IP Routing Protocols   Routers running distance vector routing protocols, such as *Routing Information Protocol* (RIP) or *Cisco's*

Interior Gateway Routing Protocol (IGRP) broadcast their entire routing table periodically to each of their directly attached neighbor routers. If a large number of neighbor routers attach directly to the backbone routers, then two adverse effects can occur:

- The backbone routers have to exchange more routing information with directly attached neighbors. This introduces more router overhead that could impact the speed at which the router can switch packets.

- A potentially more serious issue is the bandwidth consumption associated with the periodic updates. This is particularly relevant for large routing tables. In the case of RIP, the routing table is broadcast to and from each remote router every 30 seconds. Hence, this is equivalent to broadcasting the entire routing table across each serial link every 15 seconds in one direction only. Remember also that in a flat design, all remote offices connect directly to the central site, some of which may be small and therefore might have relatively low bandwidth serial links. The effect of these periodic routing updates on a 56Kbps link, for example, can be quite pronounced.

A very important point should be made in relation to the use of distance vector routing protocols while considering the issues encountered with a flat WAN design as the network grows. A scalable *Internet Protocol* (IP) routing protocol such as *Open Shortest Path First* (OSPF) or Cisco's *Enhanced Interior Gateway Routing Protocol* (EIGRP) should be used on a large or growing network. If a crude distance vector protocol like RIP version 1 or IGRP is used, scalability problems will occur regardless of whether a flat or hierarchical WAN topology is employed.

Remember:
- As the network grows, a scalable IP routing protocol such as OSPF or EIGRP is required regardless of the type of WAN topology.

Now having made that point, you will see that even with a scalable IP routing protocol, potential routing protocol issues need to be faced with a flat WAN design.

Number of Router Neighbors   In a network of this size, it is likely and desirable that a scalable routing protocol such as OSPF is being used. Scalable IP routing protocols such as OSPF and Cisco's EIGRP rely on the formation of a neighbor relationship with each directly connected router. This whole area is discussed in detail later in the relevant IP routing chapters.

In a flat network topology, these routing protocols form neighbors between the main site and each remote site over the WAN links. If the number of OSPF or EIGRP neighbors gets too large, the following issues can arise:

- The topological database can get excessively large, placing memory resource restraints on the main office router. This is an even greater issue with EIGRP than OSPF because in EIGRP, the size of the database is directly proportional to the number of EIGRP neighbors. In OSPF, the size of the database is proportional to the number of IP subnets on the network.

- The large number of neighbors can cause router convergence problems again, particularly in the case of EIGRP. When a router running EIGRP loses a route without a backup route, it queries each of its neighbors for another route to that destination. EIGRP does not converge until it receives a reply from each of those neighbors. Therefore, if the number of neighbors is very large and the WAN links are slow, for example 56k, a strong possibility of a route convergence problem exists. The maximum number of neighbors that can be supported depends on a combination of the following parameters:

  - The routing protocol itself, for example, OSPF or EIGRP.
  - The speed of the WAN links over which these neighbors are being formed and more significantly, the bandwidth percentage utilization on these links *excluding* routing update traffic.
  - The amount of memory available on the backbone routers.
  - The number of routes or subnets in the overall enterprise network.
  - The stability of the network, in other words, how often *Local Area Network* (LAN) or WAN segments go down or change state.

These issues will be discussed in detail in the upcoming chapters on IP routing protocols. As you will learn, it is not possible to come up with hard and fast rules as to what the maximum number of allowable neighbors is. However, I would suggest that the following number of neighbors could be comfortably supported by a backbone router, without having to worry unduly about the issues mentioned:

- EIGRP: 20 neighbors
- OSPF: 30 neighbors

These are not by any means firm maximum values for these protocols. If you go beyond these values, then the issues mentioned would need careful consideration in order to ensure that no adverse effect occurs in network performance.

Route Summarization Difficulties   A flat structure does not readily facilitate route summarization, which results in larger routing tables as the network grows. Minimizing the size of the IP routing table is desirable regardless of the routing protocol being employed. This is true for a number of reasons:

■ A large routing table increases the delay or latency associated with routing table lookup.

■ More WAN bandwidth is consumed as a result of larger routing tables, particularly in the case of a routing protocol that uses periodic updates.

■ Even for a link state protocol like OSPF that uses incremental updates, it is still desirable to reduce the size of the routing database in order to impose less memory and processing requirements on the routers.

■ By failing to implement route summarization on a large network, the convergence time of the routing protocol can increase.

■ Route summarization, as well as improving the convergence time, can also make the network more stable. You will revisit this entire area in the context of scalable IP routing.

Although it is certainly true that it is more difficult to implement route summarization with a flat WAN design, it is by no means impossible. However, the extent to which route summarization can be performed is usually reduced. Consider the network shown in Figure 2-6, which uses OSPF as its routing protocol. Each serial link could be placed in a separate OSPF area and all routes in each area could be summarized into a single route, assuming that the IP addressing has been planned accordingly. Now consider the extent of the summarization. In this flat-structured example, each OSPF area contains only two subnets. These two subnets could be summarized into a single route, which is better than no summarization. However, it is not as extensive as the level of summarization that can be achieved on a well-designed hierarchical WAN.

Broadcasting Issues   On a flat WAN structure that uses point-to-point WAN technology such as serial leased lines, the number of broadcast domains that directly connect to the backbone routers is increased. For example, referring back to the network in Figure 2-2, the remote sites connect to the main site using serial links.

Figure 2-6
Route summarization with a flat structure

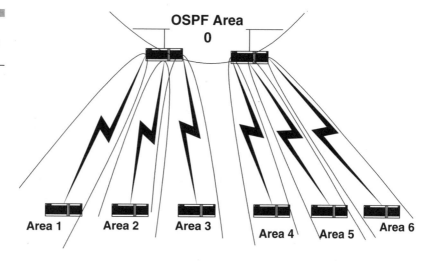

The increased number of broadcast domains can have several implications. In the case of leased line serial links, broadcasts are sent and received on each serial interface that connects to a leased line. These broadcasts may be routing updates or other types of broadcasts that relate to the network applications. An excessive number of inbound broadcasts in particular can potentially place a processing strain on the backbone routers, which are the last devices on the network that should be slowed down due to needless processing. However, even with a flat leased line topology, broadcasting need not be a problem in the WAN. As you will see in subsequent chapters, some IP routing protocols such as OSPF and EIGRP are more efficient in their use of WAN resources. Also, through proper choice and design of the network applications, broadcasting in the WAN can be minimized.

On a flat network that uses PVCs such as Frame Relay or ATM, the effect of a large number of PVCs connecting to the backbone router can be potentially more serious. This is because ATM and Frame Relay (like X.25 and ISDN) are not broadcast media. These media do not support broadcasting by default, but routers can forward broadcasts across such media by simply replicating the broadcast across each of the PVCs.

Refer to the network shown in Figure 2-1. A PVC from each remote site connets to the central site. Two basic topological implementations of Frame Relay and ATM are available:

- Point-to-point
- Point-to-multipoint

As you will see in more detail in the next chapter, point-to-point implementations involve putting each PVC on a separate IP subnet. Point-to-multipoint, on the other hand, entails placing more than one PVC on an IP subnet. It would be quite conceivable to design the network of Figure 2-1 with a multipoint configuration such that the entire set of PVCs connecting into the central site is all on the same IP subnet. At first sight, it might seem that a multipoint configuration would resolve the problem of excessive WAN broadcast domains connecting to central site routers, but this is not necessarily the case. A single IP subnet is normally synonymous with just one broadcast domain. However, it must be remembered that, because-WAN media such as Frame Felay and ATM are not true broadcast media, the packets are simply replicated across each PVC rather than broadcast in a single copy across all PVCs. Therefore, the normal idea of a broadcast domain does not hold true on these media. In fact, the same level of packet replication occurs regardless of whether the configuration is point-to-point or multipoint. A point-to-point implementation has more broadcast domains, but a multipoint configuration has more hosts that must each receive their own copy of the broadcast.

The whole issue of broadcasts in the WAN is very significant and something that will be revisited during the course of this book. In the preceding paragraphs, the issue has been highlighted for a number of reasons:

■ It is important to be clear about how broadcasting really works on non-broadcast media such as ATM and Frame Relay. A weak understanding of this topic could result in a fundamental WAN design flaw.

■ As a rule, it is desirable to reduce the amount of broadcasts that backbone routers have to send and receive. Excessive broadcasts can slow the backbone routers down because broadcasts are usually process switched rather than layer-3 switched. As you will see, if the backbone routers are slowed, then so is the entire network.

■ It is true that a flat design increases the amount of WAN broadcast processing that the backbone routers must do. It is equally true that minimizing the level of broadcasts in the WAN is a definite design goal. Other ways of achieving this goal are to make an appropriate choice of IP routing protocol and intelligent application design for example. The network designer should not dismiss a flat WAN topology due to the issue of broadcasting alone. The likely extent of broadcasting in the

WAN should be quantified, and also methods for reducing these broadcasts should be examined as part of the design process.

Conclusion

Thus far, the advantages of a flat WAN topology have been discussed along with the limitations associated with such an implementation. The potential problems with a flat design relate to the handling of broadcasts, and in particular the IP routing protocol, regardless of how sophisticated the protocol in use is. These issues usually come into play as the network grows. Generally, flat networks do not scale as well as the next topic to discuss— hierarchical topologies. Bear in mind that this is a rule of thumb. In every network design, few absolutes can be found. Every network is different and must be designed on its own merits and requirements, with its own priorities and constraints being taken into consideration.

Hierarchical

A hierarchical WAN design involves the deployment of an additional layer of sites between the most remote sites and the central site(s). This is also referred to as bringing an additional tier into the WAN hierarchy. A typical WAN hierarchy consists of the following:

- A central main site as the Tier-1 site, which is also sometimes called the core or backbone site.
- Tier-2 sites connect directly to the Tier-1 site using the designated WAN technology, (such as leased line, Frame Relay, and so forth).
- Tier-3 sites connect directly to Tier-2 sites but not to the Tier-1 site(s). Connectivity to the core of the network is provided for Tier-3 sites by Tier-2 sites.

Figure 2-7 shows a diagram of a network deploying a classic hierarchical WAN topology. Note that more than one Tier-1 site can exist. Often two or more Tier-1 sites are connected via a campus or *metropolitan area network* (MAN) backbone, as is the case in Figure 2-7.

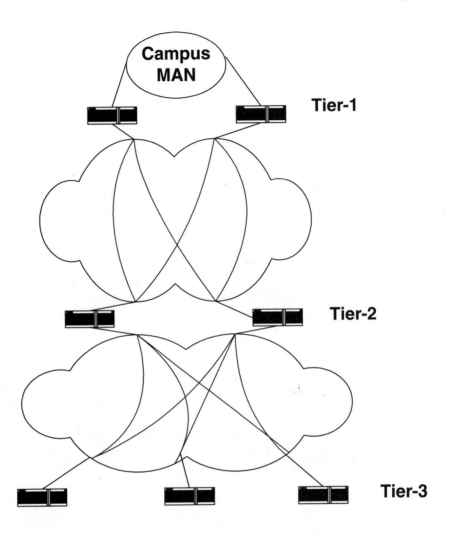

Figure 2-7
Multiple tier-1 sites
connecting to a
campus MAN

Some of the advantages offered by a hierarchical WAN design will now be discussed. This will be followed by a summary of some of the potential disadvantages and tradeoffs that are entailed in a hierarchical design. As always with network design, no one solution fits all networks.

PVC and Leased Line Aggregation

Leased lines or PVCs from the Tier-3 sites are aggregated at the Tier-2 sites rather than connecting all the way back to the central Tier-1 site. The rationale behind doing this is as follows:

Cost-effective Bandwidth Deployment

By aggregating leased lines or PVCs at the Tier-2 sites, the overall amount of WAN bandwidth purchased can be reduced.

Consider a network where over 100 remote sites exist. A remote site in this context is defined as any site other than the Tier-1 campus. Assume, for example, that 70 of these sites only require a 56k leased line connection to the Tier-1 site. Assume that the average utilization on these 56k links is less than 50 percent. The remaining 30 sites require 112k and run at a typical utilization of 60 percent. In a flat structure where each of these sites connect directly into the core, a very significant waste of expensive WAN bandwidth would occur.

Alternatively, by aggregating groups of 10 56k sites and two 112k sites to a Tier-2 site, a potential exists for cost saving. The total bandwidth purchased between the remote sites and the Tier-1 site for these 12 sites on a flat design is as follows:

$$(10 \times 56k) + (2 \times 112k) = 784k$$

The estimated utilized bandwidth is as follows:

$$(560k \times 50\%) + (112 \times 60\%) = 347.2k$$

This means that the overall average utilization on these links back to the head office is as follows:

$$347k / 784k = 44.3\%$$

This is not a very cost-effective utilization on serial links that are likely to be long in distance on a geographically dispersed WAN.

These 12 sites could be aggregated into a single site Tier-2 site where their leased lines would terminate. The Tier-2 site could be designated because of its geographic proximity to this group of Tier-3 sites.

The Tier-2 site could, in this example, provide connectivity over a channelized T-1 to the central Tier-1 site.

If an $n \times 56k$ link with $n=8$ was chosen for the channelized T-1, then the utilization would be as follows:

$$347k / (8 \times 56) = 347k / 448k = 77.5\%$$

This is a higher level of utilization that still has some room for increased traffic levels. The upshot of this solution is that effectively less bandwidth has been purchased between these 12 sites and the main office site. The same amount of bandwidth is purchased from the Tier-3 sites to the Tier-2 site. However, less bandwidth is required between the Tier-2 and Tier-1 sites to support this level of utilization. The cost of leased line bandwidth is usually proportional to the amount of bandwidth and the length of the leased lines. Therefore, in this example, it is less expensive than purchasing the 784k to run from Tier-3 sites to the central site.

In summary, a number of significant points occur here:

(i) The degree of cost saving from leased line aggregation at Tier-2 sites to some extent depends on bandwidth utilization levels, although in practice usually some under-subscription occurs. Again, you must check the carrier's pricing plan.

(ii) The cost saving can be equally true of Frame Relay or ATM PVCs. However, in the case of these technologies, usually a flexible bandwidth offering includes a number of variables. Each of these parameters will be discussed in the next chapter. For the moment, it is necessary that you very carefully clarify the Frame Relay or ATM pricing options with the service provider.

(iii) The choice of Tier-2 sites often relates to their WAN link aggregation function. Therefore, parameters such as geographic proximity to Tier-3 sites and the Tier-1 site could come into play. However, certainly other factors determine the choice of the Tier-2 sites on the network, which are discussed in the next section.

(iv) The preceding example was quite simple and was intended to illustrate the principle of using Tier-2 aggregation to reduce WAN costs. Obviously, it should not be used as a blueprint given the many variables associated with WAN bandwidth costs.

Shorter Leased Line Distances

In considering the previous point about cost-effective bandwidth deployment, it is generally possible that by aggregating the leased lines at a Tier-2 site, the total average distance of the leased lines on the network is reduced.

Clearly, this requires an analysis of the geographic distances between the sites. PVC-based technologies such as ATM or Frame Relay may or may not have a pricing structure that relates to the physical distance between the sites connecting the PVC. However, it is often true in practice that some relationship exists between PVC distance and cost. It may be, for example, that if the PVC extends beyond a particular geographic zone, then the cost will increase. Again, at the risk of sounding repetitious, you must carefully clarify all of these details with your service provider.

Reduced Core Router Ports or Interfaces

Another advantage of PVC or leased line aggregation is that the number of WAN router serial ports or WAN interfaces is reduced. In the case of leased lines, fewer serial ports are required on the Tier-1 routers. This potentially reduces routing overhead on the Tier-1 routers, as well as presenting a possible cost saving with respect to router ports.

If Frame Relay or ATM is being used, it is unlikely that much of a difference in terms of the number of router interfaces will occur because these technologies can run multiple PVCs on the same physical serial interface. However, PVC aggregation at Tier-2 does mean that fewer PVCs terminate at the main office site. This has the benefit of reducing router processing at the Tier-1 site. An example of this has already been discussed in relation to broadcasting over Frame Relay and ATM.

Less Routing Protocol Neighbors

For larger networks, a scalable routing protocol such as OSPF or EIGRP should be used. As shown when discussing flat topologies, these protocols can have a practical limitation on the number of neighbors supported on each Tier-1 router.

These routing protocols rely on neighbor formation with directly connected routers, and neighbor relationship is formed on each serial link or PVC. The potential problem caused by the upper limit on IP routing neighbor relationships can be alleviated using a hierarchical design rather than a flat one. This is achieved because fewer leased lines or PVCs connect to the Tier-1 site with a hierarchical design.

Route Summarization

IP route summarization greatly increases a network's stability and scalability, as was already discussed. A hierarchical design facilitates route summarization much more easily than a flat WAN structure.

Figure 2-8
Hierarchical route
summarization

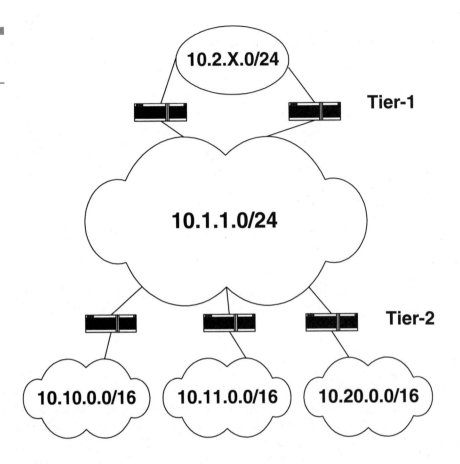

For example, consider the network shown in Figure 2-8. This is a relatively straightforward example of hierarchical route summarization and is a useful illustration.

This network uses a private Class A 10.0.0.0 addressing structure with 24-bit subnet masks being used on all LAN and WAN subnets. Cisco's EIGRP is the IP routing protocol. Each Tier-2 site summarizes all the networks that attach to it from the Tier-3 side. This includes Tier-3 LAN segments, Tier-3 WAN links, and Tier-2 LAN segments. These subnets are all summarized into a single route 10.x.0.0/16, where x is between 10 and 20 inclusive. Tier-2 sites connect to Tier-1 over a multipoint Frame Relay cloud, which is addressed as 10.1.1.0/24. All the Tier-1 LAN segments are addressed as 10.2.x.0/24.

This summarization scheme would reduce routing table and topology database size. This in turn would improve the network's scalability, speed up route convergence, and ultimately increase the network stability.

Broadcast Control in the WAN

A hierarchical design will not in itself reduce the level of broadcasts that are being passed in the WAN. However, one difference it makes is that because fewer sites are now connecting directly into the Tier-1 site, the Tier-1 routers have fewer broadcasts to process both inbound and outbound. This serves to minimize any overhead incurred by the backbone routers due to broadcast handling.

Disaster Recovery

The most fundamental goal of a disaster recovery plan is to ensure the backup availability of the Tier-1 core resources. In other words, network connectivity to some form of backup Tier-1 site must be achievable.

In a flat design, this means that connectivity would be required from every remote site to the disaster fail-over site. For example, in the case of a Frame Relay WAN topology, this could be achieved by having a backup PVC from every site on the network to the disaster recovery site. It could be difficult to administer the execution of this plan due to the number of sites and PVCs involved, and for the same reason it could be prohibitively expensive. Figure 2-9 shows an example of this type of disaster recovery.

It is easier to perform fail-over from just the Tier-2 sites rather than from every remote site on the network. In a hierarchical design, such as in Figure 2-10, this is all that is required. A disaster recovery plan could be executed without interfering with any of the Tier-3 sites, which would likely make for a smoother transition as well as providing a potentially more cost-effective solution.

Issues with a Hierarchical Design

WAN Costs

As this chapter has established, WAN costs can be a disadvantage of a hierarchical design as well as an advantage. More often than not, as a network scales or grows, a hierarchical design provides a more cost-effective solution. However, nothing is ever cut and dry in network design. The designer has to ascertain whether this is true of the particular network that he or she is designing. If it is true that a hierarchical design can provide more cost-effective scaling on a network, then at what point in terms of network size does this become true? These questions can only be answered strictly on an individual basis. Every network is different, and even more significantly, every telecommunications service provider has its own pricing plans that need to be carefully understood. It is necessary to cost out *all* solutions before concluding that a hierarchical design will reduce the WAN costs.

Additional Router Hops

Hierarchical design introduces an extra router hop between most of the remote sites on the network, namely the Tier-3 sites and the central Tier-1 site. Additional router hops always mean increased latency or delay on the network.

In the case of a Tier-3 site accessing core resources at the central site, one additional router hop exists as compared to a flat design. For Tier-3 sites

Figure 2-9
Disaster recovery with a flat topology

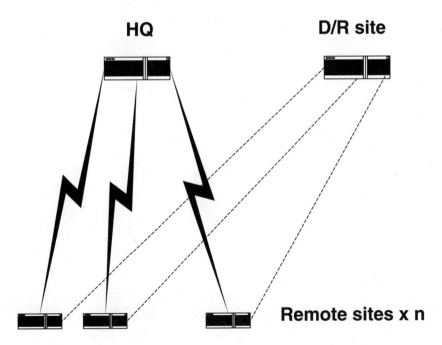

HQ

D/R site

Remote sites x n

communicating with each other, at least two additional hops are available. This is demonstrated in Figure 2-11. With a hierarchical design, it is wise to limit the number of router hops and maximum network diameter.

The network designer should strive to achieve the following goals in terms of maximum number of router hops:

- A maximum of three hops from a Tier-3 LAN to the Tier-1 LAN.

- A maximum of six hops from any Tier-3 LAN to any other Tier-3 LAN. Six hops should only be necessary for communication between two dispersed Tier-3 sites that ultimately connect to the main office resources via different Tier-1 routers. This is demonstrated in Figure 2-11.

Figure 2-10
Disaster recovery with a hierarchical topology

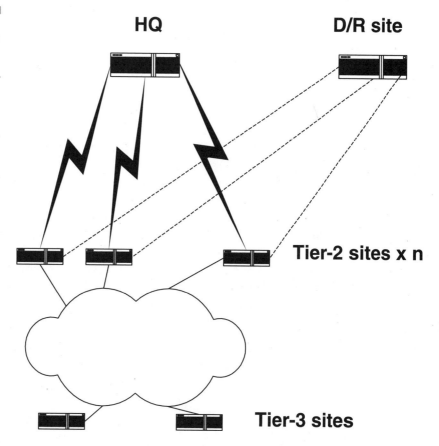

HQ   D/R site

Tier-2 sites x n

Tier-3 sites

Figure 2-11
Minimizing the
network diameter

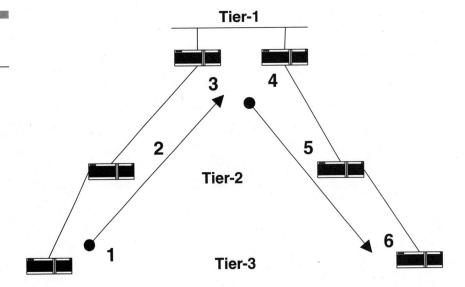

Using Layer-3 switching or multilayer switching on the routers can minimize the actual latency associated with a router hop. These technologies enable the router to cache routing information that is extracted based on real traffic flow. The cache provides layer-3 and layer-4 information that facilitates a one-to-one lookup. This is distinct from a routing table lookup, which is one-to-many and is therefore slower. Layer-3 and multilayer switching is also faster because it is primarily hardware-based rather than looking up a software-derived routing table. All major router manufacturers support layer-3 switching and multilayer, although usually configuration constraints such as access lists, need to be understood in order to implement the feature.

The deployment of Layer 3 switching is discussed in detail in Chapter 8.

Remember:
- Try to minimize the number of router hops required to communicate across the network.
- Use layer-3 or multilayer switching, where possible, to reduce the latency associated with router hops.

Conclusion

In our discussion so far, you have seen that a flat or single layer design may be the only requirement in a small- to medium-sized network, such as the classic star or hub and spoke configuration. A geographically dispersed network that does not include a clearly defined central site may also be better suited for a flat design because it is difficult by its nature to impose a hierarchy on it.

A hierarchical WAN topology is often necessary for larger networks; however, you have seen that it is difficult to ascertain the exact point at which a hierarchical design becomes the best solution. To successfully decide on the correct design, you must understand the issues such as leased line and PVC aggregation, WAN costs, routing protocol operation, and route summarization.

The Hierarchical Layers

This section discusses some of the key issues in relation to the functionality of Tier-3, Tier-2, and Tier-1 sites. At different layers in the hierarchy, these sites form part of an overall design, and they each have functions above and beyond the simple provision of network connectivity.

The Tier-3 Layer

The networking functions and policies implemented at Tier-3 are examined in this section.

Implementing Policies at Tier-3 The routing, security, and other network policies that can be implemented at Tier-3 will now be discussed.

Routing Policies Static routes are sometimes used on the Tier-3 routers in order to reduce the sizes of their routing tables and also to minimize the routing updates on the WAN links. The disadvantage of static routes is that they place an administrative overhead on the network. Redistributing the static routes into the dynamic routing protocol can reduce this administration.

If OSPF is the routing protocol, routing overhead can be reduced at the Tier-3 sites by placing them in stub areas. This will be discussed in detail during the chapter on OSPF.

Other policies that can be implemented at Tier-3 in order to control routing overhead on the network. Route filters could be configured on the Tier-3 routers so that they only advertise their directly-connected networks. Tier-3 routers don't have a responsibility to give routing information to any downstream neighbors because Tier-3 is effectively the end of the line stub. Consider the example of Figure 2-12. The Tier-3 router is configured using a route filter to advertise only its four directly connected networks — three physical and one loopback network. This filtering prevents any unnecessary routing updates from wasting expensive WAN bandwidth.

If just a single active link exists between the Tier-3 and Tier-2 site, then the principle of split horizon prevents routing information from being advertised back to the WAN link over which it was learned. However, if more than one link exists from Tier-3 to Tier-2 sites, as is the case with most resilient designs, then route filters must be used. This is because routes learned over the primary interface can be advertised out the backup interface and vice versa.

Remember that the principle of filtering unnecessary traffic can be applied to any unnecessary traffic and not just routing updates. For example, application-related traffic does not need to be advertised back into the core if it does not relate to services that are located at that Tier-3 site.

Remember:
- Route filters can be used on Tier-3 routers so that only directly connected networks are advertised across the WAN links into the Tier-2 sites.
- Similarly, any unnecessary application traffic can be prevented from going back into the core by filtering at Tier-3.

Security Policies The Tier-3 sites are by definition at the edge of the network. Therefore, the only type of security policies that can be implemented here are as follows:

- Controlling what enterprise resources local users have access to.

If it is necessary to prevent some local Tier-3 LAN users from having access to certain enterprise resources at the Tier-1 router, then this policy should be implemented on the Tier-3 router. Filtering at this point is more efficient than allowing that traffic to cross the WAN before it is denied by a router access list and dropped. Generally, it is a good idea to put security filters as close to the source as possible for the reason just described.

- Controlling the level of access that the rest of the corporation, and the outside world in general, have to the local Tier-3 LAN.

Most commonly, the local Tier-3 LAN does not contain important enterprise servers, so this is less of a concern as the first. However, it is certainly not irrelevant, particularly in the case of specialized applications and departments.

Consider the example of a law department, which is not part of the company's main business and happens to be located at one of their Tier-3 sites. They might share the same router for WAN access as the rest of the users on that site, but they may have special security requirements. In this case, inbound and outbound filters may have to be configured on the Tier-3 router to completely isolate the Law LAN segment from not only the other local users, but the rest of the organization apart from the legal department.

Remember:
- When controlling access for Tier-3 LAN users to certain core resources, it is more efficient to place the filters as close to the source as possible.

Tier-3 as Part of the Design Model   When implementing a layered structure, adhere to it. It is not advisable to add small new routers below the most remote layer, for example. This would start to add a layer of Tier-4 routers, which would gradually compromise the original design and open a back door to the network. In a three-tiered model, any new site, however small, should be a Tier-3 site. In other words, this site must directly attach to one or more Tier-2 sites.

It is a common problem in relation to the operational management of existing networks that some small new sites might be added and made to hang off an existing Tier-3 site. This may seem convenient at the time, but if the original network design is gradually eroded, then there will come a point where the original design is simply no longer in place, and the network may start to behave or misbehave accordingly.

Adding another tier also adds more router hops. A hierarchical design should be scaled by widening the network rather than adding another layer and hence more router hops.

Remember:

■ Don't introduce a Tier-4 for even very small sites. Scale by widening the network rather than introducing another layer.

The Tier-2 Layer

The networking functions and policies implemented at Tier-2 are examined in this section.

Functions of the Tier-2 Layer   The Tier-2 layer has two fundamental functions:

■ To provide network access to LAN users that are local to that particular Tier-2 site.

■ To act as an aggregation point for a number of Tier-3 sites, providing access to the network backbone to each of these sites.

Because the Tier-2 layer does more than just provide network access to local users, a number of network functions can be implemented at this layer.

■ Policy implementation:

  ▪ Route filtering and manipulation

  ▪ Packet manipulation, for example, protocol translation, *Network Address Translation* (NAT), and IP tunneling

  ▪ Filtering of application traffic for security or network efficiency

■ Remote access services for telecommuters or mobile users

■ Internet access

■ Protocol redistribution if required

Although it is possible and in some cases desirable to implement these functions at Tier-2, the real issue is that they are not carried out on the main Tier-1 routers. Any functionality that entails significant router overhead such as filtering or packet manipulation should be devolved away from the Tier-1 routers that provide WAN connectivity to the rest of the network. If these routers slow down, then so does the entire network.

Services such as remote access and Internet access are just as likely (if not more so) to be provided at the Tier-1 site. If these services are provided at the core site, it is advisable to use specialized routers in order to offload this functionality from the main WAN routers.

Application and route filtering are examples of functions that can be effectively implemented at Tier-2, such as the filtering of unnecessary application or routing updates from propagating to Tier-1 or Tier-3 sites. Some filtering may also be performed at Tier-2 for security purposes. How exactly this is done is determined by the application and routing requirements.

Choosing a Tier-2 Site The following is a summary of the main issues to be considered when evaluating the suitability of a site for the Tier-2 function.

Geographic Location A site is often designated as being a Tier-2 site because of its geographic location, and a key function of Tier-2 sites is to provide a WAN aggregation point for a set of Tier-3 sites. A Tier-2 site may be chosen because it has one or both of the following characteristics:

- Having this site as the Tier-2 site would minimize the average leased line distance from the Tier-3 sites and the Tier-1 sites. Note that it is even more important to minimize the distance to the Tier-1 site because it is the highest bandwidth link.

- This site may be in a particular geographic region where tariffs are more favorable from the telecommunications service provider.

Local Users and Resources Tier-2 sites are often bigger and busier in terms of the operations of the corporation or enterprise. They may be of increased strategic importance within the company.

Tier-2 sites might typically have a greater number of local users or LAN clients. More significantly, they might also have a number of applications servers present locally. If clients at various Tier-3 sites access these servers, then it would make sense to designate this site as being Tier-2.

Technical Support Availability Given that Tier-2 sites are strategically important within the networking infrastructure, it is often a key practical concern to ensure the availability of adequate technical support staff at such a site.

Even in this age of remote network management, often no substitute exists for some competence on the ground. This factor is not to be underestimated when deciding which sites become Tier-2 sites.

Designing Tier-2 Sites I will now discuss the design parameters that must be addressed in relation to Tier-2 sites.

Traffic and Capacity Planning The Tier-2 site must be able to comfortably aggregate the total traffic from its downstream Tier-3 sites along with its own local traffic that is destined for the Tier-1 site.

Estimates should be made on the likely levels of WAN utilization from each Tier-3 site and the Tier-2 site itself. Some room for growth above this total should then be incorporated into the bandwidth capacity on the Tier-2 to Tier-1 links. It is important to incorporate room for growth and increased traffic conditions when purchasing leased lines. In the case of packet-switched technologies such as Frame Relay or ATM, this may be less of an issue. These technologies usually allow for a flexible bandwidth profile that can be easily modified.

Scaling Within the Layered Structure The first issue that has to be decided is the question of how many Tier-3 sites a Tier-2 site should support. The factors to consider are as follows:

(i) Increasing the ratio of Tier-3 sites for each Tier-2 site can maximize the benefits of a hierarchical structure. These include serial line or PVC aggregation and route summarization.

(ii) Having too many Tier-3 sites terminating at a Tier-2 site can place increased processing overhead on the Tier-2 routers. Given the importance of Tier-2 sites to the routing architecture, this is clearly undesirable. Of course, the use of multilayer or layer-3 switching on the Tier-2 routers is of course advisable.

It is very difficult to put a concrete number on the maximum number of Tier-3 sites for each Tier-2. Its difficulty lies in the fact that so many variables must be considered—the WAN technology itself, the IP routing protocol, and the requirements of the network applications, to name a few. However, in the interest of attempting to to solve this problem, I personally would be reluctant to have more than 15 to 20 Tier-3 sites per Tier-2 site.

When scaling the network, add more Tier-2 sites if that is what is required to support growth in the number of Tier-3 sites. As with Tier-3 sites, scale the Tier-2 layer by widening the network. A site should be either Tier-2 or Tier-3. Avoid falling between two stools, and introducing improvised sites that have both Tier-3 and Tier-2 characteristics. Remember this will only serve to erode and invalidate the original design.

Remember:

■ The Tier-2 portion of the network should be scaled by widening the network rather than by introducing another layer and more router hops.

Tier-2 Resilience   The Tier-2 layer of the network must provide two types of resilience:

■ **Resilient network connectivity for Tier-3 sites**   This can be achieved by connecting each Tier-3 site to separate Tier-2 sites. Typically, one connection is treated as primary with every Tier-3 site having a designated primary Tier-2 site. The other connection is to the designated backup Tier-2 site. If the second connection is purely for backup purposes, then no traffic is passed over it unless the primary link fails. The alternative is to run the two links in a load-sharing manner. Alternatively a different technology, such as ISDN, could be used to provide redundant backup for the main WAN connections. The relative merits of these different approaches are discussed later in this chapter in the section on WAN resilience.

■ **Resilient connectivity to the Tier-1 core**   Again, the approach can be to dual home each Tier-2 site to different Tier-1 sites (or at least different Tier-1 routers if only one Tier-1 site exists). The alternative is to use a different technology to backup the primary connection, such as the use of ISDN to backup Frame Relay. It can be more prevalent to use load sharing on resilient links between Tier-2 and Tier-1. The reason for this is that the bandwidth levels are higher and it may not be cost-effective to have very high-capacity connections lying in a purely redundant mode.

The Backbone: Tier-1

The Tier-1 layer of the hierarchy is also known as the network backbone or core and can take the form of a single site or multiple sites. More than one Tier-1 site may exist for the following reasons:

■ The corporate structure of the organization may dictate that multiple central sites be available, each serving a different major function.

■ A second Tier-1 may be prudent for the purpose of network resilience. A typical design scenario might have half of the Tier-2 sites connecting to one Tier-1 site and half to the other.

Figure 2-12
Route filterign at Tier-
3 sites

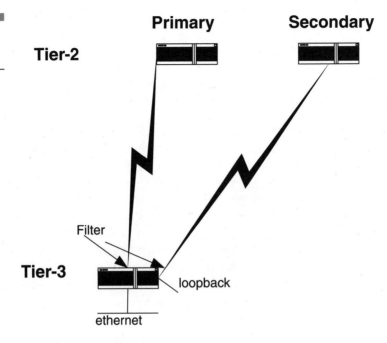

In the case of multiple Tier-1 sites, they are usually (but not necessarily) within close geographic proximity to each other. The Tier-1 sites may be connected by a campus backbone if the buildings are only a mile or two apart. If they are more spread out, then a *Metropolitan Area Network (MAN)* may be used to provide inter connectivity.

This chapter centers on WAN design elements rather than the campus, which is dealt with in a later chapter. For the moment, let's just say that a typical campus backbone could use the following:

- ATM.
- Fast Ethernet or Gigabit Ethernet over fiber. It would need to be over fiber to overcome any distance limitations
- Point-to-point fiber or alternatively *Synchronous Optical Network (SONET)*
- *Fiber Distributed Data Interface* (FDDI) could be used, but that is more likely to be a legacy solution because FDDI is being phased out by the other technologies mentioned previously.

Figure 2-13 shows a schematic of a typical campus backbone at Tier-1, with Gigabit Ethernet over Fiber being the backbone technology.

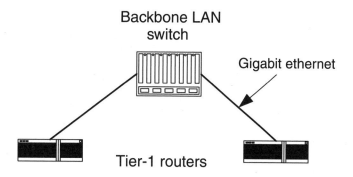

Backbone LAN
switch

Gigabit ethernet

Tier-1 routers

R3 has no WAN
responsibility here

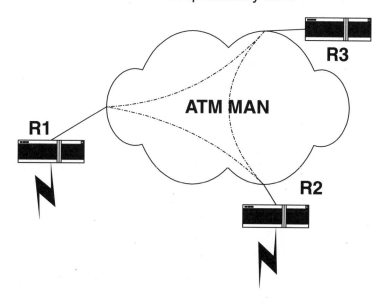

A Metropolitan backbone usually stretches over longer distances than a campus, such as a city and its suburbs. It often uses services provided by a public carrier such as ATM or SONET. However, it is not unusual for a large corporation to purchase and manage its own private MAN.

The use of an ATM MAN to interconnect the Tier-1 sites is shown in Figure 2-14. This ATM service could be purchased from a service provider. Alternatively, it could take the form of a privately managed ATM switch, which is connected to over fiber links.

The design of the Tier-1 site relates not only to the core site itself, but also to how it fits into the overall network design, which is very important when you bear in mind the importance of the backbone.

A well-designed Tier-1 site or campus should exhibit the following characteristics:

■ Minimal unnecessary traffic

Minimize any unnecessary traffic crossing the WAN links between the Tier-2 and Tier-1 sites. Similarly, the Tier-1 backbone should be kept as free as possible from overhead traffic.

If the Tier-1 core or backbone becomes congested, then effectively, the entire network is congested in terms of accessing enterprise resources. It should be a fundamental design goal to ensure that the only traffic crossing the Tier-1 backbone is for accessing core resources. It is usually inevitable that some overhead traffic due to the routing protocol and applications will be present on the Tier-1 backbone, however this should be minimized. The Tier-1 site(s) should be kept as "lean and mean" as possible. All unnecessary traffic should be kept off the backbone, particularly broadcasts.

Remember:
■ Minimize unnecessary traffic going into Tier-1 from Tier-2. Also mini mize any unnecessary traffic between Tier-1 sites.

■ Minimal overhead on Tier-1 routers

Network policies such as routing policies and security should be implemented as much as possible at the Tier-3 and Tier-2 sites. If at all possible, packet filtering should not be implemented at the Tier-1 layer. The configuration of access lists on core routers (as with any router) increases overhead and slows the router down. In many cases, having an access list on a router interface means that the router must compare every packet that passes that interface against this access list. This can have an adverse effect on router performance, particularly if the access list is very long or poorly designed.

At times, it is essential to implement a particular policy on the Tier-1 routers because technically, it cannot be done elsewhere on the network. If this is really the case (and you should be sure that it is), then ensure that the filters or access lists are well-designed and as short as possible. A well-designed access list should have the most restrictive statements at the top of the list. This way, the router should not have to scroll down through most of the list before deciding that the packet has to be dropped.

Layer-3 or multilayer switching should be employed on the Tier-1 routers to speed up the switching of packets at the network core. Having access lists or filters configured on these routers does not preclude the use of multilayer switching. However, it may impose additional configuration constraints that need to be understood on the vendor's router.

Remember:

- Try to avoid implementing policies at Tier-1. In cases where it is unavoidable, minimize the overhead on the Tier-1 routers by configuring efficient filters or access lists.
- *Use layer-3 switching regardless of whether or not filters are configured.*

In line with the principle of minimizing overhead on the Tier-1 routers, the following functions should *not* be implemented on the Tier-1 routers that provide WAN connectivity to Tier-2:

- Internet access

- Remote access for telecommuters or mobile users

- Any specialized functions such as protocol translation or IP tunneling

Other routers that are located at the Tier-1 site or campus specializing in these tasks should provide these functions because all of these tasks involve a high degree of overhead. Remote access and Internet connectivity involve security checking, filtering, or access lists and possible packet manipulation such as NAT. Protocol Translation and, to a lesser extent, IP tunneling also involves increased overhead.

It is better to offload these functions to specialized routers and allow the main Tier-1 WAN routers to do what they do best — to route packets efficiently.

- Adequate capacity

Adequate bandwidth capacity must be present at two points:

(i) On the WAN links from the Tier-2 sites to the Tier-1 site(s). The network designer must plan for the aggregation of all Tier-3 and Tier-2 WAN traffic.

(ii) On the Tier-1 LAN or campus backbone. Enough bandwidth must be available to service the traffic to and from the applications and enterprise servers. This should cater for the aggregation of all Tier-3 and Tier-2 traffic to the core along with local Tier-1 traffic. All applications including the Internet should be accounted for.

- Resilience

Resilience at the backbone is even more critical than at any other point in the network. The isolation of the Tier-1 site due to a network fault would mean that the corporation's enterprise services would be unavailable. The following steps should be taken to ensure the resilience of the backbone site:

1. Consider using more than one Tier-1 site. Connect the sites together using a campus backbone or possibly a MAN. Figure 2-13 and Figure 2-14 demonstrate this type of architecture. Every Tier-2 site connects to each Tier-1 site, usually in a load-sharing manner called dual homing, as explained earlier.

2. If it is decided not to have a second Tier-1 site, then at very least, a minimum of two Tier-1 WAN routers should be used. Every Tier-2 site should be dual-homed to each of the Tier-1 routers.

3. Ensure that all Tier-1 routers have dual power supplies and also *uninterruptible power supplies* (UPS).

WAN Design Parameters

In designing a WAN, certain questions need to be asked in order to characterize the goal that is to be achieved. The fundamental parameters against which a WAN design is assessed are summarized in this section. These are the parameters that drive the WAN.

Cost

The WAN is the single most expensive element of any corporate network. When designing a network, the engineer must address a wide variety of complex issues such as the application characteristics, the routing protocol requirements, and so on. However, when it comes to designing the WAN the most fundamental driving force is cost.

The issue of cost is often the single greatest factor influencing the type of WAN technology used and the type of structure it takes. WAN costs have been discussed a number of times during the course of this chapter, and this is certainly not the last time that they will be referred to. Every network design is made within budgetary constraints and because of its cost, the WAN is a particularly sensitive area. The following points, however, should be kept on mind in relation to WAN costs:

(i) Clearly understand all the factors that influence the pricing from a telecommunications carrier. They can vary dramatically from company to company or even between geographic regions. Make no assumptions as you strive to avoid any hidden catches. If my advice seems slightly paranoid, then let me assure you that my paranoia has developed from much experience!

(ii) Perform a costing over the lifetime of the network. It is unwise to choose a solution that is the least expensive for a two-year span only. Any special deal should be viewed with a healthy skepticism and analyzed thoroughly.

(iii) Analyze other elements that contribute to the total cost. Bear in mind that support is the second most expensive element to owning a network. For example, it might appear attractive to have a private ATM network where you could apply generous bandwidth profiles without incurring additional cost. A key element here is the the cost of attracting and maintaining a technical support staff of the requisite skill level, which might make this solution prohibitively expensive.

(iv) Finally, although cost is hugely significant, it isn't everything! It is not much use implementing the least expensive solution if the network fails to perform to any satisfactory level of performance. Situations have occurred where, for this very reason, a network had to be radically redesigned with a more expensive solution. The network then ultimately cost much more than if this solution had been implemented in the first place.

Availability and Performance

Network availability in the WAN depends on the following factors:

- The reliability of the WAN technology as provided by the telecommunications carrier.

■ The amount of resilience that has been built into the WAN. This topic will be discussed in the very next section.

The WAN is often a traffic bottleneck, because it is usually the slowest part of the network in terms of bandwidth. Latency in the WAN is usually the largest component of the end-to-end delay between a client and server. This latency is inversely proportional to the bandwidth and directly proportional to the packet size used by the application (however, large packets improve throughput).

It is evident that the WAN is a key element in determining network performance for users that are not local to the main office site. The performance of the WAN is dependent on two basic factors:

(i) The amount of WAN bandwidth.

No matter how well designed and engineered your network is, a time may come when it will be necessary to provide more bandwidth. Although it is extremely important to design your network such that WAN bandwidth is used as efficiently as possible, it is also important to recognize when you can go no further in terms of design.

(ii) The efficiency with which the WAN bandwidth is used.

This is probably a far more significant factor than the previous point. Solving a performance problem by simply purchasing more bandwidth effectively involves throwing money at the problem without addressing its cause. It is also a luxury that most companies cannot afford.

It is essential to understand the traffic patterns on WAN in question. This means understanding the client-server traffic flows across the WAN.

It is necessary to understand which users or clients need to access which resources. The location of these resources along with an estimate of their bandwidth consumption must be established. The identity as well as physical and logical location of all clients and servers should be known on a well-managed network.

The applications on the network should be understood in as much depth as possible. This principle is applicable to any type of network design and beyond the WAN. For example, the degree to which the application depends on broadcasts or multicasts should be understood. It is the application that determines the main traffic that has to be supported by the network. "Designing from the top down" is a somewhat well-worn cliché, but it does make a valid point.

It is important to establish detailed figures on the application parameters, particularly those that relate to bandwidth consumption. Assess the current values for these parameters and project future growth during the network's lifetime. A lifetime of no more than five to 10 years maximum should be projected, as it is impossible and unrealistic to look any further into the future in this rapidly changing technological environment that we operate within. The application bandwidth utilization should be assessed in a lab if you are not satisfied with vendor estimates. Having clients and a server attached to the same LAN switch and using a LAN analyzer with port mirroring on the switch to monitor traffic levels would suffice in the lab.

It is always a design goal to minimize the amount of client-server traffic crossing the WAN, where possible. The technical and practical feasibility and financial viability of locating servers locally rather than centrally should be examined. Sometimes re-engineering the application can dramatically reduce WAN bandwidth consumption and increase performance. For example, in a Windows NT environment, forcing clients to authenticate the domain logon across the WAN has a very negative effect on performance, as users may have to drag down their user profiles across a busy WAN link. This can particularly cause problems if multiple users are logging in simultaneously, for example, at the beginning of the working day. One resolution to such a problem would be to locate a *Backup Domain Controller* (BDC) locally. Thus, authentication could occur on the local LAN.

As a general means of ensuring that applications are working in an efficient manner, a similar and rigorous examination of all applications on the network, including Mainframe and any other legacy systems, should be performed.

Redundancy and Resilience

The provision of effective resilience is an extremely important design goal. Its complexity is often underestimated. For this reason I will now lay further emphasis on some of the key relevant issues.

Options for Achieving Resilience   Resilience is required at each layer of the WAN hierarchy. In a three-tiered hierarchical topology, resilience is required on the WAN connections between Tier-3 and Tier-2 and between the Tier-2 sites and the core.

In terms of achieving this resilience, a number of fundamental options exist:

Figure 2-15
Example of partial-
mesh frame relay
/ATM

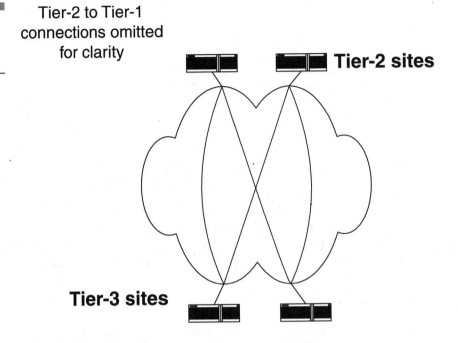

Tier-2 to Tier-1
connections omitted
for clarity

Tier-2 sites

Tier-3 sites

- It is possible to back up "like with like." This means using the same technology as backup to the primary WAN link. An example of this would be using full or partial-mesh Frame Relay to provide backup PVCs to primary Frame Relay connections. This is shown in Figure 2-15.

- In this type of scenario, the next question to be answered is whether the backup links should act in a load-sharing mode with the primary or whether they should be used strictly for backup purposes. Strict backup means the backup links only carry traffic when the primary links fail.

The issues to consider when making this choice are as follows:

- Load sharing can make the IP routing more complex, particularly if the backup link is of a lower bandwidth than the primary, because no standardized IP routing protocols support unequal cost load balancing. Therefore, to achieve load balancing with OSPF, for example, the metrics would have to be manipulated to fool the protocol into seeing equal cost paths. This is not a satisfactory practice and may cause other problems, as you will see in future chapters.

- In the case of Frame Relay or ATM, using a PVC explicitly for backup is usually less expensive. This cost issue can vary depending on the service provider. However, most providers offer deals on backup PVCs on the proviso that the PVC is only utilized if the primary PVC fails.

- When using leased lines to backup other leased lines, it will not be cost-effective to leave one leased line in idle standby. When using serial links to backup other serial links, it is better to do equal cost load balancing. If it is required that no degradation in service occurs if one link fails, then clearly the two links together would run at no more than a 50 percent average utilization in normal conditions.

- Use an alternate technology to act as backup to the primary WAN connections, such as using ISDN to provide a backup for leased lines. This type of backup is not usually done in load sharing mode, although the backup technology can be configured to kick in when a particular load level is exceeded on the primary link.

How Real Is the Resilience?

One final and very important point needs to be made in relation to resilience in the WAN. The designer must have a clear understanding of the extent to which the resilience applies.

Consider the typical design scenario where redundant WAN links are on each site on the network. Although that might seem satisfactory, the designer must be able to answer the following questions:

- Is the local loop ducting that connects the primary and backup circuits to the local central office switch different? If not, then no redundancy in the local loop exists.

- Sometimes companies use different service providers in an attempt to achieve resilience. If so, are the local loop connections over different cables? Often, one service provider is just leasing the local loop from the other service provider.

- If separate providers are being used, it must also be ascertained whether one provider is simply leasing space on the other's local central office switch. If this is so, then you certainly do not have the redundancy that should be achieved by using a second carrier. Remember that a second carrier almost always increases the cost of the network, because you miss out on bulk discounts. The administrative overhead of maintaining a relationship with a second service provider for the same network should also be taken into consideration. By not having one single point of contact with one service provider, you will probably increase the cost of supporting the network.

- Are the primary and backup circuits terminating on different central office switches?

- If the primary and backup circuits are terminating at the same central office, then at the very least they must be terminating on completely different equipment racks.

- Now apart from the local loop, what about resilience elsewhere? Can you be sure that the primary and backup circuits are taking completely different paths from source to destination through the service provider's network?

Choosing the WAN Technology

In this chapter the design issues encountered with the different major *Wide Area Network* (WAN) technologies will be examined. The driving forces that influence the choice of WAN technology will also be studied.

W A N technology is traditionally segregated into three fundamental categories. Synchronous serial or point-to-point leased lines will first be addressed from a network design perspective.

The second category to be studied is packet-switched WAN technology. Frame Relay, X.25, and ATM can all be loosely described as packet-switched technologies. Frame Relay has largely superceded and is replacing X.25. Therefore, the latter technology will not be discussed in this chapter because it is very unlikely that a new network would be designed around X.25. ATM technically can be described as cell relay because it switches fixed-length cells rather than variable-length frames. It is nonetheless categorized with Frame Relay. The motivations for deploying ATM will be addressed, as well as the main design issues associated with its implementation.

The third category is dial-up WAN or circuit-switched WAN. This will be covered in the form of ISDN. The specific design challenges that relate to the different applications of ISDN will be studied in this chapter.

Design Considerations for Serial Links

Synchronous serial links or leased lines are the most traditional of the WAN technologies in widespread deployment on modern networks. Although it is the simplest type of WAN technology, the following issues should be taken into consideration when deploying serial links on your network:

■ The use of serial leased lines is often the most expensive type of WAN bandwidth. For leased lines to be cost-effective, they should be exhibiting over a minimum of 50 percent bandwidth utilization because the subscriber is being charged for the purchased speed of the link independent of utilization levels. When deciding on an appropriate leased line speed, existing traffic levels should be catered for, while leaving some room for growth.

- Leased lines are less flexible than other WAN technologies in terms of modifying the available bandwidth. Technologies such as Frame Relay and ATM allow for the purchase of a flexible bandwidth profile that can usually be adjusted with ease. This flexibility is not necessarily true of leased lines. Therefore, a good degree of capacity planning should be done prior to purchasing a serial line.

- Synchronous serial lines have the advantage of producing less overhead than packet-switched technologies such as Frame Relay or ATM.

- The choices of data link layer (layer 2) protocol on serial lines are as follows:

  - **HDLC**   This is a derivative of IBM's SDLC, which was developed to support a single protocol, namely SNA. HDLC was never fully standardized in its support of multiple protocols and, for this reason, is a proprietary protocol. Most major networking vendors have their own implementation of HDLC. The upshot of all of this is that HDLC cannot be used on a serial link that connects two routers from different vendors.

    The advantages of HDLC are simplicity of operation and configuration. It also entails minimal overhead. These advantages are not to be underestimated and they mean that HDLC can be an adequate layer 2 serial link protocol in a single router-vendor environment.

  - ***Point-to-point protocol*** (**PPP**)   PPP is a sophisticated data link layer WAN protocol that can be applied to serial links or ISDN. It will be discussed in more detail in the upcoming section on ISDN. Although it is more complex than HDLC, the only major additional features it provides is that it is a standard (and that could be important) and also has the support of CHAP authentication.

    Authentication might not be as critical on a serial link as on an open network like ISDN. Nevertheless it is good practice as part of your security policy.

  - **SLIP**   Don't even think about it! It has been superceded by PPP.

- Redundancy on serial links can also be expensive if serial lines are used to backup other serial lines. Particularly if it is required that there is no possibility of degraded service in the event of a link failure. Potentially more cost-effective solutions include the following:

- Purchasing two serial lines that together support the total WAN utilization from a site. These links can then be configured to operate in load balancing mode. If one link fails, the network may exhibit degraded service due to congestion. This is the classic tradeoff of cost versus performance. Some words of caution about load balancing IP over serial links will be offered in the chapters on IP routing.

- Using an alternate technology such as ISDN to restore network connectivity in the event of a serial line failure. ISDN can also be used to backup the serial lines if a certain traffic load is exceeded. This is sometimes termed *bandwidth top-up*.

- It is often worthwhile to implement compression on serial links. Compression algorithms improve throughput across those expensive serial links. The relative improvement in throughput is dependent on the exact type of compression being used and on the protocol to which it is applied. Although the advantage of compression is obvious, it does have a couple of potential drawbacks:

  - Compression can be CPU intensive for the device that implements it.
  - It usually increases latency, which can add up if compression is implemented over multiple serial links between the source and destination. This can also cause a problem for very time-sensitive applications such as SNA or LAT.

For these reasons, compression should only be used on slower WAN links between 56k up to a maximum of 128k.

A number of options must be considered when employing compression. It can be implemented through software running on the router. Alternatively, it can be implemented using hardware that is either integrated or external to the router. The choice here is made against the parameters of cost and performance, which of course vary with the different vendors.

When evaluating compression performance, the different types of compression must be considered against the type of applications and traffic that is on the network. Most vendors of compression hardware or software support the following types of compression:

- **Full data compression** This is sometimes called *link compression* because it compresses all data that crosses the link, header, and payload. Different vendors at either the hardware level or software level support this type of compression. This type of compression is appropriate on point-to-point serial lines. The percentage improvement varies depending on the compression product and the nature of the traffic being compressed.

- **Header compression** This type of compression is often implemented within the router software and is applicable to traffic that is mainly composed of header, for example Telnet, LAT, or Xremote sessions. In the case of Telnet, a 20-byte TCP header and a 20-byte IP header with just 1 byte of payload exists. Header compression can be very CPU-intensive because it is more difficult to only compress the header.

- **Payload compression** This is also CPU-intensive due to the complexity of only compressing the payload. Payload compression can be appropriate for packet-switched media link Frame Relay or ATM because the data link header must remain intact when traversing these media. In other words, the DLCI or ATM VPI/VCI cannot be manipulated through compression when crossing a public network. It is also cost-effective due to the more efficient use of bandwidth. For example, multiple small IP packets could be in the same Frame Relay packet and become the compressed payload. Note that payload compression is not only CPU-intensive, it also increases latency. It should generally not be used if most of the data is traversing a path that consists of more than three router hops. This is of course just a rule of thumb, and it is also dependent on how delay-sensitive the traffic is.

Remember:

- Compression can be suitable on low-speed WAN links.

- Different types of compression have various levels of CPU-intensity and latency associated with them.

- Choose the correct type of compression (header, payload, or data) to suit the predominant traffic that is on the WAN.

- **IP Unnumbered** This is a feature supported by most router vendors. Its intention is to help conserve IP address space in the WAN. The router serial interface uses the IP address of another router interface such as a LAN interface. Most WAN media types support IP Unnumbered including HDLC, PPP, Frame Relay, and ATM. Although it does indeed conserve IP subnets, only use IP Unnumbered if no other option is available. A main reservation is that Ping cannot be used to test IP connectivity to the serial interface. SNMP must instead be used to actively monitor the interface. In a well-designed network that uses *Variable Length Subnet Masking* (VLSM), this feature usually should be unnecessary.

Remember:
- With IP Unnumbered, Ping cannot be used to test the WAN links.

Designing IP over Frame Relay

The design options and challenges of running IP over a Frame Relay WAN will now be examined.

Broadcasting over Frame Relay

Frame Relay is a non-broadcast medium. This does not mean that broadcasts cannot be sent out on a Frame Relay network; it means that broadcasts cannot be sent efficiently on this medium. The router must send individual unicast copies to each peer on the Frame Relay. This means of transmission is not broadcasting at all; it is simply replicated unicasts. Consider the network shown in Figure 3-1. Any broadcast destined for the WAN from R1 must be replicated to each of the routers from R2 through R5. This may work for just four remote sites, but imagine what would happen if 40 remote sites existed.

Any broadcast or multicast traffic such as routing updates or application advertisements could cause excessive bandwidth consumption and router overhead associated with the broadcast replication. The non-broadcast nature of the Frame Relay medium limits the scalability in terms of the number of Frame Relay peers that any one router can have. This issue is encountered regardless of whether it is point-to-point or point-to-multipoint Frame Relay implementation.

Remember:
- It is important to understand the scalability issues associated with Frame Relay's support of broadcasting.

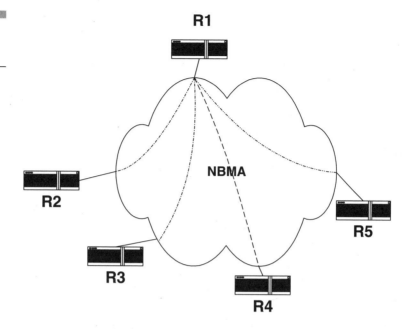

Figure 3-1
Broadcasting and
NBMA networks

Using Sub-Interfaces in an IP Environment

Routers manufactured by a number of the major vendors have the ability to support sub-interfaces in Frame Relay. A single physical interface can then be divided into multiple sub-interfaces. Each sub-interface must relate to a different network or subnet for routing purposes, just like physical router interfaces. A single or multiple PVCs can be run over a sub-interface.

The same Frame Relay WAN network can support routers that use a mixture of both sub-interfaces and main physical interfaces. This is unusual in practice because the designer tends to opt for either the use of logical sub-interfaces or the main physical interfaces.

The use of sub-interfaces can provide the following design and operational advantages:

- **Eliminate any split-horizon issues**: The split-horizon principle dictates that a router will not advertise routes back out the interface over which it learned them. This is a prudent way of helping prevent routing loops with distance vector routing protocols. However, it has the potential to create connectivity problems with Frame Relay. In the network of Figure 3-1, if R1 had split-horizon enabled on its serial interface, then it would not advertise the local LAN subnets from the other sites back out that interface. As a result, R1 would have an entry in its IP routing tables for all of the remote LANs, but none of the remote routers would receive these updates. Basically, no means would exist for the remote LANs to communicate with each other. Times occur when such communication is not required, but this is certainly not always the case.

■ The use of sub-interfaces means that R1 would receive an update about each remote LAN on a different sub-interface. It would not advertise it back out that particular sub-interface, but it would advertise it out all the other sub-interfaces. Thus, each remote router would learn about the LAN attached to all the other routers. A sample topology is shown in Figure 3-2.

Although overcoming the split-horizon issue is often touted as a major advantage of sub-interfaces, most routing protocols either have split-horizon disabled on Frame Relay interfaces or else support the ability to disable it through configuration.

Point-to-Point and Multipoint Multiple PVCs can be defined for a main physical interface that is using Frame Relay. Such an interface is said to be a point-to-multipoint interface. With sub-interfaces, an option usually is available to employ them as point-to-point if only one PVC is being

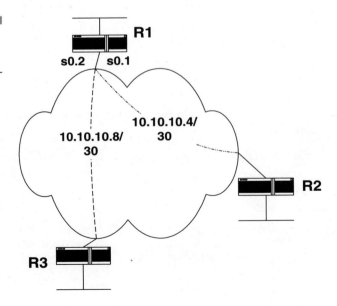

Figure 3-2
Frame relay and
sub-interfaces

defined. If multiple PVCs are implemented on a sub-interface, then that sub-interface must be configured as point-to-multipoint.

So what might be the rationale in having sub-interfaces if they are going to operate in multipoint mode? The most likely reason is to conserve IP subnet address space if that is becoming an issue on the network. With multipoint Frame Relay, the Frame Relay "cloud" consists of just one IP subnet, this is also true of multipoint sub-interfaces.

Note that it is also possible to support both point-to-point and multipoint Frame Relay implementations on the same network. This is shown in Figure 3-3.

The following is a sumary of the advantages of using point-to-point and multipoint Frame Relay as well as situations when to use each implementation:

Point-to-point

- A point-to-point implementation is applicable to a star or hub-and-spoke type network because it naturally mirrors that topology.

- When communication is needed between remote sites on a hub-and-spoke type network, point-to-point is applicable because it eliminates any possibility of split-horizon issues.

- Point-to-point facilitates troubleshooting.

Figure 3-3
Point-to-point and
multipoint frame relay
PVCs

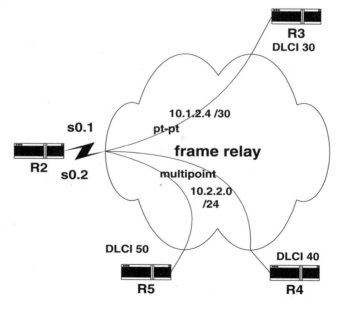

■ Configuration is potentially made easier. For example, static mapping of the DLCI to the destination IP address is never required in a point-to-point implementation. This information is resolved dynamically.

■ OSPF is easier to configure using a point-to-point implementation of Frame Relay.

■ It is often required to set certain parameters on a per-PVC basis. This potentially important feature is facilitated by the use of point-to-point sub-interfaces. For example, the CIR and the burst rate EIR could be configured on the router for each individual PVC.

Multipoint

■ When IP subnets are at a premium, a multipoint implementation is applicable because it has multiple PVCs on the same IP subnet thus conserving address space.

■ A multipoint implementation is applicable to partial-mesh and full-mesh topologies. In a meshed design communication, split-horizon is taken out of the equation. With a full-mesh topology, any connectivity issues on the *Non-broadcast MultiAccess* (NBMA) network are impossible.

■ Use Inverse ARP to dynamically resolve destination IP addresses to local DLCI. This simplifies the multipoint configuration.

The broadcasting issues are effectively the same regardless of whether it is point-to-point or point-to-multipoint. Because Frame Relay is a non-broadcast medium, broadcasts must be replicated across each PVC. This is also true regardless of whether the implementation is point-to-point or point-to-multipoint. This sometimes causes confusion because only one IP subnet for multiple PVCs is available with multipoint. An IP subnet is usually synonymous with a broadcast domain; however, this is not exactly true with Frame Relay due to the nature of the medium itself.

PVC Meshing and IP Redundancy

One reason that Frame Relay is a popular choice for the core WAN technology is its ability to provide resilience using PVC meshing.

Hub and Spoke The simplest Frame Relay topology is the classic hub-and-spoke or star as shown in Figure 3-4. Each remote site has a single PVC to the main site. Any communication between remote sites must take place through the hub site. This is obviously not a resilient design since the failure of any one PVC will cause a loss of WAN connectivity for the remote site that it services.

A second possible issue with the star topology arises if a substantial amount of traffic exists between remote sites. This means that a substantial amount of traffic exists on two PVCs instead of just one, which may not be cost-effective. Also, traffic between remote sites in a star topology always requires at least two router hops, and it is always a design goal to minimize router hops. Therefore in this instance, providing a PVC directly between the sites that exchange a significant amount of data may be justified.

Partial-Mesh Topology   A partial-mesh topology means that most sites (or indeed all sites) have at least two PVCs connecting to the Frame Relay network. Therefore, the failure of any one PVC will not cause a loss of WAN connectivity at any site. Figure 3-5 shows a typical partial mesh design.

A potential problem with the partial mesh is that a single point of failure still exists at the main site router. This could be overcome by dual-homing the remote sites to different hub site routers as shown in Figure 3-6. This is sometimes called a *dual partial-mesh*. The hub routers could be located at different sites for better redundancy. In this case, the two hub routers would have to be inter-connected using two PVCs (for redundancy), or alterna-

Figure 3-4
Hub and spoke (Star)
NBMA network

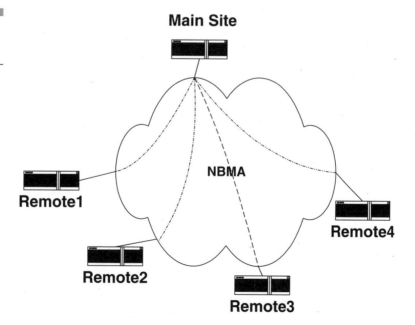

Figure 3-5
Frame relay partial
mesh

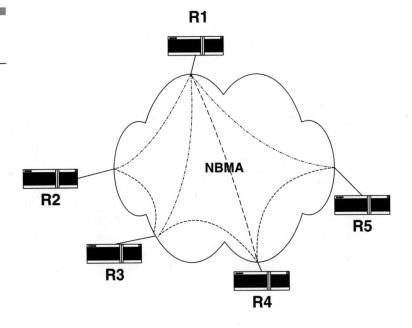

Figure 3-6
Dual-homed partial
mesh

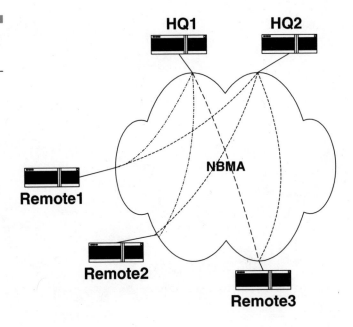

tively, a resilient campus backbone could be used if the two sites are in close geographic proximity to each other. It is not always practical for a company to have two central sites because only one site may be well-suited for housing its main applications resources. But even in such a scenario, two hub site routers should be present.

Full-Mesh Topology   A fully meshed topology entails directly connecting each site together. This is shown in Figure 3-7. Clearly this results in a fully redundant design albeit at a cost.

In Figure 3-7, four sites are fully meshed. A total of six PVCs are required to enable this topology.

More generally, it can be stated that in order to provide full meshing for n sites, the total number of PVCs required is n $(n\text{-}1)/2$. For example, in order to provide full meshing for 10 sites would require $10{\times}9/2 = 45$ PVCs and so on. In terms of resilience in a network of n sites, n PVCs are present from each site and all of these PVCs would have to fail in order to isolate a given site. This sounds impressive; however, if one PVC fails due to a local problem, then it is quite possible that multiple PVCs will fail. This is because absolute resilience is difficult to achieve in the local loop to the Frame Relay switch. So it would be disappointing to find out that, after spending all this money on resilience, all the PVCs happen to be terminating on the same piece of common equipment in the local central office! Personally, I believe

Figure 3-7
NBMA full mesh

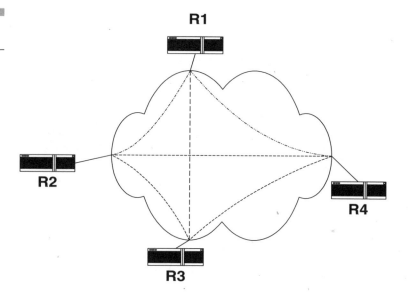

the use of partial meshing with added backup using an alternate technology such as ISDN is a better and more cost-effective solution than the full mesh.

The obvious main limiting factor for full meshing is cost. However, some provided services give competitive rates for PVCs that are used exclusively for backup purposes. So, such a solution should not be discounted on the basis of cost alone without proper cost analysis.

Dynamic Routing over Frame Relay

When using a dynamic routing protocol with Frame Relay, a number of issues must be considered:

Neighbor Formation   Due to the non-broadcast nature of Frame Relay, problems may arise with IP routing protocols that rely on neighbor formation. The routers may have to be configured specially to facilitate neighbor formation on the Frame Relay interfaces. This can be particularly evident in the case of OSPF, which will be discussed in Chapter 5, "Scalable IP Routing I."

Another issue in relation to neighbors is the limitation on the number of routing protocol neighbors. As will be discussed in the chapters on OSPF and EIGRP, if the number of neighbors formed over Frame Relay goes beyond a certain limit, router resource problems may occur due to the memory being consumed by the topology database. Convergence problems can be encountered with EIGRP if too many neighbors have to be queried for a backup route in the event of a link failure. These convergence problems are more likely on PVCs that have a low CIR since routing update packets may be dropped or delayed if the link is busy.

Bandwidth Consumption   Routing protocols that exchange routing information using periodic broadcasts can consume an excessive amount of the Frame Relay bandwidth. This happens to a greater extent as the network grows and the routing tables become larger. Consider the network shown in Figure 3-8 and assume that a total of 450 routes or subnets exist on the network. Without any route summarization, this would then be the total number of entries in each routing table. The total CIR from the hub site is 128k; therefore, the average CIR per PVC to each of the 20 remote sites is 6.4k. As a general rule, a RIP packet can carry 15 networks; hence, 30 RIP packets are required to broadcast this routing table. Therefore, at least 30 RIP packets are sent on each PVC every 30 seconds. The net result is that the RIP updates are consuming a large proportion of the CIR, poten-

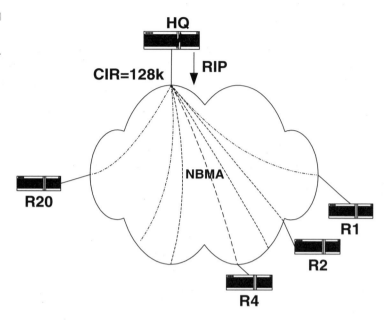

Figure 3-8
Author...need caption

tially to the detriment of other traffic. The converse possibility of RIP packets being dropped at times of heavy traffic is of equal seriousness. In that case, routes could be going in and out of a hold-down state, causing routing problems on the network.

A link state routing protocol like OSPF uses incremental updates rather than periodic broadcasts. The fact that routing updates only need to be sent across Frame Relay when a subnet changes state makes this type of protocol vastly more efficient in a Frame Relay environment. This is one of the reasons why link state routing protocols are more suitable for larger networks.

Static routes of course do not entail any bandwidth overhead. However, they do require more administration that may be prohibitive as the network scales.

Router Overhead   Apart from the inefficient manner in which a distance vector routing protocol like RIP uses periodic broadcasts, additional inefficiency is caused by the non-broadcast nature of Frame Relay. Instead of sending a single broadcast copy of the routing updates out to all PVCs, the updates have to be replicated across each individual PVC. This effectively is like sending a unicast across each PVC. This can place undue processing overhead on a core router if an excessive number of broadcasts have to be replicated periodically on each PVC.

Convergence   Convergence problems can occur on Frame Relay if routing update traffic is dropped on slow PVCs. This can happen on excessively busy PVCs, particularly if an inefficient routing protocol such as RIP or Cisco's IGRP is being employed. This creates the possibility of routing loops if a link goes down and the resulting routing update gets dropped or delayed on one or more of the PVCs.

A second type of generic convergence problem could occur if the PVCs are frequently over utilized. In the case of a distance vector protocol, routes may time out of the routing table if a succession of periodic updates are missed. Problems could also be experienced with link state protocols but only if the PVCs are extremely busy. If a number of successive hello packets are dropped, then the OSPF neighbor relationship could be lost across the PVC. This could cause a stability issue with the neighbor being recreated and dropped again as the traffic conditions change.

In the particular case of Cisco's EIGRP, when a route is lost, the router may have to query its neighbors for a possible backup route. An EIGRP router will not converge until it receives a reply to the query from each of its neighbor routers. It is not uncommon to see this type of EIGRP convergence problem on slow or very busy PVCs. In Chapter 6, "Scalable Routing II—EIGRP and Protocol Redistribution," methods to resolve this problem will be discussed.

Metric Calculation   The network designer must be careful about how the routing metric is calculated for Frame Relay. The perceived Frame Relay bandwidth influences the calculation of the routing metric for protocols such as OSPF or Cisco's EIGRP. The interface bandwidth is a configurable parameter, but on most vendors' routers, it has a default value. This default value won't necessarily match the CIR. Therefore, a potential anomaly exists between the actual CIR on the PVC and the committed speed of the PVC as the router sees it. It is important to be aware of this issue, and it is good practice to match the configured router interface bandwidth with the actual CIR. This is a general rule intended to give predictable routing paths. Consider, for example, the case where one PVC is intended as backup for another PVC. The backup PVC has a significantly lower CIR and is only intended to carry significant traffic if the primary PVC fails or is congested. However, the interface bandwidth for each PVC could possibly be seen as the same default value. In such a scenario, a routing protocol such as OSPF would see the two PVCs as equal cost paths and load balance across them.

A poorly designed or controlled routing metric can cause unnecessary additional hops. Consider the network displayed in Figure 3-9. The network

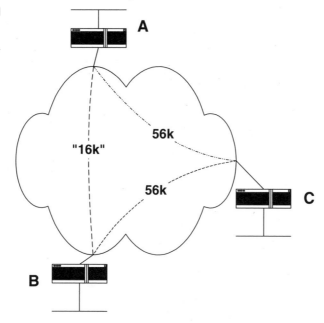

Figure 3-9
Author...need caption

"16k"

56k

56k

A

C

B

is a full mesh with all PVCs having a 64k CIR. Site A has a direct PVC to site B, but this has been mistakenly configured to have an interface bandwidth of 16k. OSPF would then send all traffic from A to B via C; thus, an additional hop has been needlessly incurred. This is a rather trivial example, but it illustrates an important issue that can occur in a less obvious manner on a large network.

When protocols such as OSPF and EIGRP are examined in more detail, other instances will be discussed where the interface bandwidth may require configuration. For the moment, the most important point to remember is that the router does not necessarily see the PVC as operating at the real CIR. If this is not understood and controlled, it can lead to undesirable routing effects.

Split-horizon As previously discussed, split-horizon can be an issue on multipoint Frame Relay networks. If the split-horizon feature were enabled on a core router, then passing routing information between the various remote sites would be a problem. However, as already mentioned, most routing protocols either have split-horizon disabled on Frame Relay interfaces or they support the capability to disable it through configuration.

Frame Relay Traffic Management

Frame Relay enables a flexible bandwidth offered by the service provider to the subscriber. This is potentially a very cost-effective advantage of employing this technology. However in order to unlock its full benefit, a good understanding is required of the network and the applications it supports.

A *Committed Information Rate* (CIR) can be purchased, meaning that the service provider will guarantee throughput at a rate up to this CIR value. A second parameter, called the *Enhanced Information Rate* (EIR), can be specified. This is the maximum possible data rate that can be supported by that Frame Relay connection. The subscriber is said to be able to "burst" up to this maximum data rate. Obviously, the maximum EIR or total burst rate value that could be purchased is the physical speed of the link into the local Frame Relay switch.

The service provider will not guarantee transmission of packets once the CIR has been exceeded. When the transmission rate from the subscriber into the Frame Relay network exceeds the CIR, all packets get marked "Discard Eligible" at the local Frame Relay switch. This essentially means that the data will be delivered through the Frame Relay network, provided no congestion is encountered. If congestion does occur along the path to the destination, then any packets marked "Discard Eligible" will be dropped.

Different PVCs may have different CIR and burst rate values as required to fit the bandwidth utilization profile on a given network. For example, one PVC may be used to provide backup for a primary PVC.

The congestion messages in Frame Relay take the form of *Backward Explicit Congestion Notifications* (BECN) or *Forward Explicit Congestion Notifications* (FECN). BECN messages that are sent by the Frame Relay network back to the source upon detection of congestion are useful when the source controls the information rate, as is the usual. FECN messages can be used if the destination controls the rate at which information is exchanged across the PVC. Up until recently, the usefulness of FECN and BECN messages has been limited because not all higher-layer protocols are capable of processing this type of congestion notification.

Earlier generation routers had limited abilities to dynamically learn most of the Frame Relay traffic parameters from the local Frame Relay switch. Newer routers support the ability to react to parameters' settings learned from the switch. Other parameters can be configured on the router to help manage the Frame Relay traffic and how the bandwidth is divided amongst different types. Some vendors call this *Frame Relay traffic shaping*.

Frame Relay traffic shaping can provide the following facilities on a per-virtual circuit basis:

- Rate enforcement at the router interface. The average and peak information rates can be configured. Hence, the router will know when the CIR has been exceeded without necessarily relying on feedback messages from the Frame Relay switch. If a feature like this is being implemented, then obviously it must be ensured that all the parameter values match on the router and switch.

- Automatic throttling back upon the receipt of a BECN from the Frame Relay network.

- The ability to apply configurable priority and queuing features that will help determine the traffic profile and prioritization between the different protocols in the events of congestion. This is usually described as providing a designated *quality of service* (QOS) for different network applications. For example, a time sensitive application could have its own dedicated queue at the router interface in order to avoid having to compete with other traffic. An important point to note about prioritizing protocols by implementing separate queues is that this prioritization is only relevant if packets are actually queued up at the router interface when accessing the Frame Relay network. This may not necessarily be the main bottleneck between source and destination. Also at other points along the path in the Frame Relay network, this prioritization is no longer in effect.

It is evident that traffic-shaping provides a potentially powerful tool that enables subscribers to have increased control over the type of traffic profile that occurs across their Frame Relay network. For this feature to be effective, careful analysis must be done on the traffic that is accessing the Frame Relay network. This should include auditing the type of traffic, its source and destination, its volume, and what percentage of packets is being dropped.

Controlling the DE Bit   Apart from setting the CIR and EIR at the router interface, most types of routers provide a number of other configurable features that could help resolve Frame Relay congestion problems.

The first of these such features to be discussed is the ability to control what packets get marked "Discard Eligible." During heavy traffic periods when the CIR has been exceeded, switches in the Frame Relay network will mark packets "Discard Eligible" by setting the DE bit. Traffic marked DE will be the first to be dropped if the Frame Relay network cannot transport all traffic up to the burst rate. The ability to configure the router to decide what types of packets get marked DE gives the subscriber more control over what type of packets should be dropped during heavy traffic conditions.

For example, the router could be configured so that IP packets greater than 1,000 bytes that are going over a particular DLCI will be marked DE by the router. This may be desirable in a scenario where interactive IP traffic takes precedence over batch IP traffic.

Broadcast Management If excessive broadcasts in the form of routing updates or NetBIOS traffic, for example, are utilizing a large portion of Frame Relay bandwidth, then a particular queue could be dedicated to broadcasts. This type of feature is often termed *broadcast queuing* and could be used to help curb the problem of excessive broadcasts on Frame Relay. This can be particularly useful at a hub site where broadcasts need to be replicated on several different DLCIs to the remote sites. The idea behind a broadcast queue is to limit the amount of Frame Relay bandwidth that broadcasting consumes. The broadcast queue usually has priority at transmission rates below the configured maximum for the queue, thus guaranteeing an allocation of bandwidth for broadcast traffic.

Private Frame Relay

Instead of purchasing a Frame Relay service from a telecommunications carrier, it is also possible to implement Frame Relay privately. Frame Relay switches can be purchased and configured by the enterprise network support staff. The only element of the network that must be purchased or leased from a service provider is the bandwidth to connect the sites together via the Frame Relay switches.

In terms of topology, private Frame Relay is exactly the same as public Frame Relay and faces the same issues. The only difference is the Frame Relay switches are located on certain designated sites on the enterprise network, instead of being in the service provider's *Central Office*, (CO). Just as with public Frame Relay, one Frame Relay switch can service multiple sites. The only requirement is physical connectivity with adequate bandwidth.

One of the advantages of going private is that the enterprise is no longer purchasing a CIR and EIR, so they can be more cavalier in their bandwidth usage in the WAN. In fact, private Frame Relay radically changes the cost model. The fixed costs rise, such as the cost of purchasing Frame Relay switches. An end-to-end path providing adequate bandwidth must be put in place between the various sites. The cost of variable access bandwidth is reduced. The CIR and EIR values can be set to generously high values, provided that this does not cause congestion on the private Frame Relay backbone. A detailed cost analysis should be performed before implementing private Frame Relay.

Other issues apart from cost must also be considered. A private Frame Relay implementation requires a skilled staff to support the network. In today's networking industry it can be difficult to recruit and retain such staff. If staff of a reasonably high caliber is not available, the cost of support may get prohibitively high because consultants may have to be hired on a frequent basis. If, however, such staff is available within the company, then private Frame Relay can represent a very efficient solution because support and troubleshooting issues can be resolved in-house without having to coordinate any third parties.

ISDN Design Issues with IP

ISDN is a circuit-switched WAN technology that has a number of niche applications within the networking marketplace. Dialup WAN has its own set of design challenges that will now be studied.

IP Routing over ISDN

Both static and dynamic IP routing are frequently employed over ISDN. Here I will examine the issues associated with the different routing alternatives.

Static Routes The routing traffic associated with dynamic routing protocols can cause ISDN calls to be initiated, resulting in prohibitively expensive ISDN bills. For this reason, static routes are often a preferred option for ISDN.

When implementing static routes, it is important to remember that, like all routes, they are unidirectional. Therefore, they must be configured in each direction. Consider the network shown in Figure 3-10. A static route exists on each router, enabling connectivity to the 10.1.40.0/24 main office

Figure 3-10
Author...need caption

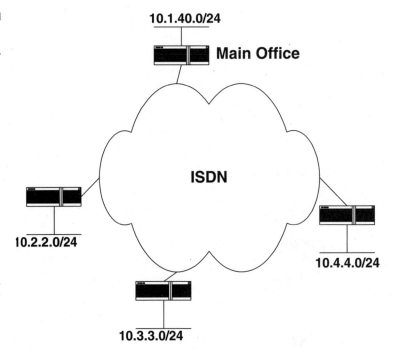

LAN over ISDN. A static route must also lead to each remote LAN 10.x.x.0/24 on the main office router. Therefore, the main office router requires a separate static route for each remote LAN that points to the ISDN network. This can result in significant administrative overhead as the number of remote sites grows. This is one potential disadvantage of using static routes in this manner.

Dynamic Routing over ISDN   The use of a dynamic routing protocol on the ISDN portion of the enterprise network usually poses challenges for the network designer. Regardless of whether the routing protocol is distance vector or link state, routing traffic must be propagated across the ISDN network. A certain amount of thought must be put into avoiding excessive ISDN costs due to calls initiated by the routing protocol itself. The type of solution employed can depend on the nature of the routing protocol itself.

Distance Vector Routing Protocols   Most distance vector routing protocols propagate routing information through the periodic exchange of routing updates between neighbor routers. If this is not controlled or manipulated in some way, then the ISDN line may be kept up indefinitely as a result of these updates.

The router can be configured to prevent routing updates from bringing up the line but also to enable the routing updates to flow once the line is up. Therefore, a full routing table can be learned over ISDN once the call is made. The main problem with this is that because the routing updates cannot bring up the line or keep the line up, the routing protocol has no control over when the line will drop. So, when the line drops due to a lack of traffic, routes will eventually time out of the routing table and must be relearned when the next ISDN call is made. This can lead to periods when no route is available to a destination for a certain period of time after the call is made. The almost random manner in which ISDN routes move in and out of the routing table can lead to unpredictable results.

A number of proprietary solutions are available such as Cisco's snapshot routing where a snapshot of the routing table is taken while the ISDN line is up. These routes are then retained in the routing table and only need to be refreshed on a long and configurable time interval. For example, the snapshot routes could have a configured update interval of two days, resulting in an ISDN call only occurring every two days in order to refresh the routing information.

Link State Protocols   Link state protocols such as OSPF do not require periodic updates. Instead, updates are exchanged incrementally upon a change in the network topology such as a link failure or the addition of a new subnet. These protocols, however, do rely on the formation of formal neighbor relationships with attached routers. Neighbor relationships are formed and maintained through the exchange of periodic hello packets. These packets must be prevented from bringing up the line through appropriate filtering. Another problem with the use of a link state protocol is that every time the ISDN line changes state, the link state protocol floods the network with link state advertisements. This can significantly increase the routing-related overhead on the network.

OSPF uses the hello protocol to form neighbor relationships; this, along with its link-state nature, has traditionally made full OSPF operation difficult over ISDN. The OSPF demand circuit is a more sophisticated solution to the problem of running OSPF over ISDN. It is based on RFC 1793 and is supported by all vendors in the industry. The difficulties of using OSPF over ISDN and the demand-circuit feature are discussed further in Chapter 5. The general design challenges posed by running OSPF over ISDN are also discussed in this chapter along with some viable solutions.

Using ISDN for Redundancy

ISDN is frequently used as a means of providing backup to serial or Frame Relay links in the event of link failure. It is also commonly employed, as a cost-effective option, to provide additional bandwidth when required. This is a simple principle but can be at the root of a number of network problems usually due to poor configuration or a badly thought out design. For this reason, some of these problems, as well as corresponding solutions, will now be discussed.

Floating Static Routes Dial-on-demand is usually implemented using floating static routes over the ISDN network. Routes to the rest of the network are learned dynamically over the primary interface, but if this interface fails, a static route points at the ISDN interface. The static route is configured with a higher administrative distance, hence it will not normally be preferred. This effect can also be achieved by running the same dynamic routing protocol over the ISDN but with a higher cost metric.

When configuring and testing ISDN dial-on-demand, caution must be exercised again to ensure that unwanted spurious dialing does not take place. The network and router configurations must also be engineered to avoid keeping the ISDN link up for an excessive amount of time. Dialer scripts can be configured on the router defining the exact type of IP traffic that can initiate a call. For example, the router could be configured to prevent any IP broadcasts from initiating an ISDN call, but any other type of IP traffic is allowed to generate a call. The type of traffic that can generate a call is termed *interesting traffic,* and a dialer script is sometimes called an *interesting traffic list*. Thus when the router sends interesting traffic to a destination using the ISDN network, a call is generated. An interesting traffic list is different from an access filter because once the line is up, traffic that is *not* defined as "interesting" can be sent out the ISDN interface if that is its next hop to the destination. Returning to the example, IP broadcasts could be sent out the ISDN interface once the line is up even though they cannot be allowed to generate a call. The ISDN interface has an idle timer that will cause the line to drop if outgoing interesting packets are not detected for a certain time interval. This prevents the line staying up indefinitely after data transfer is complete, and it will not be reset by "noninteresting" traffic.

In designing an interesting packet list, any traffic that will cause excessive ISDN calls will be filtered. However, this must be balanced against the requirement for IP communication at the application level. It is possible, for example, to specify RIP packets as uninteresting (as they must be to avoid keeping the line up with periodic updates every 30 seconds); however, the RIP updates could pass once the line is up, enabling the exchange of routing information over ISDN.

The interesting packet list could be of a loose specification if the ISDN is purely used for backup in the instance where a main WAN link has failed. The rationale here may be that all IP traffic should flow across the ISDN just as it does across the main serial link that the ISDN is backing up. If all IP traffic is specified as interesting, then a large ISDN bill is likely. However, the reasoning might be that this is a necessary evil while the main link is being repaired, and the onus is then on the network administration in order to minimize the downtime associated with the main serial links.

Dial Backup   Dial-on-demand routing, as implemented by static routes or a dynamic routing protocol, is often confused with dial backup, which is not the same thing. A dial backup implementation entails the use of one WAN link or WAN technology to track another. The backup link is only used in the event of a failure on the primary line. For example, an ISDN interface on a router could back up the main serial interface. Thus, the ISDN only comes up if the serial interface that it is tracking looses line protocol.

The ISDN only comes up after the primary interface has been down for a configurable delay time to protect against the effects of a flapping serial link. The router can also be configured to bring up the backup interface if a certain load is exceeded on the primary interface. Otherwise, the backup interface only dials if the layer 2 protocol goes down on the primary. This is a serious limitation of dial backup. For example, if the LAN interface on the remote router goes down, dial backup will not take any action. Consider the scenario shown in Figure 3-11 where the remote office has a serial link to HQ1 where LAN A resides. In the event of this link failing, the backup ISDN interface dials HQ2 and provides access to a backup LAN. The problem is that if a failure occurs on the LAN switch at HQ1, no action will be taken by the remote router because line protocol has not been lost on the primary serial interface. Even if LAN A and LAN B are the same LAN or IP subnet, a problem still would exist because traffic would continue to be sent over the serial link since its line protocol did not fail. With dial-on-demand, this would not be a problem because the loss of the route to LAN A would be detected by the routing protocol.

The main advantage of dial backup over DDR is technical simplicity. The definition of the interesting packet list is less likely to be critical because the possibility of an ISDN call being made is nonexistent unless the main interface loses line protocol.

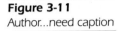

Figure 3-11
Author...need caption

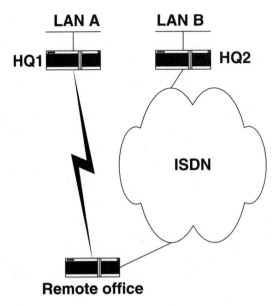

The ISDN lines should be tested on at least a monthly basis if a dial backup configuration is being employed. This is necessary because a particular serial link may not fail for a long period of time and so the ISDN is not guaranteed to still be functioning properly without periodic testing.

Remember:

- Dial backup, as opposed to DDR, will not respond to a failure on a remote LAN.

What Happens When the Line Changes State? As already explained, with a dial backup solution, the ISDN link is only availed of when the primary link fails. Therefore when the ISDN is initiated, a change is made to the network topology. It is important that all potential side effects of utilizing ISDN have been thought out and tested. This point can be illustrated by way of an example of a poorly designed dial backup solution where the consequences for IP connectivity had not been properly tested.

The network shown in Figure 3-12 is an example of ISDN dial backup. Each remote serial link is backed up by ISDN, which dials Router C at the Main Office. The network administrator noticed that when Router A's serial link went down, the backup ISDN interface did dial up. However, local users still cannot access an IP-based server at the Main Office.

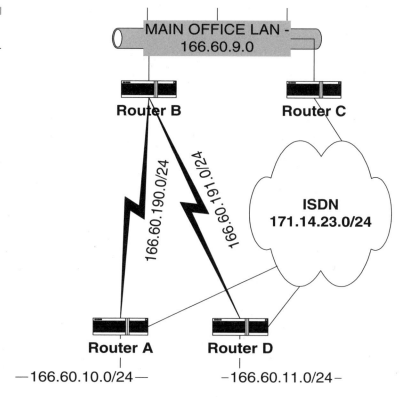

Figure 3-12
Author...need caption

The problem here is that the IP addressing, and hence routing, changes when the ISDN is brought up. The ISDN belongs to a different Class B network; hence, RIP version 2 will summarize the 160.60.0.0/16 route, which will then become a discontiguous network. The solution here is either to disable automatic summarization on the remote routers or to make the ISDN network part of the same Class B as the serial links. (This type of problem will be examined again in each of the IP routing chapters.) The basic point is that the situation can change dramatically when ISDN kicks in. You must have analyzed and tested the different networking scenarios after a link fails, otherwise, it gets overloaded. In the case of dial backup, it is easy to forget about an issue like this because the ISDN could be inactive for a very long time before being called into use.

PPP and Multilink PPP

The PPP is a layer 2 protocol derived from HDLC that can run over any DTE/DCE interface. It supports multiple layer 3 protocols and can support both synchronous and asynchronous transmission. The basic properties of PPP have made it ideally suited for ISDN networks.

PPP has a layer 2 *Link Control Protocol* (LCP) component, which negotiates link layer establishment, management, and link termination. PPP also supports a family of *Network Control Protocols* (NCP), which negotiates the support of most of the more common layer 3 desktop protocols including IP, IPX, DECNET, and Appletalk.

The main LCP parameters to be negotiated are error detection tests, authentication, compression, and multilink PPP.

Authentication   The most popular type of authentication used across PPP link is *Challenged Handshake Authentication Protocol* (CHAP). Although, other security protocols such as the more sophisticated TACACS or the simpler *Password Authentication Protocol* (PAP) are also supported. The advantage that CHAP offers over PAP is that the password is encrypted with CHAP and therefore cannot be detected by a network analyzer. If a password is not encrypted, then it is not secure; this makes CHAP the ubiquitous choice of PPP authentication protocol. A further advantage of CHAP is that it is no more difficult to configure or manage than PAP.

Error Detection   Upon link establishment, PPP sends a "magic number" onto the link. This is simply a unique bit stream. If it detects the receipt of this exact bit stream at the same end of the link (that is, back at the point from where it was sent), PPP concludes that a loop is on the circuit. This test is often presented as a further example of PPP's sophistication, but it is certainly not the only WAN data link protocol with the capability of loop detection.

Compression   STAC or predictor compression can be configured for PPP. The throughput improvement can vary depending on the desktop protocol being transported. For example, IP would usually show a slightly higher compression ratio than IPX. When configuring compression, as with authentication, it is important to ensure that the configuration is consistent at both ends of the link. This may sound trite, but these are the simple errors that cause far too many problems in practice.

Multilink PPP   A recent enhancement to PPP is *Multilink PPP* (MPPP). In the case of traditional PPP over ISDN, problems have occurred in obtaining an efficient utilization of the two B channels simultaneously. The router can be configured to bring up the second B channel either when an ISDN call is made or when a certain load threshold has been exceeded.

Traffic normally just propagates across the first channel until the second channel is actually needed to support the throughput. This is often demonstrated by the fact that the second channel sometimes drops on an ISDN call as its idle-timer expired, while the first channel remains up.

When the bandwidth requirements increase, the second channel gets utilized. Packets can be sent out randomly on either channel. However, traffic across both channels is not guaranteed to take an identical path through the public ISDN network. Thus, both channels are not guaranteed to experience equal delay while getting to the destination. Hence, packets arriving out of sequence at the destination router is highly probable. This can cause problems with unreliable protocols or extremely time-sensitive protocols. Even with reliable protocols, a very high number of retransmissions can nullify the effect of using both channels. For example, instances with TCP-based applications have occurred where a high percentage of TCP retransmissions meant that the throughput was not significantly greater with two channels rather than with one.

The solution to this problem is Multilink PPP. With this enhancement, a sequencing feature has been added, which ensures that data is reassembled in the correct order at layer 2. This eliminates the need for higher layer retransmissions. MPPP is negotiated during the LCP set-up stage, and both ends of the link must be configured to support it. The sequencing capability of MPPP enables it to view the two B channels as a logically aggregated link.

Designing IP over ATM

In this section, the use of ATM as a WAN technology will be examined. The arguments for and against its deployment along with the design issues and challenges that it presents.

Benefits of ATM

ATM is often generally described as a packet-switched WAN technology, similar in may respects to Frame Relay. Technically, ATM is a cell relay technology because data is transferred across an ATM network in fixed-length, 53-byte cells.

ATM was the first technology to attempt a full end-to-end integration of the LAN and WAN. This gave rise to the development of ATM technologies such as *LAN Emulation* (LANE), which enables the seamless integration of legacy Ethernet and token ring LANs with ATM local area technology.

The original driving forces behind the development of ATM were manifold:

■ Increased bandwidth

ATM can run over multiple media types from copper pairs to single-mode fiber. The access speeds can scale from T-1 to bandwidths in excess of 155Mbps in line with the SONET bandwidth hierarchy.

■ Diversity of application

The dividing line between voice and data applications has become increasingly vague over the last decade. Traditional data networks are now being designed to carry a diversity of traffic types such as voice, data, video, and multimedia. ATM is capable of accommodating multiple types of traffic by specifying different QoS parameters for various end-to end connections.

■ Single end-to-end technology

ATM is a WAN technology that employs PVCs or SVCs. It is also possible to implement ATM in the LAN courtesy of LANE. LANE is complex to implement and administer. Partly because of this large campus, LANs that have not yet migrated to LANE are opting for Gigabit Ethernet as a less complex technology that satisfies LAN bandwidth requirements.

■ Network resilience

ATM has a layer 2 routing protocol called PNNI, which can make forwarding decisions throughout the ATM network. Forwarding decisions can be made based on virtual circuit QoS requirements. It is also capable of dynamically rerouting failed PVCs. These routing decisions are made exclusively at layer 2 based on ATM NSAP addresses. They are therefore transparent to layer 3, provided that the appropriate IP to NSAP address mappings are in place on the routers.

With regard to the ATM implementations within the industry, the need for increased bandwidth has proven to be by far the single greatest driving force for the technology. ATM, as a single end-to-end technology, is a nice concept but its complexity is a stumbling block. In addition, the advent of Gigabit Ethernet has further depressed the use of ATM in the LAN. The requirement for resilience and QoS-based data forwarding can be implemented by other technologies such as Frame Relay at layer 2 or IP at layer 3. *Multi-Protocol Label Switching* (MPLS) also provides an efficient solution for resilience and the provision of different QoS levels for various types of traffic. Although MPLS is still a new and maturing technology, it is gaining a significant foothold particularly within the ISP marketplace.

The net result of all of this is that most, but certainly not all, ATM networks are not very complex implementations that primarily satisfy a need for high bandwidth. QOS is typically the second reason why ATM is chosen. Resilience is more often incorporated into the physical and logical network design rather than being implemented through the ATM switches.

In this section, WAN technology is focused on and that is the context in which ATM is examined. The ATM virtual circuits discussed will relate to VCs between routers rather than end-to-end VCs between end-user devices.

ATM Design Issues

The design challenges presented by the use of ATM as a WAN technology will now be studied.

Topology and Architecture   ATM, like Frame Relay, uses virtual circuits for communication in the WAN. Both switched and permanent virtual circuits can be implemented. ATM PVCs is a more mature technology than SVCs and hence have a much broader implementation base. For this reason, the main elements of the discussion will focus on ATM PVCs.

Most of the fundamental issues relating to the design and implementation of an ATM PVC WAN are quite similar to Frame Relay. These issues include the following:

Sub-interfaces   The majority of ATM routers in the marketplace support the ability to divide a physical ATM interface into multiple logical sub-interfaces. Each of these sub-interfaces must be on a different layer 3 network or subnet. The sub-interface can be configured to support a single or multiple PVCs.

The deployment of sub-interfaces has the familiar driving forces such as cost of router ports, resolving split-horizon issues in the WAN, and also the facilitation of troubleshooting.

Point-to-Point Versus Multipoint   Sub-interfaces can be configured to support a single ATM PVC, in which case, they are designated at point-to-point sub-interfaces. A VPI/VCI pair identifies the PVC. The virtual circuit in ATM is termed a virtual channel and is identified by a *virtual channel ID* (VCI). Virtual channels can be placed in logical groups called virtual paths that are, in turn, denoted by a *virtual path ID* (VPI). Path determination can be implemented more efficiently by the ATM switches if forwarding decisions are made, based on the virtual path ID rather than for each virtual circuit. The VPI and VCI values are agreed between the customer and service provider in the case of public ATM. The network administrator has full control over the VPI/VCI conventions for a private ATM network. The VPI/VCI pair is very similar in principle to the DLCI in Frame Relay, and like the DLCI, the VCI is of local significance only.

The router sub-interface must be configured as point-to-multipoint in order to deploy multiple PVCs on the same sub-interface. With this configuration, the same sub-interface supports multiple VPI/VCI pairs, each of which must be mapped either statically or dynamically to the IP address at the other end of the PVC. Point-to-multipoint PVCs may be used in a situation where IP subnet address space is being exhausted. Figure 3-13 displays a network that contains both point-to-point and multipoint sub-interfaces. The router interface serial 0.1 contains a single PVC on the 10.1.2.4/30 subnet and is a point-to-point sub-interface. The serial 0.2 sub-interface is configured to be point-to-multipoint and supports two PVCs that are on the 10.2.2.0/24 IP subnet. Although it is quite possible to do so, it is unusual in practice to combine point-to-point and multipoint sub-interfaces.

Broadcasts   ATM, like X.25 and Frame Relay, is a non-broadcast medium in nature. This means that a single copy of a broadcast cannot be flooded across all PVCs. Instead, the broadcast is replicated across each PVC, which can put processing strain on a central site router that attaches to a large number of PVCs.

ATM Overhead   ATM offers some clear benefits and motivations for its deployment. However, it is also a relatively overhead-intensive layer 2 pro-

Figure 3-13
Author...need caption

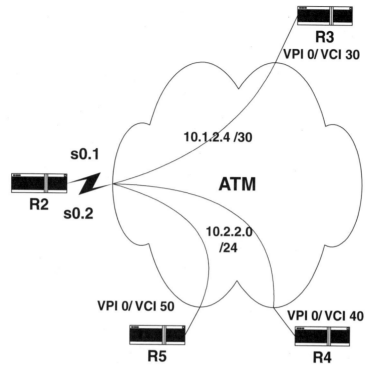

tocol. Two elements of the overhead associated with ATM are now discussed.

An ATM cell consists of a 48-byte payload and a 5-byte header. Although the principle of fixed length cells achieves a certain amount of efficiency through consistency of delay and cell size, a large percentage of overhead is associated with this cell format. The high ratio of header to payload within ATM is sometimes called the *cell tax*.

IP packets must be segmented into 53-byte ATM cells at the ATM adaptation layer, which prepares cells for layer 2 ATM transmission. The ATM adapter at the receiving end must reassemble the ATM packet for transport up to the higher layers in the IP stack. This process is called *segmentation and reassembly* (SAR) and is overhead intensive. SAR occurs not only when sending to the ATM network and receiving from it but also at each router hop through the network. This is because the router must reassemble IP packets from the ATM cells in order to make routing and switching decisions. The issue of SAR overhead is referred to again for this reason when ATM redundancy is discussed in the next section.

Redundancy A resilient topology can be accomplished through PVC meshing or by backing up the ATM with an alternative technology. If another technology such as ISDN is used to provide redundancy, then an adequate amount of bandwidth must be used to match the ATM PVC, thus avoiding degraded service when the dial backup is required. This may entail primary rate ISDN or multiple ISDN B-channels.

A full mesh or partial mesh of PVCs may also be used for network redundancy purposes. In order to provide a full mesh for n nodes, the number of PVCs required is

$$n \times (n\text{-}1)/2$$

So, obviously a cost issue is associated with achieving a full PVC mesh.

Aside from cost, the issue of increased hop count in getting to the central site over a backup PVC must be considered. If the PVC between RB and RA (shown in Figure 3-14) fails, a redundant path exists via RC. This incurs an additional router hop with a resulting increase in latency. Extra router hops are minimized as a design goal, but in most cases may be a necessary evil. The latency associated with a router hop is greater in ATM because of the issue of SAR. The router switches packets not cells. The router must

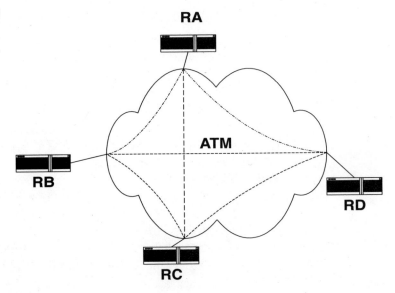

Figure 3-14
Author...need caption

reassemble the 53-byte ATM cells before performing the routing table or cache lookup. When a destination interface has been selected, the packet is again segmented into ATM cells. This SAR function increases the latency associated with router hops and should be kept in mind when designing ATM networks.

Remember:

- The SAR function increases the latency associated with a router hop; therefore, unnecessary router hops should be particularly avoided with ATM.

OAM One of the main motivating factors behind the deployment of sub-interfaces is the manner in which they facilitate troubleshooting. Line protocol on the router's physical interface is lost only if communication with the ATM switch is broken. If sub-interfaces are employed, the status of the line protocol on a point-to-point sub-interface will provide information on the associated PVC. Although this is true of Frame Relay point-to-point sub-interfaces, it is not always the case with an equivalent ATM implementation. In order to ensure that the failure of an ATM PVC results in the loss of line protocol on the point-to-point sub-interface, a feature known as the *Operation and Maintenance* (OAM) protocol should be enabled. This is a very useful troubleshooting and management protocol that should be incorporated in the configuration of the ATM network. It also speeds up the convergence of the routing protocol since the time to initially detect the PVC failure is minimized. OAM messages are periodically exchanged between the router and the switch. Equivalent messages are also transferred end-to-end across the ATM network. The use of OAM improves the router's capabilities as an ATM troubleshooting tool.

Remember:

- OAM should be used to facilitate troubleshooting of the ATM network and PVCs. It also improves network convergence.

Resource and QoS Parameters The user can avail of similar flexibility in bandwidth offering that Frame Relay affords. With ATM, a *Sustainable Cell Rate* (SCR) and a *Peak Cell Rate* (PCR) can be purchased from the service provider. This is very much an equivalent idea to CIR and EIR in Frame Relay. Thus, as with Frame Relay, the customer has a certain amount of control over access speeds and can tailor this to application requirements.

It was also observed with Frame Relay that class of service or QoS queuing and prioritization techniques could be configured on a per-VC basis. This is also true of ATM and in fact, was incorporated into the early development of the protocol.

Other ATM QOS parameters exist apart from the PCR and SCR. These can be requested at the user network interface and are intended to provide better service for various delay-sensitive and loss-sensitive applications.

- *Cell Loss Ratio* (CLR)

  This is the ratio of dropped cells to the total that was throughput across the connection. This ought to be a very small number. The CLR is a parameter that may be set at a particular maximum value for an application that is sensitive to packet loss such as an UDP-based data application.

- *Cell Delay Variation* (CDV)

  The CDV is the average variation in delay across the ATM connection over a specific time interval. A maximum CDV value may be requested from the ATM network for applications that do not tolerate a large variation in delay such as voice and video.

- *Cell Transfer Delay* (CTD)

  The CTD is the total end-to-end latency or delay across the ATM connection. This value may be set for time-sensitive voice or data applications.

ATM also supports a number of fundamentally different classes of service that relate to how bandwidth is allocated on the ATM network.

The ATM forum has specified four service categories:

- *Constant bit rate* (CBR)

  This service category ensures a CBR across the ATM PVC. CBR is a prerequisite for high-quality voice and video transmission. This is the most expensive type of service on a public ATM network because the provider must allocate sufficient bandwidth along the entire path of the PVC in order to meet the specification. The CBR is equivalent to the SCR value purchased from the service provider. If traffic is sent across the PVC at a rate in excess of the SCR, packets may be dropped during times of congestion in the ATM network. The *Cell Loss Priority* (CLP) bit in the ATM header can determine what traffic is dropped in such instances. This bit is set by the user and can be used as a very basic attempt to give prioritization to delay-sensitive or high-priority applications in cases where multiple types of traffic are passed over the same PVC.

■ *Variable bit rate* (VBR)

The bit rate can vary in line with network conditions with this service category. A predefined maximum PCR can be achieved across the PVC when network congestion is completely absent, which of course cannot be guaranteed. An average throughput can be negotiated between the ATM access device and the switch for a particular time interval. A guaranteed maximum bit rate can also be negotiated for a short time interval. The VBR class of service is suitable for bursty data applications that are not particularly time-sensitive.

■ *Available bit rate* (ABR)

ABR is a specific type of VBR. A feedback loop is implemented between the ATM switch and router (or whatever ATM adapter is accessing the network). The adapter requests a particular bit rate but will accept whatever the current network utilization permits. If the bit rate provided by the switch is lower than the requested rate, then the switch may increase after a certain time interval when the network is underutilized. Similarly, if the original rate requested by the adapter is granted by the switch, it may reduce that rate if the network utilization grows.

Despite the apparent complexity of ABR, it is less expensive than the CBR or VBR class of service due to limited guarantee on the allocation of bandwidth.

■ *Unspecified bit rate* (UBR)

UBR has absolutely no guarantee of bit rate. All cells sent by the access device may be dropped by the network or may be successfully transported to the destination. The achieved throughput depends entirely on network conditions. For this reason, UBR is frequently compared to "flying on standby."

The *ATM adaptation layer* (AAL) prepares a cell for transmission by performing SAR and other transmission functions. Different AAL protocols are defined in order to support optimized transport of traffic types that have different requirements and characteristics. The various AAL protocols have different characteristics in terms of bit rate profile, connection-oriented/connectionless nature, and timing characteristics.

AAL1 is connection-oriented and provides CBR. Constant delay is achieved by implementing connection timing end to end between the source and destination. This CBR and delay makes AAL1 ideal for delay-sensitive applications such as voice and video.

AAL4 and AAL5 are the most popular ATM adaptation layer protocols used for data transmission; both supply a VBR. The difference between the two protocols is that AAL4 is connectionless; AAL5 is connection-oriented.

The type of AAL protocol that is to be used on an ATM PVC is selected and configured on the router and ATM switch. Different AAL protocols can be run on different PVCs; thus, a particular PVC could be used for voice and video traffic and another PVC could be dedicated to data.

The following table displays a summary of the main AAL protocols. AAL2 has yet to be formally standardized and is therefore omitted. The applications that are likely to relate this AAL include packet video or a video stream that has a bursty nature due to the implementation of compression algorithms. AAL3/4 has not been discussed because it is the standard applied to SMDS, which was intended as a migration technology to ATM.

Feature	AAL1	AAL 3/4	AAL 4	AAL 5
Bit Rate	Constant	Variable	Variable	Variable
Connection mode	Connection-oriented	Connection-oriented	Connectionless	Connection-oriented
Timing required between source and destination?	Yes	No	No	No
Traffic type example	Voice / Video	Data (SMDS)	Data	Data

The ability to support different AAL protocols makes ATM a suitable protocol in supporting applications that have different characteristics and networking requirements.

The ATM bandwidth and transmission profile can also be tailored in other ways to enable the support of traffic types with different transport requirements. The CLP bit can be used to give a higher priority to delay-sensitive applications such as voice and video. The SCR and PCR can also be shaped to meet the needs of a diversity of applications. In addition, queuing and protocol prioritization techniques can be implemented on the router on a per-PVC level. The exact manner in which this is performed depends on the router vendor. The area of QoS is intended to support such a diversity of application types in the most efficient possible manner. QOS principles and techniques are applicable to ATM or Frame Relay transmission as well as to IP encapsulated traffic. For this reason, QOS will be discussed again in the final section of this chapter on voice and data integration.

Private ATM

The question of whether the ATM implementation on the enterprise should be private or public centers around many of the same issues involving a Frame Relay implementation. However, it could be stated with some degree of justification that the stakes are higher on either side of the argument.

A private implementation of ATM entails purchasing or leasing the bandwidth for the WAN infrastructure and privately owning the ATM switches. The switches must therefore be configured and managed by the end user or their representatives. Private ATM provides the following potential advantages:

■ Reduced cost of bandwidth

This is a potential advantage that requires specific verification for the network in question. The infrastructure bandwidth still has to be put in place, however no further services needs to be purchased after this investment is made. A full cost analysis should be performed to confirm the cost-effectiveness of private ATM in relation to the cost of bandwidth.

■ Bandwidth only limited by physical medium

The end user can afford to be reasonably cavalier in its bandwidth deployment once the infrastructure is put into place. This should be of benefit to applications such as voice that require a steady level of guaranteed bandwidth.

■ Flexibility to alter bandwidth profile

No service contracts with regard to bandwidth profile exist, so the user has ultimate flexibility in altering these parameters as the applications and traffic profiles change on the network.

■ Single point of network management

Eliminating at least one other party from the network support loop can facilitate troubleshooting. The ATM switches could be analyzed without having to rely on the honesty or competence of the service provider's staff. By eliminating the service provider, one less party is likely to engage in political finger pointing.

Having discussed the possible benefits of using a private ATM implementation, it is now appropriate to issue some stern words of caution. The following issues must be studied before attempting to embark on private ATM:

■ Availability of expertise

Even the more straightforward ATM implementations require a significant level of expertise among network support staff. Few organizations have a sufficient number of staff members at this level. In the current marketplace, such expertise is difficult and expensive to secure and retain; but without it, a private ATM implementation is completely unrealistic. I would suggest that this issue is the greatest stumbling block for private ATM.

■ Cost of support

This is closely related to the issue of expertise. Support is the second largest element of network cost of ownership after the WAN costs. The problem is that it can be difficult to precisely quantify. Without adequate network support staff, downtime is likely to accrue. Eventually, the support of the network may have to be outsourced to consultants or a service provider. This may effectively put the end-user's organization back in the position of having public ATM only via a cumbersome and costly route.

■ Cost of bandwidth

A full-cost analysis must be performed to determine if it is cost-effective for the enterprise to purchase its own bandwidth infrastructure. The factors that determine this result include the price and support packages available from service providers, the projected lifetime of the network, and the cost of the infrastructure itself.

Remember:

▪ Although private ATM offers potential advantages, it cannot be implemented without the presence of skilled support staff.

Voice and Data Integration

Voice can be transported over the WAN as another IP-based application, or alternatively it can be transported directly in HDLC, Frame Relay, or ATM. Given the ubiquitous state of the Internet and its IP-based nature, applications such as voice, video, and multimedia are increasingly being encapsulated in IP. A basic configuration for running voice over IP requires a voice-capable router as shown in Figure 3-15. These *voice-over-IP* (VoIP) packets form another application that has specific characteristics and requirements. The key differentiating feature of voice and video is its time-sensitivity and resulting requirement for constant delay and bit rate.

Some fundamental points must be noted before designing the transport of voice on an IP network.

- UDP-based transport

  VoIP uses UDP as its transport layer protocol. The IP packets carrying voice must arrive in real time. A small amount of packet loss may be tolerable but a large variation in delay is not. Therefore, TCP reliability with retransmissions is not of use for voice applications.

  A UDP port is similar to any other UDP application thus identifies the VoIP traffic. The difference is that this UDP application must get priority when accessing or leaving interface queues. It must be guaranteed a certain QoS through the network in order to satisfy its real-time transmission requirements.

- Frame Relay

  If VoIP is being transported over Frame Relay, then it is important that the CIR on the PVC is not exceeded. Exceeding the CIR is likely to result in dropped packets and possible variations in delay as interface queues fill along the path of the PVC. A reliable TCP-based data application can tolerate these lost packets and delay variations better than voice. As the percentage of packet loss increases, voice quality will degrade in direct proportion.

Figure 3-15
Author...need caption

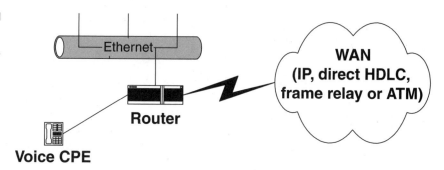

A number of actions can be taken to minimize packet loss on a Frame Relay PVC carrying voice traffic:

- Use dedicated PVC for voice between the sites.

  The average bit rate required for voice transport on this PVC should not exceed the CIR. Having dedicated PVC for voice is by no means essential, and other solutions are available for ensuring good VoIP quality.

- Ensure that the PVC has a CIR that is high relative to its average throughput.

  If budgetary constraints prohibit this, then the following steps can be performed in attempting to achieve a good QoS for voice traffic.

- Ensure that only data traffic is marked DE.

- Create a separate high-priority queue for voice.

- ATM

  When running VoIP over an ATM backbone, the AAL1 encapsulation should be used to provide a CBR and connection-oriented class of service.

  The SCR should not be exceeded in order to avoid degradation in voice quality. The steps that can be taken to ensure that packet loss, as a result of the SCR being exceeded is minimized are identical to those just described in relation to the Frame Relay CIR.

  - The use of dedicated PVC for voice is an expensive solution with ATM.

  - Ensure that the PVC has an SCR that is high relative to its average throughput.

    If budgetary constraints prohibit this, then the following steps can be performed in attempting to achieve a good QoS for voice traffic:

  - Ensure that only data traffic has the CLP bit set.

  - Create a separate high-priority queue for voice.

Typically, voice integration takes place on a network that is already supporting other IP applications whose characteristics may be radically different from those of voice and video. This poses new design and implementation challenges for the network support personnel. Applications that are of a time-sensitive nature must be integrated with existing data applications that are likely to be more of a loss-sensitive nature. This integration must be implemented successfully to support the new applications without degrading the performance of in-situ data applications. To achieve this design goal, the following general steps should be followed:

- Network audit

  An audit of the existing IP network should be performed paying particular attention to the following parameters:

- Device resources and capability

  The first issue to be ascertained is whether the devices on the network support the capability for transporting voice traffic in terms of the hardware platform and software feature set. Many different implementations of voice support currently are available in the marketplace. Each has to be assessed specifically for that vendor platform.

  CPU utilization and memory utilization should be measured at peak and average traffic levels for each device on the network. This is to determine if the additional voice traffic will place a significant strain on existing resources as well as giving an initial indication of the level of upgrade that is required, if any.

- Network and media utilization

  Bandwidth utilization statistics should be measured at peak and average traffic levels on all IP subnets on the network. Particular emphasis should be placed on the WAN links because this is a potential bottleneck if additional traffic is placed on the network. These measurements serve as a benchmark in determining whether bandwidth upgrades are required on the network after the projected level of voice traffic has been estimated.

- QoS features and support

  QoS features and policies should be implemented on a voice and data network even in scenarios where an abundance of bandwidth is present. It is difficult to predict traffic profiles and patterns on a network. Although average utilization may be moderate, peaks could exist due to bursty data traffic that may impinge on the quality of voice transport. Even if the current data traffic profile is relatively consistent and predictable, this very possibly could change dramatically with the addition of even one new data application. The design of an integrated voice and data network should enable significant growth and change in both voice and data application, just as scope for growth is provisioned into the design of a data network. For this reason, QoS is important on a voice and data network even if its necessity is not immediately apparent.

The capability of all devices to support QoS must therefore be assessed. These devices include, at a minimum, the routers and WAN switches. If a public implementation of Frame Relay or ATM is in place, then the QoS offering of the service provider must be evaluated and compared to the equivalent capabilities of the CPE devices. The main function of QoS is to ensure that time-sensitive applications such as voice and video do not suffer service-affecting delays during peaks in the traffic on an integrated network.

Most methods for achieving a certain QOS for various traffic types entail a similar principle. The high priority traffic is distinguished based on an identifying parameter such as UDP port number, IP precedence, or DE/CLP bits. It is then given preferential treatment when accessing and leaving interface queues on the WAN switches and routers. This may involve giving the traffic a higher priority for leaving the queue, or alternatively, the high-priority traffic may be given a dedicated queue of its own.

The different options for implementing QoS varies depending on the exact features supported by the vendor. It is therefore important to understand precisely the QoS alternatives and their operation on the router and WAN platforms on the network.

In general, two fundamental sources of delay can inhibit voice traffic:

(i) Serialization

(ii) Queuing

Serialization is the process of sending a packet onto the transmission link. Delay can be incurred for large packet sizes, thus, the packets must be fragmented to minimize serialization delay. For example, a 1,300-byte packet may typically be fragmented into 13 100-byte packets. A queuing mechanism must also be in place to compliment the fragmentation process for the purpose of minimizing the delay of time-sensitive traffic. Without a queuing policy, all fragments of the 1,300-byte packet would be transmitted before any other packet could be sent. Apart from techniques such as queues that give priority to traffic "tagged" with a particular port number of bit sets, other fundamental ways can minimize queuing delay. Small packet sizes are usually given a higher priority for leaving the interface queue. This has the effect of reducing latency incurred simply because a large packet is being transmitted.

The following are some standard techniques for identifying traffic that is to be prioritized:

(i) IP Precedence

The three *type of service* (ToS) bits in the IP header can be used to distinguish traffic that is to be given a higher priority. These bits are Delay, Throughput, and Reliability. The delay bit could be set for VoIP traffic to tag it as delay-sensitive and therefore a candidate for preferential queuing. Because this tagging is occurring in the IP header, it must be established how this information can be given to the Frame Relay or ATM protocol at layer 2. Some standards are currently being ratified by IETF and the ATM forum for the mapping of QoS parameters between layers 2 and 3. It is important to clearly understand the degree to which the WAN switch and router vendors support such capabilities.

(ii) *Real Time Protocol* (RTP) Reserve

RTP can be used to provide header compression in order to minimize latency. Queuing priority is also given to the UDP ports used to transport voice traffic. As with IP precedence, it is important to verify that the layer 3 QoS can be mapped to layer 2 on the device platforms in question.

(iii) *Resource Reservation Protocol* (RSVP)

RSVP enables end-user devices to request guarantees on certain QoS parameters such as bandwidth throughput and delay. The capability to meet the requested RSVP guarantees at layer 2 must again be verified before implementing this protocol.

Remember:

- The main function of QoS is to ensure that time-sensitive applications such as voice do not suffer service-affecting delays during peaks in the traffic on an integrated network.

- The main sources of delay are serialization and queuing.

- Preferential queuing techniques can be applied to delay sensitive traffic based on layer 2 parameters such as the DE/CLP bits or ATM CBR. Alternatively, the traffic can be identified by layer 3 QoS parameters such as IP precedence. In this case, it must be ensured that the layer 3 QoS can be mapped to layer 2 for efficient transmission over the WAN.

■ Formulation of a dial plan

A dial plan must be in place to map destination phone numbers to DLCI or VPI/VCI pairs in the case of running voice directly over Frame Relay or ATM.

If voice is to be encapsulated in IP, then the mapping must be between destination phone numbers and destination IP addresses. Unlike running IP data packets over PSTN or ISDN, the ultimate destination is not necessarily called directly at the source. Instead, series of call legs may be present along the path, as shown in Figure 3-16.

The number of call legs can vary depending on whether the voice is encapsulated in IP or being run directly over Frame Relay, HDLC, or ATM. The first call leg is always from the voice CPE to the local router. For direct Frame Relay or ATM operation, the next voice call is from the local DLCI or VPI/VCI to the local WAN switch. Subsequent call legs require mapping between the layer 2 address and the dialed numbers. The second last call leg is from the destination WAN switch to the destination WAN router port, again using a DLCI or VPI/VCI. The final call leg is always between the destination router and the destination voice CPE. For voice encapsulated in IP, the second call leg points to the destination IP address. Therefore, once this call is made from the originating router, the traffic will be routed like normal IP traffic along the path to the destination router. A VoIP mapping table must tell each device the number to call to get to the next hop.

Figure 3-16
Author...need caption

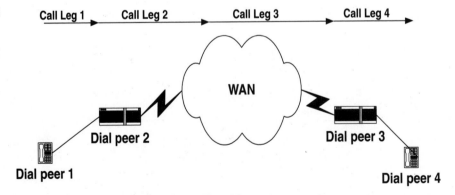

A fixed digit dial plan (for example, all numbers could be 4-digit or 6-digit) enables greater simplicity in planning, administration, and call processing. This, however, may not be possible on a network that is geographically diverse or spread across different countries.

The dial plan should not be formulated until the router equipment vendor for VoIP has been selected and assessed. The reason for this is that significant variations still exist between the VoIP implementations of different vendors in the marketplace.

■ Telephony network test

The VoIP network should be tested for basic connectivity in a laboratory. Having verified that all connectivity requirements have been satisfied, traffic levels should then be measured. A certain amount of test traffic can be generated on the network. Projections can then be made from these measurements concerning what the real traffic levels associated with VoIP are likely to be. These figures must then be compared with earlier audit results in regards to bandwidth utilization on the WAN links in order to assess if sufficient bandwidth exists on the network. The QoS strategy should be planned in this phase. Tests should be incorporated by adding data traffic to the telephony test network and measuring QoS parameters such as bandwidth utilization, throughput, delay, and packet loss for the voice and data applications.

■ Integration of telephony network with IP network

The rollout of voice support on the IP data network can commence when the following is in place:

■ It has been ascertained that the bandwidth infrastructure can support the addition of the projected bandwidth requirements for VoIP.

■ A QoS strategy has been planned and laboratory tested.

Fundamental IP Routing Design

Designing an IP Addressing Plan

Designing the IP addressing plan is of paramount importance for a good network design. It is the foundation upon which a scalable logical network design is built. As you will see in this chapter, many of the benefits provided by the more sophisticated routing protocols, such as rout summarization and *variable length subnet masking* (VLSM) can only be realized to a limited extent (if at all) in the absence of a well-designed IP addressing plan.

Choice of Major Network Addresses

If one intends to connect the enterprise network to the Internet without employing address translation, then a registered network address must be received from the InterNIC. Given that all available Class A and Class B networks have been allocated, this most likely would have to take the form of a Class C network or a contiguous block of Class C networks.

Alternatively, a private address range could be used. This is an increasingly popular approach whereby a special reserved address is used that must remain private to that enterprise network. Such addresses cannot be used to attach to the Internet. In fact, if routes within these private ranges are advertised to an ISP router, the packets are immediately dropped. Connectivity to the Internet can be achieved through *Network Address Translation* (NAT) from the private address range to a public registered address obtained from the InterNIC. Most likely, a significantly larger number of internal private addresses will exist than registered ones. The firewall router can usually overcome this by storing detailed layer 4 information about each HTTP session. This uniquely identifies each session by layer 4 port numbers enabling multiple unregistered addresses to share the same registered address. This procedure in NAT is sometimes termed *overloading*.

RFC 1918 details private address ranges for Classes A, B, and C networks:

Class A: 10.0.0.0

Class B: 172.16.0.0 to 172.31.0.0 inclusive

Class C: 192.168.0.0 to 192.168.255.0 inclusive

Clearly the choice of the one private Class A network 10.0.0.0 provides the most IP address space. It also can make design easier because given the amount of available address and subnet space, the design may not have to be overly stringent. Efficient use of IP address space is less of an issue with the private Class A network. However, this scheme also can let bad designers off the hook temporarily, which can create other problems once the network is rolled out.

Private Class B and Class C networks are sometimes used for the purposes of isolating certain sections of the corporate network. For example, if two corporations merged, then a private Class B network may be used to interconnect the two enterprise networks. Figure 4-1 displays a logical diagram of such a scenario. In this case, enterprise A has a registered Class B 143.10.0.0 and enterprise B also has a registered Class B 163.4.0.0. They have gone into partnership and regularly require connectivity between the two networks. However, they do wish to retain a certain amount of isolation between the two networks. They also intend to retain separate methods of accessing the Internet. In this case, the links between the two corporations are addressed using the 192.168.1.0 private Class C network. This is a neat way of interconnecting the two networks while maintaining control over the propagation of routes and retaining some form of isolation between the two networks. It also means neither enterprise will have to waste registered addressing on the interconnection between the two networks.

Subnet Planning

The importance of carefully planning the IP addressing scheme cannot be overstated. A well-constructed subnet plan is critical if the network is to scale easily. Even on small networks unforeseen problems can arise that are only encountered after the network is commissioned. The root of such problems is often poor planning and design of the IP addressing scheme. On many networks, the only adequate solution is to re-address the entire network. This may be accomplished without too much difficulty on a small network. However, on large networks, this is a major task that usually must be

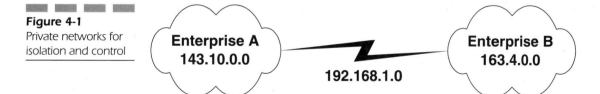

Figure 4-1
Private networks for isolation and control

Enterprise A
143.10.0.0

192.168.1.0

Enterprise B
163.4.0.0

performed in stages rather than a once off cut over to the new scheme. In fact, re-addressing a large network is in itself a project that requires extensive planning. Getting the IP addressing plan right the first time is very important and can save the corporation a vast sum of money.

Traditionally, the most basic form of subnet planning centered around the choice of the subnet mask on the network. If a classful routing protocol that did not support VLSM were being used, then the mask would have to be chosen with great care. The selection of a subnet mask usually involves the asking of two questions:

- How many routed subnets are required on the network?
- What is the likely maximum number of hosts on any one of those subnets?

If n bits are used for subnetting, then 2^n subnets are available. This assumes that subnet-zero and the broadcast subnet are available. Some routers need to be configured specifically to enable the use of these two special subnets.

If n bits are remaining as host address space, then 2^{n-2} host addresses are allowed per subnet. The subnet address itself and the broadcast address cannot be used as the host address; hence, two must be subtracted in the calculation.

For example, consider a Class B network 150.47.0.0. It is required to have a total of 90 subnets in order to accommodate the WAN links and LAN segments at each site. The busiest LAN segment does not have more than 200 hosts on it. The IP routing protocol in use is RIP version 1. What subnet mask should you choose?

This exercise can be approached in either one of two ways. The number of subnet bits required to support 90 subnets can be calculated, or you can evaluate the number of remaining host bits needed to ensure that each subnet supports up to 200 hosts.

Consider how many subnet bits are required to support 90 subnets.

$2^6 = 64$
$2^7 = 128$

Therefore, seven bits are required for subnetting. This leaves nine bits for hosts:

$2^{9-2} = 510$

hence, ample address space is available for the maximum number of hosts per subnet. This results in the following mask:

255.255.254.0—this can also be denoted as a 23-bit or /23 mask.

In this example, a 24-bit mask would also suffice. This mask would allow for 256 subnets that could each support 254 hosts. In fact, this may be a better choice because a 255.255.255.0 or /24 mask is very easy for a network support staff to interpret.

The following is an example in which a Class C address is being used; hence, address space is tight, and only one mask meets the requirements.

The Class C network is 211.4.3.0, and the requirement is that seven subnets be addressed. No more than 30 hosts are on any one subnet. This time the problem will be tackled from the host end.

$$2^{5-2} = 30$$

Therefore, five host bits exactly meet the requirement for host address space. This leaves three bits for subnet address space:

$$2^3 = 8$$

which is adequate to support the number of subnets. This results in a 255.255.255.224 or /27 mask, and it is the only mask that meets the subnet requirements in this case.

As stated at the outset of this section, answering the traditional questions of how many subnets were required and how many hosts they should support was paramount in choosing a mask. This was so because the IP routing protocol typically only supported the use of one mask on a given Class A, B, or C major network. These are still fundamental questions that determine the choice of any subnet mask. However, nowadays it is more likely, especially on large networks, that a protocol supporting VLSM is being employed. This enables the same major Class A, B, or C network to be subnetted with more than one mask. Therefore, different portions of a network may employ a different mask for optimum efficiency in address allocation.

Along with VLSM, another key feature of good IP address planning is the provision for route summarization. It is appropriate to discuss in some detail these two elements of the IP address plan.

VLSM

VLSM means implementing more than one mask on the same major Variable Length Subnet Masking network. It enables a more efficient use of IP address space, both in terms of hosts and subnets. On a network that does not have an abundance of IP address space, it can be essential. In order to implement different masks for the same major network, it is required to have a routing protocol that supports VLSM. Such routing protocols are called *classless routing protocols*. They carry the mask information along with the route advertisements, therefore enabling the support of more than one mask. Examples of classless routing protocols include OSPF, RIP version 2, Cisco's EIGRP, BGP, and IS-IS.

Consider the example shown in Figure 4-2 where a private Class B 172.25.0.0 is being used on the enterprise network. It may be decided that one mask could be used for the LAN segments and another for the serial links between the sites. In this case, a /24 mask could possibly be used on each LAN segment. This enables 254 hosts per subnet. However, to use a /24 mask on a leased line serial link would be a waste of IP address space because no more than two hosts can be on a point-to-point link. A /30 or 255.255.255.252 mask is appropriate for a point-to-point link because with two host bits, each subnet can support two hosts. Therefore, no IP address space is wasted.

Now look at this example in some more detail. Assume that no more than a total of 150 LAN segments will be on this network, which means one LAN subnet per branch office. The LAN subnets can then be designated from the following range:

172.25.1.0/24 to 172.25.150.0/24

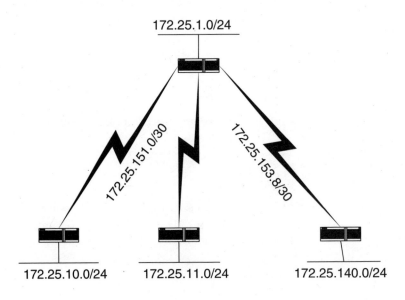

Figure 4-2
Variable length subnet masking

172.25.1.0/24

172.25.151.0/30

172.25.153.8/30

172.25.10.0/24   172.25.11.0/24   172.25.140.0/24

If each site requires a subnet to connect to the main office over a serial link, then approximately 150 serial link subnets are required. To meet this requirement, one or more subnets of the Class B 172.25.0.0 that has not already been allocated can be further subnetted with a /30 mask. This is the principle of starting with the shortest mask and then "subnetting the subnets."

Here, 172.25.151.0 can be chosen as the next available subnet. Instead of giving it a /24 mask, it will have a /30 mask and additional subnets as a result. How many additional subnets are created by changing the mask like so? Moving from /24 to /30 gives an extra six subnet bits, and hence, 64 additional subnets.

The first of these subnets is 172.25.151.0/30 (that is, subnet zero). The next subnets after subnet zero are 172.25.151.4/30, 172.25.151.8/30, and so on. Notice that with a /30 mask the subnet address in the final octet moves up in multiples of four. Networking personnel who are slightly uncomfortable about working with binary may find it convenient to remember this. The idea of deducing subnet addresses directly from the mask will be re-examined later. To return to the previous example, evaluate in binary what the last two /30 subnets are. Here the network portion of the final octet is shown in bold:

2nd last subnet: **111110**00 = 248

Last subnet (broadcast subnet):   **111111**00 = 252

Thus, the last two subnets (that is, the numerically highest subnets) are 172.25.151.248/30 and 172.25.151.252/30.

You now have a total of 64 subnets of 172.25.151.0 for serial links; however, approximately 150 are required. So the next available subnet of 172.25.0.0 can be chosen to support another batch of serial links. Using 172.25.152.0/30 gives another 64 subnets, resulting in a total of 128 WAN links that are subnetted with a /30 mask. Another 22 are required, so taking 172.25.153.0/30 provides more than enough subnet address space to support the current WAN links and leave room for the potential growth of up to 42 more.

A number of points are worth emphasizing in relation to VLSM:

■ **Start with the shortest mask**. Plan the subnets that support the most hosts. This is typically the mask used on most or all of the LAN segments.

■ **Choose one or more *available* subnets and subnet further**. This is sometimes called "subnetting the subnets." It is important to remember that this can be done only with one or more subnets that have not already been used up.

■ **Aim to use contiguous subnets where possible**. Although it is not essential, it certainly makes very good sense to choose a continuous range of addresses and apply a particular mask to them. As will be highlighted in the next section, when route summarization is discussed, efficient allocation of IP addresses is not done merely for the sake of neatness, it is often essential for good network design. In the previous example, the range from 172.25.1.0 to 172.16.150.0 has been assigned to the LAN segments. The advantage of this type of consistency is that it can be determined from the third octet address that this is a LAN segment and also that the mask is 24-bit. As the upcoming sections will demonstrate, the advantages of contiguous addressing go beyond ease of administration. For effective route summarization, contiguous subnets are mandatory.

Planning for Route Summarization

Route summarization means summarizing a group of routes into a single route advertisement. The net result of route summarization and its most obvious benefit is a reduction in the size of routing tables on the network. This in turn reduces the latency associated with each router hop because the average speed for routing table lookup will be increased due to the reduced number of entries. Reducing routing table size is particularly critical on large networks where each routing table may contain several hundred entries. The most obvious problem is the increased latency observed due to the large routing tables. On a large network, traffic may have to traverse more router hops, which serves to compound the issue.

Without the use of route summarization, routing on the Internet could be virtually inoperable. The average Internet router has approximately 75,000 entries in its routing table. This figure, which is growing constantly, is with route summarization being implemented. Clearly the latency associated with each Internet router hop could add up to be a prohibitive tally if each router had the massive routing tables that would ensue without route summarization.

Reducing the size of the routing tables on the network avoids unnecessary use of extra router memory resources storing and maintaining large routing tables. By summarizing routes and reducing routing table size, routing overhead is also reduced as each update contains fewer entries. This reduces the amount of bandwidth consumed by the routing protocol. This is particularly beneficial for a distance vector routing protocol where the periodic updates can consume a significant amount of bandwidth, particularly on WAN links.

Apart from reducing routing tables sizes, route summarization has another less obvious but potentially equally significant benefit. It can improve the stability of the network by containing the propagation of routing traffic after a network link goes down. Essentially, this speeds up convergence resulting in a more stable network. The way in which this happens varies slightly depending on the routing protocol in question. For this reason, this topic will be discussed in more detail in the appropriate sections of the book.

For the moment, it can be generally stated that the basic principle is as follows. If a specific subnet goes down, the attached router usually queries its neighboring routers for a possible alternate route. If these routers do not know of an alternate path to the destination, then they query their neighboring routers. This process can continue until the edge of the network is reached. On a large network this can cause convergence problems. However, if a router only has a summary route to a group of destinations, then it will not propagate a query in relation to a specific subnet within that group of routes. This is because that router never had a route to that specific subnet, so it will not react to it going down. Consider Figure 4-3 where router R2 gets a summary 172.16.0.0/16 route from R1. If 172.16.3.0/24 goes down, then with most routing protocols, R1 would relay that information to R2. In this case, R2 does not propagate any routing messages to its attached routers in relation to this event. The reason is that R2 never had a specific route to 172.16.3.0 and therefore does not react to a change in its state. This principle has useful and far-reaching consequence that improves convergence on large networks. For that reason, it will be discussed in more detail in the chapters on OSPF, and in particular, EIGRP.

Having highlighted the benefits of route summarization, it is necessary to study what must be done to enable it to happen. Firstly, a routing protocol must be running on the network that supports configurable route summarization. This exact topic is discussed in more detail later in the chapter.

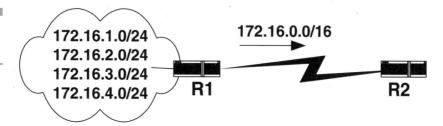

Figure 4-3
Route summarization and convergence

Apart from ensuring that a suitable routing protocol is used, additional elements are necessary when planning and designing a network that employs effective route summarization. In fact, the most important element to enabling route summarization is the formation of an appropriate IP addressing plan. Route summarization has four fundamental rules.

Contiguous Address Blocks   This is essential for route summarization. Appropriate planning must be done to ensure that the network can be divided into distinct logical regions. These regions then can have their routes summarized at appropriate boundary or aggregation points. This can only be done if a contiguous block of subnets exists within each region.

Consider the network shown schematically in Figure 4-4; all the subnets within region A fall within the range 10.2.0.0 to 10.2.255.0. They are not necessarily 24-bit masks, but the first three octets are always within that range. Similarly, the first three octets of all of the subnets contained in region B fall in the range from 10.3.0.0 to 10.3.255.0. Hence, router RA can summarize all of the subnets in region A in the single entry 10.2.0.0/16 in the routing updates to RC. Likewise, RB can summarize all routes in region

Figure 4-4

Contiguous address blocks

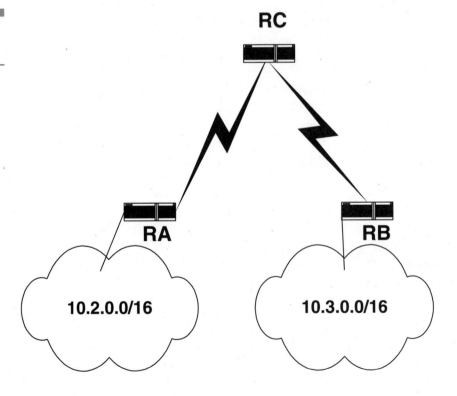

B as 10.3.0.0/16. If region A and region B each had 70 subnets, then instead of receiving a total of 140 routes from RA and RB, RC receives just two. This example is simple for the purpose of clarity but it does illustrate the power of route summarization.

If region A contained even one subnet of the form 10.3.x.y, then this summarization would no longer be valid and hence could not take place. This is also true if region B had even one route of the form 10.2.x.y. This would constitute a discontiguous network, which would either prevent summarization from being used, or at the very least, reduce the amount of summarization taking place.

It must be noted that the idea of a "region" is not a technical term. This term is being used in the context of a group of routers and subnets that are connected together, which can be thought of as a subdivision of the main enterprise network. In an OSPF network, for example, this could correspond to a particular OSPF area.

Do Not Over-summarize The configuration of route summarization can be done in one of two ways. The first method is to be very stringent about the generation of summary routes. A summary route in this case is configured to exactly summarize a precise range of explicit routes. For example, consider the range of subnets 172.16.64.0/24 to 172.16.127.0/24. This range could be summarized by a single route 172.16.64.0/18 (This example will be worked through at the end of this section). That summary route 172.16.64.0/18 exactly covers every subnet within the range and nothing outside it. This is the most precise and stringent form of summarization.

Sometimes in practice, the range of subnets 172.16.64.0/24 to 172.16.127.0/24 might be summarized as 172.16.0.0/16. Although every subnet within the designated range does have the first two octets as 172.16.x.0; this is also true of subnets outside this range. In fact, any route with a third octet value between 128 and 255 is outside our range, yet would be summarized by 172.16.0.0/16. Summarizing routes in this less stringent manner is termed *over-summarization*. It is only valid and acceptable if the over-summarized subnets are never going to be used elsewhere on the network. If in our example the subnets 172.16.128.0/24 to 172.16.255.0/24 were to be employed on an entirely different part of the enterprise, then a discontiguous network would be created as illustrated in Figure 4-5. In such a scenario, this type of over-summarization may cause a routing problem because the router shown would receive conflicting information. It receives an update on one side that all 172.16.0.0 subnets are to be found through its serial 0 port, however it is learning about specific subnets of 172.16.0.0 through serial 1.

Figure 4-5
Over-summarization

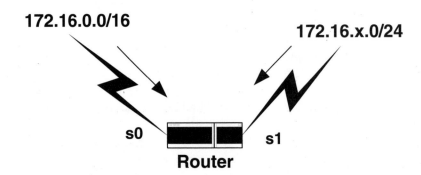

Over-summarization has the benefit of simplicity, but it must be based on the valid assumption that the additional subnets are not (and never will be) used elsewhere on the network. Sometimes over-summarization is employed because it is eventually planned to use the additional subnets in that region of the network; hence, the underlying assumption is valid.

Common Higher Order Bits Across the Range   Networking professionals use different approaches to calculate summary addresses, mainly depending on what their appetite for binary is. The binary method compares the lowest subnet address in the range that is to be summarized with the highest address and determines what they have in common in terms of higher order bits. The number of common bits between the bottom and top of the range gives the summary mask. This is best illustrated by way of example.

Consider the case that was previously discussed where it was required to summarize 172.16.64.0 to 172.16.127.0. Obviously, the first two octets are common throughout the range. However, it is in the third octet that the calculation must be performed because some third octet values fall within the range and some do not.

Compare the bottom and the top of the range in binary:

64 = **01**000000

127 = **01**111111

It can be seen that the first two bits are **01** throughout the range. The value of the remaining six bits varies from all zeros to all ones. The bottom of the range is 172.16.64.0—this becomes the summary address.

The fact that the first two bits of the third octet are common gives results in a summary mask of /18 or 255.255.192.0. The address can be thought of as indicating the bottom of the summarized range, and the mask indicates the end of the range; therefore, the summary address is 172.16.64.0 255.255.192.0. This exactly summarizes the range of addresses or subnets: 172.16.64.0 to 172.16.127.0.

Alternative approaches that avoid the use of binary can be used to calculate summary routes. When VLSM was discussed, it was stated that a 252 mask means that the subnets move up in multiples of four. Similarly a 248 mask, which corresponds to six bits, causes the subnet addresses to move in multiples of eight. For example, consider 192.168.5.0 255.255.255.248. The first subnet after subnet-zero is 192.168.5.8, the next is 192.168.5.16, and so on. Similarly, a 240 mask (4 bits) has subnet addresses that move in multiples of 16. Table 4-1 indicates the multiples that correspond to different subnet masks.

An alternate approach to calculating summary addresses can be applied by memorizing this table. For example, if the Class B network 140.10.0.0 was subnetted with a 24-bit, the first 16 subnets would be 140.10.0.0/24 to 140.10.15.0/24, inclusive.

If it were required to summarize those first 16 subnets into a single summary route, then it could be noted that this is simply a block of 16. Hence, the third octet of the mask is 240. The summary address would therefore be 140.10.0.0, 255.255.240.0, or 140.10.0.0/20. This can be verified using the binary method that the bottom and top of the range (0 and 15 respectively) have the first four bits in common; hence, the mask is 240 in the third octet.

If the second method, the "non-binary" method, is used to calculate summary routes, then a rule is used to check the validity of the summary route. If, for example, the summarization is being done in blocks of 16, then the lowest address must be divisible by 16.

Consider the earlier example where the range of 172.16.64.0 to 172.16.127.0 was summarized using the single route 172.16.64.0 255.255.192.0. The summary route has 192 as the third octet value, and from our table that means the summarization is being done in blocks of 64. The third octet value of the lowest address is 64, which of course is divisible by 64. This is helpful in verifying that this is a correct summary route.

Table 4-1

Author - need a
table caption

Mask	128	192	224	240	248	252	254
Address Multiples	128	64	32	16	8	4	1

Use Bit Boundaries Where Possible   In returning to the two examples of route summarization that have been discussed so far, the range 172.16.64.0 to 172.16.127.0 was summarized using the single address 172.16.64.0/18, and the range 140.10.0.0 to 140.10.15.0 was summarized using the single address 140.10.0.0/20. These examples were deliberately chosen so that they could be summarized into a single route. This of course is not always the case with a range of addresses or routes that are to be summarized. These particular examples could be summarized into a single address because the range of addresses coincided with a *bit-boundary*.

A bit-boundary occurs when two addresses have *n* identical higher order bits, and the remaining bits range from all zeros to all ones. In the first example studied, the summary address summarized a range of addresses whose third octet value varied. Comparing the third octet value of the top and bottom of the range showed that the first two higher order bits were common and the remaining bits ranged from six zeros to six ones. This means that the range of addresses 172.16.64.0 to 172.16.127.0 coincide with a bit boundary. Hence, they can be summarized into a single address, which in this case is 172.16.64.0 255.255.255.192.

Likewise, the range 140.10.0.0 to 140.10.15.0 coincides with a bit boundary. In this case where the first four bits of the third octet are all zeros and the remaining four bits vary from all zeros to all ones, the following is true:

0   =   **0000**0000

15 =   **0000**1111

Because the first four bits are common, the third octet summary mask is .240. This range can be summarized into one address because the lower order bits range from all zeros to all ones.

Now what if it is required to summarize a range of addresses that do not coincide with a bit-boundary? The first fact that must be acknowledged is that the range cannot be summarized with a single address. The best that can be achieved is to find bit boundary ranges that form subsets of the overall range and summarize these. The ultimate goal is to have the minimum number of summary addresses that cover the entire range.

Returning again to the previous example, assume that it is now required to summarize the range 140.10.0.0 to 140.10.40.0 in as few statements as possible. Again, it is the third octet where the address varies, so this is where the action is in terms of calculating summary addresses. The addresses 0 to 40 do not coincide with a bit-boundary so the summarization entails more than one statement. To verify that 0 and 40 does not constitute a bit-boundary, write the two numbers in binary:

0   = 00000000

40 = 00101000

Only the first two higher order bits are common, but even then the remaining bits do not vary between all zeros and all ones. Therefore, this is not a bit boundary.

Now smaller ranges between 0 and 40 that coincide with a bit-boundary must be identified. the range 140.10.0.0 to 140.10.31.0 coincides with a bit-boundary with the first three bits being common:

0   = **000**00000

31 = **000**11111

The first three common bits sets the mask at 11100000 or .224 in the third octet. Therefore, the summary address for the subset range 140.10.0.0 to 140.10.31.0 is as follows:

140.10.0.0 255.255.224.0

A portion of the range has been successfully summarized in one statement, but what about the remainder? A second subset range that coincides with a bit-boundary can also be identified between 32 and 39:

32 = **00100**000

39 = **00100**111

The first five bits are common and the remaining three bits vary across the full range. The summary address for this portion is as follows:

140.10.32.0 255.255.248.0

This leaves just one address in the range namely 140.10.40.0, which has to be given a 24-bits mask.

And so to recap on this example: The range of addresses 140.10.0.0 to 140.10.40.0 can be summarized using the following three statements:

140.10.0.0 255.255.224.0

140.10.32.0 255.255.248.0

140.10.40.0 255.255.255.0

This is the most efficient summarization that can be done when a range of addresses does not coincide with a bit-boundary. For this reason, it is very important to plan your IP addressing scheme so that routes that are to be summarized within particular areas of the network fall within bit-boundaries. This minimizes the number of route summarization statements required and basically maximizes the benefits of route summarization.

Remember:

■ Plan for route summarization by using contiguous blocks of addresses where possible.

■ Do not over-summarize unless it is valid to do so.

■ Choose address ranges that coincide with bit-boundaries.

Categorizing IP Routing Protocols

I will now examine the different types of IP routing protocols and how they are categorized. In particular, distance vector protocols will be compared to link state routing protocols. The difference between classless and classful routing protocols will also be explained.

Distance Vector and Link State Protocols

Traditionally IP routing protocols have fallen into two basic categories: distance vector and link state. A distance vector routing protocol exhibits the following characteristics:

■ Routing tables are built up using the principle of "routing by rumor." That is, each router tells all neighbor routers about its own directly connected subnets. They in turn tell their neighbor routers and so on. This simple principle enables all routers to have a route to each subnet on the network.

■ Routing updates are exchanged between connected routers in the form of periodic updates.

■ The routing updates that are transmitted consist of the router's routing table, which it periodically sends to each router to which it is directly attached. The entire routing table is usually transmitted out of each interface that has the protocol enabled with the exception of routes that would violate split-horizon, that is, routes that were learned over that particular interface.

■ Each router calculates its own routing table based on the routing table of neighboring routers. An algorithm, such as the Bellman-Ford algorithm, is used to take the existing metric associated with a route and add the metric incurred over the link to the neighbor router. This then becomes the neighbor's metric for that route. This is a very significant principle because it means that with distance vector routing protocols, an implicit inter-dependence exists between each router's routing table. This indirectly results in many of the limitations associated with distance vector routing.

The other category of IP routing protocols, link state routing protocol, takes a slightly more sophisticated approach and is characterized by the following properties:

- Routers maintain a database or all links (that is, subnets) on the network. This database includes all information on the routers that are attached to each of these subnets.

- It is the links rather than routes that get advertised in routing updates, which are incremental rather than periodic. In other words, routing updates only occur after a network topology change.

- Each router independently calculates its routing table from the information contained in the database, which is shared by all routers in the domain. Although the database consists of information about every subnet on the network, the routing table is the router's best path to each of these subnets. It is important to be clear about the terminology. A link can be thought of as any IP subnet, and a route is the best path to that subnet from a given router.

The fundamental differences between the distance vector and the links state approach to IP routing results in significantly different characteristics between the two families of protocols. As will become evident when the criteria for evaluating a routing protocol is examined, link state protocols are more suitable for large or growing networks.

Classful and Classless Routing

The distinction between classful and classless routing protocols is very clear and distinct. A routing protocol that does not carry the mask as part of the route advertisement is said to be *classful*, whereas one that does include the mask with the update is a *classless* routing protocol. Although it is true that this is a simple and clear distinction, it is one that has far-reaching consequences.

Remember:

■ Classful routing protocols do not include the mask with the route advertisement, whereas classless protocols do.

■ As a consequence, classful routing protocols cannot support VLSM.

A classful routing protocol cannot support VLSM. This is because the update does not include the mask, therefore only one mask can be allowed for a given major Class A, B, or C network.

Now we will discuss in more detail how classful routing protocols deduce the network mask. In addition, a sometimes misunderstood issue concerning what classful protocols have in relation to route summarization will be discussed.

Classful Route Advertisements and Summarization

How do classful routing protocols know the mask associated with a route if it is not carried within the update? Consider the network shown in Figure 4-6, and assume the routing protocol is the classful RIP version 1. Router R1 advertises the 148.20.1.0 subnet to R2. The mask is deduced by R2 as it assumes that because its serial 1 interface is also a subnet of 148.20.0.0 with a /24 mask, then it must also be the mask for 148.20.1.0. In terms of the operation of a classful routing protocol, if a router receives an update about a subnet of a particular major network over one of its interfaces, which is also in that major network, the router assumes consistency of the mask. The router must make this assumption, otherwise it has no way of

Figure 4-6
Classful route
summarization

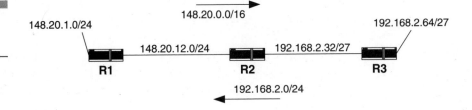

deducing the subnet mask. A consequence of this type of operation is that VLSM cannot be supported by classful routing protocols.

What if a router receives an update about a subnet on an interface that is not part of the same major network? Referring again to Figure 4-6, R2 must advertise the subnets of 148.20.0.0 to R3. The problem here is that the interface over which R3 will receive this information is not part of the Class B network 148.20.0.0, so R3 has no way of assuming what the subnet mask is. In this case, the subnets of 148.20.0.0 that R2 knows about (that is, 148.20.1.0/24 and 148.20.12.0/24) must be summarized as the Class B 148.20.0.0/16. This is called route summarization upon crossing a major network boundary. It happens with classful routing protocols simply because it has to. The router R3 in Figure 4-6 has no way of knowing the subnet masks for the explicit subnets of 148.20.0.0; hence, it must assume that no subnetting is taking place. Examining the routing updates flowing in the other direction, R1 similarly has a summary route to the Class C network 192.168.2.0/24 rather than to the two explicit 27-bit subnets.

Route summarization usually increases network efficiency by reducing routing overhead; however, it must be planned for carefully. This type of automatic route summarization is something that cannot be avoided in a classful routing environment if a major network boundary is crossed and, as we shall see, can potentially cause routing problems.

Choosing a Routing Protocol

The choice of routing protocol can have a critical bearing on network performance and the feasibility of implementing a set of design requirements. A routing protocol must be evaluated against a number of fundamental parameters. In this section, these performance parameters are reviewed, and the discussion will make it evident how some of them are deeply interrelated. After first performing this basic evaluation that is about to be discussed, some subtle points in relation to the network design may also make one protocol more favorable to another. These finer points will be addressed in the upcoming chapters on the more ubiquitous IP routing protocols in use on modern networks. Now, it is appropriate to explain the features that are characteristic of an IP routing protocol that meets the network design requirements.

Scalability

One of the most fundamental issues that determines the choice of IP routing protocol is scalability. That is, how effectively will the routing protocol support a large network or one that is likely to grow? The scalability of a routing protocol is determined by factors such as how efficiently it processes routing updates and how quickly it can react to changes on a large network.

Routing Updates

The scalability of the IP routing protocol is always partly determined by the efficiency with which it processes routing updates. Traditional distance vector routing protocols exchange routing information by periodically broadcasting their routing table to all directly attached routers. This is a crude and inefficient method of building and maintaining routing tables for a number of reasons:

- **Incremental updates are preferable to periodic exchanges.** The periodic broadcast of the entire routing table can cause excessive bandwidth consumption, particularly on slow WAN links or if the routing table is large. These updates are usually unnecessary if a topology change has not been made on the network. It is vastly more efficient to only transmit routing information when a network topology change has occurred, such as the loss of a link or the addition of a new subnet. The use of incremental rather than periodic updates is employed by the more scalable routing protocols such as OSPF, IS-IS, Cisco's EIGRP, and BGP.

- **Multicasts are preferable to broadcasts.** Older distance vector routing protocols, such as RIP version 1 and Cisco's IGRP, use broadcasts to exchange routing information. Consider the case where a stub Ethernet segment is being advertised into a RIP network. Because the Ethernet segment is participating in RIP, the local router will broadcast its entire routing table on the Ethernet every 30 seconds. This is a waste of bandwidth, however that is not necessarily the main issue because bandwidth is not always at a premium in the LAN. More seriously, every station must process the broadcasts on the LAN even though they are not running RIP. This would not be the case, unless the routing protocol uses a multicast group to transfer routing information. Only devices that are members of the group must process the updates. The use of multicasts is an enhancement that RIP version 2 offers over its predecessor.

■ **Network Diameter.** All IP routing protocols have an associated maximum hop count that determines the network diameter or maximum possible number of router hops between any source and any destination on the network. Most so-called scalable routing protocols have a maximum hop count of at least 100 so they do not pose any limitations on the maximum network diameter. RIP, however, has a maximum hop count of 16 hops. This is intended to prevent the "count to infinity" problem with degrading metric that can be characteristic of a routing loop on a RIP network. Some technology analysts cite this as a major reason why RIP is unsuitable on large networks. Although RIP (regardless of version) is not even close to being a scalable routing protocol, this is not the most compelling reason for RIP's lack of scalability. Certainly in the context of the enterprise network, if more than 15 hops is required between any source and any destination, then the network must have been poorly designed.

Routing Protocol Stability

The stability of a routing protocol can be tested during a network transition such as the loss of a link or other form of topology change. The routing protocol reacts to the topology change and propagates the information about the change through the network. During the time that it takes the routing protocol to distribute this information, routers will be working off inconsistent information. In other words, some routers will be aware of the change and some will not. This inconsistency can result in a particular type of routing problem called a *routing loop*.

Distance vector routing protocols have a potential susceptibility to routing loops because they do not maintain any additional information about the network topology other than the routing table. A link state routing protocol maintains a database of all subnets on the network and has topological awareness of what routers are attached to these subnets; therefore, it is less likely to act on misinformation immediately following a topology change.

Consider the network shown in Figure 4-7. Assume that RIP is the IP routing protocol, keeping in mind that the principle about to be illustrated is true of any distance vector routing protocol.

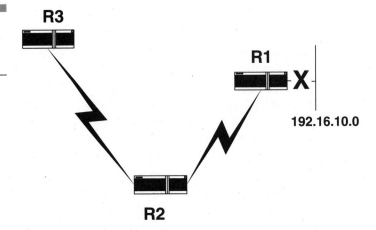

Figure 4-7
Routing loops and
distance vector
protocols

Now, let us work through the following hypothetical scenario. R1's Ethernet 192.168.10.0 fails, so this route is missing from the next periodic update that R1 sends to R2. Upon receipt of this update, R2 deletes the route to 192.168.10.0 from its routing table. Immediately after receiving this message from R1, R2 receives its next periodic update from R3. The R3 router has not yet found out that 192.168.10.0 is no longer accessible, so its routing update will include this route with a hop count of 2. R2 has just deleted the same route, hence it will put the route to 192.168.10.0 with a next-hop address of R3 and a hop count of 3 in its routing table. R2 sees the 192.168.10.0 route as being new, and if R3 is two hops away from that destination, then R2 assumes itself to be three hops away. In its next update to R3, R2 includes this spurious route to 192.168.10.0. R3 learned this route from R2 originally, but it now sees it as having an increased metric. R3 now places this route in its routing table with a hop count of 4. After the next received update from R3, R2 shows the route with a hop count of 5 and so on.

This phenomenon is known as *counting-to-infinity*. It can occur if routers have inconsistent information about a network change, and it is characterized by spurious routing information being exchanged with a continuously incrementing or worsening metric. This example dealt with RIP and hop count, but the count to infinity phenomenon could conceivably happen with any distance vector routing protocol.

Distance vector routing protocols have incorporated the following features to help safeguard against this type of routing loop:

- **Define a maximum metric**   To prevent the count to infinity continuing until the bit registers overflow, a maximum possible metric is defined after the route is deemed inaccessible. In the case of RIP, a hop count of 16 indicates an inaccessible route.

- **Split-Horizon**   This principle states that a routing protocol should not advertise that routes back out the interface over which they were learned. In our example, this would have prevented R3 from sending an update to R2 about 192.168.10.0 because R2 learned about the route over that serial interface.

- **Route Poisoning**   When a router detects a failure on a directly attached network instead of just deleting it from its routing table and forgetting about it, it *poisons* the route. This means advertising the route as inaccessible to each of its attached routers. In the case of RIP, a lost route would be advertised with a hop count of 16. The neighbor routers acknowledge the route poison message by returning a *poison reverse* message, which confirms that they now know that the subnet is down. Each router that receives a poison message also passes it on to its own directly attached neighbor routers. These messages are *triggered updates,* meaning that they are sent immediately and do not have to wait for any periodic update timer to expire. Thus in theory, the entire routing domain should quickly learn that the subnet in question has gone down.

- **Hold-down timer**   A router that receives a poison message does not delete the corresponding route from its routing table, instead it places the route in a *hold-down* state. A router will continue to advertise the route as being inaccessible (that is, with an infinite metric) while the route is in hold-down. However, it will ignore any updates about the route that do not have a better metric than the original metric. This avoids the possibility of the routing loop characterized by a worsening metric counting-to-infinity.

These features just described are incorporated into distance vector routing protocols in order to increase their stability against routing loops. The downside is that distance vector routing protocols are slow to propagate definitive information about a topology change. They are said to be slow to converge. Protocol convergence is the topic that will be discussed next.

This can be thought of as the *stability tradeoff* that is inherent to distance vector routing protocols—slower convergence for increased stability.

Remember:

- Distance vector routing protocols have features incorporated such as hold-down timers that improve stability against routing loops. The trade-off is slower convergence.

Before moving on to talk about routing protocol convergence, some final comments about routing loops should be mentioned. Routing loops usually occur as a result of a network topology change or a configuration change on one or more routers. The time lag required for all routers to become aware of the change can provide a potential window for the development of a routing loop.

While a routing loop is active on the network, a router (RA) may send packets for a particular destination to an attached router (RB). The problem is that RB's path to the destination is through RA; hence, the packets bounce or loop between the two routers. In the example I discussed in relation to Figure 4-7, packets destined for 192.168.10.0 could loop between the routers R2 and R3.

Other possible reasons for routing loops exist that are usually more likely on larger networks. These include problems due to device configuration errors or due to poor design. No routing protocol is completely immune against the possibility of a routing loop. Distance vector protocols have features such as hold-down, whereas link state protocols do not need hold-down timers due to their greater awareness of the network topology. However, routing loops can still occur with either distance vector or link state protocols. Good design practice, as will be discussed in the upcoming chapters, is the key to minimizing the possibility of routing loops.

Remember:

- Routing loops can occur with both distance vector and link state protocols. By good design the possibility of routing loops is minimized.
- No matter how much redundancy is in the network, one potential single point of failure is always possible—the routing protocol, which is why it should be chosen with care.

Speed of Convergence

Network convergence can be defined in a number of ways. A clear and basic definition of network convergence is the time that elapses from a topology change occurring on the network until every router is aware of this change. If a topology change occurs, such as the loss or addition of a subnet, then a time lapse occurs before every router on the network is aware of this change. During this time interval, which is called the *convergence time*, some routers are operating off inconsistent information. Hence, the convergence time can also be thought of as the time lag from a topology change occurring to the point where all routers in the network have consistent routing information in relation to the affected subnet.

The speed of convergence can vary dramatically on a network depending on a number of factors not least of which are the operational characteristics of the routing protocol itself. The following issues should be considered when attempting to predict convergence times:

Failure detection mechanism   This may or may not be independent of the routing protocol depending on the type of failure. For the more sophisticated routing protocols that converge quickly, the initial detection of the failure is often the largest component of the convergence time. For the network shown in Figure 4-8, OSPF is the routing protocol. If R1's Ethernet switch connection goes down, then R1 detects this failure after the loss of three Ethernet keepalives. R2, however, does not detect this failure until four OSPF hello packets are missed from R1. In other words, this is the OSPF dead interval, which is 40 seconds by default on Ethernet. The two routers, R1 and R2, report the failure to the routers to which they are connected. However, because R1 detected the failure before R2, the convergence process begins in WAN1 slightly sooner than in WAN2.

Update mechanism   It must be ascertained whether the routing protocol uses triggered updates as soon as a link changes state, or whether it is required to wait for the next periodic update. The use of periodic updates slows down convergence in proportion to the length of the update interval. The use of hold-down timers with distance vector routing protocols is a necessary evil. This feature, however, can dramatically increase the convergence time, because a router does not place a backup route in the routing table until the hold-down timer has expired. For RIP, the update interval is 30 seconds and the hold-down time is 180 seconds. The values of these

Figure 4-8
Failure detection and
convergence time

timers can be altered through configuration; however, this should only be done as a last resort because it can lead to unpredictable routing results. Also, the timers must agree on all RIP routers within the domain.

Advanced distance vector protocols and link state protocols always use incremental triggered updates. This is not only a more efficient means of transferring routing information; it also speeds up convergence by immediately sending only the minimum amount of information required.

With the more sophisticated protocols such as OSPF and Cisco's EIGRP, the concept of a hold-down timer does not exist. It is unnecessary because these protocols maintain information about the network topology in terms of a database. Therefore, when a route is lost from the routing table, more information is available for the router to access without relying on potential spurious updates from neighbor routers. The exact convergence mechanism for each of these two protocols will be discussed in detail in the relevant upcoming chapters.

Route calculation algorithm   The exact manner in which a backup route is calculated when a primary route fails has a great bearing on the convergence time. An example of RIP convergence is examined later in this chapter, highlighting the crude manner in which a backup route is selected and propagated through the RIP domain.

Other, more sophisticated protocols have inherent delay associated with route calculation. For example, an OSPF router typically waits five seconds between receiving a *Link State Advertisement* (LSA) and recalculating its routing table. This is prudent as it protects against the routing protocol, becoming unstable due to a flapping link; however, it does slightly increase the convergence time.

EIGRP does not have an initial delay like OSPF. However, if an EIGRP router does not have a backup route, it will query each of its neighbors for such a route and will not conclude its calculation until all of them reply. This mode of operation can sometimes make EIGRP slow to converge.

Before choosing any routing protocol for a network, it is important to understand how exactly the protocol attempts to converge. This requires a clear understanding of the protocol in terms of update mechanism and route recalculation methodology. Different protocols should always be evaluated because all protocols converge in a slightly different manner. As a result, on two different networks, different protocols may converge at significantly different speeds and with differing reliability. As a measure of the importance of the entire issue of network convergence, examples of RIP, OSPF, and EIGRP convergence will be studied in this book.

Media characteristics The medium on which the topology change occurs can influence the speed of detection. Examples of this are the HDLC, Frame Relay LMI, or Ethernet keepalive intervals. Another example is with ATM where, if OAM is not being used, failure detection can be slower because the routing protocol has to wait longer before a loss of line protocol occurs on the ATM PVC.

After the attached router has detected failure, appropriate routing update messages must be propagated through the network as part of the convergence process. The speed with which this occurs depends on the different LAN and particularly WAN media that must be traversed. For example, routing traffic may be dropped on busy or slow WAN links, which can slow down convergence sometimes to extreme levels.

The extent to which convergence is affected by slow WAN links depends to a certain degree on the nature of the protocol itself. If a router running EIGRP is actively requesting a backup route, it will query each of its neighbors and will not attempt to calculate the backup route, until each neighbor replies. This can mean convergence problems if an EIGRP router has many neighbors that are formed over slow serial links.

Routing Metric

If a router running a particular IP routing protocol receives multiple advertised paths to a particular destination network, it chooses the path with the best metric and place in its routing table. If the best metric is true of more than one path, then each of these least cost paths are placed in the routing table, and equal cost load balancing is performed. Different routing protocols use different metrics, in other words various routing protocols each have their own way of deciding the best path to a destination. The metric should be sufficiently sophisticated to ensure that the routing protocol's interpretation of the best path is a realistic one.

Considering the network shown in Figure 4-9, if RIP was the routing protocol in use, then Router A would see two equal cost paths to 10.10.0.0 and would load balance accordingly (assuming the implementation of RIP supported load balancing).

OSPF uses an administrative cost value as its metric. The OSPF cost is inversely proportional to bandwidth, hence OSPF would ensure that Router A chooses the T-1 path to 10.10.0.0.

It should be ensured that all routers in the domain have a common benchmark for calculating the metric associated with each link. For exam-

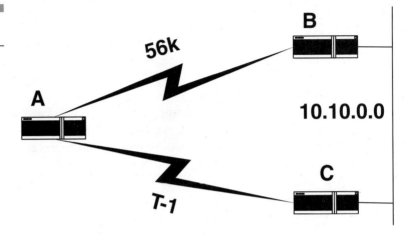

ple, the routers may have to be configured so that the interface bandwidth that OSPF uses to calculate its metric matches the actual speed of the link. This can be an issue for serial links of varying speed or Frame Relay PVCs when the router cannot dynamically learn the CIR.

Routing metric only should be manually manipulated for good reason, such as deliberately biasing one path over another for backup applications. Routing metrics is examined in more detail when multiprotocol route redistribution is discussed in a later chapter.

Remember:
- If a routing protocol uses bandwidth as part of its calculation, ensure that the interface bandwidth as indicated by the router matches the actual speed of the link.

One of the limitations of the conventional routing metric is that all traffic tends to travel over the least cost path as decided by the routing protocol. Returning to the simple example of Figure 4-9, if a very large amount of traffic was sent over the T-1 link to the point where it got congested, it may be desirable to send some traffic over the higher cost path. In fact, traffic travelling over this path may experience a better quality of service during periods of congestion. In other words, most conventional routing metrics cannot respond to dynamic changes on the network, such as increased loading, on the least cost path. This can cause compounded problems on very large networks and on the Internet.

Support of VLSM

For a network where anything less than an abundance of available IP address space is available, then VLSM is likely to be a requirement. VLSM enables a very efficient use of IP address and subnet space. Classless routing protocols such as OSPF, RIP version 2, EIGRP, IS-IS, and BGP support VLSM because they include the mask along with the updates. Classless protocols, such as RIP version 1 and IGRP, cannot support VLSM. This provides another reason why such protocols are unsuitable on medium to large networks.

Discontiguous Networks

If a block of subnet addresses belonging to the same major Class A, B, or C network is distributed across different regions of an enterprise network, and these regions are logically separated by subnet addresses that are not part of the same major network, then a discontiguous network is formed. It is said that a picture tells a thousand words, so examine Figure 4-10 for an example of a discontiguous network.

Although not entirely desirable, discontiguous networks are not necessarily a problem in themselves; it depends on the routing protocol being employed on the network. Classful routing protocols must automatically summarize networks based on class when a network boundary is crossed. This in itself means that classful routing protocols cannot support discontiguous network.

In the example shown in Figure 4-10, Router A receives a summary route 172.16.0.0/16 from both Router B and Router C. Hence, it does not have a specific route to either 172.16.18.0 or 172.16.27.0. These networks become inaccessible from Router A because it has two conflicting summary routes to 172.16.0.0, while it is also directly connected to another 172.16.0.0 subnet. Thus, a fundamental routing problem has occurred.

If a classful routing protocol is being used, only one way to solve the problem exists, and that is to remove the discontiguous network by putting subnets of 172.16.0.0 on the serial links between Router A and the other two routers. The addressing on the serial links could be changed or they could take the form of secondary addresses. The discontiguous network condition would no longer exist because the 172.16.0.0 network boundary would not be crossed by any of the routers; therefore, summarization would not take place.

Figure 4-10
Discontiguous
subnets

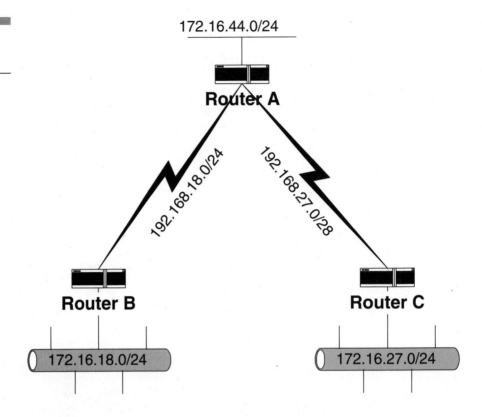

When using a classless routing protocol such as RIP version 2, another solution is available. RIP v2 enables automatic summarization to be turned off through router configuration. If this feature is turned off on Router B and Router C, a discontiguous network is avoided and Router A receives specific routes for the 172.16.18.0 and 172.16.27.0 subnets. Other classless routing protocols, like OSPF, do not perform any summarization even if a major network boundary is crossed. Hence, no configuration is required to support discontiguous networks.

Route Summarization

As a network grows, the number of IP subnets grows, which in turn is likely to produce larger routing tables. These large routing tables can have two negative effects. Additional memory resource requirements can be placed on the routers. Also, the latency associated with routing table lookup is increased if process switching is used.

Figure 4-11
Summarization and
reduced routing
overhead

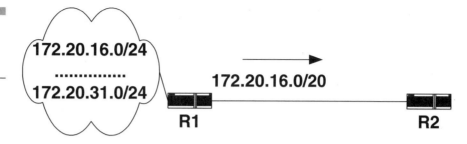

Apart from reducing the size of routing tables, thoughtful employment of route summarization can improve network stability. The unnecessary propagation of triggered updates can be reduced when a link fails. For an example of this, consider the network in Figure 4-11. R1 has a route to each specific subnet in the range 172.20.16.0/24 to 172.20.31.0/24, however it only advertises a single route 172.20.16.0/20 that summarizes these 16 subnets. One of the effects of this is if 172.16.23.0/24 changed state, then R1 would not send a triggered update to R2. Because R1 is not actually advertising this specific route to R2 in any case, it will then tell R2 that it has gone down.

This effect of route summarization can significantly reduce the amount of routing traffic on the network following a topology change. It can therefore speed up convergence and make the network more stable. Another positive side effect is in the event of a flapping link; a persistent flow of triggered updates does not occur every time the link changes state.

In the chapter on EIGRP, a further use of route summarization will be demonstrated that can dramatically reduce convergence time in the particular case of this routing protocol. This is where summarization can be used to control the propagation of query packets for a specific route that has failed. A further niche application of route summarization can overcome difficulties encountered when redistributing subnets of varying mask length into a protocol that does not support VLSM.

In Figure 4-12, R2 borders a domain that has a classless routing protocol with one that uses a classful routing protocol, in this case RIP version 1. Both domains use the Class B network 150.10.0.0. In the RIP v1 domain, this is subnetted using a 24-bit mask. In this example, just two subnets are shown in the classless domain: 150.10.10.16/28 and 150.10.9.0/24. If the classless routing protocol were redistributed into RIP on R2, then the 150.10.10.16/28 subnet would not be included in the redistribution because RIP v1 does not support VLSM. Summarizing 150.10.10.0 with a 24-bit mask on R1 could avert this problem. Then the route would be redistributed

Figure 4-12
Summarization and
VLSM

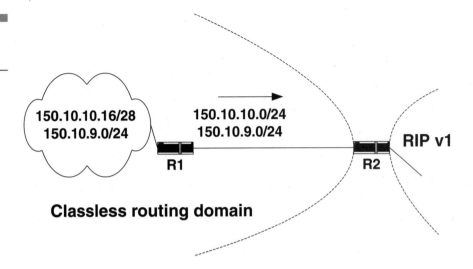

Classless routing domain

successfully by R2 into RIP because it has a mask that is consistent with the 150.10.0.0/24 mask in the RIP domain. In this example, just one route was shown, but of course the same principle is applicable to any subnets that are subnetted with a mask longer than that used on the same major network in the RIP v1 routing domain.

Having discussed some of the benefits and uses of route summarization, it should be clear that route summarization is certainly not something that is done purely for aesthetic purposes. It is therefore important to employ a routing protocol that supports the ability to do configurable or manual summarization. Manual summarization gives the network designer control as to where in the network route summarization should take place, rather than just across major network boundaries. Classful routing protocols do automatic summarization when a major network boundary is crossed. This might sound useful and indeed sometimes it is; however, it has also been demonstrated that it renders these protocols incapable of supporting discontiguous networks. With a classless routing protocol, even if it automatically summarizes routes when crossing a major network boundary, the feature can be disabled to support discontiguous subnets. Classless routing protocols also support manual or configurable summarization. This is a topic that will be addressed specifically in each of the upcoming chapters on OSPF, EIGRP, and BGP.

In conclusion, the general benefits of route summarization include the following:

- Reduction in routing table size, resulting in less routing overhead and lower latency at each router hop.
- Reduction in triggered updates and route flapping.
- Route summarization is a possible method of containing the propagation of routing traffic after a link changes state. This can speed up convergence.
- The redistribution of subnets with variable masks into a protocol that does not support VLSM can be facilitated using route summarization.

Before moving on, some words of caution are worth noting in relation to route summarization.

Sub-optimal Routing   One possible tradeoff that sometimes has to be faced with route summarization is sub-optimal routing. This occurs when a router has a summary route to a group of destinations that points to a particular next hop, and that router may have another shorter path to a specific member of that group that it cannot use because it is only receiving a summary route.

Sub-optimal routing is best illustrated with an example. In the network shown schematically in Figure 4-13, the summary route 150.10.0.0/16 is advertised over a configured summarization boundary between Router B and Router A. Router B summarizes all of the 150.10.0.0 subnets and no other router advertises subnets of 150.10.0.0. This results in a single point of summarization. If Router A has to route to 150.10.17.0, it must use the summary route via B, even though there is a lower cost path via D. This is sometimes termed the summarization versus optimization tradeoff. However, it is less likely to be an issue if the IP addressing plan and network architecture has been carefully designed.

The Longest Prefix Rule   Most IP routing protocols use the longest prefix rule when selecting a path to a destination. This means that the most specific match to the destination is chosen from the routing table regardless of metric.

In Figure 4-14, Router A is intended to receive only a summary route for 150.10.0.0/16. This summarization has been successfully configured on Router B but was overlooked on Router C. Hence, Router A learns all of the specific subnets of 150.10.0.0 from Router C.

Figure 4-13
Route summarization
and sub-optimal
routing

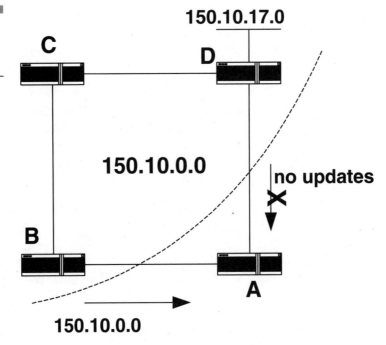

150.10.17.0

C   D

150.10.0.0

no updates

B   A

150.10.0.0

Figure 4-14
Routing to the
longest prefix match

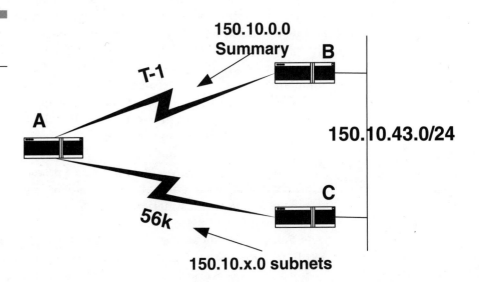

150.10.0.0
Summary   B

T-1

A

150.10.43.0/24

C

56k

150.10.x.0 subnets

To get to 150.10.43.0, Router A choses the path over the 56k link to C rather than the T-1 link to B. This is because A receives a specific route to 150.10.43.0/24 over the 56k link. This is a more specific match than 150.10.0.0/16 to the destination in question. The routing metric of the summary route is better as it is learned over a T-1 link; however, the metric does not come into play here. Router A does not compare the metric for 150.10.43.0/24 with that of 150.10.0.0/16 because they are not regarded as being the same route due to the different prefix lengths.

The principle of longest prefix match is very important in scalable IP routing and can cause much confusion. It is important to remember that the routing protocol will always choose the path with the longest prefix match to the destination. It should be noted that the routing metric is only used to compare paths to the same destination. If the prefix lengths are different between two routes, then technically they represent route to different destinations.

Often a particular boundary where summarization is done has at least two routers for redundancy. A typical example is the use of two Area Border Routers in OSPF. In such a scenario, it is very important to ensure that configuration is done correctly on each router. If this is not the case, then specific routes will "leak" through, effectively invalidating the route summarization.

Remember:

■ Remember that routing protocols normally route to the longest prefix match regardless of metric. Hence, if route summarization is misconfigured at one point in the network, then it may be rendered useless.

Understanding Load Balancing

Most IP routing protocols load balance across equal cost paths. This basically means that the routing protocol will place multiple paths to the same destination in the IP routing table if the metrics are equal.

It is important to understand exactly how traffic is balanced across the paths. The mechanism for load balancing depends on whether the router is using process switching or layer 3 switching.

With process switching the router must consult the IP routing table for every packet being switched between its interfaces. If layer 3 switching is used, then the first packet on a particular source-destination data flow is process switched, but the result of the routing table lookup is stored in a high-speed cache. Subsequent packets in the same data flow are switched by consulting this cache rather than the routing table.

Load balancing is done on a per packet basis if process switching is being employed. With layer 3 switching, load balancing is achieved across equal cost paths by caching an equal number of destination flows against each path. A potential problem may occur when load balancing is done in this manner. If a disproportionate number of very busy destinations happens to be cache against the same path, one path might be significantly busier than the other(s).

Some proprietary routing protocols, such as Cisco's IGRP, support unequal cost load balancing. The problem of using this with layer 3 switching could be even more serious than with equal cost load balancing. More destinations would be cached against the lower cost path. Again, these may not necessarily be the busiest destinations, so the net result could be counterproductive.

Policy-based routing is discussed in Chapter 7, "BGP and Internet Routing," along with BGP. One of the applications of policy-based routing, even outside of a BGP environment, is that it provides a sophisticated method for performing load balancing. Different next-hop paths to a destination can be specified depending on the source address. Thus, policy-based routing provides a mechanism for making routing decisions based on source address as well as destination address. This has an application for load balancing where certain source addresses can be sent over one path and other sources routed on the second path as controlled by the network administrator.

Remember:
- Load balancing over multiple paths can give unpredictable results if layer 3 switching is used on the router. Use policy-based routing for the most efficient implementation of load balancing.

Security

The routing protocol should support the ability to authenticate routing updates. Ideally this authentication should use encrypted passwords. The more sophisticated routing protocols, such as OSPF and BGP, support authentication, with OSPF also supporting MD5 encryption. Authentication is not worth implementing if the passwords are not encrypted. Following is an example used to illustrate this point.

Some time ago I worked as a consultant helping two recently merged companies interconnect their networks in a secure and controlled manner. One company used OSPF with simple password authentication, while the other company used a proprietary routing protocol. A DMZ LAN with a firewall was used to connect the two enterprise networks together. The company running OSPF made the mistake of not filtering hello packets being sent onto the DMZ LAN. They possibly thought that because the other company was not using OSPF, redistribution had to be configured, which would be done in a controlled manner. Also, the OSPF packets were password protected in any case. However, I put a laptop PC running a standard type of network analyzer software on the DMZ LAN. I was then able to see the hello packets from the OSPF router. They included the IP addressing information as well as the password, which was being sent in clear text! All I needed to form an OSPF neighbor with this router was another router with a fastethernet interface. I could then have received the entire link state database for that corporation. This would have enabled me to configure spurious routes using loopback interfaces that mimicked all of their subnets. I could have advertised these subnets with a more favorable metric, thus redirecting all traffic with that enterprise to my router! Essentially, I could have crashed their network. If MD5 authentication were used, this potential for a security breach would not have existed.

Remember:
- On a secure network, authentication of routing traffic should be implemented. The passwords should also be encrypted.

When To Use Static Routes

Static routes do not scale well even on medium-sized networks due to the amount of administrative overhead that they entail. However, static routes do have a number of niche applications:

Stub networks   Small LANs on the edge of the enterprise networks are sometimes termed *stub networks*. In terms of our hierarchical model, these would be no greater than Tier-3 sites, or more likely, sub-offices of Tier-3 sites. For these stub sites, usually only one path runs into the core of the enterprise network. If a dynamic routing protocol were run to these sites, then the stub router would have a large routing table with each entry having the same next-hop address. In this case, it may be more efficient to simply have a static route or default route pointing at this next-hop address. The router that connects directly to the stub router must then have a static route for the stub LAN, since it obviously cannot learn about this subnet dynamically. It must also redistribute the static route into the dynamic routing protocol that is being used on the enterprise network. Otherwise, the network core routers will not have a route to the stub network.

Dialup connections Certain issues are associated with running dynamic routing protocols over dial-up connections such as ISDN. Periodic routing traffic due to hello messages or periodic routing updates can bring up the ISDN line, resulting in excessive usage charges. Although efficient methods are available to run dynamic routing over dialup connections by using good design and configuration, the issue is often avoided entirely by the use of static routes.

Problems with administrative overhead can come into play on large networks. If a large number of remote sites have ISDN as a backup connection to the central site, then the central site routers must have a static route to each of these remote LANs.

Security Static routes are a prudent choice for connecting to the ISP or for links to business partners. Dynamically routing protocols advertise information about your network. Route filtering can be employed so that only essential routes are advertised to these parties. However, route filtering can be poorly configured. Even aside from this, it can be easy to hack through a dynamic routing protocol; hence, static routes offer the greatest security on these types of connections.

To correct VLSM problems It has already been discussed how route summarization can be used to solve problems encountered when redistributing variable mask length subnets into a protocol that does not support VLSM. Static routes can also be used to provide an equally effective, if somewhat less, elegant method of solving the same problem.

Returning to the example of Figure 4-12, the same problem could be resolved by configuring a static route on R2 for 150.10.10.0/24. This is similar in principle to summarization because the static route is summarizing the 150.10.10.16/28 subnet with a 24-bit mask. This static route could then be redistributed into RIP on R2.

Routing Information Protocol

Having examined the main issues and features surrounding IP routing protocols, we will now discuss our first specific example of an IP routing protocol and that is the Routing Information Protocol (RIP).

RIP Version 1

RIP version 1 is the most traditional and simplest routing protocol that is still in popular use on many LANs and WANs. Its popularity stems from the fact that it was the first standardized IP routing protocol to be supported by all major vendors in the industry. Its simplicity further fueled its growth as a ubiquitous routing protocol. However, along with its simplicity comes a number of limitations which are problematic in today's era of increasingly complex internetworks. The limitations of RIP version 1 include the following:

- A maximum network diameter of 15 hops is inadequate for large networks.

- The hop-count metric is unsophisticated and can lead to sub-optimal routing decisions.

- The periodic exchange of routing tables with neighboring routers every 30 seconds is a crude way to exchange routing information and leads to the unnecessary use of valuable WAN bandwidth.

- Convergence is slow. A hold-down timer must expire before RIP updates its routing table with a change in state of a particular link. This, coupled with the fact that periodic update timers have to expire in order to further propagate the routing changes to neighbor routers, results in a slow convergence time for RIP. The issue of convergence becomes particularly evident as the network scales make RIP very slow to react to changes on a large network. The reason for the use of a hold-down timer is to provide for stability against the possibility of routing loops, which can occur when different routers are making routing decisions based on inconsistent information. The hold-down timer tells RIP to "wait and see" before reacting to a network change. The tradeoff here is slow convergence for increased stability.

- VLSM is not supported because RIP updates do not include mask information. This results in the potentially inefficient use of IP address space.
- Address summarization cannot be manually configured. RIP networks are simply summarized based on class when a network boundary is crossed.

These issues render RIP unsuitable for use in large networks because of its poor scalability, speed of convergence, and inefficient bandwidth usage. The motivation for the development of an enhanced version of RIP is obvious and it came in the form of RIP version 2, which addresses many of its predecessor's limitations.

RIP Version 2

RIP version 2 is a classless version of RIP v1, meaning that RIP v2 updates include the subnet mask along with the route. This offers some significant enhancements over version 1.

RIP version 2 supports the following:

- Route summarization—Like RIP version 1, summarization is automatically performed when crossing classful network boundaries. However, an extremely useful differentiating feature is that automatic summarization can be disabled. This feature has an application in resolving problems caused by discontiguous networks.
- VLSM can be supported because RIP v2 updates contain the subnet mask until version 1.
- *Classless Inter-Domain Routing* (CIDR)—This most fundamentally means that routing can be performed while ignoring the constraints of network class type. Each network or subnet is routed on the basis of its network address and mask without any regard for it being Class A, B, or C.
- Updates are multicasts that use the 224.0.0.9 reserved Class D address. This is distinct from version 1, which simply broadcasts the updates out of each router interface that is running RIP. Multicasts are a more efficient means of transferring routing information because the updates are addressed to the 224.0.0.9 group address. Therefore only stations in this multicast group (that is, RIP v2 routers) will process these packets. All stations process broadcasts. This can be particularly

inefficient on a LAN that may have only two routers, whereas all other stations must interrupt their CPUs to process RIP broadcasts every 30 seconds.

■ Security—RIP version 2 supports authentication of routing updates. This can take the form of simple password exchange or the preferable option of Message Digest authentication. MD5 ensures that the passwords are encrypted rather than sent in clear text. This prevents a network analyzer from easily picking up the passwords.

The classless nature of RIP v2 enables support for VLSM and discontiguous subnets. However, some issues still remain with version 2. Convergence is not any faster than version 1, which of course is a major problem on large networks. Also, the maximum network diameter of 15 hops is an issue. Hop count is still used as the sole routing metric. This is a crude and unsatisfactory method of evaluating the best routing path to a destination. RIP version 2 (like version 1) would see a T-1 and a 56k link as equal cost even though one path happens to be 23 times faster than the other one.

Before moving on to demonstrate an example of RIP convergence, one point must be clarified concerning RIP's capability for load balancing. Load balancing is neither specified nor denied in the RFC for RIP. A number of proprietary implementations of RIP support load balancing, including most of the major router vendors. The net result is that most industrial implementations of RIP will load balance across multiple equal-cost paths. It is often assumed that RIP cannot load balance due to its overall unsophisticated nature. Also remember that what RIP perceives as equal cost merely means equal hop count.

RIP Convergence

Arguably, the most fundamental reason why RIP is unsuitable for large networks is its slow convergence. An example of RIP convergence will be used to demonstrate this, using the network shown in Figure 4-15.

Consider what happens when R1's Ethernet link fails:

1. R1 sends a route poison update to R3 and R4 for the 131.5.5.0 network. R3 and R4 propagates this poison message to their attached routers using triggered updates.

2. After receiving a poison reverse message from R3 and R4, R1 deletes the 131.5.5.0 route from its routing table.

Figure 4-15
RIP convergence
example

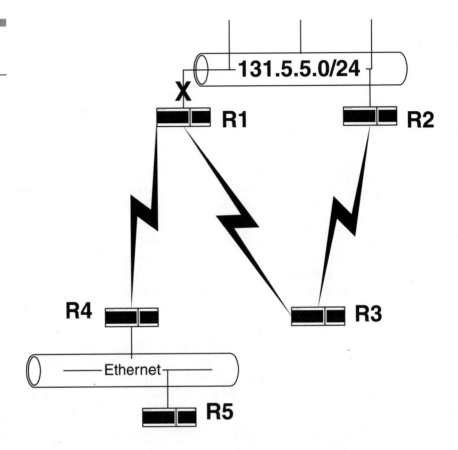

3. R1 sends a query to its neighbors R3 and R4. This takes the form of a broadcast for RIP v1 and a multicast with RIP v2. R4 responds with a poisoned route, but R3 responds with a route to 131.5.5.0 that has a metric of 2 hops.

4. R1 places the route via R3 in its routing table because the original route to 131.5.5.0 has been deleted.

5. The next periodic update from R1 to R4 includes the new path to 131.5.5.0, but is ignored because the route is still in hold-down on R4 and R5.

6. Convergence does not take place until the 131.5.5.0 routes come out of hold-down on R4 and R5. They then learn the new path with the next periodic update from their neighbor router.

7. Therefore, the convergence time on R5 is the total of the detection time, plus the hold-down timer, plus up to two periodic update intervals (R1 to R4 and R4 to R5). The update interval for RIP is 30 seconds and the default hold-down time is 180 seconds. Therefore, the total convergence time in this example is the detection time plus up to 240 seconds. Given that this is a very small demonstration network should suggest the convergence problems presented to medium to large networks.

Scalable IP Routing I—OSPF

Open Shortest Path First (OSPF)

OSPF is a sophisticated and standardized link state IP routing protocol. It was designed with the intention of being a scalable protocol that could support large networks. This goal was certainly achieved, and today, OSPF is a popular choice for medium to large enterprise networks. *Internet Service Providers* (ISP) also commonly use OSPF as their *Interior Gateway Protocol* (IGP), not only because of its scalability, but due also to its interoperability across multivendor platforms.

Why Use OSPF?

Before moving into the heart of a discussion on OSPF and its design applications, it is worthwhile to summarize why OSPF might be an appropriate choice of IP routing protocol:

■ Scalability

If one word were needed to justify the employment of OSPF, it would be scalability. A number of reasons can explain why OSPF is suitable for large and growing networks, and they are all interrelated in some way.

▪ Hierarchical Structure

OSPF supports the ability to divide the network into multiple areas that have a certain degree of autonomy from each other. In such a structure, a backbone area (which is always designated as Area 0) exists and a number of other areas that, barring exceptional cases, must directly attach to Area 0. A sample topology of an OSPF domain that consists of a backbone area and three other areas is shown in Figure 5-1. The RIP element to the network can be ignored at this point for clarity purposes.

▪ Speed of Convergence

Each router running OSPF maintains a database of the logical topology of the network. This increased intelligence of OSPF means that it can converge faster without having to resort to the crude convergence methods of distance vector protocols.

▪ Route Summarization

A consequence of a well-planned hierarchical design is that each area can be summarized into contiguous blocks. OSPF also supports the

Figure 5-1
OSPF multi-topology

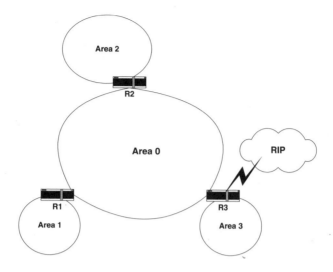

capability to summarize routes that are redistributed from another routing protocol.

- Efficient Update Processing

  Incremental, rather than periodic, updates are sent when a network topology change occurs.

- OSPF uses well-known multicast addresses rather than broadcasts to transfer routing information.

- VLSM

  Because it is a classless protocol, OSPF supports VLSM, enabling an efficient use of IP address space.

■ Standardization

OSPF is an IETF standard. The most recent version of OSPF, termed version 2, is specified in RFC 2328. This ensures interoperability across different vendor platforms, which is now more important than ever with the integration of different services on IP networks.

So having briefly highlighted the reasons why OSPF might be applicable on a network, one might ask if OSPF has a downside. The potential cons of OSPF are as follows:

■ Complexity

OSPF is without dispute a very complex routing protocol. Engineers who have a less than sound understanding of its operation and complexity should never apply it to a network. Therefore, it not only requires significant expertise to design OSPF networks, but the same is true of adequately supporting them.

At first sight, this may seem like a major disadvantage; however, this is not necessarily the case. If a complex OSPF design involving multiple areas is appropriate, then the network in question is likely to be large and reasonably complex. The complexity will therefore extend to areas other than the IP routing protocol, requiring proficient design and support staff in any case. If implementing an OSPF network proves to be too much in terms of complexity, then so will other elements of the network.

■ Design Restrictions

For a large network that also needs to incorporate scope for growth, multiple OSPF areas normally should be used. Certain rules pertain to how traffic should move between these areas, which can impose some design restrictions, as we shall see. Although there is a solution to every problem, some solutions with OSPF turn out to be more complex than if an area structure was not in place.

■ Resource Utilization

OSPF increases router memory requirements due to the fact that each OSPF router maintains a topological database of the network. The routing table is calculated from this database, which consumes more memory than the routing table.

Running OSPF also increases the average router CPU utilization. In order to recalculate the routing table following a topology change, the *Shortest Path First* (SPF) algorithm is run. This is a processor-intensive activity that could potentially restrain the performance of low-end routers.

How OSPF Operates

OSPF is arguably the most misunderstood of all IP routing protocols. Many engineers in the industry have a moderate working knowledge of the protocol, but a significantly fewer number have what would be considered a satisfactory understanding of how OSPF actually operates. For a design engineer who does not work in a hands-on environment, this is particularly dangerous because such an engineer may not be fully aware of the limitations of his or her knowledge. OSPF is a very complex protocol that can be understood at various levels. Although it is true that much of the time a detailed understanding of every aspect of the relevant RFCs is not required, it is equally true that a number of key concepts must be clearly understood before doing any design work with OSPF. At various stages during this chapter, these concepts will be explained in a concise manner. This is necessary because too often, engineers make poor OSPF design decisions due to a subtle yet fundamental misunderstanding of the protocol's operation.

Link State Advertisements (LSAs)

OSPF routing information is exchanged by directly encapsulating OSPF packets within IP packets, there is no layer 4 component to the communication, and OSPF packets are identified to IP by protocol number 89.

Unlike distance vector routing protocols, which advertise routes in the updates between neighbor router, OSPF advertises link states. A link simply means a subnet on the network. The difference between routes and links may seem subtle, but it is significant. A route is the best path to a destination. OSPF does not exchange routes. Instead, information on all the subnets on the network as well as what routers attach to these subnets is exchanged. When all of this information has been exchanged between all routers on the network, each router has a database of all the subnets on the network and also has information on what routers attach to each subnet. This is called the *link state database*. From the link state database each router independently calculates its IP routing table, which is a list of the best paths to each destination. The link state database is sometimes thought of as a complete map of all the subnets or links on the network, whereas the IP routing table is each router's view of its best path to each of these subnets.

It is a significant principle of link state routing protocols that each router *independently* calculates it own best path to each destination. With distance vector routing protocols, routes are advertised rather than links. This means that each router calculates its routing table by taking into consideration the best path that its neighbor routers have to that destination and simply increments the metric incurred to get to that neighbor, unless it has a more direct route itself. This interdependence between the routing tables imposes a limitation on how quickly a distance vector routing protocol can converge in a loop-free manner.

Figure 5-2 shows a high-level flow chart indicating how the link state database and then the routing table is built. The link state database can

Figure 5-2
OSPF routing table
calculation

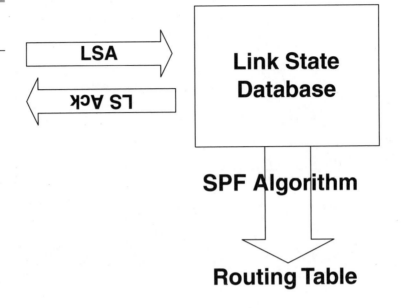

impose additional memory resource requirements on the router. The memory requirements are proportional to the size of the databases. This should be discussed with a technical support advisor who is familiar with the router vendor's equipment prior to purchase or before migrating to OSPF as the main routing protocol.

LSA Types LSAs are grouped into a number of different categories of LSA. Each LSA type relates to the contents and function that it serves. Here is a brief overview of the different LSA types:

■ Type 1

These are termed router links and they indicate the state of the router's links or attached subnets. The information provided includes router ID, link status, and cost. Type 1 LSAs are only flooded within the area where the particular router is resident.

■ Type 2

Type 2 LSAs or network links describe networks and the routers attached to these networks. Type 2 LSAs are generated by designated routers on broadcast multiaccess networks. They are only flooded within the area where the particular network resides. In some ways, Type 2 LSAs can be thought of as containing similar information to Type 1 packets, but the manner of presentation is different. With Type 1, the link information is given with respect to the router; with Type 2, it is sorted with respect to the network. The use of Type 2 LSAs, in addition to Type 1, helps facilitate a more efficient layout of link state information in the database and therefore can speed up the running of the SPF algorithm.

■ Type 3 and Type 4

These LSAs are called Summary LSAs and are generated by the *Area Border Router* (ABR). An ABR is a router that typically borders the backbone area 0 and at least one other area. Referring back to Figure 5-1, R1, R2, and R3 are all ABRs. Type 3 LSAs are a summary of Type 1 LSAs within a particular area. The summary information includes the network and metric. These LSAs are injected into the backbone by the ABR. Summary information is used because OSPF does not propagate detailed link state information beyond the local area. It is important not to confuse Type 3 summary LSAs with route summarization. Type 3 LSAs will be generated by the ABR regardless of whether or not route summarization is being used. Hence, the Type 3 packets may or may not include route summarizations for that area.

Type 4 LSAs contain information that describes reachability to *Autonomous System Boundary Routers* (ASBRs). An ASBR connects OSPF to another routing domain or *autonomous system* (AS). An ASBR must therefore be running OSPF along with another routing protocol. Referring again to Figure 5-1, R3 is an ASBR because it is running OSPF and RIP, thus forming a boundary between the two ASs.

■ Type 5

External LSAs or Type 5 packets are generated by the ASBR and indicate the status of routes that belong to another AS but are being redistributed into OSPF by the ASBR. These LSAs are propagated within OSPF except to stub areas.

■ Type 6

Multicast OSPF (MOSPF) uses Type 6 LSAs to propagate multicast group membership information throughout the AS.

■ Type 7

The ASBR generates Type 7 LSAs in a *Not-So-Stubby-Area* (NSSA). Type 7 packets are particular to a NSSA. The Type 7 packets are flooded within the NSSA, and the ABR converts the Type 7 to standard external Type 5 LSAs before distributing them to the backbone.

- Type 8

  Type 8 LSAs are external attribute LSAs for BGP routes that have been redistributed into OSPF.

OSPF Packet Types   Like LSAs, OSPF Packets are grouped into a number of categories.

- Hello

  Hello packets are exchanged periodically between OSPF routers with the purpose of forming and maintaining neighbor relationships.

- Database Description

  Database Description Packets (DDPs) are used when two neighbor routers are exchanging link state databases. Each DDP contains a summary of the link state information contained in that router's link state database. DDPs are sent and received at the beginning of the database exchange process in order to avoid each router unnecessarily sending the full detailed contents of its database to a router that may already have that information.

- Link State Request

  During database exchange, a router compares the summary information received in the DDP with the link state information it already has in its own database. If the DDP contains more up-to-date information about an existing link (as indicated by a sequence number) or a new link, then the receiving router will issue a *Link State Request* (LSR) for detailed information about this entry in the link state database.

- Link State Update

  A LSR is responded to with a *Link State Update* (LSU) that contains detailed information about one or more entries in the sending router's link state database.

- Link State Acknowledgement

  During the exchange , a router will acknowledge the receipt of a DDP by sending a *Link State Acknowledgment* (LSAck). In fact, all OSPF packet transmissions are reliable apart from hellos and therefore require an acknowledgement.

Neighbor and Adjacency Formation

OSPF uses hello packets to form and maintain neighbor relationships with directly attached routers. The hello packet is the only type of periodic information transfer that takes place in OSPF. Neighbors can be formed on each interface that has OSPF enabled. Multiple neighbors can be formed on the same interface, for example on a *local area network* (LAN) segment. The router maintains an OSPF neighbor table with each neighbor router indicated by a router ID. The router ID is the highest IP address of any of the router's active interfaces, or alternatively, a loopback interface will supercede any physical interface.

Neighbor Formation   For a neighbor relationship to be formed between two OSPF routers, the routers must agree on the following parameters:

Area ID   The segment that connects the two routers together must appear as being in the same area on each router.

Hello and dead intervals   The dead interval is the amount of time a router will wait without receiving a hello packet before declaring the neighbor to be down. It is usually four times the hello interval. These two parameters must match on the respective router interfaces that connect to the common OSPF network segment. The parameters are configurable. The default hello and dead interval on a broadcast, or point-to-point segment, is 10 seconds and 40 seconds respectively. On a non-broadcast network or a point-to-multipoint network, the corresponding default values are 30 seconds and 120 seconds.

Authentication   OSPF supports simple authentication along with MD5. The interface authentication parameters must match in order for neighbor formation to take place.

Stub area flag   Both routers must agree whether or not the area through which they are attempting to form neighbors is a stub area. The area cannot be configured as stub on one router and not on the other.

Adjacency Formation   After an OSPF neighbor relationship has been formed, the two routers may proceed to form a full adjacency. This entails exchanging link state databases. Not all OSPF routers on a particular segment may necessarily need to become adjacent with each other. On a broadcast network for example, a *designated router* (DR) and *backup designated router* (BDR) are elected using the hello protocol. These act as centralized points for the exchange of routing information across the segment. Thus, all routers do not need to exchange link state databases with each other; they only do this with the DR and BDR.

On this type of broadcast network (for example, an Ethernet segment), each router only forms an adjacency with the DR and BDR, and it sees all other OSPF routers as two-way neighbors. It is possible only on a broadcast or multiaccess network for a router to have neighbors to which it is not adjacent.

The following is a sequential list of the different states that neighbor formation and eventually adjacency formation goes through. Most of the states are quite self-explanatory:

Down   No information has been detected on the segment.

Attempt   The router has not received any hello, but is attempting to send a hello packet.

Init   A hello packet has been received; now bi-directional communication has to be established.

Two-way   At this point, a two-way neighbor relationship has been formed. This means that the two routers have agreed on the key parameters contained within the hello packets.

Exstart   This indicates that the routers have begun to negotiate the exchange of databases.

Exchange   This is the initial stage of information exchange.

Loading   This is the final stage, which enables database exchange.

Full   This final state indicates that a full adjacency has been formed.

Figure 5-3 shows a schematic diagram highlighting the different stages of neighbor and adjacency formation. In this case, the R1 and R2 form neighbors across the serial link. After reaching the two-way neighbor state, they begin to attempt adjacency formation. On a serial link, OSPF neighbors will become adjacent because no concept of a designated router exists on a point-to-point network.

The database exchange is done in a master/slave manner with the higher router ID (R2- 10.10.2.1) becoming the master and beginning the exchange process. R2 sends R1 a summary of its link state database in the form of DDPs. R1 likewise sends DDPs to R2. The received DDPs are acknowledged

loopback 10.10.1.1/24

loopback 10.10.2.1/24

Figure 5-3
Neighbor and
Adjacency formation

loopback 10.10.1.1/24

loopback 10.10.2.1/24

R1

R2

by each router by sending a LSAck packet back to the source. The neighbor relationship on each router is now in the Exchange state.

Consider the scenario where R1 has received summary information in the DDP for the network 10.99.99.0/24, but it does not have any entry for this network in its own database. R1 then sends a LSR to R2 for detailed information on this network. R2 then replies with a LSU containing detailed information on the 10.99.99.0/24 link including the cost metric and which router IDs are attached to this subnet. R1 acknowledges the LSU with a LSAck packet.

This process is complete when all the LSRs have been answered for each router. This means that both routers have identical link state databases. The databases are said to be synchronized and the neighbor state is now indicating a full adjacency between router ID 10.10.1.1 and router ID 10.10.2.1.

SPF Algorithm

The SPF or Dijkstra algorithm is used by OSPF to calculate the routing table from the link state database. The database can be thought of as an entire topological map of the network including all subnets and indicating which routers are attached to these subnets. The database effectively contains all destinations and all possible paths to these destinations. The routing table contains only the best path to each destination *as seen by that router*.

The OSPF Routing Metric   The OSPF routing metric is cost. Each link has an OSPF cost associated with it by default. The cost relating to any link can be manipulated if necessary through router configuration in order to influence routing decisions. The cost is inversely proportional to bandwidth and is normally calculated as follows:

$$Cost = 10^8/Bandwidth$$

The 10^8 figure is configurable on most routers on the market. It may be necessary to increase this figure if links with speeds of greater than 100Mbps exist on the network such as ATM 155Mbps or Gigabit Ethernet. These links would have an OSPF cost of less than one, which is undesirable due to the possibility of a rounding error and potentially unstable mathematical calculations. This figure, which is termed the OSPF reference bandwidth, may also be increased to give better metric granularity. It is important to remember that if this figure is altered, then it should be changed on every router on the network to ensure consistency in the metric calculation.

Remember:

■ If the OSPF reference bandwidth is altered, this must be performed on all routers on the network to ensure consistency in metric calculation.

The total metric associated with a path to a destination is simply the cumulative cost of each link along the path.

Note also that the metric calculation is based on the interface bandwidth that the router sees, which might not match the actual speed of the link. Particular care should be taken in relation to serial links or Frame Relay PVCs. Most routers on the market have a default bandwidth setting that is unlikely to match the real speed of the link. This should be rectified through configuration; otherwise, unpredictable routing paths may be chosen. For example, two parallel serial links that are of significantly different speeds could be treated by OSPF as equal-cost paths. As a result, load balancing may unintentionally occur.

Remember:

■ Ensure that the bandwidth used by OSPF to calculate a metric matches the actual speed of the link, and is not just a default value set by the router. This is particularly relevant for serial links of varying speeds.

Load Balancing with OSPF   Up to six equal-cost paths can be entered in the routing table. The number of equal-cost paths supported can vary in actuality on different vendor platforms.

In earlier chapters, concerns about equal-cost load balancing were discussed, particularly when multilayer switching or layer 3 switching is being employed. The same concerns hold true with OSPF load balancing. Be careful that an excessive number of busy destinations are not cached against one particular path. If this happens, then a disproportionate amount of traffic will use one path above the other and true load balancing will not take place.

Remember:

■ Be careful doing load balancing when layer 3 switching or multilayer switching is enabled on the router.

OSPF Convergence

One of the main reasons why OSPF is chosen for so many networks is its speed of convergence. So how does OSPF converge? The following is a high-level description of how it operates:

If a router detects that an attached link has gone down, it updates its link state database and sends a LSA to each of its *adjacent* neighbors. Each of these neighbors updates its database and floods the LSA to its adjacent neighbors. This flooding of the LSA continues throughout the network until all OSPF routers have received it. If the network architecture consists of multiple OSPF areas, then the LSA is just flooded within the local area. The LSA is only flooded outside of the local area if the change of link state causes a change in the equivalent Type 3 summary LSA that is sent by the ABR.

After receiving a LSA, each router updates its link state database and waits for a predetermined delay time before recalculating its routing table using the SPF algorithm. This is called the *spf-delay time* and is intended to protect against flapping routes. A typical value for this timer is five seconds. It is a good feature of OSPF, although technically, it does slow down convergence. Consider the case where a flapping serial link resulted in a continuous flood of LSAs, and all routers on the network persistently recalculated their routing tables. It is likely that the network would not converge until the link stopped flapping. Aside from a very serious convergence problem, the SPF recalculations can be very CPU-intensive on the routers. With the delay time in place, the LSAs would continue to flood in the case of a flapping link; however, the routing tables would not get recalculated because an LSA containing conflicting information would have been received before the first calculation had begun.

See Figure 5-4 for an illustration of the following example of OSPF convergence.

1. R1's Ethernet link goes down. R1 then sends a LSA to its adjacent neighbors, in this case R3 and R4.

2. R3 and R4 update their link state database. R3 floods the LSA to R2, while R4 floods the LSA to R5.

Figure 5-4
OSPF convergence
example

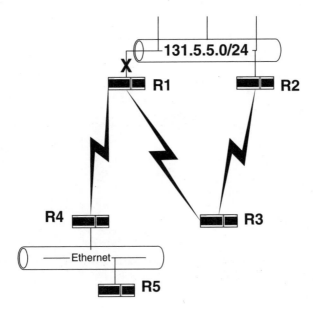

3. After each router receives the LSA, it updates its database. It then waits for the duration of the spf-delay timer (typically five seconds) and then recalculates its routing table.

Because each router had a database of the network, it will already have the backup path to 131.5.5.0/24 via R2 in its database. This path will be placed in the IP routing table after the SPF calculation is done.

The total convergence time should just be a matter of a few seconds. In this example, it is likely to be approximately six seconds with the largest component of the delay being the spf-delay timer.

OSPF Network Types

OSPF has the concept of a network type where it actually distinguishes between links that are part of fundamentally different topologies. Some OSPF characteristics and modes of operation vary depending on the network type. Five network types are defined in OSPF:

- Broadcast
- Point-to-point
- Non-broadcast
- Point-to-multipoint
- Virtual link

The first four of these will be discussed in this section. Many people do not even realize that virtual links are defined as another OSPF network type, and with good reason, since they relate entirely to the logical topology and have no relationship to any physical characteristic of the links. For this reason, virtual links will be discussed separately in the next section of this chapter.

Broadcast Networks and Designated Routers

This refers to broadcast media such as Ethernet, token ring, or FDDI LANs. A DR and BDR are elected on OSPF broadcast networks. This provides a more efficient means for routers to exchange LSAs on the network, by providing centralized points to update the entire segment. Each ordinary (that is, non-designated) router sends its LSAs to the designated router rather than to all other routers on the network. The DR is then responsible for ensuring that all routers on the broadcast segment have their topology database updated with the same information.

On a broadcast type network, all routers see each other as neighbors, but they are only adjacent to the DR and BDR. Therefore, each "ordinary" router only exchanges databases with the DR and DBR, reducing unnecessary traffic on the segment. Also, if a router detects a topology change, it only sends the LSA to the DR and BDR because LSAs are only sent to adjacent neighbors. The DR is adjacent to all routers and hence is responsible for flooding the LSA to all routers on the broadcast segment. This is obviously far more efficient than having each router unnecessarily flood LSAs to every other router on the segment. The BDR monitors the DR, and if it does not detect the DR flooding the LSA, it will assume the responsibility. The manner in which LSAs are flooded on broadcast networks is shown in Figure 5-5 where the backup designated router has been omitted for clarity.

If R3 detects the loss of a link, it sends a LSA to its adjacent neighbors (that is, the DR). The DR floods the LSA to its adjacent neighbors, which is every router on the segment. Each of these routers floods the LSA to their adjacent neighbors in turn. In Figure 5-5, R1 is shown to have an adjacency over its serial link.

Figure 5-5

LSA management on OSPF broadcast networks

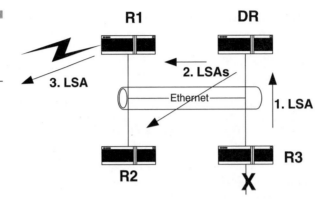

So how does a router send LSAs to only the DR and BDR without having the other OSPF routers processing the packet? OSPF distinguishes between designated routers and ordinary OSPF routers by placing them in two separate multicast groups:

224.0.0.5—All OSPF routers

224.0.0.6—All OSPF DRs

For example, in the network shown in Figure 5-5, R3 would send its LSA to the DR using the 224.0.0.6 address. The DR would then flood the LSA to the other routers, using 224.0.0.5 as the destination multicast address.

If OSPF does not automatically see the network segment as being a broadcast medium, it can be configured to appear as a broadcast network for the purposes of OSPF. The idea of configuring a router so that OSPF "sees" the network as a network type other than what it actually is has applications when running OSPF over NBMA topologies such as X.25, Frame Relay, or ATM, as will be shown later.

One question in relation to OSPF broadcast networks still needs to be answered, and that is how the designated routers are elected. Here are the criteria:

■ Priority

This is the overriding parameter that determines which router becomes the DR. The router with the highest priority becomes the DR, and the next highest becomes the BDR on a segment. The OSPF priority is a parameter that is configurable on the router interface. If a particular router attaches to multiple LAN segments, then it is a good idea to avoid the same router becoming the DR on more than one segment. Although the DR does not store any more information than any of the other routers, it is likely to be busier in terms of database exchange and LSA processing. A router could be made the DR on one segment by raising the interface priority for that segment to a large value. Likewise, it could be prevented from becoming the DR on other segments by configuring a priority value of zero on those corresponding appropriate interfaces.

- Router ID:

  The router ID in OSPF is the highest IP address on the router. If a loopback address is configured, then it overrides any other address. If the interface priority value is equal on all routers on the segment, then the router with the highest ID becomes the DR on the segment. The router ID address does not even have to belong to a network that is participating in OSPF. If the OSPF priority is left at its default value, the router ID becomes relevant in deciding the designated router election. The router ID is an important concept in OSPF. It is a parameter that is contained in the hello packets, and a router lists its OSPF neighbors by their corresponding router ID.

  Bogus loopback addresses can be used to conserve address space. For example, on a network that uses the class B 148.4.0.0, subnets of network 10.0.0.0 could be used for the loopback addresses, and hence would define the router IDs. In this example, network 10.0.0.0 may not even participate in the OSPF routing process, so routers would not have a route to any of the loopback subnets. This is not necessarily a problem so long as loopback addresses are not being used for any other purposes such as DLSW peers. My own preference is to include the loopback interfaces in the OSPF process so that basic router connectivity can be verified without pinging each of the physical interfaces.

The principle of succession with DRs is very simple—the incumbent remains king until it dies. In other words, if a new router is commissioned on a segment that happens to have a higher router ID (or priority) than the DR, it does not become the DR until the existing designated router goes down. This is a good mode of operation from a network stability point of view. It is different from the idea of a root bridge election in spanning tree where a new bridge could potentially force a reconvergence of spanning tree.

One final point to emphasize in relation to designated routers is that the whole concept of having a DR is purely for traffic management purposes. The DR is not a master router and does not have any more information or intelligence than any other router. Remember also that the designated router is simply the DR on that broadcast segment; that is, the DR principle is of local significance only. These points are stressed because they frequently cause confusion.

Point-to-Point Networks

In the case of serial leased lines or point-to-point Frame Relay using sub-interfaces, OSPF automatically detects that this is a point-to-point network. A neighbor relationship can then be formed with the router at the other end of the link.

This network type does not use the concept of a designated router because it would have no meaning on a point-to-point link. Hence, all OSPF packets use the 224.0.0.5 multicast address.

Non-broadcast Networks

Some *wide-area network* (WAN) media such as X.25, Frame Relay, and ATM are non-broadcast by nature. Given that X.25 is a technology that is being phased out, the discussion will be confined to Frame Relay and ATM. The issues that are about to be discussed are identical in relation to each technology.

Consider the network shown in Figure 5-6. In this example, the WAN technology happens to be Frame Relay. Assume that it is a multipoint Frame Relay implementation and the routers are not using sub-interfaces. A multipoint Frame Relay or ATM router interface would be seen by OSPF as a non-broadcast network. On a non-broadcast network, neighbor formation usually cannot occur unless the neighbor is statically defined. Cases occur where Frame Relay Inverse ARP can facilitate neighbor formation. This happens when Inverse ARP is enabled on multipoint Frame Relay, and the OSPF hello interval matches at each end of the PVC. In this section, OSPF neighbor formation will be discussed in a variety of scenarios, so assume that the network topology is not doing you any favors.

Because OSPF sees the medium as a non-broadcast network type, it does not send multicast hello packets out the router interface because multicasts are treated the same as broadcasts by non-broadcast media. This means that the neighbors must be statically defined on the routers.

The second issue encountered with this topology is that, to be more exact, OSPF sees the Frame Relay (or ATM) medium as not just non-broadcast but as *non-broadcast multi-access* (NBMA). OSPF assumes on a multiaccess medium that every host has connectivity to every other host like on a LAN. So what does OSPF do with a network where all hosts have connectivity to each other? Yes, you've guessed it. It elects a designated router. However two problems are encountered with this. First, unless the NBMA network is fully meshed, the assumption about all sites having direct connectivity to each other is not valid. In Figure 5-6, only Router A has connectivity to the other two sites; hence, it is the only possible candidate for becoming the designated router. Apart from the requirement for a full mesh, another reason exists for why DRs are undesirable on WAN media. WAN links are significantly less reliable than LAN links; therefore, the likelihood of losing connectivity to the DR is substantial. This could cause network stability problems because LSAs obviously cannot be sent to the DR while it is down. In addition, a requirement would exist for a DR election on the WAN.

Remember:

■ OSPF over NBMA media can involve static neighbor configurations and also the election of a designated router in the WAN.

■ A DR is undesirable in the WAN because it assumes a full-mesh PVC structure. In addition, instability can occur when the WAN links to the DR go down.

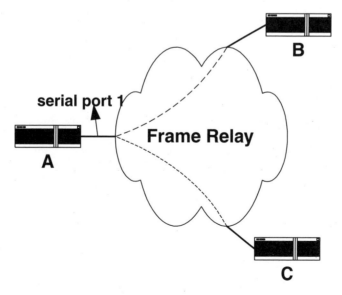

Figure 5-6
OSPF over frame relay

Clearly the use of OSPF over Frame Relay or ATM can potentially cause significant problems that require a better solution. A number of solutions, however, will now be discussed.

The simplest solution is to use Frame Relay or ATM point-to-point sub-interfaces. OSPF will then see each PVC as a separate point-to-point network type. On a point-to-point network, neighbors are dynamically discovered using multicast hellos, and no concept of a DR exists. Thus, the two fundamental issues posed by the NBMA topology are resolved.

Remember:

■ The use of point-to-point sub-interfaces enables OSPF to see each PVC as a separate point-to-point network, removing the DR issue and the requirement for static neighbor configuration.

Situations occur where point-to-point sub-interfaces may not be used, such as with legacy router equipment that does not support the feature. Also if IP subnet space is at a premium, point-to-point sub-interfaces may not be used because they each require their own subnet. Now some other ways of facilitating the use of OSPF over Frame Relay and ATM will be discussed.

Most router vendors support the capability to change the OSPF network type on an interface in order to facilitate neighbor formation and resolve other issues. This enables OSPF to "see" the router interface as a particular network type other than the one that it would be by default. For example, the use of OSPF over multipoint Frame Relay could be facilitated by configuring each FrameRelay router interface to be an OSPF broadcast network. If a multipoint Frame Relay or ATM network is configured as an OSPF broadcast network, some issues need to be remembered:

■ Configuring the medium to be a broadcast network for the purposes of OSPF does not make it a broadcast medium! If in the case of multipoint Frame Relay, the appropriate PVCs are not in place between the routers or if the necessary Frame Relay mapping statements are not configured, then OSPF will not work as desired. This leads to a more basic secondary point and that is that altering the OSPF network types should be thought of as something done solely for the purposes of OSPF. It does not alter the physical or logical topology of the medium in question.

■ By configuring the NBMA medium to be a broadcast network for the purposes of OSPF, dynamic neighbor discovery is supported. Hence, any requirement for static neighbor configuration is eliminated. However, a designated router will be elected, which is less than desirable on the WAN for the reason previously given.

■ If a multipoint network is configured as a broadcast network, then it is essential that the designated router has a PVC to all of the other routers. For example, in the network shown in Figure 5-6, Router A is the only suitable choice for the DR on this segment because it is the only router with a PVC to each of the other two.

If the issue of running OSPF over Frame Relay or ATM is going to be resolved by altering the OSPF network type that the routers see on these interfaces, then there is, in my view, a better alternative to making it appear like as a broadcast network.

This leads to the next sub-section, which discusses another OSPF network type that has not yet been introduced: point-to-multipoint.

NOTE: *The routers on your network can be configured to see the NBMA medium as a broadcast medium for the purposes of OSPF. This enables dynamic neighbor discovery without using point-to-point sub-interfaces. However, it does involve having a designated router in the WAN.*

Point-to-Multipoint Networks

As previously mentioned, a multipoint Frame Relay main interface would be seen by OSPF as a non-broadcast network. Other than statically defining neighbors, one option is to manually configure the network to be point-to-multipoint for the purpose of OSPF. This enables the router with the multiple PVCs to form a neighbor relationship with each router to which it has a PVC. A point-to-multipoint network type in OSPF operates like a series of point-to-point links going over the same physical interface. The router interface could be a main Frame Relay or ATM interface. Alternatively, the interface could be a multipoint sub-interface supporting multiple PVCs.

For the network shown in Figure 5-6, configuring the Frame Relay interface on Routers A, B, and C to be seen by OSPF as point-to-multipoint would enable dynamic neighbor formation without the use of point-to-point sub-interfaces.

The advantage of configuring Frame Relay to be point-to-multipoint rather than a broadcast network type is that point-to-multipoint does not use a designated router because OSPF does not assume full interconnectivity between all hosts on such a network. This makes the point-to-multipoint network type preferable for partial-mesh Frame Relay or ATM. It is also more desirable to avoid having a designated router on WAN segments from a network stability viewpoint.

Remember:

■ Configuring the routers to see the NBMA topology as a point-to-multipoint network type is preferable to using a broadcast network type because point-to-multipoint does not use a DR.

One word of caution must be mentioned in relation to the entire issue of configuring different OSPF network types for NBMA router interfaces. It is sometimes possible to form neighbors at each end of a PVC, even if OSPF sees different network types at each end of the PVC, but only if the hello intervals match.

In some instances, for example if point-to-point sub-interfaces were being used at one end of the PVC and not at the other, OSPF could see a different network type at each end of the PVC. Neighbor formation does not occur unless the hello intervals match. It is important to remember that some router vendors give a shorter hello interval for broadcast and point-to-point networks than for point-to-multipoint or non-broadcast networks. Hello intervals can be altered by reconfiguring the router.

Remember:

■ OSPF neighbors can be formed across links where the network type does not agree at each end, but only if the hello intervals match.

Designing Within the Hierarchical Structure

Within a given OSPF area, all routers share the same link state database. If the entire OSPF network is a single area (which it can be), then this could create the following scalability problems:

■ LSA flooding across the entire network

After each topology change, resulting LSAs flood throughout the entire network. This consumes bandwidth on the WAN links, but more seriously, it forces every router on the network to run the SPF algorithm. Unnecessary SPF calculations should be avoided since traffic forwarding is often suspended during a SPF calculation.

- Increased frequency of SPF calculations

As the network grows, so does the number of links. Therefore, statistically more topology changes per unit time will occur on the network. This is another reason why more frequent and possibly unnecessary SPF calculations would be performed on every router on the network.

- Increased link state database size

The size of the link state database is directly proportional to the number of links on the network. The size of the database that each router must hold grows with the network. This increases the memory resource requirements on each router as well as increasing the CPU utilization and delay associated with SPF calculations.

- Increased routing table sizes

Each router would have to maintain at least one, if not more, best paths to each subnet on the network. Larger routing tables result in increased memory usage on each router. It also increases the latency associated with routing table lookup. Very large routing tables can also make troubleshooting more difficult.

OSPF solves this scalability problem by allowing the network to be segregated into multiple areas that can each have a certain amount of autonomy in making routing decisions.

Areas reduce link state update overhead. Each router within an area has the link state database for that area only. The link state database associated with a particular area contains detailed information about the links contained within that area and summary information about links on the rest of the network.

Because each router's database only contains detailed information about links within its local area, it is not necessary to flood all LSAs throughout the entire network. Usually LSAs are confined to the area in which they originate. You will see how this happens when ABRs are discussed. Therefore, any unnecessary flooding of LSAs and the resulting SPF calculations performed by the routers are minimized.

The area structure facilitates route summarization. By choosing a contiguous block of addresses to reside in each area, route summarization can be performed at the ABR. This can significantly reduce routing tables and link state databases across the network.

Rules for the OSPF Area Structure

OSPF is a complex protocol. Sometimes in practice, the simple matter of a single link failing can produce additional effects. This may be because the loss of a single route could mean that a basic OPSF principle is violated. The following is a summary of some of the principles in relation to OSPF area architecture of which the design or support engineer should always be particularly mindful.

■ If a multi-area structure is to be used, then OSPF requires the definition of a backbone area, which must be designated as Area 0.

If the network consists of only one area, then this area does not necessarily have to be designated as Area 0. However, I think it is preferable that it is configured as Area 0 so that if it is ever decided to migrate to a multi-area structure, the amount of reconfiguration and redesign is minimized.

■ All OSPF areas must connect to Area 0 in the form of an ABR. An exception to this rule is the use of an OSPF virtual link. Generally, virtual links are not considered good design practice and are usually only used as part of interim solutions. A typical multiarea OSPF topology is shown in Figure 5-7. Three regular areas, 10, 20, and 30, attach directly to Area 0. The ABRs are R1, R2, and R3.

■ All inter-area traffic must cross the backbone Area 0. Hence, all routers in a given area must have a route, default or otherwise to Area

Figure 5-7
Multi-area OSPF
topology

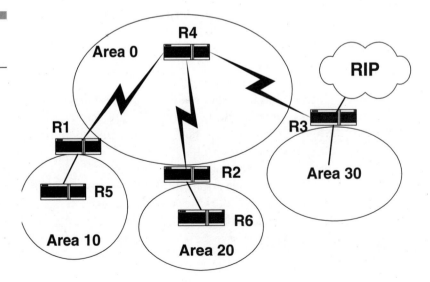

0. Referring to Figure 5-7, traffic from R5 to R6 could never take a direct path without violating the rules of OSPF (again excluding the possibility of a virtual link, which will be discussed later). Traffic from R5 to R6 must take the path R5-R1-R4-R2-R6. In other words, traffic can only exit an area via the ABR. This might seem like additional router hops are needlessly incurred and, in some cases, this may be the situation; however, in a true hierarchical structure, most of the traffic terminates at a head office site rather than another peer level site. Also, and more importantly, the overall benefits of a hierarchical design usually outweigh any sub-optimal side effects.

An important issue in relation to inter-area traffic must be emphasized because it is frequently misunderstood. As previously mentioned, it is a rule of OSPF that inter-area traffic must cross the backbone. Inter-area traffic should not traverse directly between "non-zero" areas. However, this is not to say that inter-area traffic will not take the direct path if a route is available. For example, in Figure 5-7, consider the case where a serial link was commissioned between R5 and R6 and it was placed in Area 10 or Area 20, as shown in Figure 5-8. Would traffic between the

Figure 5-8
Illegal OSPF inter-area routing

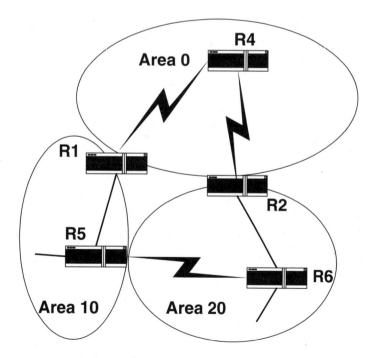

local LANs that these routers support cross this serial link? Two questions arise here: *Would* it and *should* it? To answer the second question first, the traffic certainly should not cross this link because it violates the principles of OSPF. But the answer to the other question is that yes it would cross the direct link, if this is the best path according to the IP routing table. This is something that can be easily overlooked. Although it is a rule that inter-area traffic should cross the backbone, it is the responsibility of the network designer to ensure that this happens. OSPF cannot take care of this by itself. Remember that it is the IP routing table that makes the forwarding decisions, and it is not always aware that the best path to a destination is in violation of an OSPF principle.

Remember:

- Inter-area traffic can potentially "leak" between areas without crossing the backbone if a least-cost path is provided. The network designer must ensure that such a path does not exist.

- Areas cannot be "broken up." In other words, a single area cannot have two ABRs that have no physical path between them. This is also called a discontiguous area. In the example shown in Figure 5-9, R1 and R2

Figure 5-9
A discontiguous OSPF
Area

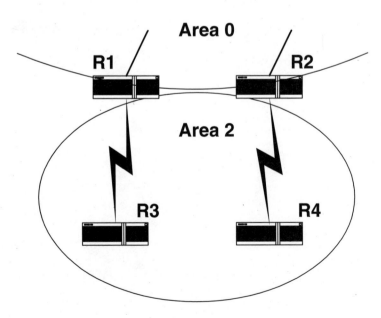

are ABRs both bordering Area 0 and Area 2. It is quite typical to have two ABRs for resilience; however, a direct path must exist between them. This would mean that traffic between R3 and R4 would have to go from Area 2 to Area 0 and back to Area 2. The hierarchical principles of OSPF deem that traffic within the local area should not have to enter Area 0. In such a scenario, connectivity between the two ABRs would have to be provided within Area 2. Otherwise, Area 2 would have to be split into two distinct areas.

Instances also occur where the backbone area can become discontiguous. These scenarios will be discussed along with possible solutions in the upcoming section on OSPF virtual links.

Routing in the OSPF Hierarchy   The different link types in OSPF have been discussed, but the different route types to which these give rise have yet to be discussed. The three fundamental types of OSPF routes are as follows:

■ Intra-area routes

These are routes that have originated within an area to which the router is attached. In the case of an ABR, a route that originates in any of the areas where it is resident is seen as an intra-area or internal route. For example, in Figure 5-7, R1 borders Area 10 and Area 0; hence, any routes that originate in either of these area are seen by R1 as intra-area routes. When an OSPF router is building its routing table from its database, intra-area routes are the first to be calculated and placed in the routing table.

■ Inter-area routes

An inter-area route is one that originated in an area to which the router is not attached. Referring again to Figure 5-7, any route that originates in an area other than Area 10 appears in R5's routing table as an inter-area route. In R1's routing table, any route that originates in an area other than Area 10 or Area 0 appears as inter-area.

Inter-area routes are the next types of routes that are calculated from the link state database and are placed in the IP routing table after the intra-area routes have been resolved.

If a router has an intra-area path and an inter-area path to the same destination, it will choose the intra-area path and place that in the routing table.

■ External routes

External routes are routes that originated in another routing protocol or AS. These routes were redistributed into OSPF by an *autonomous system boundary router* (ASBR), which is running OSPF and another routing protocol. In Figure 5-7, R3 is an ASBR that is running RIP and OSPF. If R3 redistributes the routes that it has learned via RIP into OSPF, these routes appear to routers in the OSPF domain as external routes.

External routes are the last types of OSPF routes to be calculated from the database after intra-area and inter-area routes.

A Word About the Backbone Area Obviously, the backbone Area 0 is the single most critical element of the OSPF network because it provides the path to shared enterprise resources. Like the core of any network, it should not experience traffic congestion; otherwise, the entire network is potentially congested. For this reason, a number of rather loose design rules often are quoted for Area 0, these include:

■ Keep the number of routers in Area 0 small.

■ Avoid having end users in Area 0.

■ It is often thought that backbone area routers must be very high-performance ones with an abundance of memory and CPU processing power. This is not necessarily true. The link state database for Area 0 is not necessarily significantly larger than other areas; hence, memory requirements are likely to be similar. In relation to CPU utilization, additional processing power above and beyond the norm is only required if the SPF algorithm is run frequently due to a large or unstable area.

These rules are well intentioned and, in many cases, carry a certain amount of validity. However, they are by no means written in stone. The reason I say this is because I have seen poor OSPF designs implemented (as described later in the chapter) because the designers were overly concerned about keeping Area 0 as small as possible and not allowing end users within this area. The extent of their concern caused them to seriously compromise other aspects of the design.

The engineer must be clear about what he or she intends to achieve by all of this. The designer wants to avoid excessive flooding of LSAs and frequent SPF recalculations in Area 0. These factors are determined as much by the number of links in Area 0 as by the number of routers it contains. Therefore, if Area 0 contained a very large number of serial links that connected Tier-1 sites to Tier-2, a possibility exists of much LSA traffic and

SPF recalculations even if Area 0 only contained a few routers. Having said that, I think it is a valid aspiration to keep Area 0 from getting excessively large in terms of routers and links that it supports. But keep in mind the reasoning behind this principle.

As for the idea of not allowing end users in Area 0, I really do not understand the reasoning. End users on a LAN segment do not contribute to increasing the number of routers, links, or the database size. In fact, the end positioning of end users is largely irrelevant to the routing protocol. The network design issue that relates to end user positioning is to ensure that they take the shortest physical and logical path available to the enterprise resources. Thus, placing end users at a corporate HQ or Tier-1 site within Area 0 is by no means out of the question. The only possible argument in favor of this point is that a large number of end users may increase the traffic being processed by the router, which in extreme cases could impinge on the memory and CPU resources required for OSPF.

Scaling Limitations for OSPF Areas

It is difficult to place limits on the maximum number of routers per area and the maximum number of areas that can be supported on an OSPF network. However, this has not stopped some vague rules of thumb gaining circulation within the industry. The most typical figures are as follows:

Maximum number of routers per area	50-100 routers
Maximum number of OSPF areas	50-100 areas

Two points in relation to these figures must be kept in mind. The first is that they are very much rules of thumb and pretty crude ones at that. The second point to note is that although these figures are by no means accurate guidelines, a maximum value is given to these two parameters, and OSPF cannot necessarily be expected to scale indefinitely. The important thing is to understand why these parameters have maximum values.

Areas can only be so large for the reasons already discussed. Namely the amount of LSA traffic becomes too extensive, SPF calculations are too frequent, and link state databases and routing tables are too large. Therefore, the figure for the maximum number of routers per area is really a reflection on the maximum size of the area rather than just the number of routers within it. The "size" of the area is determined by the number of links and routers it contains.

The number of areas that can be supported is limited because each of these areas must connect to the backbone. Therefore, a very large number of areas result in a large number of ABRs that are also part of Area 0.

Just to show that few hard and fast rules exist, results from an Internet Draft OSPF standardization report from the late 1990s are displayed. As shown in the results, an extremely large mean deviation is evident in terms of area size and the number of areas. The average area size seems to be a little large. Of course, one issue does not get referred to here and that is, just how well are these networks operating?

Parameter	Minimum	Mean	Maximum
Routers in domain	20	510	1,000
Routers per single area	20	160	350
Areas per domain	1	23	60

Areas and IP Addressing   In order to get the full benefit of a hierarchical OSPF structure with multiple areas, each area should relate to a contiguous IP address range in order to facilitate the summarization of routes advertised by each ABR.

It is a good idea to take the first n bits from the subnet portion of your major network address and use them for area designation. The number of bits that can be used is determined by how much address space is available. The choice of how many bits are used for area designation also decides how many areas can be supported; therefore, make this choice with care.

If a private class A 10.0.0.0 is used, then most likely plenty of address space is available. In this case, you may be afforded the luxury of using the entire second octet to designate the OSPF area.

For example, 10.1.X.Y could denote Area 1, 10.2.X.Y could be designated to Area 2, and so on. Note that, with the exception of Area 0, the numbering of OSPF areas is entirely arbitrary. However, if you are using an entire octet to denote the area, then it is a good idea to match up the two values for ease of administration.

With a class B major network, address space is not necessarily as plentiful. Consider the example of 172.20.0.0, where it is decided to have at least 10 OSPF areas and to leave room to scale up to 15 areas. Therefore, four bits are required for area designation. The first area would have a range of 172.20.0.0 to 172.10.15.0—this could be (but does not have to be) Area 0. The next area's range is 172.20.16.0 to 172.20.31.0, and so on.

It is not essential to OSPF operation that a certain number of bits are used for area allocation. However, if area address allocation is not performed in a contiguous manner, the benefit of route summarization will not be realized, which may in turn result in scalability problems.

Remember:

■ For contiguous address allocation, use the first n subnet bits to designate the OSPF area. The value of n depends on how much address space is available and it also decides how may areas can be supported.

OSPF Routers

Most of the different functional types of routers that are encountered in OSPF have been mentioned. They will now be discussed more formally here, not only to clarify the terminology, but also to discuss their functionality in more detail and how it relates to the network design.

Backbone Routers This type of router does not have any special functionality. It simply refers to a router that only has interfaces in the backbone Area 0. Such a router holds the link state database for Area 0 only. The only backbone router shown in Figure 5-7 is R4.

Internal Routers An internal router is one that is entirely within an area other than Area 0. All of its interfaces are within that area for which it holds the link state database.

Area Border Routers ABRs have strategic importance in OSPF from both a design and operational perspective. An ABR is resident in at least two areas. In other words, it has interfaces in these areas.

Ignoring for the moment the concept of virtual links, which will be discussed in the next section, an ABR must border Area 0 and at least one other area.

The ABR holds the link state database for each area that it borders. It should therefore ideally only border two areas in order to avoid having to store an excessive amount of network topology information. The ABR is responsible for advertising Type 3 summary LSAs into the backbone. These contain summary information about the specific Type 1 LSAs contained within that area's link state database. These Type 3 LSAs may or may not contain route summarization, depending on whether route summarization has been configured on the ABR. Thus, even if route summarization is not configured on the ABR, it will only advertise a summary of what is contained within the area in order to reduce the size of the link state databases elsewhere on the network outside of that particular area. In some ways, the ABR can be thought of as "cheating" the rules of link state protocols by advertising routes (or best paths) to the backbone rather than links.

Each area should have two ABRs for resilience; otherwise, the loss of an ABR would isolate the entire area from the rest of the network. Ideally, these routers should be geographically dispersed for ultimate resilience such as in Figure 5-10. Here each internal router is dual-homed to the two ABRs. The traffic can be distributed in a load sharing or a primary and backup manner. If leased lines are being used, then it is more cost-effective to perform equal-cost load sharing, although, Frame Relay or ATM may provide cost-effective backup solutions as well. With a backup scenario, half of the routers within the area could use ABR1 as their preferred route out of the area, and the other routers could use ABR2.

Sometimes the two ABRs are co-resident on the same LAN. This is a less satisfactory solution in terms of resilience because the two routers are within the same building and possibly even the same wiring closet.

Another point to be very mindful of when implementing multiple ABRs is that certain configuration parameters must be identical on each router. One of the most important of these is the manner in which router summarization is configured. If a configuration inconsistency exists between the two ABRs, then the route summarization on the correctly configured router may be rendered ineffective. Remember that OSPF always routes to the longest prefix match; hence, if specific routes are being advertised through some "backdoor" such as a misconfigured ABR, then the summary routes

Figure 5-10
ABR Resilience

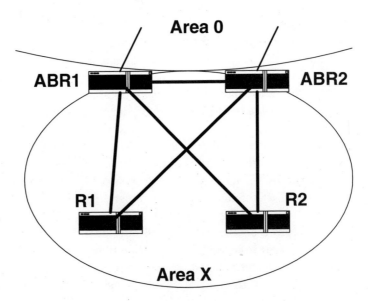

will be ignored. Of course, it also means that the link state databases and routing tables across the network will contain all of the specific routes for that area, which defeats the whole purpose of route summarization.

Just to recap on some of the design issues relating to ABRs:

- They should ideally only border two areas, area 0 and one other.
- Two ABRs should be present for resilience.
- The two ABRs should ideally be geographically dispersed.
- Each ABR should share the same functions and configurations, particularly in relation to route summarization.

Autonomous System Boundary Routers The entire OSPF routing domain is termed an *autonomous system* (AS). Another definition of an AS will be encountered when BGP is discussed. For the purposes of OSPF, an AS can be thought of as a network or part of a network that is running a particular routing protocol. An OSPF domain that includes several different areas is still one AS. If another routing protocol is being run on the enterprise network, then this is a separate AS. Multiple routing protocols are run on a network for a number of possible reasons:

- The network is migrating from one routing protocol to a more sophisticated and scalable protocol. Altering the routing protocol on a medium to large network is an extensive job that should not be attempted with a single straight cut-over. Therefore, when changing a network's routing protocol, migrating is a better strategy than an "overnight" replacement.
- During a merger or acquisition where two networks are being interconnected.
- Other routing protocols may be used for the parts of the enterprise network that connect to business partners.
- Legacy equipment may not support the main routing protocol on the core of the network.
- A proprietary routing protocol may be in place on the edge or core of the network. This may not be supported by all routers on the enterprise network.
- Technical reasons may prompt the use of a particular routing protocol for niche applications. The following are a few examples:
  - As you will see, the use of OSPF over ISDN is potentially complicated and requires appropriate planning. If this planning is not done, then

it may be necessary to use static routing or another dynamic routing protocol for the ISDN portion of the network.

- The connection to the Internet typically entails static routes. This represents another AS that must communicate with the core of the enterprise network.

An OSPF router that also connects to another AS is termed an *Autonomous System Boundary Router* (ASBR). This router must be running OSPF and at least one other routing protocol (static routes also represent another AS).

Consider the example of Figure 5-11 where the ASBR has two interfaces in the OSPF domain, while its other two interfaces are running RIP. The ASBR enables routers in the OSPF domain to connect to subnets of 172.31.0.0 by redistributing RIP into OSPF. Likewise, routers in the RIP AS can see the OSPF 10.0.0.0 subnets if the ASBR is redistributing OSPF into RIP. When a router redistributes in each direction between two routing protocols, this is termed *mutual redistribution*.

Redistribution policies can be implemented on the ASBR. For example:

(i) Only selected subnets of 172.31.0.0 might be advertised into the OSPF domain. These policies can be implemented using route filters and may be done in order to reduce the number of external routes within the OSPF link state database. An *external* route in OSPF is one that did not originate within OSPF but was redistributed in by the ASBR instead. You will see why it may be desirable to reduce the number of external routes within the OSPF domain.

Figure 5-11
ASBR bordering RIP
and OSPF domains

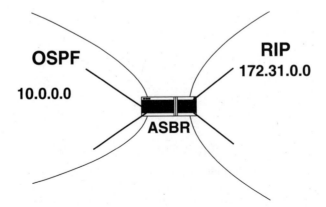

(ii) Route filters may also be used to ensure that only certain subnets of 10.0.0.0 are advertised within the RIP domain. This may be done for network efficiency reasons such as reducing the number of routing table entries that are advertised periodically within the domain. Security is another possible reason why certain subnets might be hidden from the other domain.

The exact manner in which route filtering is performed can vary depending on the router vendor. Different vendors use different terminology such as filter lists, distribute lists, or route filters. Regardless of the vendor platform, a very important issue about route filtering and OSPF is that being a link state routing protocol, OSPF advertises links rather than routes. Therefore, a potential problem exists with applying route filtering to OSPF. Instances occur where route filters can be applied to outbound OSPF updates, and as a result, all links associated with the networks that are being filtered are omitted from the OSPF LSAs. However, route filters certainly cannot be assumed to work for inbound OSPF filtering. OSPF must first of all receive the LSAs before it can calculate the routes; hence, it does not filter routes inbound.

So what is the solution to the problem of route filtering with OSPF? The exact solution again varies in accordance with the router vendor. Cisco, for example, uses what are called *route-maps*, which are a powerful configuration tool that enable inbound and outbound route and LSA filtering. Route-maps not only enable filtering, but also enable the manipulation of routing parameters such as metric. Juniper networks have something very similar to route-maps, only they call it *policy language*.

Remember:

■ Route filters do not work well with OSPF due to its link state nature. Various router vendors have proprietary solutions for LSA filtering and route manipulation with OSPF.

Aside from metric, one of the routing parameters that can be manipulated upon redistribution into OSPF is *metric-type*.

Two kinds of external routes are defined in OSPF, E1 and E2. The difference between them relates to how their metric is calculated as the links are advertised throughout the OSPF domain. When redistributing another routing protocol into OSPF, a metric must be specified for all of the external routes at the point of redistribution. For example, when redistributing from RIP to OSPF, the hop count metric of the RIP routes must be converted to an OSPF cost. The metric assigned at the point of redistribution is termed the *external cost*. OSPF E1 and E2 routes calculate metric differently after the external cost has been assigned:

■ Type 1 (E1): The cost is calculated by adding the external cost to the sum of the internal costs incurred for each link the packet crosses. This is the normal manner by which the metric is incremented as a route is advertised throughout the domain. This should be used when you have multiple ASBRs that are located at distinctly different points in the network in order to avoid sub-optimal routing to the various external subnets.

■ Type 2 (E2): This type of route does not add the internal metric to the external metric. Hence, E2 routes appear with the same metric that was assigned on redistribution at each point throughout the OSPF domain. Routes can be redistributed into OSPF as E2 routes if only a single ASBR exists or if the two ASBRs are directly attached to each other. Hence, the internal metric to reach each ASBR from within the OSPF domain should be identical. The advantage of using E2 routes is predictability in their metric.

■ In general, it is a good idea to specify a high-cost metric at the point of redistribution, particularly in the case of E2 routes where the metric does not increment beyond the external cost. This protects against a scenario where, for example, a conflict may occur because some of the external routes actually exist as internal routes with the OSPF domain due to error or poor configuration. By specifying a higher metric for the external routes, valid internal routes are accessed without attempting to leave the OSPF domain through the ASBR. This is a safeguard that should not be necessary in theory because an external route is the last type of route that OSPF calculates from the database, but it is good practice nonetheless.

Redistribution normally should be performed at more than one point for resilience. This means at least two ASBRs are performing the same redistribution task. Although it is certainly a good idea to have multiple ASBRs for network resilience purposes, it can also introduce complexity and potential problems as a result of the mutual redistribution procedure.

In Figure 5-12, redistribution is performed on two routers, ASBR1 and ASBR2, each of which borders the RIP and OSPF domains. Each router is performing mutual redistribution between RIP and OSPF; that is, RIP is being redistributed into OSPF and vice versa on each router.

By performing mutual redistribution at multiple points within the network, routing loops becomes a possibility. For the scenario in Figure 5-12,

Figure 5-12
ASBR Resilience

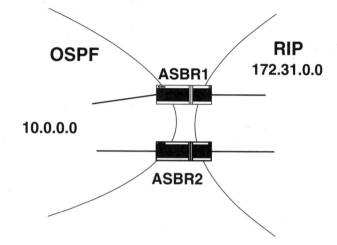

routes from the 10.0.0.0 OSPF domain are redistributed into RIP on ASBR1. These routes are then advertised within the RIP domain, and it is possible that they will be redistributed back into OSPF by ASBR2. Likewise, the 172.31.0.0 routes that are redistributed into OSPF by one router could be redistributed back into RIP by the other ASBR. A potential result of this is that routers in the RIP domain may attempt to route to some 172.31.0.0 subnets through the ASBR rather than internally within RIP. This type of scenario is termed a *redistribution loop* and may result in a routing loop. There are of course, normal routing safeguards such as split horizon, but these should not be relied upon. Neither should the fact that OSPF tags routes that it receives through redistribution as being external and should therefore ignore external routes if it learns the same routes internally to OSPF.

To absolutely safeguard against redistribution loops, the following filtering policy should be configured on each ASBR:

■ Filter the routes redistributed from RIP to OSPF so that only the 172.31.0.0 routes get advertised within the OSPF domain. In other words, do not advertise native 10.0.0.0 OSPF routes back into the OSPF domain.

■ Similarly, the only routes redistributed into RIP that should be advertised within the RIP domain are the 10.0.0.0 subnets that are native to OSPF.

In general, the purpose of redistribution filtering is to ensure that routes originated within a particular routing protocol domain do not get re-advertised back into that domain. When performing this route filtering, bear in mind the issues faced when applying route filters to OSPF.

Remember:

■ Filtering should be performed at the point of redistribution to prevent routes "looping" back into the protocol from which they originated.

Finally, to dispel a couple of misconceptions about ASBRs:

■ They do not have to connect directly to Area 0.

■ They also do not have to be ABRs.

In fact, no real restrictions exist in relation to what type of router can be an ASBR in terms of its OSPF functionality. Special types of areas called *stub areas* and their different variations are to be discussed next. You will then see that it is only if you want to configure these types of areas on your network that restrictions are then imposed on ASBRs.

Stub Areas

A stub area does not propagate the advertisement of external Type 5 LSAs. The filtering is performed at the ABR. Although the ABR maintains any Type 5 LSAs that it has learned within the backbone, it does not advertise them into the "non-zero" area that it borders. Hence, routers within this area will not have any Type 5 LSAs in their database and, as a result, their routing tables will not contain any external routes.

In terms of configuring a stub area, each router must agree that the area in question is a stub area in order to form a neighbor relationship.

In order to provide the routers within the stub area with a routing capability to external ASs, the ABR automatically injects a default route into the stub area.

The following are some other rules in relation to stub areas that are worth noting:

■ Area 0 cannot be a stub area.

If Area 0 were a stub area, then the routing capability of the entire OSPF domain to an external AS would be hindered. The concept of a stub area is to reduce the amount of external LSAs that are advertised to non-zero areas and to use default routes to compensate for the loss of routing information.

- An ASBR cannot be present within a stub area.

  Clearly, an ASBR cannot exist within a stub area because it would not be able to advertise its external LSAs. It is possible for an ASBR to border a stub area as an ABR. This way it would still advertise the Type 5 LSAs to the backbone.

The advantages and rationale behind the use of stub areas is as follows:

- Smaller link state databases.

  External links are "memory hogs" in the router, due to their format within the link state database. This is one of the driving forces behind the use of stub areas.

  The other positive consequences of the small link state databases are that they are faster and require fewer SPF calculations. Also, the memory requirements on the routers are potentially reduced.

- Smaller routing tables.

  Resulting from the smaller link state databases.

- Less LSA traffic.

- Less issues with route flapping.

  By not having Type 5 LSAs within the database, routers in a stub area can remain blissfully unaware of topology changes within an external AS. This makes them immune to route flapping in the external AS and can therefore improve stability within the OSPF domain.

Some of the potential disadvantages of stub areas include:

- A potential exists for sub-optimal routing, particularly if external routes are being redistributed into OSPF from multiple sources. The routers within the stub area are simply using default routes, so they may not always take the shortest path.

- Multiple ABRs also create the potential for sub-optimal routing. One ABR may be preferable to another for a given external AS network; however again, only default routes are being used. These are examples of design tradeoffs.

A typical application of stub areas is in a hub and spoke topology. Of course again, as is usual in network design, a few hard and fast rules exist. It is a question of understanding what a stub area is, how it operates, and how to configure it. After understanding the benefits that stub areas provide, while being mindful of any possible tradeoffs, the decision must be made if they are appropriate to your network design requirements.

The extent of the benefits of stub areas depends on how much Type 5 traffic is being redistributed into the OSPF domain. Generally, stub areas improve the scalability of the network. They also can reduce investment requirements for large routers at remote sites by reducing the memory requirements on these devices. The potential for sub-optimal routing depends on how the external routes are redistributed into OSPF. If just one ASBR exists or two ASBRs that are locally connected for resilience, then effectively all traffic to an external AS takes the same path. So, no sub-optimal routing occurs. This may not be the case if external routes are being redistributed from multiple geographically dispersed ASBRs.

Totally Stubby Areas

This is a Cisco Systems proprietary feature that is mentioned due to the extensive market penetration that this vendor has achieved to date in the enterprise network market place.

A totally stubby area is similar in principle to a stub area, but it blocks LSA Type 3 and 4 as well as Type 5. Thus, with this type of area, the ABR will not advertise external routes or inter-area summary LSAs that it learns from the rest of the network.

A router within a totally stubby area does not have Type 3, 4, or type 5 LSAs within its database; therefore, its routing table only includes intra-area routes for that area. No external or inter-area routes will be present in the routing table and routers within the Totally Stubby Area must use the default route injected by the ABR to access these networks.

The rationale for using totally stubby areas is the same for stub areas. The benefits associated with reducing link state database and routing table sizes are clearly even greater. However, the potential exists for sub-optimal routing in a resilient environment with default routes being used not only to attach to external ASs, but for inter-area routing also.

Not-So-Stubby Areas (NSSA)

A NSSA is an area that acts like a stub area in that the ABR does not advertise external Type 5 LSAs learned via the backbone. The difference between a NSSA and a stub area is that a NSSA accepts external routes that are *not* learned via the backbone. The use of NSSA is a standard described by RFC 1587.

If an area is configured to be a NSSA, routers other than the ABR that act as ASBRs redistribute external routes into OSPF as Type 7 LSAs. This is a special LSA-type used for NSSAs. The Type 7 LSAs propagates throughout the NSSA and is converted to normal Type 5 external LSAs before being advertised to the rest of the OSPF domain.

So having given a description of what a NSSA is, a question that needs to be answered to those of you not already familiar with this concept: What is the point of having NSSA within the network?

This question is best answered by way of examples. The first example pertains to routing in the Internet and was probably one of the driving forces behind the development of the NSSA concept.

The network in Figure 5-13 is for an ISP. The ISP is using OSPF for its own network and running BGP in order to route to other ISPs. The OSPF areas that ultimately connect to customer networks are configured as NSSAs. The connection to the customer networks may be running RIP or more likely static routes that must be redistributed into OSPF so that the customer's network is available to the ISP and can then be advertised to the

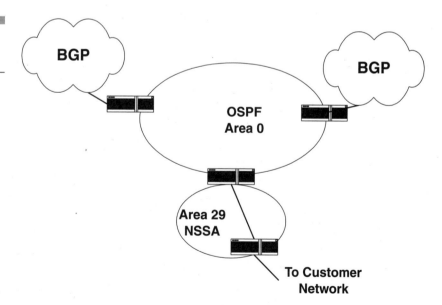

Figure 5-13
Application of NSSA
within an ISP

entire Internet. These OSPF areas cannot be stub areas; otherwise, the customer's networks would not be visible to the ISP. If they were configured to be ordinary (that is, not stub) areas, then all external LSAs that the ISP network knows of would be injected via the ABR. These would in fact be the BGP routes potentially relating to the full Internet routing table. Obviously, these routes at the very least would have to be filtered from the customer network, and even then would place heavy resource constraints on the non-backbone routers.

A better solution is to configure the areas as NSSA. This way the customer networks get redistributed into the ISP's OSPF domain. This in turn prevents the advertisement of any external routes learned via the backbone, which in this case could be the routing table of the Internet.

Another potential application of a NSSA is shown in Figure 5-14. In this case, ISDN is used to provide backup for routers within a non-zero area. For this example, a protocol other than OSPF is being used on the ISDN network. Even if static routing is used for the ISDN, these static routes must be redistributed into the OSPF area; hence, it cannot be a stub area. With a NSSA, these backup ISDN routes will be redistributed into the OSPF area in the event of link failure. However, any policy requirements to prevent external LSAs from the backbone from entering Area 29 can also be satisfied.

Figure 5-14
Application of NSSA
with ISDN

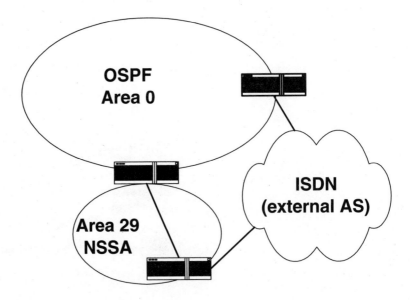

The NSSA principle can also be used if one or more non-zero areas are running another routing protocol, such as when connecting to business partners or supporting legacy equipment. Such a scenario is shown in Figure 5-15. Connectivity to these external networks can be maintained with a NSSA, without flooding each of the non-zero areas with other external LSAs from the backbone. Thus, the OSPF overhead is minimized due to external links.

Virtual Links

In a multi-area OSPF network, it is a requirement that all areas connect directly to the backbone. This is a fundamental rule of OSPF, but like most rules, an exception is supported. The concept of the OSPF virtual link allows for this exception because it enables a non-zero area to connect to the backbone Area 0 via a third area.

A schematic example of a virtual link is shown in Figure 5-16. The ABR for Area 8 connects to Area 6 rather than the backbone. This violates the area connectivity rules of OSPF, so a virtual link must be configured

Figure 5-15
NSSA for legacy
support

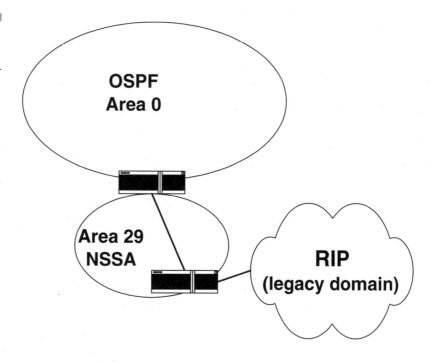

Figure 5-16
OSPF Virtual link
topology

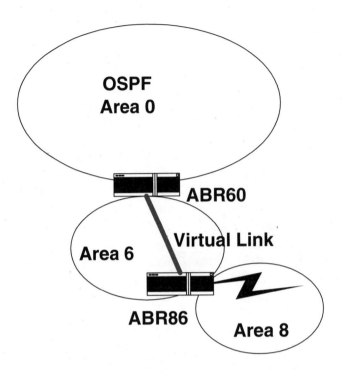

between ABR86 and ABR60. This is similar in principle to configuring a tunnel between Area 8 and the backbone. The two ABRs shown in Figure 5-16 form the endpoints of the tunnel. The ABR86 router borders Areas 8 and 6, therefore maintaining the database for each of these areas. When the virtual link is configured, ABR86 will also have elements of the Area 0 link state database. This critically could be described as a patch solution enabling Area 8 to connect to the rest of the OSPF domain.

Virtual links are generally not recommended as good OSPF design practice and are regarded as a last resort solution for practical requirements when all other options have been exhausted. One of the reasons for disfavoring virtual links is that with a virtual link in place, each packet must be encapsulated and tunneled through the virtual link using up router CPU cycles and potentially adding latency to protocol convergence. A second more generic reason why virtual links should be used as a last resort is that by providing an exception to such a fundamental OSPF design rule, virtual links gradually erode the OSPF design and may defeat the purpose of having a hierarchical routing structure on the network. For this reason, alternative solutions should always be evaluated before implementing virtual links.

Apart from the basic idea of enabling an area to connect to the rest of the OSPF domain without directly attaching to Area 0, some other specific examples of when a virtual link may be implemented will now be discussed.

Using Virtual Links for Redundancy Consider the network shown in Figure 5-17, where it is required to provide a redundant connection out of Area 10 in the event of the ABR failing. One or more routers in Area 10 could have a backup connection to routers in Area 8. This would protect against the failure of Area 10's ABR, as well as providing redundancy in the event of a router's path to the ABR becoming unavailable.

A virtual link would be required for the direct connections between Area 8 and 10, as shown in the diagram. It is necessary because the OSPF area rule would be violated if traffic from Area 10 were to route to Area 0 via Area 8 in the event of a failure within Area 10.

My view is that the use of a second ABR in Area 10, along with resilience in the paths to these ABRs, would be a better solution. Apart from avoiding virtual links, I think it should be an aspiration of the network designer to

Figure 5-17
Using a virtual link for redundancy

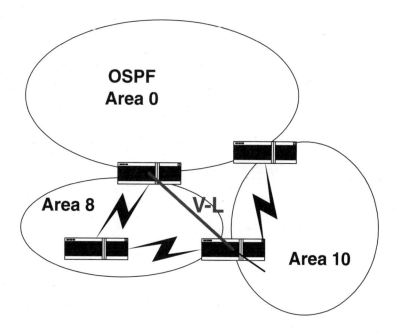

build resilience into the design of each area. In other words, traffic should not have to be rerouted outside an area as a result of a single link failure within that area.

Discontiguous Areas   Another application of virtual links is to prevent areas becoming discontiguous or "broken up."

Figure 5-18 shows an example of the backbone Area 0 being discontiguous. In this design, the ABRs are Tier-2 sites that each connect to one, and only one, of the Tier-1 sites. (For clarity, only the remote areas 20 and 30 are shown.) The campus backbone at the Tier-1 site has been put in Area 1. The fact that each of the Tier-2 ABR routers connect to just one of the Tier-1 sites means that Area 0 has become discontiguous. With this topology, a virtual link is required across Area 1.

If ABR20 had a backup link to R2, and likewise ABR30 had a backup connection to R1, then the backbone would not be discontiguous.

Another way of resolving the discontiguous backbone problem is to simply place the Tier-1 campus backbone in Area 0 rather than Area 1. Sometimes designers are over zealous in trying to prevent end users from being in Area 0, but I would certainly advocate that ahead of using virtual links.

The topology shown in Figure 5-18 can also result when a virtual link is used across a transit area for merged networks. One alternative to using virtual links is to redesign such that just one merged Area 0 exists.

Figure 5-18
Virtual link and discontiguous backbone

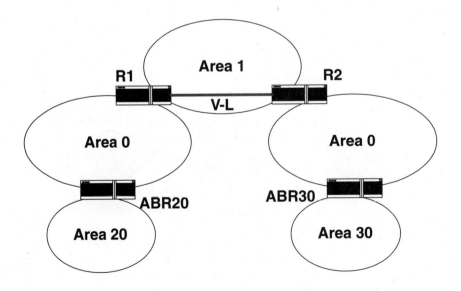

Another possible solution would be to treat the two networks as separate ASs and route between them using BGP. The solution chosen depends on factors such as the total size of the network and policy requirements such as security.

A Final Word on Virtual Links   Virtual links often tend to occur on real networks by accident rather than design. The network designers are sometimes forced into a corner and have to use virtual links as a solution for accommodating poorly planned growth. The use of a virtual link, as a short term fix if an area became discontiguous due to a failed link, is a more appropriate application rather than as part of a long-term design strategy.

Finally, a rule about virtual links that has not been mentioned thus far is that they cannot be configured across stub areas. This is because a stub area can hardly be intended as a transit area to the backbone.

Remember:

■ Only use virtual links as a last resort or interim solution.

TIP: *Virtual links cannot be configured across stub areas.*

Variable-Length Subnet Masking (VLSM)

OSPF, being a classless routing protocol, supports VLSM. This enables the optimum use of the IP address and subnet space.

If OSPF is being redistributed into a protocol that does not support VLSM in a multiprotocol environment, then any subnets that have a mask different to the one in the classful routing domain will not be successfully redistributed.

A number of ways are available to solve this problem. The simplest method is the use of static routes. Conside, for example, the network of Figure 5-19. OSPF is being redistributed into RIP v1 on R2. The 201.10.10.4/30 network will not be redistributed successfully because this class C network

Figure 5-19
VLSM redistribution
from OSPF to RIP

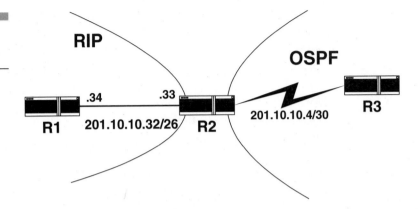

is using a 26-bit mask within the RIP domain. Connectivity could be achieved by configuring a static route on R1 for the 201.10.10.4/30 network with a next hop of 201.10.10.33. This type of solution can become overhead-intensive if a large number of VLSM routes are being redistributed. This solution also can become overhead-intensive if the RIP domain contains a large number of routers because each will require a static route to the various VLSM subnets.

Although static routes can always provide a possibly cumbersome solution, the next topic to be discussed, route summarization, provides an elegant solution to this problem, provided certain conditions are met.

Route Summarization in OSPF

The merits and importance of using route summarization have already been espoused on more than one occasion so far in this book. All of these motivations apply to OSPF, as for other routing protocols. Before dealing with the two different types of route summarization in OSPF, the following is a brief recap on the main benefits that route summarization provides:

■ Smaller link state databases, which reduce LSA traffic and SPF calculations.

■ Reduction in routing table size, resulting in less routing overhead and lower latency at each router hop.

- Reduction in updates related to route flapping. If a specific route flaps that is part of a summary route, LSAs will not propagate throughout the OSPF domain since the summary route is unaffected.

  Route summarization is a possible method of containing the propagation of routing traffic after a link changes state. This can speed up convergence because the impact of a topology change is localized.

- The redistribution of subnets with variable masks into a protocol that does not support VLSM can be facilitated using route summarization.

How OSPF Summarizes

Route summarization does not take place automatically in OSPF, even if major network boundaries are crossed. This feature, combined with the fact that OSPF routing updates include full-mask information, also enables OSPF to automatically support discontiguous networks without any additional configuration.

NOTE: *OSPF automatically supports discontiguous networks.*
Route summarization is never automatic in OSPF, even when crossing a major network boundary. It must be manually configured.

Two types of route summarization can be configured in OSPF:

Inter-Area Summarization This type of summarization should be configured on an ABR, that is, routers that have interfaces in Area 0 and one other area. The purpose of this type of summarization can be threefold:

- To reduce the size of routing tables and link state databases for the OSPF process. Area 0 routers would see summary routes to each of the other areas. Non-area 0 routers would also see summary routes from the adjacent non-zero areas.

- By summarizing the routes that get injected into the backbone from each area, and hence propagated into all other areas, convergence can be improved and overhead reduced. For example, if a specific route is lost in a given area, the OSPF SPF or Dijkstra algorithm only needs to be recomputed for that area. This would not be the case if that specific route had been injected into each of the other areas.

■ Inter-area summarization also can be used to make different sets of routes of the same major network all appear as if they use the same mask. This can be a useful trick if OSPF is being redistributed into a protocol that does not support VLSM. The following is an example of this.

In Figure 5-20, R2 is an ABR for Area 2, which contains the 150.10.9.16/28 and 150.10.10.32/27 subnets. R1 is in Area 0, but it is also an ASBR redistributing between RIP and OSPF. Within the RIP domain, the 150.10.0.0 class B network is being used with a 24-bit mask; therefore, the subnets within Area 2 cannot be redistributed into RIP. Summarizing the routes with 24-bit masks, such as 150.10.9.0/24 and 150.10.10.0/24, could solve the problem. They would now be successfully redistributed into RIP. This assumes that these 24-bit subnets are not already allocated within the RIP domain. Also, the mask must be shorter in the classful domain in order for the summarization solution to work.

Remember:

■ Inter-area summarization can be used to resolve the issue of redistributing variable length subnets into a protocol that does not support VLSM.

Although OSPF does support discontiguous networks, they should be avoided where possible since they hamper the ability to use route summarization.

Figure 5-21 shows a simple, but very effective, contiguous addressing plan that facilitates inter-area route summarization. Each area summarizes all internal routes as a single, 16-bit 10.x.0.0 summary route. This

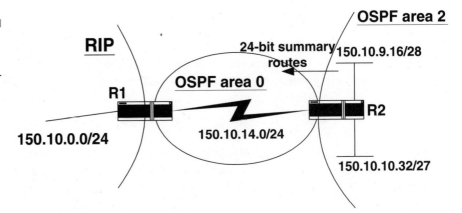

Figure 5-20
Route summarization
and LBSM

Figure 5-21
OSPF and contiguous
addressing

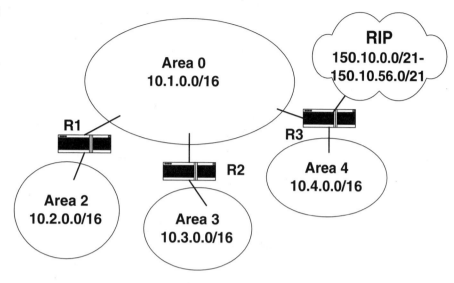

only can be achieved with an addressing scheme where each area is assigned a contiguous block of IP subnets. The masks that are implemented on these subnets can be anything above 16 bits.

On a network that does not use a class A major network address, it is unlikely that an entire octet can be used to designate the area. It is then a matter of choosing the "first n bits" from the subnet mask in order to denote the area. This was described earlier in the chapter, when hierarchical addressing schemes were discussed. The n-bit boundary then forms the inter-area summarization mask. For example, an area might contain several subnets of 172.16.0.0, all with a 24-bit mask. If three bits were used to denote the area, then eight different OSPF areas can be supported. The summarization mask for each area would be 19 bits. Examples of these ranges would include 172.16.0.0/19, 172.16.32.0/19, 172.16.64.0/19, and so on up to 172.16.192.0/19 and finally 172.16.224.0/19.

Now for a final word of caution in relation to implementing inter-area route summarization in OSPF. It is prudent to have two ABRs for resilience in each area. If this is the case, ensure that the exact same summarization policy is implemented on each router. If a specific route "leaks" into the backbone through a poorly configured second ABR, the summary route will be rendered meaningless due to the longest prefix rule. This can happen particularly in the case where the second ABR is operating in standby mode and a configuration error might not be noticed until it goes live on the network.

Remember:

■ With dual ABRs, ensure that the same summarization is configured on each router.

External Route Summarization   External routes consume a great deal of router memory. Route summarization, default routes, and stub areas are mechanisms for minimizing the effect of external routes.

External route summarization is used to aggregate the routing updates that are redistributed from another routing protocol into OSPF. This summarization is normally configured on the ASBR. OSPF will view another routing protocol or another OSPF process as a separate AS.

Referring again to Figure 5-21 where R3 is an ASBR, the RIP domain contains the routes 150.10.0.0/21 through to 150.10.56.0/21. This range of addresses could be summarized as a single route 150.10.0.0/18. Of course, in order to achieve this route summarization, the external AS must represent, at least in part, a contiguous address range.

As was mentioned with inter-area summarization, if multiple ASBRs are used for resilience or redundancy, ensure that the identical route summarization policy is implemented on each router.

OSPF and ISDN

OSPF has traditionally been problematic over ISDN for two main reasons:

■ The hello packets would tend to keep the line up unless a complex dialer list is configured. This, in any case, would break the OSPF adjacency over the ISDN network. Another possible solution is to make the hello and hold times very long. This is also less than ideal.

■ Every time the ISDN link changes state, the OSPF area would be flooded with LSAs.

OSPF Demand Circuit

A newer OSPF feature that complies with RFC 1793 is the OSPF demand circuit. The primary application for this feature is to facilitate a more effective implementation of OSPF over dial-up networks such as ISDN and also backup serial link applications.

The demand circuit feature addresses one of the basic issues of running OSPF over ISDN by suppressing the hellos, and periodic LSA refreshes once the initial adjacency is formed. The adjacency then is maintained without requiring periodic hello packets. The demand circuit will only become active if topology changes occur within the area.

If combined with a higher cost metric, the ISDN link then can provide dial-on-demand or dial backup while still remaining part of the OSPF topology. The use of the demand circuit feature is not restricted to ISDN. It could be applied to a redundant serial link that uses the demand circuit feature for backup purposes. Deploying the demand-circuit feature on the network should not be done without carefully considering the following issues:

■ The demand circuit feature is relatively new, and all legacy routers must support it. If an OSPF demand-circuit is being employed in a particular OSPF area, then all routers in the area must support the feature even if they are not using it. Otherwise, they will not be capable of interpreting the LSAs relating to the demand circuit.

■ As stated earlier, the demand circuit will come up (initiating a call in the case of ISDN) each time there is a topology change within the OSPF area. For this reason, many calls may be generated in an area that incurs relatively frequent topology changes, such as an area with many WAN links. This can mean that the use of a demand circuit is very debatable within Area 0, for example. In fact, a stub area is a good place to implement the OSPF demand circuit due to the lower proportion of topology changes and resulting LSAs.

Remember:

■ The OSPF demand circuit should not be used in an area that has frequent topology changes in order to avoid excessive ISDN calls.

Other ISDN Solutions

OSPF can be run over an ISDN network that is being used for backup with reasonable efficiency using a dial backup solution where the ISDN (or even a backup serial link or PVC) tracks the primary serial interface. An ISDN call is only initiated when the serial line fails or is experiencing an excessive traffic load. The OSPF neighbor is only formed after the ISDN connection comes up and is removed when the dead timer expires after the call is cleared down.

One of the biggest issues faced when designing OSPF over ISDN is deciding in what area the ISDN subnet(s) should be placed. It has already been shown that in the case of a solution based on the OSPF demand circuit feature, it may not be wise to place the ISDN network in Area 0 due to the extent of topology changes. Area 0 is, however, a popular choice for the ISDN network because it is often a backup solution for the WAN core, which is usually in Area 0.

Other issues are encountered if the ISDN network is part of Area 0. Consider the network shown in Figure 5-22. This is a three-tiered network with the Tier-2 routers being ABRs. Both Tier-2 and Tier-3 routers dial the main office over ISDN if their serial link fails. The ISDN network is exclusively in Area 0. This may be an appropriate solution for the Tier-2 sites; however; a problem exists with the Tier-3 sites. When they dial the main office, they suddenly become ABRs and must receive the link state database of Area 0 after the ISDN call is made. The other problem is that any route summarization configured on the Tier-2 ABR now becomes compromised and all of the specific routes leak into the backbone from the Tier-3 router. This can cause instability on the network.

Another possibility is to keep ISDN in its own exclusive area. This would be similar to the topology of Figure 5-22. The only difference being that the ISDN would be in a unique area, for example Area 99. The problem here is that every remote router would require a virtual link across Area 99 in

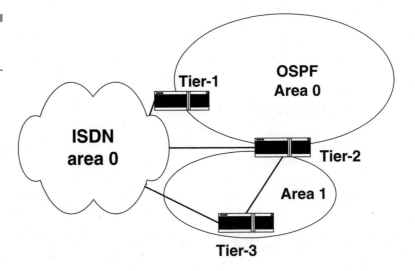

Figure 5-22
ISDN s part of area 0
only

order to connect to the backbone. This type of solution is unsuitable on several counts. It is complex, ugly, compromising of the OSPF hierarchy; entails the additional routing overhead associated with virtual links; and on a large network would entail extensive administrative overhead.

Now consider a third possibility that, in my view, is preferable to the previous two. It is often overlooked that ISDN does not have to be just one IP subnet and therefore does not have to belong to just a single area. Virtual dialer interfaces can be configured on the routers that are being dialed into, and each of these can represent a different IP subnet. This is analogous to the difference between multipoint and point-to-point Frame Relay. This solution is shown in Figure 5-23, where the ISDN connection on each of the Tier-3 routers in Area 1 is also within Area 1. The Tier-2 ABR has downstream ISDN in Area 1, and its own upstream ISDN is in Area 0. Dial

Figure 5-23
ISDN deployed across
multiple areas

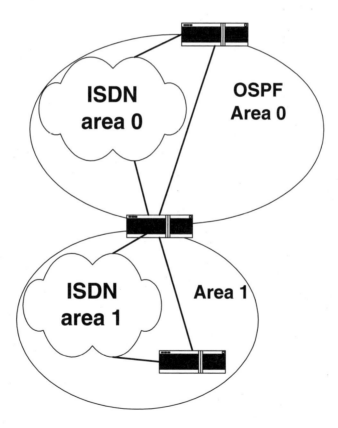

backup could be used to ensure that the ISDN only comes up if the serial interface fails. Dialer filters also are required to ensure that OSPF packets are not interesting packets that could potentially keep the line up even after the serial link is restored. This is also a better solution because a failure within Area 1 is dealt with exclusively within Area 1; thus, the hierarchy of the OSPF design has not been compromised like in the previous solutions.

Remember:
- For Tier-3 sites, ISDN backup should be performed by dialing the local ABR. This obeys the hierarchical design, where a link failure in a given area is dealt with within that area.

Conclusion

As with other topics in this book, a set of design rules will not be summarized. The reason is that every network and its requirements are different and should always be designed on its own merits. It is important to clearly understand the technology and all of the design issues, but to generalize is inappropriate and potentially misleading. OSPF, as previously mentioned, is a complex protocol. Understanding it well enough so that you can apply it to a network design is the first challenge. The other challenge is to understand the network and its design goals. The solution involves applying OSPF in as simple a manner as possible to effectively meet these design requirements.

Scalable IP Routing II— EIGRP and Protocol Redistribution

The *Enhanced Interior Gateway Routing Protocol* (EIGRP) is a Cisco proprietary IP routing protocol. It has a reasonable level of deployment on medium to large networks due in part to Cisco's dominant position in the enterprise network marketplace. For this reason, it is appropriate to include a chapter dealing with this protocol.

EIGRP was developed as a scalable routing protocol in a similar genre to OSPF. Similarities exist between the two protocols as well as differences that vary from being subtle to fundamental. Comparisons between the two protocols are inevitable and are made very frequently by enterprises that are in the process of deciding on the core IP routing protocol for their network.

Cisco's predecessor to EIGRP is IGRP, which may sound similar but is actually a fundamentally inferior protocol. EIGRP can scale up to reasonably large network sizes, whereas IGRP was really only a moderate improvement on *Routing Information Protocol* (RIP) version 1.

EIGRP Operational Characteristics

Protocol Overview

EIGRP is in some ways a dichotomy between a distance vector protocol and a link state routing protocol. Technically, it is a distance vector routing protocol, but it does exhibit several link state characteristics that improve its scalability. The reason it is a distance vector routing protocol by definition is due to the fact that it advertises routing table entries rather than link states in its updates.

Before discussing EIGRP in detail, the following is a very high-level summary of the protocol's operation:

- EIGRP uses direct IP encapsulation as its transport mechanism. Update packets are encapsulated directly in IP packets and are identified by protocol number 88.

- Information exchange is achieved through multicasts rather than broadcasts. Routers running EIGRP are part of the multicast group address 224.0.0.10, and all routing information packets are sent to this address.

- Formal neighbor relationships are created and maintained with attached routers. These relationships are formed dynamically using multicast hello packets.

- Each EIGRP router calculates its routing table using the updates it receives from each of its attached neighbors. However, it also keeps a copy of each of its neighbor's routing tables. All of this information constitutes a topology database that is unique to each router on the network. The purpose of the topology database is to provide information on backup routes if a path to a destination is lost.

- Only certain paths qualify as valid backup routes to be placed in the topology database. The method for calculating and selecting these paths is the *Diffusing Update Algorithm* (DUAL). DUAL is intended to provide a loop-free topology without the traditional distance vector requirement for hold-down timers that slows down convergence.

- If an EIGRP router detects a lost route and does not have a valid backup path in its topology database, it will query each of its neighbors for such a path.

- EIGRP uses immediate incremental updates after a topology change occurs rather than periodic routing updates. Therefore, a minimum amount of bandwidth is consumed by routing updates.

- VLSM is supported due to the classless nature of EIGRP, whereby routing updates include the subnet mask.

- EIGRP automatically summarizes routes based on class when a major network boundary is crossed in the same manner that a classful routing protocol must. However, because EIGRP is a classless routing protocol, this feature can be disabled when it is required to support discontiguous networks. EIGRP also supports the capability to manually configure route summarization within the network.

- The idea that EIGRP supports the integrated routing of IP, IPX, and AppleTalk is a misnomer. Cisco has a proprietary routing protocol for IP called EIGRP, they have one for IPX called IPX EIGRP, and a Cisco-proprietary routing protocol for AppleTalk called AppleTalk EIGRP is also available. The three protocols, presumably for marketing reasons, are all called by the same name. Although they do employ similar but certainly not identical principles, they are three different routing protocols that support three different routing tables and three different topology databases. This point is emphasized because clients have been naïve enough to think that EIGRP was a single routing protocol that could route IP, IPX, and AppleTalk if those desktop protocols were being used on the network.

EIGRP Concepts and Operation

EIGRP Packet Types   EIGRP has four basic packet types that need to be understood:

- *Hellos and Acks* are packets used for the discovery and recovery of neighbors. Hellos are multicast messages that use the 224.0.0.10 address. Acks are unicast packets. Hellos and Acks are not transmitted reliably. The main purpose of these packets is to establish and maintain neighbor relationships, which are discussed in the next section.

- *Updates* are routing updates, which are of a unicast nature when neighbors are building up each other's topology changes. Updates use multicasting for incremental topology changes. Update messages always use reliable transmission, which requires an acknowledgement.

- *Queries* are sent when a router does not have a feasible successor in its topology database for a route that is lost. The queries are sent to each neighbor and they require an acknowledgment. Queries are multicast in nature unless they are in response to a received query.

- *Replies* are sent in response to queries. They are unicast packets that are sent to the originator of the query. Replies are also transmitted reliably. During the stage when a router is exchanging queries and replies for a particular route, the router is said to be in an EIGRP *active* state for that route.

Neighbor Formation   The parameters that must be agreed upon, in order to allow neighbor formation to take place in EIGRP, are not particularly stringent. Like OSPF, EIGRP uses hello packets to form and maintain neighbor relationships. Significantly, and unlike OSPF, neighbors can be formed even if the hello interval and hold times do not match. One of the effects of this is that EIGRP has fewer potential difficulties in running it over a NBMA medium.

The *hello interval* is by default five seconds on the following network types:

- Broadcast LAN media

- Point-to-point

- Multipoint circuits with a bandwidth *greater* than T1 including ISDN PRI, Frame Relay, and ATM

Hello packets are sent every 60 seconds on multipoint circuits that have a bandwidth *less* than T1, although it should be noted that network types are not defined with the same level of formality in EIGRP than in OSPF. For example, the network type of a medium is not a parameter that can be reconfigured on the router.

An EIGRP neighbor is declared down and removed from the neighbor table if no hello packets are received from it for the duration of the *hold time*. The value of the hold time is included within the hello packet. By default, it is three times the hello interval. However, since it is included within the actual hello packet, it will not be automatically adjusted to reflect a change in the hello interval.

Even if hello and hold times are not required to match, EIGRP routers must agree on some parameters in order to form neighbors:

■ *Autonomous system* (AS) number

The EIGRP routing domain must be assigned an AS number that must agree on every router within the domain in order for neighbor formation and hence EIGRP routing to take place.

■ Metric k-value multipliers

The parameters that EIGRP uses to calculate a routing metric must be consistent to enable neighbor formation. The nature of the EIGRP metric will be discussed in more detail shortly. For the moment, it is sufficient to know that these k-value multipliers are almost never altered from their default values; hence, this is unlikely to ever be an issue hindering neighbor formation.

EIGRP will form neighbors with every router on each of its interfaces that is participating in the EIGRP process for the overlapping network. Hence, a router can potentially form an EIGRP neighbor relationship with the same router on several different interfaces, or with several different routers on the same interface.

In Figure 6-1, Router A will see Router B as an EIGRP neighbor three times, with a neighbor relationship being formed over each token ring segment. The same would be true of Router B. In Figure 6-2, each router on the collapsed Ethernet backbone will see the other routers as EIGRP neighbors.

Sometimes having a large number of EIGRP neighbors can cause problems with convergence speed after a link or subnet is lost. This can be true especially if the neighbors are formed over serial links, which may already be burdened with other traffic, causing a slow response to EIGRP queries.

The following issues relating to a potentially excessive number of EIGRP neighbors should be kept in mind either when designing or troubleshooting a very large EIGRP network.

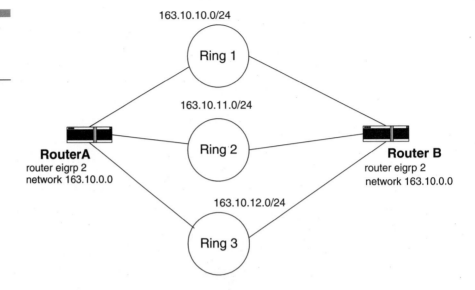

Figure 6-1
Multiple EIGRP
neighbors with the
same router

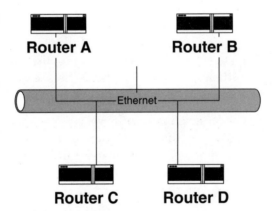

Figure 6-2
Multiple EIGRP
neighbors on the
same interface

- **Memory constraints**: A very large number of neighbor relationships result in a large topology database. The appropriate Cisco documentation of the Technical Assistance Center should be consulted if it is suspected that the routers do not have enough memory to support a large EIGRP network.

- **Convergence problems**: If a router running EIGRP detects a lost link and does not have a backup route or feasible successor, it sends a query to each of its neighbors. When a neighbor receives a query for a route to which it does not have a feasible successor, it will query each of its neighbors for a successor for that route. If the number of neighbors is large, then this could have a snowballing effect, which could produce a convergence problem. The likelihood of such a problem occurring increases if the queries are taking place over heavily utilized serial links. Also, imagine what could happen in the case of a flapping link. Safeguards against this possibility will be discussed later.

EIGRP Parameters and Terms

EIGRP Routing Metric   An EIGRP metric calculation has the potential to be extremely complex as it has the ability to consider bandwidth, delay, reliability, load, and *Maximum Transmission Unit* (MTU), as shown in the following formula:

$$\text{Metric} = \text{K1} \times \text{BW} + [(\text{K2} \times \text{BW})/ (256 - \text{load})] + \text{K3} \times \text{Delay}]$$
$$+ [\text{K5}/(\text{reliability} + \text{K4})]$$

By default, the so-called k-value multipliers have the following values:

$$\text{K1}=1, \text{K2}=0, \text{K3}=1, \text{K4}=0, \text{K5}=0$$

In the default case, the formula then becomes:

$$\text{Metric} = \text{Bandwidth} + \text{Delay}$$

The manner in which bandwidth is calculated as part of the metric is as follows:

$$\text{Bandwidth} = [10^7/\text{BW}] \times 256$$

where BW is the bandwidth that the router interface sees in kbps.

The bandwidth value used to calculate the metric to a destination is the *minimum bandwidth* associated with any link along that path to the destination.

Delay is calculated as the following:

$$\text{Delay} = [\text{Delay in 10s of microseconds}] \times 256$$

The delay value in the metric calculation is related to the *total delay* associated with all of the links along the path to a destination. Thus, the EIGRP metric is calculated from bandwidth and delay. The metric value is better (that is, numerically lower) with a higher minimum bandwidth and a lower total delay, which makes sense.

The k values must agree in order for neighbor formation to take place, but, I would never recommend changing these parameters. The first reason is that the change would have to be made on every router within the EIGRP domain. Secondly, and even more significantly, by making the K2, K4, or K5 multipliers anything other than zero, metric calculation becomes extremely complex and very unpredictable. It is important for support and design engineers to be able to intuitively know the best path to a destination without the aid of a computer program for each metric calculation.

Remember:

■ The EIGRP metric is calculated from the *minimum* bandwidth and *total* delay incurred along the path to the destination.

A significant point in relation to the bandwidth calculation must be mentioned. The figure that EIGRP uses for its metric calculation is the bandwidth, as shown on the router interface. This may not match the actual bandwidth or speed of the medium, particularly in the case of serial links.

The default bandwidth on a Cisco router's serial interface is 1544 kbps or 1.544 Mbps, in other words a T-1. This is true of serial interfaces that support point-to-point leased lines or Frame Relay. If the true speed of the link is anything other than T-1, then the router interface should be reconfigured to reflect the true speed. Otherwise, EIGRP is not using the real bandwidth in its metric calculation. Another typical problem is when one WAN link is used to backup another serial link that is of a higher speed. However, if the routers are not configured with the true bandwidth, then EIGRP will regard the paths as equal cost and load balance accordingly.

Remember:

■ Note that the default bandwidth on a Cisco router's serial interface is T-1. To avoid unintended EIGRP routing decisions, this should be reconfigured as necessary to reflect the true speed of the link.

The EIGRP Topology Table A router running EIGRP retains a list of all the routes that it has learned through the EIGRP process. In effect, it is like holding a copy of each neighbor's routing table. This information forms what is known as the EIGRP topology table or the topological database. The best path calculated to each destination is placed in the IP routing table, while other paths learned from neighbors are retained in the topology table.

Therefore, EIGRP retains two tables that hold routing-related information, the IP routing table, and the topology table. The holding of additional information and intelligence about the network topology enables EIGRP to find backup routes and convergence faster and in a more stable manner than a traditional distance vector protocol without the use of hold-down timers.

The topology table can be thought of as simply keeping a copy of each neighbor's routing table. This is clearly a significantly more intelligent approach to the usual distance vector method of calculating a routing table as RIP or IGRP does. However, it still falls short of the link state method of OSPF where the link state database provides a complete topological picture of the network. An EIGRP router does maintain significant information about its immediate surroundings. It should be noted, however, that because they do not have a complete topological map of the network, the routers do not converge independently without having to query their neighbors.

The topology table consists of information complied from the routing table received from each neighbor; therefore, its size is in direct proportion to the number of neighbors a router has. This is one reason why EIGRP is more susceptible to a limitation on the number of neighbors it can have, since the size of the topology table is more likely to be determined by the number of neighbors rather than the size of the network. As a very general rule of thumb, it is inadvisable to have more than 20 EIGRP neighbors on any router. However, this also depends on other factors such as the speed of the links to these neighbors, which will be explained when convergence is discussed in detail.

The topology table is arranged such that each destination is listed, along with all neighbors that can reach that destination with an associated metric.

Successor This is a very confusing piece of terminology. If a route to a destination is called a successor, one could be forgiven for assuming that it refers to some kind of backup route. However, with EIGRP, the term is used to describe the best route to a given destination as selected by the EIGRP routing metric. This route gets placed in the IP routing table and is also held in the topology table. Multiple equal cost routes (up to six) can be placed in the routing table.

If a successor refers to the best path to a destination, then what is used to describe a backup or alternate path? The following section will answer this question.

Feasible Successor In simple terms, a feasible successor is considered to be a valid backup route to a destination. It is kept in the topology table but not in the routing table. Despite being a relatively simple concept, the idea of a feasible successor has a precise and technical meaning.

In order to define what exactly constitutes a feasible successor, some more EIGRP terms need to be introduced. The actual metric associated with a successor or route in the routing table is called the *feasible distance*. The metric that a neighbor router advertises for a destination is called the *advertised distance*. The advertised distance is the neighbor's metric for that destination. A feasible successor is a path that is advertised by a router whose metric for the destination is lower than the feasible distance. In other words, a particular router will consider a path to be a feasible successor if it advertised by another router that is closer to the destination than itself. To put it purely in EIGRP terminology, a path through another router is a feasible successor if that router's advertised distance is less than the feasible distance. This is true regardless of how high the metric is to get to that router.

If this sounds confusing, then perhaps an example will provide some clarity. Consider the network shown in Figure 6-3. The best path that Router A has to 130.10.0.0 is through B with a metric of 15. This is the feasible distance that A has to 130.10.0.0, and this path gets placed in the routing table as the successor route along with being held in the topology table. A potential backup path also exists through C to 130.10.0.0. C's advertised distance for this destination is 10. Thus, A considers this path to be a feasi-

Figure 6-3
EIGRP feasible
successors I

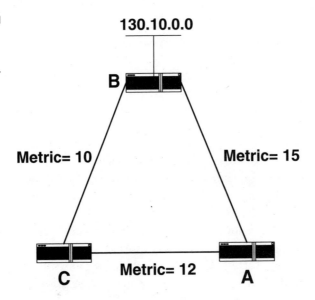

ble successor because the advertised distance is less than A's feasible distance for that route. The total metric associated with this feasible successor path is 22. The path to 130.10.0.0 through C then gets placed in A's topology table.

Now, consider what would happen on the same network but with the metrics shown in Figure 6-4. The advertised distance that C sends to A for the 130.10.0.0 route is now 16, which is greater than A's feasible distance. Therefore, this path will not be a feasible successor and is not placed in A's topology table. This is true despite the fact that the total metric associated with the path via C is 19, which is less than the metric it had in Figure 6-3 where it was a feasible successor.

The rationale behind requiring that C's advertised distance is less than A's feasible distance is that this is the only way of ensuring that C's path to 130.10.0.0 is not through A. This is a safeguard against routing loops that is integral to EIGRP's DUAL algorithm.

Remember:

- A feasible successor for a route is a path advertised by a neighbor that has a better metric to the destination than the current metric. This is independent of the metric associated with the link to that neighbor.

Figure 6-4
EIGRP feasible
successors II

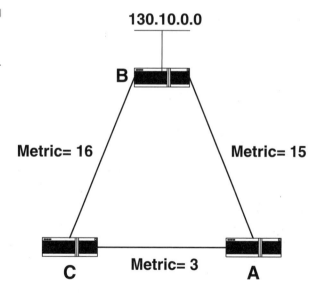

EIGRP Convergence

Convergence and DUAL

When a router running EIGRP detects a lost route, the following sequence of events may unfold:

- It will check its own topology database for a feasible successor to that route. If a feasible successor is found, this path is placed in the routing table as the new successor path and the router updates its neighbors with this new path.

- If the topology database does not have a feasible successor, then the router will query each of its neighbors for such a successor. During this process whereby the router is trying to find another route to succeed the one that was lost, the router is said to be in an *active* state for that route.

- Each neighbor that receives a query will examine its own topology table for a feasible successor. If it finds a feasible successor, then it will send a query reply with this information. If it does not have a feasible successor, it will in turn query its own neighbors. This flood of queries can spread throughout the network if none of the routers has a feasible successor.

- The router that sent the original query then waits to receive a reply from all of its neighbors. When each of these replies has been received and it is calculated that at least one of them has a feasible successor, it will recompute its topology database in accordance with the DUAL algorithm.

- The feasible successor is placed in the routing table as the new successor or best path to the destination. The router then updates each of its neighbors with the new route. Convergence will then have taken place, and the route will appear in the routing table as being in a passive state.

The network in Figure 6-5 can be used to provide a sample scenario of EIGRP convergence.

1. R1 detects the failure of the 131.5.5.0/24 Ethernet segment.

2. It has no feasible successor because the path through R3 has an advertised distance greater than R1's feasible distance.

3. It therefore goes into active mode for this router, querying R3 and R4.

4. R4 replies with no feasible successor.

Figure 6-5
EIGRP convergence
example

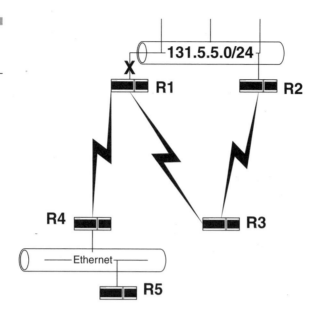

5. R3 replies with a path that has an advertised distance greater than the feasible distance. R1, in the absence of a "better offer," accepts the new path from R3 and places it with the new metric in the routing table and topology table.

6. It advertises the new path in a flash update to R3 and R4.

7. Each router acknowledges all update packets.

For this simple network, the convergence time is just a few seconds. All routing packets are processed and sent immediately. The only limiting factor is the CPU utilization on the routers and the speed and utilization on the links. For a very simple example like this, these limiting factors are unlikely to come into play, and the actual convergence time is likely to be just two or three seconds. However, as the upcoming section will demonstrate, this is not always the case when a large number of neighbors must be queried over heavily utilized links.

Convergence Problems with EIGRP

EIGRP transports use a window size of one. In other words, every single packet (that is of a reliable nature, such as Query, Update, and Replies) must be acknowledged before a higher sequence packet can be transmitted.

With the EIGRP DUAL algorithm, the router will wait until it receives a reply from all queried neighbors before proceeding with any possible recalculation of its routing table or topology table. Even if the querying router does not receive a reply from just one neighbor, the request will time-out. The route is then said to be *stuck-in-active* (SIA), and an appropriate EIGRP error message will be generated.

Remember:

■ The DUAL algorithm must wait until all neighbors have replied to the query before calculating a new path. This is true because the EIGRP does not have full topological awareness.

This can create an issue if one or more neighbors are slow to respond on a multi-access network. For example, a routing update that requires multiple packets would have to be interrupted if one neighbor was slow to acknowledge the receipt of the first packet.

A workaround exists for such a scenario as reliable multicast packets that have not been acknowledged from "slow" neighbors are retransmitted as unicasts. This helps reduce the escalation of unnecessary traffic on the network.

The reason the DUAL algorithm must wait for all neighbors to respond before performing any calculations is because EIGRP routers do not have full topological awareness. Merely maintaining a copy of each neighbor's routing table does entail a certain amount of dependence in terms of routing information between EIGRP routers. The EIGRP topology table is therefore no substitute for OSPF's link state database, which contains a full topology of the network and enables each router to independently calculate its routing table. The requirement for EIGRP to wait for all neighbors to respond does not create a problem, assuming that each neighbor can promptly respond to queries. This is not always the case in practice, however, and situations occur where EIGRP can experience convergence problems for one of the following reasons:

(i) If a router has a very large number of neighbors to query, then its CPU utilization may be overwhelmed with the amount of EIGRP traffic that must be processed after a topology change.

(ii) In the case where a router is querying neighbors over serial links that are heavily congested with other traffic. As a result, EIGRP query request and query reply packets may be getting dropped.

(iii) If the AS is so large that routers keep on querying their respective neighbors and the convergence timer expires.

The solution for issue (i) is to place an upper limit on the number of EIGRP neighbors. No hard and fast figure exists for the maximum number of neighbors because it also depends to an extent on item (ii), namely the speed of the links to each neighbor.

Two fundamental reasons explain why an upper limit should be set on the number of EIGRP neighbors that any router has:

■ The size of the topology table is directly proportional to the number of EIGRP neighbors because the topology table contains the routing table of each neighbor. Additional memory requirements are placed on the routers if the topology table is too large.

■ Convergence problems can occur if too many neighbors must be queried after a network topology change. This type of problem is more likely to occur if a number of the links to the neighbors are heavily utilized.

In relation to item (ii), the best approach is to avoid regular occurrence of the problem through good design. In addition, ensure that serial links are not so heavily loaded that these timeouts occur on a regular basis.

If the problem is persistent, then some appropriate EIGRP parameters can be manipulated. By default, EIGRP occupies a maximum of 50 percent of the bandwidth on a link. This can be altered from its default value using the following command:

```
interface serial 0
bandwidth 56
ip bandwidth-percent eigrp 1 75
```

With this configuration, EIGRP 1 could use up to could use up to 42Kbps (0.75 x 56) for its traffic. Keep in mind that this only sets the maximum amount of bandwidth that EIGRP can utilize, and in the stable passive state, EIGRP will generally occupy only a small amount of link bandwidth.

The bandwidth parameter that EIGRP uses to calculate how much actual bandwidth it may use for EIGRP traffic is the bandwidth that is displayed using the "show interface" command. The value of the bandwidth parameter can be altered from its default value. It may often be altered to a value above or below the actual physical bandwidth in order to influence routing decisions or satisfy policy requirements. Later in this chapter, it will be evident why the interface bandwidth regularly requires configuration on Cisco router serial interfaces.

The EIGRP active timeout can also be increased from its default value of three minutes using the "timer's active-time" router configuration command, thus reducing the likelihood of getting router SIA messages.

A very important point to note from the previous discussion is that these measures are really only addressing the symptom of a problem rather than the cause. In a well-designed environment, these EIGRP parameters should not have to be changed from their default values.

You should also, of course, note that the default values of EIGRP parameters should not be changed, unless it is clearly understood that by doing so a problem will be fixed without creating other side effects.

Finally, in relation to the problem scenario mentioned in item (iii), where queries keep on propagating throughout a large network resulting in convergence timeouts, it is a goal of good EIGRP network design to limit the extent to which queries can needlessly propagate though the network. Three different techniques have been used in an attempt to achieve this goal, and they have been met with varying success:

Use of a Second AS   I have seen EIGRP networks designed with multiple AS numbers with a view to curtailing the propagation of query packets. This quite simply does not work in practice—a fact that was not acknowledged on these networks until a real convergence problem existed. The network in Figure 6-6 has two ASs, 10 and 20, segregating the network. R2 performs mutual redistribution to enable communication between the two ASs. The sole purpose of having more than one AS is to bind queries within each AS. However, this does not really work in practice. When R3 detects the loss of the 50.20.0.0 subnet, it queries R2, which replies to the query. However, instead of presenting a barrier to the propagation of the query, R2 also generates a new query and sends it into AS 10. Thus, while technically the original query has been blocked, a new one was generated by R2, which defeats the purpose of having an AS boundary.

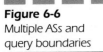

Figure 6-6
Multiple ASs and query boundaries

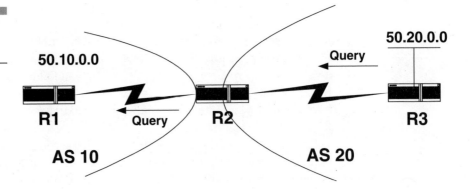

Distribute Lists   If a router running EIGRP receives a query for a particular route that is not contained in its own routing table, then it will reply that it sees the route with an infinite metric and will not propagate the query any further. The fact that EIGRP routers do not propagate queries for routes about which they do not know provides a mechanism for bounding queries. The first of the methods that employs this principle entails the use of distribute lists.

Distribute lists or router filters can be used to curtail the amount of routing information contained in the EIGRP updates that are advertised throughout the AS. This type of filtering can be done to ensure that routers do not include any unnecessary routes in their routing tables, such as to networks that they would never need to attach to.

The network shown in Figure 6-7 displays a simple scenario that can be used to illustrate this point. The remote sites serviced by the Routers B and C only require to connect to the main office 10.1.0.0. Route filters can be configured on A to prevent 10.2.0.0 from being advertised to B and to similarly stop 10.3.0.0 being advertised to C.

Figure 6-7
Route filtering and
query boundaries

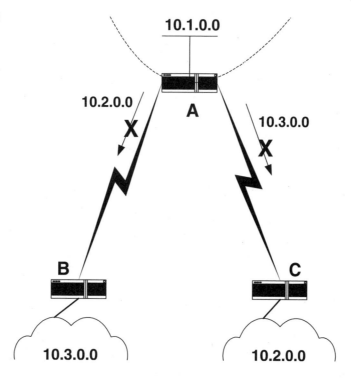

If A sends a query to B for 10.2.0.0 in the event of that subnet going down, B will reply with infinity and will not propagate the query any further. C will similarly bound a query for the 10.3.0.0 route.

Although this is an effective method of bounding queries, it can have limited application. Route filtering can only be performed if it is certain that downstream routers will never require the filtered routes.

This leads us on to the final and most efficient solution for bounding queries, route summarization.

Route Summarization   Route summarization employs the same principle that has just been discussed, namely that an EIGRP router will not propagate a query relating to a route that is not in its own routing table.

The network of Figure 6-8 can be used for illustrative purposes. Routers B and C each have a large number of downstream subnets. In the case of Router B, the subnets are all 24-bit and take the form 50.3.x.0/24. Likewise, the subnets downstream of Router C take the form 50.2.x.0/24. Both Router B and Router C summarize the respective subnets on the 16-bit boundary so that B advertises a single route 50.3.0.0/16 and C only advertises 50.2.0.0/16.

Now consider what happens when the 50.3.17.0/24 link fails. Assuming that it does not have a feasible successor, B sends a query to A. If A does not have a feasible successor, it will propagate the query to C. The router at C will not have an entry in either its routing table or topology database for 50.3.17.0/24. It only has an entry for 50.3.0.0/16, which is not the same route. Therefore, it will reply to the query stating that the router has an unreachable or infinite metric and will not propagate the query to downstream routers.

Thus, the range of the query has been effectively limited through use of route summarization. Route filtering was not required. As is always the case with a scalable network, the IP addressing plan must be first implemented in a contiguous manner in order to facilitate route summarization.

The example just demonstrated involves the use of manual summarization configured on Routers B and C. Manual summarization is a feature of EIGRP that will be discussed in more detail in an upcoming section of this chapter. Limiting the scope of queries is one of its most powerful applications and a major reason why route summarization is very important on large EIGRP networks.

Remember:

- Route summarization is the most effective method of limiting the propagation of queries within the network.

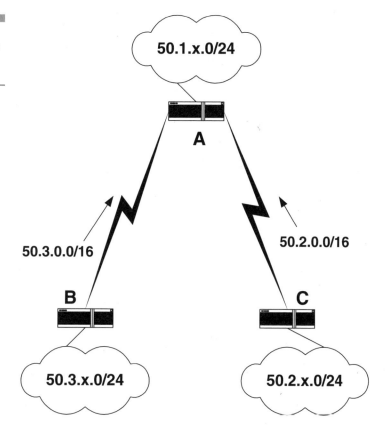

Figure 6-8
Route summarization
and query
boundaries

Load Balancing with EIGRP

EIGRP, like most IP routing protocols, supports equal-cost load balancing.
It is capable of placing up to six equal-cost paths in the IP routing table and
load balancing across each of them.

It also supports unequal-cost load balancing, which is somewhat less
common among IP routing protocols. Although unequal-cost load balancing
might sound like a very useful feature, it is not without its potential problems, which will be discussed after describing how EIGRP's unequal-cost
load balancing operates.

Consider the network shown in Figure 6-9, which shows three unequal-
cost paths from R1 to the 130.10.0.0 network. The metric values differ from
the large numbers encountered with EIGRP for the purpose of clarity and

are of relative significance only. Unequal-cost load balancing can be achieved by configuring the variance parameter on R1. The variance value is 1 by default, which refers to equal-cost load balancing. If the variance value were configured to be 2 on R1, then R1 would place the least cost path along with any path with a metric of up to twice as large in the IP routing table. In Figure 6-9, the route to 130.10.0.0 via R2 is the least cost path with a metric of 200. A variance of 2 enables R1 to also place the path via R3 in its routing table. The path via R4 could also be used if the variance were set to 3 on R1.

The potential problems associated with load sharing in general, and in the specific case of unequal-cost load sharing, relate to the type of switching employed on the router. If process switching is used on the R1, then the load sharing takes place on a per-packet basis, similar to dealing cards. However, it is certainly desirable to use some form of high-speed switching such as layer 3 switching or multilayer switching. In this case, caching a certain number of destinations against each path performs the load sharing. It may happen that some of the busiest destinations are cached against the slower path when unequal-cost load balancing is done. This may result in serious congestion and degraded service to these destinations.

The use of policy-based routing with route maps is a superior method of implementing unequal-cost load balancing on Cisco routers. With this feature, the network administrator can designate the next-hop that certain sources or destinations take. Essentially, policy-based routing enables for-

Figure 6-9
Unequal cost load
balancing

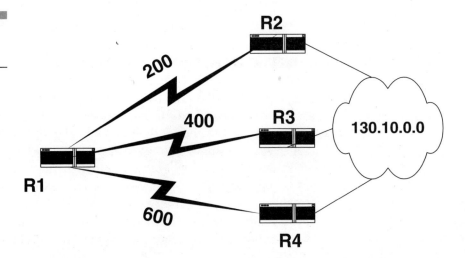

warding decisions to be made based not only on the destination address, but based on the source address also. This enables preferential treatment for certain critical hosts or time-sensitive applications.

Remember:

- Policy-based routing using route maps may be a more effective way of achieving unequal-cost load balancing rather than manipulating the "variance" parameter.

VLSM

EIGRP is a classless routing protocol that includes the subnet mask along with the advertised route. This enables the support of *variable length subnet masking* (VLSM), thus facilitating an efficient use of the IP address and subnet space, as described in Chapter 4, "Fundamental IP Routing Design."

Complications can be encountered when migrating a network to EIGRP from a protocol that does not support VLSM, such as RIP version 1 or IGRP. Consider the case where the network migration does not involve any re-addressing or more particularly, where the same major Class A, B, or C network is being employed in the old and new routing domains. If the new EIGRP domain is employing VLSM, as most likely it will, then all of these subnets cannot be successfully redistributed into the classful domain. Only subnets that use the same mask as this domain will be accepted. In the last two chapters, this same issue will be discussed. The different solutions to this issue, in relation to EIGRP, are the same as for other protocols.

(i) Static routes can be used in the classful domain to attach to the VLSM subnets. In Figure 6.10, the 201.10.10.0 Class C network is subnetted with a 28-bit mask in the legacy IGRP domain. Therefore, the 30-bit serial links cannot be redistributed from EIGRP. In the example shown, a static route to 201.10.10.4/30 specifying a next-hop of R2 could be configured on R1. If the number of VLSM subnets is large, then there is the usual administrative overhead issues with static routes.

(ii) Static routes can be used to the VLSM subnets, but the mask can be altered so that it matches that of the classful domain. These static routes can then be redistributed into IGRP. This can only be done if the mask in the IGRP domain is not longer than any of the masks in the

EIGRP domain. Effectively this is "fooling" the IGRP domain by summarizing the longer mask subnets.

Returning to the example in Figure 6.10 a static route could be configured on R2 for 201.10.10.0/28, and this could then be redistributed into IGRP on the same router. The fact that the mask is 28-bit means the subnet will be successfully redistributed. This is a slightly unrealistic example since 201.10.10.4/30 is already connected to this router. However, it illustrates the principle that can be used.

(iii) Route summarization can be manually configured in the EIGRP domain for VLSM subnets in order to reduce the mask to that of the IGRP domain. These summary routes can then be successfully redistributed into IGRP. This is similar to technique (ii) in that the mask is being altered so that it matches that used in the classful domain. However, it is a more elegant solution that scales without incurring additional administrative overhead. Later in this chapter I will give an example
of this method of solving the VLSM redistribution problem. For the moment though, it brings us neatly up to the next section, namely route summarization in EIGRP.

Route Summarization

EIGRP supports two types of route summarization—automatic and manually configurable summarization. Each of these summarization mechanisms will now be discussed.

Figure 6-10
VLSM redistribution
from EIGRP to IGRP

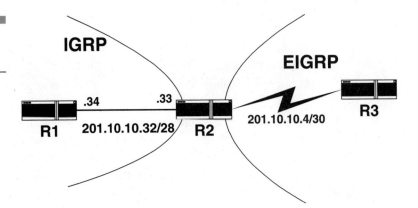

The Automatic Summarization Myth

Classful routing protocols summarize routes based on class when a major network boundary in crossed. For example, the network in Figure 6-11 is running IGRP. All of the subnets 172.16.x.0/24 will get summarized as the single Class B 172.16.0.0/16 by R1 over the link to R2 because this link is not part of that major network. This is necessary because IGRP is a classful protocol that does not advertise the mask. This type of summarization is called automatic summarization and it happens in classful routing protocols because it has to!

EIGRP also performs this identical type of automatic route summarization, not because it has to but because Cisco engineers (and possibly marketing managers) decided that it would be a good idea to do so.

The automatic route summarization feature can be disabled with EIGRP as it is a classless protocol. This may be necessary in order to support discontiguous networks. In Figure 6-11, if R3 has other subnets of 172.16.0.0 in its routing table, then it will automatically summarize them as a single route 172.16.0.0/16 on crossing the major network boundary to R2. This would result in a routing problem as R2 receives two summary routes from different directions. In order to support this discontiguous network, automatic summarization must be disabled on R1 and R3. This is something that must be done frequently on an EIGRP network, particularly when more than one major network address is being used. It is often good practice because it cannot always be ensured that discontiguous subnets will never occur on the network.

Figure 6-11
Authomatic route summarization in EIGRP

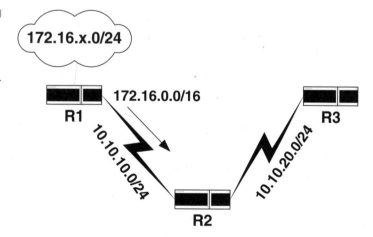

Automatic route summarization is often touted by sales engineers as a powerful selling point for EIGRP. However, it is nothing more than EIGRP behaving like a classful routing protocol when it does not have to.

Remember:

■ Automatic route summarization simply means that EIGRP summarizes based on class when a major network boundary is crossed.

■ It is often necessary to disable automatic route summarization in order to support discontiguous subnets.

The Power of Manual Route Summarization

Although automatic route summarization is not what it is sometimes presented to be, manual route summarization is a powerful and important feature of EIGRP. Throughout this book, the importance of route summarization in a scalable network design has been emphasized. At the risk of being repetitious, the following is a brief recap on the general benefits of route summarization:

■ The size of the routing table size is reduced, resulting in less routing overhead and lower latency at each router hop.

■ The size of the EIGRP topology database is reduced, resulting in less memory resource requirements on the routers.

■ Route summarization is an effective method of containing the propagation of routing traffic after a route changes state. As was demonstrated in the previous section, this can speed up convergence and improves network stability by ensuring that it *does* converge.

This is because an EIGRP router will not propagate queries for a route that is not in its own routing table. Therefore, it will not react to queries regarding a specific route when its routing table only contains a summary route.

■ The triggered updates associated with route flapping are also protected against using route summarization. This is a specific example of the previous point relating to the role of route summarization in improving network convergence and stability.

■ The redistribution of subnets with variable masks into a protocol that does not support VLSM can be facilitated using route summarization.

Some of the advantages of route summarization that again have been outlined are generic for most routing protocols. However, the manner in which route summarization can be used to curtail the propagation of routing queries is of massive significance on a large EIGRP network.

I have my reservations about the mechanism that EIGRP uses for convergence. The fact that a router must wait for all neighbors to respond to a query before proceeding with any calculation can sometimes cause serious convergence problems on very large networks, as I have observed myself. This procedure is a necessary evil because EIGRP routers do not have a full link state database of the network, so it is necessary to hear from all neighbors to protect against routing loops. This principle combined with the possibility of queries propagating to the edge of the network can result in slow convergence and indeed instability where convergence does not occur without intervention from the network administrator. A large network is more prone to these effects if many routers have a lot of EIGRP neighbors and the WAN links are busy.

The potential for such convergence and stability problems is greatly reduced by using route summarization to limit the range of the queries. For this reason, route summarization is even more important on a large EIGRP network than on an OSPF network of similar size.

Remember:

■ Route summarization is particularly important for improving EIGRP convergence and stability as the network grows.

Figure 6-12 shows a sample network employing EIGRP route summarization. Three Tier-2 sites are shown connecting to a single Tier-1 central site. The addressing has been allocated in a contiguous manner, as it must be in order to facilitate route summarization. The downstream networks for each of the four routers are as follows:

R1:172.16.0.0 to 172.16.31.0

R2:172.16.32.0 to 172.16.63.0

R3:172.16.64.0 to 172.16.95.0

R4:172.16.96.0 to 172.16.127.0

The mask for all subnets is 24-bit. Summarization can then be performed on the 19-bit boundary. For example, R1 can generate a single summary route 172.16.0.0/19 over its serial links. R2 can advertise a single 172.16.32.0/19 route over its serial link to R1 and likewise for R3 and R4.

Figure 6-12
Manual route
summarization in
EIGRP

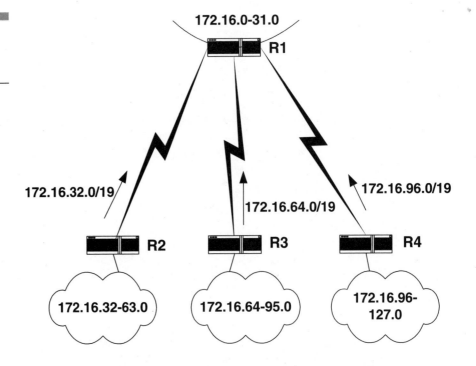

Figure 6-12
Manual route
summarization in
EIGRP

An addressing plan that facilitates this type of route summarization should be put in place prior to rolling out any EIGRP network. The route summarization that can then be employed will significantly enhance the network's scalability, convergence, and stability.

Here are some final points that are worth noting in relation to route summarization with EIGRP:

■ The metric that is applied to a summary route in EIGRP is the minimum of the metrics associated with each of the corresponding specific routes that are being summarized.

■ In relation to the router performing the summarization: If each of the specific routes are lost, then the summary route will also be removed from its routing table.

■ EIGRP always routes to the longest prefix match, because this is technically a different route to the summary. A path to 172.16.25.0/24 would always be chosen before a path to the summary 172.16.0.0/16 if

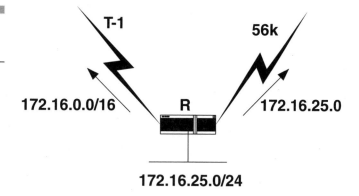

Figure 6-13
EIGRP and the
longest prefix rule

it provided a longer or more specific match. This is true regardless of the metric that each route has. The metric is only compared for identical routes, which these are not since they are of differing prefix length. It is important to be extremely clear about this principle. I have seen network designers overlook this presuming that the summary route will be chosen if it has a better metric. In a redundant design, it is critical to be careful to implement summarization on the redundant links also. Otherwise, specific routes may "leak through" the backup link, which will then be chosen ahead of the higher bandwidth primary path. This is shown schematically in Figure 6-13, where the 172.16.25.0 network would be accessed over the 56k link rather than the T-1 due to the longest prefix rule.

Remember:

- EIGRP always chooses the longest prefix match for a destination regardless of metric.

- Therefore, it is important that all "backdoor paths" have summarization configured on them.

EIGRP over NBMA Networks

EIGRP, unlike OSPF, does not have a formal concept of network type. It is also less stringent about the parameters that must agree for neighbor formation to take place. For example, it is possible for EIGRP routers to form neighbors even though the hello interval does not match. One of the results of this is that running EIGRP over NBMA networks such as Frame Relay or ATM has traditionally not involved the configuration complexity of using OSPF on the same network.

Although it is not valid to favorably compare EIGRP to OSPF for ease of operation over NBMA networks, particularly with the advent of sub-interfaces, this configuration is not as difficult as it used to be with OSPF. However, it was never an issue with EIGRP. For example, a point-to-point Frame Relay sub-interface uses an EIGRP hello interval of five seconds, whereas a multipoint sub-interface (with bandwidth less than T-1) has a 60 second hello interval by default. EIGRP neighbors could still be established across a PVC that is configured as point-to-point at one end and multipoint at the other.

Even though few difficulties are associated with neighbor formation on NBMA networks, running EIGRP over Frame Relay or ATM does pose some design challenges.

PVC Bandwidth Allocation

Ensuring that EIGRP can use enough bandwidth on each PVC to ensure network convergence without overwhelming any of the WAN neighbors is a potential issue when running EIGRP over NBMA networks.

On a multiaccess network, EIGRP divides the total bandwidth evenly among each of the neighbors. The figure used for the total bandwidth is the interface bandwidth on the router. In a case of a serial interface on a Cisco router, it is important to remember that this is T-1 speed by default, unless configured otherwise. The bandwidth that is allocated to each neighbor determines the maximum bandwidth that EIGRP traffic can consume in communicating with that neighbor. For some NBMA interfaces on Cisco routers, configuration may be required to ensure that optimum bandwidth allocation is available for EIGRP traffic on the different PVCs.

Point-to-Point NBMA Implementation Even on point-to-point sub-interfaces, the bandwidth is assumed to be T-1 on Cisco routers. It is likely that a sub-interface is a fractional T-1, in which case the sub-interfaces should be configured to reflect the true speed on the PVC. For ATM, the bandwidth should equal the *Sustained Cell Rate* (SCR), and for Frame Relay it should equal the *Committed information rate* (CIR) of each PVC.

Point-to-Multipoint NBMA Networks A point-to-multipoint NBMA topology can entail the use of multipoint sub-interfaces or simply be implemented on a main physical interface. In either case, the EIGRP bandwidth allocation issues are the same.

If all PVCs have the same CIR (in the case of Frame Relay), then the Frame Relay interface bandwidth should be set as follows:

$$\text{Bandwidth} = n \times \text{CIR}$$

where n is the number of PVCs supported on the multipoint interface.

If the PVCs are of varying CIR (or SCR for that matter), a number of configuration options are available to ensure optimum performance:

1. Convert to point-to-point sub-interfaces.

2. Group the equal-CIR PVCs into multipoint sub-interfaces.

3. Specify a bandwidth value = n × the lowest CIR.

Consider the network of Figure 6-14. A multipoint configuration is shown on Router A with three PVCs. Two PVCs have a CIR=128k and the other has a CIR = 56k.

If the serial interface bandwidth on A were set to $3 \times 128 = 384k$, oversubscription is possible on the slower PVCs. EIGRP may consume a higher percentage of its bandwidth, and the PVC will also be viewed as having a more favorable routing metric than is actually the case.

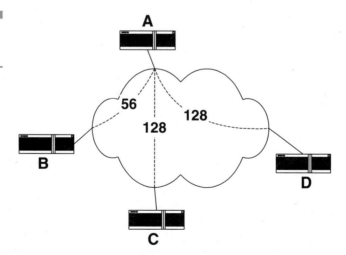

Figure 6-14
Multiple PVCs of
unequal CIR

The possibility of overwhelming the slower PVC can be avoided by grouping the two faster PVCs into a multipoint sub-interface. The configured bandwidth on this sub-interface can be set as $2 \times 128 = 256k$. The remaining PVC can be placed on a point-to-point sub-interface with a bandwidth of 56k.

If sub-interfaces are not to be employed, then the other option is to configure the main serial interface on A with a bandwidth that relates to the slowest PVC. In the example of Figure 6-14, this becomes $3 \times 56 = 168k$. This "lowest common denominator" approach is prudent because it avoids the possibility of packet pacing problems on the slower PVCs, which may result in network instability.

Remember:

- On point-to-point NBMA, set the interface bandwidth = CIR or SCR in kbps.
- On multipoint, set bandwidth = $n \times$ CIR, for n PVCs.
- On multipoint with n PVCs of unequal CIR, set interface bandwidth = $n \times$ lowest CIR.

EIGRP in a Multiprotocol Environment

The main issues that are encountered when running EIGRP on a network that also has at least one other IP routing protocol will now be discussed. This type of scenario might occur for a number of reasons, for example, when the network protocol is being migrated to EIGRP gradually from a classful routing protocol or when connections to a business partner require another protocol.

Protocol Redistribution

The points at which redistribution occurs on the network can vary depending on the nature of the multiprotocol environment. If EIGRP is being used on a particular portion of the network such as ISDN, for example, then every router that connects to the ISDN network may be performing redistribution to and from EIGRP. This type of scenario is shown in Figure 6-15.

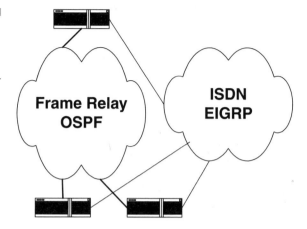

Figure 6-15
EIGRP employed on a
separate WAN
technology

**Frame Relay
OSPF**

**ISDN
EIGRP**

The other situation occurs when two routing protocols are being run on the same enterprise network, creating two distinct routing domains that are connected using at least two routers for resilience. Each routing domain uses a different protocol. This can happen when two organizations are merging or when the core routing protocol is being migrated gradually to EIGRP from another less scalable protocol such as RIP or IGRP.

The issues associated with using multiple routing protocols and their redistribution will be discussed primarily in the context of two distinct routing domains as in Figure 6-16; however, they are equally applicable to any scenario whereby multiple IP routing protocols exist on the same network.

When connecting two separate routing domains or ASs, it is advisable to have two points of redistribution for the purpose of resilience. It is imperative that the loss of a single router does not break all communication between the two routing domains. Figure 6-16 shows a network scenario where mutual redistribution is required on the routers that border the two domains. Some designers may favor an approach such as redistributing OSPF to EIGRP on Router A and redistributing EIGRP to OSPF on Router B. This does not give proper resilience since a failure of either router will break communication between the two domains. For example, if Router A goes down, then OSPF will not be redistributed into EIGRP. As a result, routers in the EIGRP domain will not have any routes to the OSPF domain.

Mutual redistribution should be performed on both routers. This ensures full connectivity between the two domains in the event of one router failing. One configuration requirement is to specify an EIGRP metric for routes

Figure 6-16
EIGRP redistribution
to and from another
routing domain

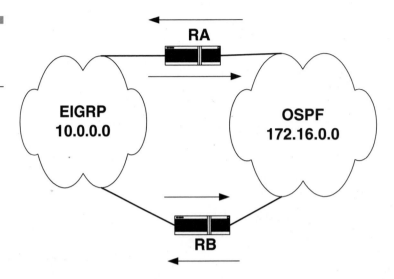

redistributed in from OSPF (or any other protocol for that matter) so that
the OSPF cost associated with each route can be converted to an initial metric within the EIGRP domain. Similarly, an initial metric must be specified
on the other routing protocol for routes redistributed in from EIGRP. As a
general principle concerning redistribution, it is good practice to make this
metric higher than the average or typical metrics within the routing
domain into which these routes are being redistributed. Although it should
not become an issue on most networks, it protects against a spurious route
being redistributed into a routing domain where that route already exists
in a legitimate sense.

Remember:

■ Routing metrics must be specified at the point of redistribution, both
for routes redistributed to and from EIGRP.

■ It is good practice to configure this metric with a value that is
artificially high.

Preventing Routing Loops

Mutual redistribution (and indeed unidirectional redistribution) must be
stringently controlled to protect against routing loops. Fundamental routing problems can occur if routes are redistributed back into the routing pro-

tocol from which they originated. Some safeguards are built into most routing protocols such as split horizon. EIGRP also labels routes that have originated from another protocol. However, these features should not be relied upon, particularly in the case where mutual redistribution is performed at multiple points within the network.

Route Filters and Route Maps Route filters or route maps can be configured on Cisco routers to protect against routing loops. Route maps are particularly powerful because not only do they provide the capability to filter routes, but they also manipulate route characteristics such as metric and administrative distances.

In relation to Figure 6-16, the following route-filtering policies should be applied to both Router A and Router B:

- *With respect to routes redistributed from OSPF to EIGRP*, only advertise the 172.16.0.0 subnets.

- *With respect to routes redistributed from EIGRP to OSPF*, only advertise the 10.0.0.0 subnets.

This policy ensures that routes originating in one routing domain are not advertised back into the same domain after redistribution.

Remember:

- When configuring mutual redistribution, use route filtering to protect against routing loops.

Route Determination

When making path selection decisions in a multiprotocol environment, a route is chosen based on the following criteria in the following order:

1. Prefix length
2. Administrative distance
3. Metric

These parameters will now be discussed, particularly regarding how they relate to routing in a multiprotocol environment.

Prefix Length Earlier in this chapter, it was described how a router always places a more specific route in its routing table in addition to any summary route it may receive. Most IP routing protocols route to the most specific or longest prefix match regardless of metric. This is because a specific route to a destination is technically a completely different route to a summary route; therefore, metric is not compared. This was demonstrated in Figure 6-13. If the specific route 172.16.25.0/24 is advertised over the 56k link, then remote routers will use this path to attach to 172.16.25.0/24 regardless of metric or routing protocol.

Administrative Distance   If a router receives two updates about a route that are of equal prefix length, then the metric is used to decide which path is placed in the routing table. However, what if the two updates come from two different routing protocols? A parameter known as the *administrative distance* (AD) is used to choose between multiple routing protocols. The administrative distance can be thought of as a credibility rating that is given to each IP routing protocol. The lower the value, the more credible or believable is the protocol. The following table shows a listing of the administrative distance value on Cisco routers for each IP routing protocol.

Notice that EIGRP distinguishes between routes that originate within EIGRP (internal EIGRP) and routes that were redistributed in from another routing protocol. It also applies a different administrative distance to these two types of routes. Therefore, if a router learns of 144.20.20.0 as an EIGRP internal route and also as an EIGRP external route, it will choose the internal path because it has the lower administrative distance of 90 as opposed to 170. This makes good sense because this route must be native to EIGRP; otherwise, it would be impossible to learn of it as an internal EIGRP route. Learning about it as an external EIGRP route may occur due to poor configuration or design.

An EIGRP summary route is given a low administrative distance of five. At first sight, this might appear to guarantee that a summary route is always chosen over specific routes, but this is not so. Why is that? Hopefully, you have guessed the answer correctly. Because the prefix is longer, a specific route is always placed in the routing table regardless of administrative distance or metric. The administrative distance parameter is only compared for routes that match in prefix length.

Remember:

■ Administrative distance is used to choose between updates received from two different routing protocols.

■ AD only comes into play if the two routes received are of equal prefix length.

Protocol	Administrative Distance
Connected	0
Static route to an interface	0
Static route to a next-hop address	1
EIGRP summary route	5
External BGP	20
Internal EIGRP	90
IGRP	100
OSPF	110
RIP (v1 and v2)	120
External EIGRP	170
Internal BGP	200

Before moving on, in relation to the previous chart, you might note with some amusement that a route learned over IGRP is placed in a Cisco router's routing table ahead of the same route learned using OSPF. Why do you believe IGRP routes are chosen ahead of a vastly more powerful and sophisticated protocol such as OSPF? Hint: These are Cisco routers we are talking about!

When to Manipulate Administrative Distance   Administrative distance values can be altered through configuration. This is something that should not be done lightly and only after careful planning. Two typical instances can occur in which AD values are manipulated:

■ To avoid sub-optimal routing

Certain niche applications exist when it may be prudent to manipulate the administrative distance in order to avoid sub-optimal routing decisions. Consider the network shown Figure 6-17, which shows two ASs, one using RIP and the other running OSPF. Router RC performs mutual redistribution between the two protocols. Router RA learns about 10.7.7.0 through OSPF and RIP as it connects to each of these routing domains. By default, it will place the OSPF route in its routing table since OSPF has a lower administrative distance. In the particular case of the 10.7.7.0 subnet, the RIP path would be optimum. It may be decided as a form of policy-based routing to allow RA the exception of using the RIP derived path to access 10.7.7.0. This could be achieved by manipulating the administrative distance of RIP to be a value less than 110 just for the specific route 10.7.7.0; all other RIP routes assume the default value of 120.

The following configuration on RA would achieve this by setting the distance to 80 for that particular route:

```
router rip
distance 80 0.0.0.0 255.255.255.255 1
!
access-list 1 permit 10.7.7.0 0.0.0.255
```

■ Floating static routes

Static routes have an administrative distance of 1 or 0 depending on whether they are configured to point to an outgoing interface or a next-hop address. Either way, a static route has a lower AD than any dynamically learned route regardless of the protocol.

It is commonplace to use static routes rather than a dynamic routing protocol over ISDN for reasons discussed earlier in this book. If ISDN is used for backup purposes, then the administrative distance of the backup static route pointing at the ISDN must be manipulated in order to make it less favorable than the dynamically learned route. This is termed a *floating static route*, which is used only if the dynamically learned route is lost due to the failure of the primary link.

Metric   Metric may seem like a simple and familiar concept, but it is important to be very clear on what exactly it means. The routing metric is used to choose between two routes that have the same prefix length and were learned via the same protocol. Metric is completely irrelevant and is not used to compare routes that are of different prefix lengths or routes that are learned from two different routing protocols.

My final word on routing metric, particularly in relation to EIGRP, is this: Do not confuse metric with administrative distance! I emphasize this point because I have seen engineers in often very responsible positions repeatedly confuse these two parameters. In fact, I have seen serious service-affecting network outages occur because the engineers who designed the network did not understand the difference. Cisco is in part to blame for this due to a very unfortunate choice of EIGRP terminology. Terms

Figure 6-17
Sub-optimal routing

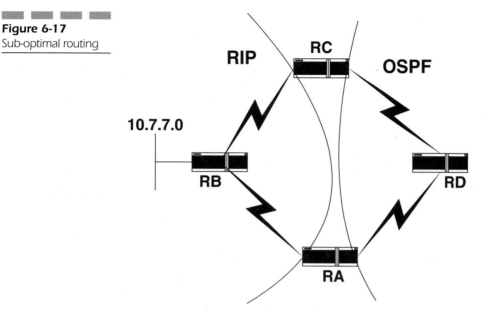

like "feasible distance" and "advertised distance" are, of course, metrics. Unfortunately, inexperienced engineers sometimes confuse these terms with administrative distance, which is an entirely different concept.

Remember:

- Do not confuse metric with administrative distance.
- Administrative distance is used to choose between routes learned via different routing protocols. Metric is used to choose between routes learned via the same routing protocol.
- Regarding EIGRP, "feasible distance" and "advertised distance" are metrics and have nothing to do with administrative distance.

Migrating from IGRP

This is a specific example of running EIGRP in a multi-routing protocol environment, but it is worth discussing specifically because it is frequently encountered in practice. Most of the issues discussed in this section are relevant to any network that is migrating from a classful routing protocol to EIGRP, or indeed happens to be running a classful protocol in conjunction with EIGRP.

IGRP is not a scalable routing protocol. In fact, the only significant advantage that it offers over RIP version 1 is a superior metric, which is similar to EIGRP's method of path selection. Most enterprise network managers that are still running IGRP are quickly migrating to OSPF or EIGRP. Given that an IGRP network must have been all-Cisco to begin with, migration to EIGRP is a popular choice.

Migration Strategy

Redistribution between IGRP and EIGRP is automatic if the same AS number is used for each protocol. This feature is sometimes part of the migration strategy as EIGRP can be gradually configured as a type of overlay network. If a failure occurs in EIGRP, then the IGRP network is still in place. Sites can be migrated in two phases.

The first phase involves enabling EIGRP. This can then be tested during normal network operation. When it is decided that EIGRP is running in a satisfactory manner, IGRP can then be disabled as part of the second phase of migration.

Although the fact that redistribution can be automatic may seem convenient and smooth, it also offers less control. For example, it may be prudent to tightly control the mutual redistribution between IGRP and EIGRP using router filters or route maps. In this case, it is better to use a different AS number for each protocol and manually configure the redistribution.

A migration approach that is synonymous with tightly controlled redistribution is to divide the network into two distinct domains such as in Figure 6-18. The backbone routers (RA and RB) provide resilient mutual redistribution, and every other site on the network belongs to one of the two domains. Initially every site is in the IGRP domain and gradually sites are phased over to the EIGRP domain until it eventually becomes the sole, new routing domain.

This is different from the overlay approach where EIGRP is gradually rolled out on the entire network. After EIGRP has been established as being stable, IGRP is then phased out, usually on the edge of the network first and then finally on the core.

The migration strategy employed depends on the topology and requirements of the network in question. In many situations, creating two distinct routing domains may only be realistic or meaningful if also a migration occurs to a new WAN technology. In this case, two different domains truly exist. As always, it's a question of designing every network on its own merits.

Remember:

■ Redistribution is automatic between IGRP and EIGRP if the AS number is the same; although, this can potentially make the redistribution harder to control.

Issues Worth Noting

Administrative Distance One very important point regarding IGRP/EIGRP network migration must be noted. Internal EIGRP has an administrative distance of 90 on Cisco routers, whereas external EIGRP routes that originated in another routing protocol have an AD of 170. This means that IGRP routes are preferred over external EIGRP routes. This is an issue that network designers frequently overlook with serious effect. A case study will be discussed in which this is one of the issues in question.

Remember:

■ The administrative distance of external EIGRP is greater than IGRP.

Discontiguous Networks With regard to the network shown in Figure 6-18, if the EIGRP and IGRP domains used different major network numbers, then the possibility of discontiguous networks being created in each domain exists. This can be resolved easily in the EIGRP domain by disabling automatic summarization.

For the IGRP domain, it is important that summary routes to the EIGRP domain do not get redistributed at multiple geographically diverse points. If different major networks were used on the two domains in Figure 6-18, then the IGRP domain would receive two summary routes to the EIGRP domain. This is not necessarily a problem in itself, as load balancing would occur. However, the presence of more redistribution points, in particular, ones that are diversely located, increases the likelihood of suboptimal routing.

VLSM Issues with VLSM can arise if the migration to EIGRP is still maintaining the former Class A, B, or C major network. An example of this is if the IGRP network uses 172.16.0.0 with a 24-bit subnet mask, while the new EIGRP domain uses 24-bit, 27-bit, and 30-bits masks for the major network 172.16.0.0. In this situation only the 172.16.0.0/24 subnets can be redistributed into IGRP, as it does not support VLSM. The problem can be resolved using static routes in the IGRP domain for the "non/24" subnets.

Figure 6-18
EIGRP migration from
IGRP

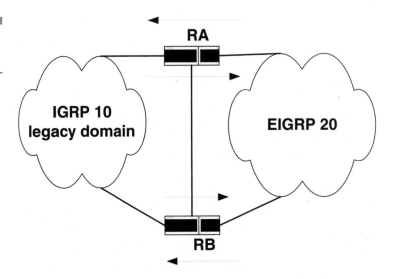

Alternatively, route summarization can be configured in EIGRP to summarize the longer masks as /24, thus enabling them to be redistributed into IGRP.

A Case Study in EIGRP Migration

A network is being upgraded from Frame Relay to ATM in the WAN as a result of growing bandwidth requirements. The project is also being used as an opportunity to change the core network routing protocol from IGRP to EIGRP.

The migration strategy is displayed in Figure 6-19 and is as follows:

1. The core site will perform mutual redistribution between IGRP and EIGRP.

2. The ATM infrastructure will be put in place and each site on the network will connect to it, while maintaining connectivity to the legacy Frame Relay network during the migration stage.

3. The Frame Relay network exclusively uses IGRP, and the ATM network only uses EIGRP.

4. The core LAN subnets are divided between the IGRP and EIGRP domains. Core resources are moved to EIGRP only after the stability of that domain has been fully verified.

Figure 6-19
EIGRP migration case study

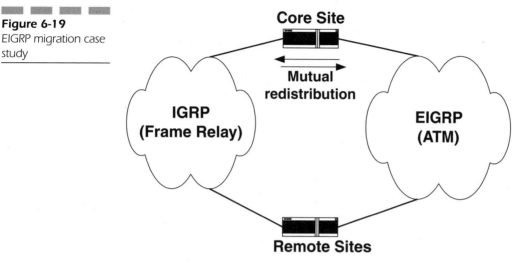

5. Each site on the network will learn about all subnets over IGRP and EIGRP, although it is assumed that the EIGRP route over ATM will always be chosen due to its better metric.

6. Eventually, all core resources will be in the EIGRP domain, and sites on the network will disconnect gradually from the Frame Relay WAN. This will leave the new ATM WAN running EIGRP in place.

During the migration stage, a very slow response is observed to certain core resources. After performing some troubleshooting, it is concluded that all of the remote sites are accessing many core resources over Frame Relay instead of ATM. This is true of the core servers that are still part of the IGRP domain. Why is this happening? The ATM network has a better metric, but this is irrelevant because a metric is used only to compare routes learned via the same routing protocol. EIGRP has a lower administrative distance than IGRP. This does not necessarily ensure that the EIGRP path over ATM is chosen. Core resources that are part of the EIGRP domain will be learned by remote routers as internal EIGRP subnets with an administrative distance of 90. These networks will be routed to over ATM as expected.

Core LAN subnets that are part of the IGRP domain will be learned by remote sites as IGRP routes and also as *external* EIGRP routes. IGRP has a default administrative distance of 100, which is less than the 170 value of external EIGRP. Therefore, these resources will be accessed over the IGRP/Frame Relay path. To resolve this issue, the administrative distance on each of the remote site routers should be configured so that IGRP is less preferable to external EIGRP.

The problem previously described may seem obvious to the more experienced readers, but it was actually inspired by a real-life network on which I worked. The issue occurred because the design engineers had not understood the difference between metric and administrative distances. The consequences of the problem turned out to be even more serious than what I referred to in this example. It again demonstrates that all issues must be carefully studied and understood before attempting to implement any significant network design or re-design. This problem, of course, would never have happened if the design had been fully tested in a lab prior to rollout!

EIGRP and OSPF: Comparison Summary

EIGRP is frequently considered against OSPF when deciding on the core routing protocol for an enterprise network. For this reason, a summary comparison will be made between the two protocols with respect to the key parameters.

Complexity of Operation

OSPF is certainly more complex than EIGRP. Some of these complexities give rise to clear benefits to OSPF. However, taking this point on its merits, it is desirable to keep a protocol as simple as possible.
Advantage: EIGRP

Design Restrictions

The hierarchical structure is formalized with OSPF by using an area-based architecture that must obey certain rules. EIGRP can support a hierarchical and scalable design without the design restrictions sometimes imposed by the area structure. It has already been demonstrated in the last two chapters that EIGRP poses less potential for design complexity to achieve resilience, redundancy, and, for example, ISDN backup.

The fact that EIGRP is that little bit more forgiving in supporting a slightly wayward design is probably one of the more common reasons why it might be used instead of OSPF.
Advantage: EIGRP

Ease of Configuration

EIGRP is easier to configure than OSPF. I sometimes think that this is a rather dubious advantage. An engineer that finds the configuration of OSPF excessively difficult probably does not understand the protocol to a sufficient degree and therefore should not be working with it.

Simplicity in itself is an advantage, although ease of configuration is not one of the most important parameters by which to judge a protocol.
Advantage: EIGRP

Scalability

OSPF maintains a link state database for the entire network. This is more information than is retained by EIGRP in its topology table. This difference is the basis for making OSPF more scalable than EIGRP.

The fact that the size of the EIGRP topology table is directly proportional to the number of neighbors is one reason why a definite upper limit is placed on the number of neighbors an EIGRP router can have.

EIGRP is significantly more scalable than any other distance vector *Interior Gateway Protocol* (IGP), but it is still not a link state protocol. Although it is technically possible to run EIGRP on networks of over 1,000 routers, I would feel that at this level the limit of EIGRP's scalability is being tested. The OSPF upper limit is closer to 5,000 routers.
Advantage: OSPF

Convergence

The two protocols have a fundamentally different approach to convergence. OSPF retains a complete topological map of the network and calculates new routes from that.

EIGRP retains limited information about backup paths and must frequently query each of its neighbors for a feasible successor. This procedure is inefficient and potentially slow and unstable. It has to be since EIGRP does not have the same topological awareness of OSPF.

The issue of convergence is one of the main reasons that OSPF is a more scalable protocol than EIGRP. Apart from speed of convergence on large networks, OSPF also converges in a more stable manner. By default, it waits before reacting to a topology change; this makes it less susceptible to flapping links.

Advantage: OSPF

Route Summarization

Both protocols support route summarization that is manually configurable. As already discussed, less constraints are associated with the manner in which EIGRP route summarization is configured.

EIGRP also supports "automatic route summarization," which is a complete misnomer. It simply means that EIGRP will summarize like a classful routing protocol has to, unless the feature is disabled.

No advantage

VLSM

Both are classless protocols that support VLSM.

No advantage

Proprietary

Being a proprietary product is always a potential disadvantage that must be considered. Even if a particular enterprise network only uses Cisco routers, it may need to connect to a business partner network that uses another vendor. This in itself may necessitate the use of a second routing protocol.

The nature of the enterprise network will continue to change significantly over the next decade, as it will support a more diverse set of applications. Many of these applications will demand more bandwidth, and their diversity will place an increased requirement for quality of service routing. Although Cisco has been the dominant player to date in the enterprise net-

work sector, it is by no means guaranteed that this level of dominance will continue in an ever-changing marketplace.
    Advantage: OSPF

Misconceptions in the Marketplace

OSPF is a standardized protocol, and it is therefore presented in the marketplace with an appropriate level of objectivity. This is not true of EIGRP, which tends to be either glorified or diminished depending on whether the sales engineer represents Cisco or not.

EIGRP is not as suitable for very large networks as OSPF is, but it is a fine protocol that can adequately support most Cisco-based networks up to this limit. I often think of EIGRP as technically very good and brilliantly marketed. It appears obvious that Cisco wanted to invent a protocol that rivaled OSPF and put a lot of thought into how it would be sold. It is comparable but slightly different to OSPF in many respects, and I assume these differences were intended as selling points.

Of these differences, some represent advantages of EIGRP and others are disadvantages, as we have just seen. Other features of EIGRP are, however, potentially misleading. Although I have, as a consultant, recommended EIGRP on a number of occasions, I have only done so for the right reasons. I am now going to highlight some features of EIGRP that have the potential to be misrepresented to the more naïve clients.

- Automatic route summarization is often presented as some major advantage of EIGRP because it does not exist with OSPF. It simply means that EIGRP behaves like a classful routing protocol unless configured otherwise. If anything, this is a disadvantage. The best thing about automatic summarization with EIGRP is that it can be disabled.

- Multiprotocol routing is a complete misnomer. Cisco has proprietary routing protocols for IP, IPX, and AppleTalk that all happen to be called EIGRP. Similarities of operation exist between the three routing protocols, but that is where the similarities end. Three separate routing tables and topology databases exist. EIGRP is sometimes presented as some kind of magic protocol that can independently route each of these desktop protocols, which is simply not the case, and it is not unreasonable to suspect a certain amount of cynicism behind this marketing ploy.

- EIGRP, unlike OSPF, does not wait before reacting to a topology change. This may be presented as an advantage in terms of convergence speed. In my opinion, it is a disadvantage with regard to network stability. The few seconds that might be saved when calculating a new route may result in a network outage due to a flapping link.

Advantage: OSPF

Conclusion

EIGRP is an adept protocol that can support most Cisco-based networks of up to, and possibly in excess of, 1,000 routers. It does have a greater limiting factor than OSPF in terms of the number of neighbors a router can support; however, this issue is often avoided through a hierarchical design.

The simplicity and lack of design constraints give EIGRP a potential edge over OSPF for certain niche applications on Cisco-based networks. Ultimately, OSPF has superior characteristics for scalability and convergence, and very large networks eventually come to a point where a threshold is crossed, making EIGRP an unsuitable choice of protocol. It is important to remember, however, that this threshold is only crossed on very large networks, making EIGRP a popular implementation on many Cisco-based networks.

BGP and Internet Routing

BGP Operation and Characteristics

Border Gateway Protocol (BGP) is an IP routing protocol that is used to route between *autonomous systems* (ASs). The concept of an AS has already been encountered in the context of it relating to an interior gateway routing protocol. From this definition a network running two interior gateway routing protocols such as OSPF and RIP effectively consisted of two ASs. This definition of an AS is a useful concept in the enterprise network arena. However, the concept of an AS will now be broadened to a more general definition of the term. An AS is also defined as a group of networks under a common control and administration. By this definition, a single enterprise that uses multiple IP routing protocols is in itself a single AS.

BGP uses this definition of an AS. A protocol such as BGP that routes between AS is known as an *Exterior Gateway Protocol* (EGP). A protocol used for routing within an AS is termed an *Interior Gateway Protocol* (IGP). The Internet is divided into multiple ASs with each *Internet Service Provider* (ISP) connecting to multiple ASs. BGP provides the routing capability between ISPs, or more specifically, between the ASs. BGP is also sometimes used for connections to a business partner's network, which is also an example of routing between two ASs. Interconnecting the networks of two merged companies is an increasingly popular application of BGP aside from the Internet.

Remember:

- As AS is a group of networks under a common control and administration.
- An IGP routes *within* the AS.
- EGPs route *between* different ASs.

BGP Overview

Before discussing BGP in a network design context, it is appropriate to review some of the protocols basic to operational characteristics:

- BGP uses TCP as its transport mechanism. Each BGP packet is encapsulated in TCP and identified by port number 179. The reliability inherent in TCP removes the requirement for explicit acknowledgement packets within BGP.

- BGP relies on neighbor formation between routers. These routers are then said to be BGP peers or neighbors. BGP neighbor formation occurs after an appropriate TCP session has been formed between the two routers.

- Two types of BGP peers relationships exist:

  - External BGP or EBGP peers are formed between routers that reside in different ASs.

  - Internal BGP or IBGP peers relationships are formed between BGP routers that reside in the same AS.

- The following BGP message types are defined:

  - Open

    This is the first message sent by each router after a TCP session has been established. An Open message includes the hold time that will be negotiated and the BGP Router ID. The *hold time* is the time that can elapse without receiving a Keepalive message before a router declares a BGP neighbor to be down and removes it from its neighbor table. The BGP router ID is calculated in the same manner as an OSPF router ID, that is, the highest active IP address on the router with a loopback interface overriding physical interfaces.

  - Keepalive

    The Open message received by each router is confirmed using a Keepalive packet. When each router has confirmed the Open message, the BGP session is now said to be *established*, enabling BGP routing information to be exchanged.

    Keepalives continue to be exchanged often enough to avoid the expiration of the hold time, which is negotiated from the Open messages.

  - Update

    Initially BGP peers exchange their full routing tables and from then on, updates are incremental after a routing table change. Each BGP update packet contains information on one AS path only. However, the information contained, which will be discussed later, can be extensive. The path information in the update includes the BGP attributes and all networks that are reachable through this AS path.

    At this point, it is worth emphasizing that although BGP is unquestionably a very sophisticated protocol, it is a distance vector protocol. Routes, rather than link states, are advertised in BGP updates, therefore technically making it a distance vector protocol.

  - Notification

    A Notification packet is sent when an error is detected. The BGP connection is closed immediately after sending such a message.

■ BGP maintains its own routing table that is separate to the main IP routing table. The router can be configured to redistribute routes between the two tables. Later in this chapter, the issues surrounding the redistribution of routes between the main IP routing table and the BGP routing table will be discussed.

Fundamental Internet Architecture

Customers who avail of the Internet connect to an ISP. Each ISP has its own network with various *points of presence* (POPs) spanning nationally or internationally. Each POP is used for connectivity to customers and may also facilitate communications with other ISPs. The manner in which ISPs communicate with each other can vary slightly depending on the part of the globe in which they reside. For example in the United States, a number of registered *Network Access Points* (NAP) exists, typically run by Telco companies that provide the service of interconnecting ISPs. Large ISPs sometimes connect directly to each other without going through a NAP. Figure 7-1 shows a schematic network diagram where ISP1 and ISP2 interconnect directly, and ISP3 connects to the rest of the Internet via its local NAP.

AS numbers are unique like IP addresses and are assigned by the *Internet Assigned Numbers Authority* (IANA). A small ISP may just have one AS, whereas a larger ISP is likely to have multiple AS numbers.

The AS designator is a 16-bit number that ranges in value from 1 to 65,535. Similar to private IP address ranges, a range of AS numbers from 64,512 to 65,530 is reserved for private use. Obviously, if BGP is being used in order to connect to the Internet, then an IANA-assigned AS number must be used.

Figure 7-1
Fundamental Internet Architecture

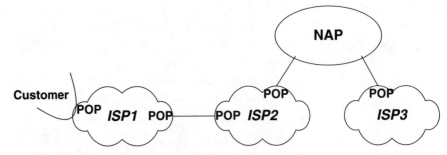

When Is BGP the Correct Option?

Using BGP is not always necessary when connecting to the Internet or to another organization's network. In fact, the use of BGP must be given careful thought and evaluation as to its necessity and consequences, prior to any implementation of the protocol.

BGP is unlikely to be necessary or desirable in the following situations:

■ A single connection to the ISP or business partner exists.

In this case, a default route to the ISP or business partner will suffice. In fact, the use of BGP would achieve little more than placing a large processing load and memory requirement on the gateway router.

■ No policy is implemented as to what path traffic should take out of the AS.

Even if multiple paths lead to the ISP or adjacent AS, BGP may not be required if sub-optimal routing can be tolerated. Instead, two default routes can be injected into the local AS, and the IGP metric determines which path is chosen. In Figure 7-2, the administered network denoted by AS65000 connects to two ISPs. A default route is used to connect to each of these ISPs. Each default route is redistributed into the IGP. Each router in AS65000 will route to the Internet using the redistributed default route that has the lower IGP

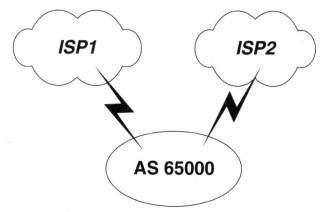

Figure 7-2
Multiple ISP
connections

metric. For example, if OSPF is the IGP, then each router in AS65000 will use the default route that it is "closer" to, in other words, the one with the lower OSPF cost.

This approach could also be used if there are multiple links to the same AS or ISP. The advantage that it provides is the reduced overhead, processing, and memory requirements on the Internet gateway routers. The downside of this non-BGP approach is the potential for sub-optimal routing as the path selection is performed by the IGP only. No control for path selection to specific networks can be exerted, because only default routes are being used.

- If the links between the ASs are heavily utilized.

  Each BGP neighbor or peer relationship requires the maintenance of a TCP session. Incremental updates will also propagate across the link. If the ISP is advertising all Internet routes (or even a significant portion of them), then this can result in heavy routing traffic that may congest the WAN link. Another potential side effect on a busy link is that the BGP traffic may get dropped.

  This can result in inconsistent routing information between the two peers, and in very serious cases, may cause the TCP session and the BGP peer to be reset.

- Insufficient memory is on the Internet gateway routers to store the Internet BGP routing tables.

  Running BGP can be resource-intensive, particularly if the Internet routing table is downloaded. Even a partial Internet routing table places heavy memory requirements on the router. The maintenance of BGP sessions incurs significant CPU utilization, so the routers must be capable of satisfying these requirements.

This all begs the question: When is BGP a requirement? BGP should be employed in the following situations:

- Multiple connections to the ISP exist.

  If multiple paths to the ISP exist and a requirement to exercise some control over what traffic traverses each path is there.

- Multiple ISPs are being used, and sub-optimal routing must be avoided.

If it is required to favor one ISP above another to route to certain destinations, then BGP must be used.

■ A requirement to manipulate routing parameters is in order to influence path selection.

Generally, when any routing policy is to be implemented for ISP path selection, BGP is employed.

■ Routing information is transiting through the AS to and from other ASs.

This scenario exists within an ISP network or that of a large enterprise where the local AS connects to more than one AS. BGP must be used if the local AS is distributing routing information between the other ASs it connects. For example, to which referring to Figure 7-2, BGP will be used if ISP1 is relying on AS 6500 to learn routes that are local to ISP2 and vice versa.

EBGP and IBGP

External BGP *External BGP* (EBGP) is run between two routers that are in different ASs. Figure 7-3 shows an EBGP session between routers R1 and R2 that are located in AS100 and AS200, respectively. Note that a router can only belong to one AS, but the two ends of a serial link can reside in different ASs. Normally, EBGP peers are required to be directly connected.

Figure 7-3
EBGP and IBGP peers

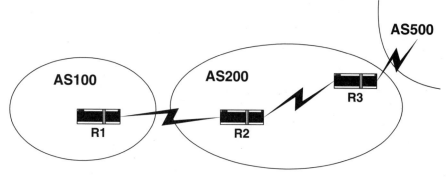

Internal BGP *Internal BGP* (IBGP) is run between routers that are located in the same AS. In Figure 7-3, an IBGP peer relationship exists between R2 and R3 as they both reside in AS200. IBGP peering is required to distribute BGP routing information across an AS in order to transit to a third AS.

Unlike EBGP, no requirement exists that IBGP peers be directly routed so long as each router has an IGP route to the other peer.

Some features and rules of IBGP will now be discussed. They must be clearly understood in order to correctly design and configure BGP networks.

- IBGP will not propagate routes that it learns from an IBGP neighbor on to any other IBGP neighbor. This feature of IBGP is intended to prevent routing loops. It will only send this routing information to EBGP neighbors. For this reason, if IBGP is being used extensively for routing within an AS, it is important to maintain a full mesh of IBGP neighbors. For example in Figure 7-4, if R5 were made an IBGP neighbor of R7, it would not propagate routing information that it learns from R7 onward to R3. Similarly, R5 would not propagate to R7 any BGP information that its learns from R3. Apart from full meshing, a number of ways to resolve problems caused by this IBGP property exists. The concept of *route-reflectors* causes this feature to be relaxed for the configured router-reflector clients. The design applications of route-reflectors along with other solutions will be explored later in this chapter.

- If a router receives an update from an EBGP neighbor about a particular network, it will propagate that route to its IBGP neighbor with the same next-hop. In other words, the next-hop address is carried into IBGP and maintained. For example, in Figure 7-4, if R6 sends an update about 166.60.0.0 to R3, R3 will receive this route with a next-hop address of 167.10.1.6. It will then advertise 166.60.0.0 to R5 with

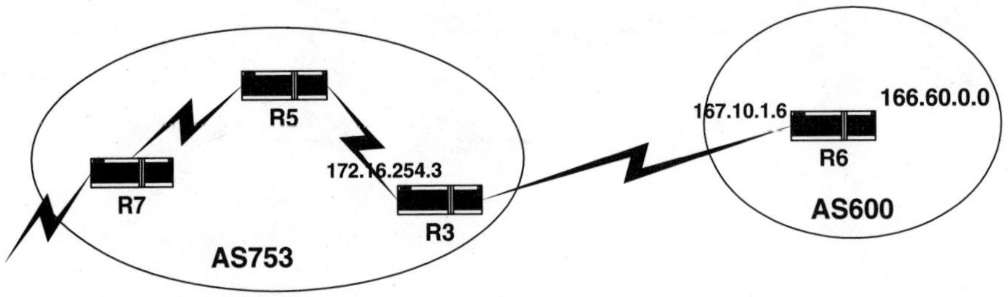

Figure 7-4
IBGP route
propagation

the same next hop of 167.10.1.6. This can create a problem if R5 does not have a route to 167.10.1.0/24.

If no way of providing R5 with a route to 167.10.1.0 exists, the other solution is to configure R3 to advertise all its routes to R5 with "itself" as the next-hop. Most router manufacturers use the next-hop-self parameter to achieve this effect. If R3 is configured to advertise routes to R5 as next-hop-self, then it will advertise BGP routes to R5 with a next hop of 172.16.254.3.

- IBGP will not advertise routes learned from one IBGP neighbor onto a third IBGP neighbor.
- The next-hop address associated with a route learned via EBGP is propagated though the IBGP domain without being altered.

Synchronization

Synchronization   The synchronization principle relates to the synchronization of BGP with the IGP. If this type of synchronization is employed, then the manner in which a BGP router deals with routes learned over IBGP is affected. The following behavior is enforced when synchronization is used:

- A BGP router will not place a route learned from an IBGP peer in its IP routing table, until it learns that same route over IGP. In other words, it will not use the BGP route until it learns it also over IGP.
- A BGP router will not advertise a route learned over IBGP to its EBGP neighbors until it learns about that route via the IGP.

Synchronization between BGP and IGP may be required in two scenarios:

- When an AS is transiting information from one autonomous system onto a third AS. If the intermediate AS advertises a BGP route that it does not yet have an IGP route to, to the third AS. There is a possibility that packets will be dropped if a BGP router in the third AS attempts to access that route. This may happen if the IGP is being relied upon to provide the path to the next-hop address in the IBGP update. If that IGP update has not yet arrived, then packets to that destination will be dropped.

For example in Figure 7-4, if synchronization were enabled, R5 would not immediately place the update that it receives from R3 about 166.60.0.0 in its IP routing table. The R7 router, likewise, would have the route to 166.60.0.0 in its BGP table but would not place it in its IP routing table until it learns the same route over IGP. R7 would not advertise the 166.60.0.0 route to its EBGP peer either. R3, on the other hand, would place the route in the IP routing table immediately since it learned about it over EBGP rather than IBGP.

Sychronization can cause a problem if IBGP is used rather than an IGP for routing within the AS. Since no routes will be learned via IGP, in this situation, the two protocols can never become synchronized and routes learned via IBGP will never be placed in the IP routing table or get advertised to EBGP peers.

- If IBGP full meshing is not in place. Synchronization can be disabled if full meshing *is* in place because there is no need to wait for the route to be learned via IGP. I use the term "BGP full-mesh" to mean an AS where every router is running BGP. It does not necessarily mean that each router is peered with all other routers. Solutions such as route-reflectors and BGP confederation can be used to achieve full BGP connectivity without full peering. These techniques will be discussed later in the chapter.

If BGP is not being redistributed into IGP, then synchronization is not required. This is because BGP and the IGP are to some extent independent and do not have to be synchronized. Redistribution may not be necessary if every router in the AS is running BGP, as is typically the case with an ISP.

Different vendors treat the synchronization issue in their own way. Cisco routers have the feature enabled by default and it may be manually disabled if synchronization between BGP and IGP is not required. Juniper Networks take a different approach in that the feature is never used on their current line of products. This is because Juniper devices are mainly targeted at the ISP market and tend to supply into networks that are BGP fully-meshed with no redistribution into IGP.

Remember:
- Synchronization dictates that a BGP router will not advertise a route to its BGP neighbors until it learns about that route from IGP.
- Synchronization is not required if there is a GP full-mesh or if BGP is not being redistributed into IGP.

BGP Stability—Problems and Solutions

Router Memory Issues   The routing table for the Internet includes in the region of 85,000 routes and 7,000 AS numbers as of the final quarter of 2000, and is in a continuous state of growth. This can translate into a memory requirement in excess of 32MB for the routing table alone. If a BGP router is indeed receiving the entire Internet routing table without any filtering, then a clear possibility is that it may at some time experience instability due to its memory limits being tested. This can be an issue even if a router is receiving a filtered version of the Internet routing table. For this reason, memory utilization levels should be frequently monitored on routers running BGP.

Route Processing and CPU Utilization   BGP maintains a TCP session with each of its neighbors. Apart from the overhead entailed in maintaining these sessions, incremental routing updates are sent to and received from each of these neighbors. This can result in a heavy CPU utilization associated with a moderate to large number of BGP neighbors. Generally if a router's average CPU utilization regularly exceeds 80-90 percent, its ability to correctly process packets can be temporarily diminished. This can have a serious and adverse effect on network operation. The CPU utilization associated with BGP increases in proportion with the number of neighbor sessions and the level of incremental updates that must be processed.

Route Dampening   A flapping link can create routing havoc on any large network, particularly on one that uses BGP. The persistent propagation of UPDATE and WITHDRAWN messages associated with a flapping link can consume link bandwidth and increase CPU utilization on each router as it updates its neighbors.

Network instability resulting from flapping routes can be reduced using a feature known as *route dampening*. This entails suppressing the advertisement of routes that flap too frequently within a short time interval. The exact manner in which route dampening is configured can vary depending on the router vendor, but in each case, the following principles are employed:

- Every time a link flaps it incurs a penalty.

- After a certain number of penalties a threshold is reached whereby the route is no longer advertised or suppressed. This is termed the *suppress-limit*. A route will continue to incur penalties even after it has been suppressed.

■ A route is given an opportunity to "recover" from its penalties through the definition of a *half-life*. The penalty value associated with a route decays or reduces exponentially, and the half-life is the time taken for the penalty to reduce by half.

■ A suppressed route will again be re-advertised when its penalty value reduces to a predefined value known as the *re-use limit*.

Figure 7-5 illustrates the principle of route dampening by showing a sample graph of penalty versus time. Route dampening ensures that unstable links will not be advertised, thus preventing routing instabilities. Routes that have been suppressed will only resume being advertised after they have remained stable for a period of time determined by the half-life value. The only compromise with this solution is that a time lag occurs from the point a route regains stability to when it is again being advertised. This additional outage time is most likely a worthwhile tradeoff for the stabilizing effect of route dampening. Parameters such as half-life, suppress-limit, and re-use limit are configurable, and their values should be chosen with regard to the recent stability history of the network.

Session Resets BGP updates about an AS path include information on the IP networks that are reachable via this path and also the routing metrics and attributes associated with these networks. If any of these attributes are manipulated by an administrator in order to implement a particular routing policy, then the TCP session relating to the BGP peer relationships must be reset.

Figure 7-5
Route dampening shown by penalty versus time

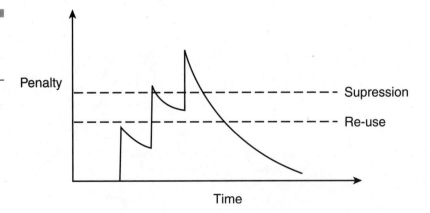

Penalty

Supression

Re-use

Time

The resetting of the TCP session causes routing table and cache entries to be flushed while the new session is being re-established. Thus, routing is interrupted while routes with the new attributes are advertised and relearned. The fact that routes disappear and eventually reappear on downstream routers potentially causes a period of instability as incremental routing updates propagate possibly through several ASs.

Most router manufactures now support the ability to reconfigure BGP attributes without resetting the TCP session. This is often called *BGP soft reconfiguration*, which eliminates any unnecessary routing updates after a configuration change. Soft reconfiguration can be configured on the router for outbound or inbound updates. For soft reconfiguration on outbound updates, all routing updates are simply resent to each neighbor after the configuration change without requiring a session reset. Inbound updates are more difficult to change without resetting the session, and the local router must store all inbound updates regardless of policy. Clearly, this can be extremely memory intensive. The new policy can be forced into effect by triggering an outbound soft reconfiguration at the other end of the session. It is important to be clear on how configuration changes are handled on the router vendor platform before configuring any related features.

IGP Redistribution into BGP

Redistributing IGP to BGP may cause instability in the BGP domain because an incremental update will be generated by BGP every time a link changes state in the IGP domain. For this reason, the redistribution of a dynamic IGP into BGP is not recommended. Here are some alternatives:

- Originate routes from the IP routing table.

   A network or range of networks local to a particular AS can be injected into BGP on a router within that AS. Each network must already reside in the router's IP routing table. These networks will then be advertised through BGP. For example, Cisco routers enabling BGP to advertise an IGP route from the IP routing table is achieved using the network command. This is more stable than redistributing the IGP into BGP. Because a major network or a Supernet can be injected into BGP, only a change in state of this network or range of networks will cause updates to propagate throughout BGP. For example, if the entire Class B network 172.16.0.0 was injected into BGP in this manner, then only the loss of all subnets of 172.16.0.0 would cause a change in the state of 172.16.0.0/16 within the BGP domain. The routes could also be injected into BGP in the form of a summarized Supernet such as 172.0.0.0/8.

■ Redistribute static routes into BGP.

Static routes can be redistributed into BGP without causing stability problems because they do not change state. Black holes (i.e., a route to nowhere) can, however, occur if the destination is down and even though the associated static route is still being advertised.

The relatively small, yet undoubtedly growing, requirement for mobile host access to the Internet highlights another limitation of redistributed static routes. This could cause a problem if there was a requirement for mobile access to an ISP directly rather than attaching to the Internet via the enterprise network. This is only an issue if the mobile host needs to retain their registered IP address, as might be the case with a mobile Web server. With simple mobile dial access to the Internet, the client is simply assigned an address from the ISP's registered IP address pool; therefore, routing is not an issue.

BGP Redistribution into IGP

Instability can also ensue within the IGP domain if BGP is needlessly redistributed into IGP or if it is not properly controlled. The instances where it may or may not be necessary to do some degree of redistribution from BGP into IGP will now be examined.

ISP Network Generally, an ISP will run BGP on all routers at each POP. An IGP is usually required to provide a route to the IBGP next-hop address. If BGP is run on all major routers within the ISP network, then redistribution from BGP to IGP should not be required. Routes from other ASs are carried through the AS using IBGP. Figure 7-6 shows a full-meshed AS for an ISP, which avoids redistributing BGP into its own IGP.

Two major benefits are derived from not redistributing BGP into IGP. First, the resource requirements on IGP routers within the network are reduced significantly. This also reduces routing overhead within the IGP domain. The second advantage is that BGP will converge faster because it can advertise routes without having to wait for an IGP update about those same routes. In other words, synchronization between BGP and IGP does not have to be employed.

Remember:

■ If all routers run BGP within an AS, then redistrubution from BGP to IGP is not required.

■ This has two benefits: (a) reduced routing overhead in IGP domain, (b) faster BGP convergence because synchronization is not required.

Enterprise Network An enterprise network will typically not run BGP on all routers. If sub-optimal routing to the Internet can be tolerated, then default routes could be redistributed into the IGP for this purpose.

However, if it is required to implement certain routing polices relating to how an adjacent AS is accessed, then BGP redistribution must be performed into the IGP. For a connection to a business partner network, this may not represent a problem as the number of BGP networks in the remote AS might not be particularly extensive. Consider the network shown in Figure 7-7. The enterprise network in question is AS5000, which connects to a business partner, AS6000, over two links. BGP is used to implement a pol-

Figure 7-6
ISP IBGP full mesh

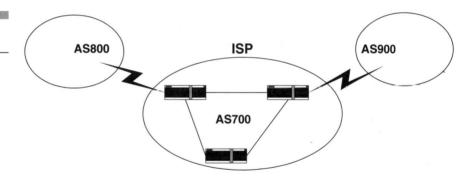

Figure 7-7
BGP redistribution into IGP

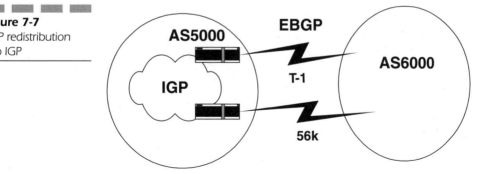

icy whereby the most important remote networks are accessed over the T-1 link and the remainder uses the 56k serial line. For security reasons, AS6000 only advertises networks to which AS5000 needs to connect. This also has the effect of reducing BGP routing overhead and also makes it feasible to redistribute these routes into the IGP domain. Hence, optimized routing as per policy can be achieved to each network in AS6000 from any router within AS5000.

If AS5000 were connecting to an ISP, then the situation would not be as straightforward. Learning the entire Internet routing table over EBGP from the ISP would place a significant strain on the resources of the EBGP routers. Redistributing all of these routes into the IGP so that each router within the enterprise network can have optimized routing to the Internet is almost certainly not an option due to the amount of routes.

A more realistic method of achieving some control over the path taken to the local ISP(s) is to accept some heavily used networks from the ISP and to use default routes for the remainder of the Internet. The routes accepted from the ISP can be filtered at the enterprise end of the link; however, it is preferable to arrange for the filtering to be performed by the ISP itself in order to prevent the unnecessary updates traversing the link from the ISP.

If BGP is redistributed into IGP, then it is likely that filtering is required to reduce routing overhead due to the very large BGP routing tables.

If redistribution or mutual redistribution is being performed between IGP and BGP, then care must be taken to avoid the possibility of routing loops. Each protocol should only redistribute routes that originated within its own routing domain. BGP should not redistribute routes that it learned from IGP back into IGP. The same must be true of routes redistributed from IGP into BGP. This can be accomplished through appropriate route filtering.

Consider the network shown in Figure 7-8. Routers R1 and R2 border the IGP and BGP domains. Mutual redistribution is configured between BGP

Figure 7-8
IGP/BGP mutual
redistribution

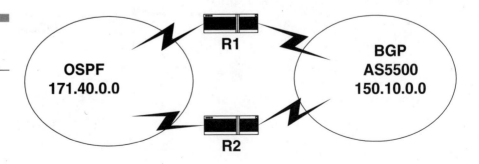

and OSPF on each router. A routing loop could occur if OSPF redistributed the 150.10.0.0 routes that it originally learned from BGP back into that protocol, or likewise, if BGP redistributed the 171.40.0.0 routes back into OSPF. Safeguards against such a scenario in each protocol exist. For example, OSPF will not redistribute external routes back into another protocol by default. However, given the potential adverse effect of a routing loop, these safeguards should not be relied upon alone. Route filtering should be configured so that each protocol will only redistribute local routes into the other protocol. For example, the 172.40.0.0 BGP routes should NOT be redistributed into OSPF, because they are originally local to OSPF.

Route filtering should be performed at the point of redistribution or mutual redistribution between BGP and IGP. This reduces the possibility of routing loops by preventing routes being advertised back into the protocol from which they were learned.

Another alternative is to accept BGP routes at the gateway router but only redistribute a default route into the IGP domain. This approach gives some control over what path is chosen when routing to the ISP(s) for particular networks. Sub-optimal routing may occur within the IGP domain when accessing the Internet gateway. In Figure 7-9, R1 and R2 access ISP1 and ISP2, respectively. If these gateway routers each receive BGP routes, then they are capable of making policy-based path selection decisions in relation to what link is to be chosen to route to the local ISP (that is, choose Link 1 or Link 2 for various destinations). That is the extent of the optimized routing that can be performed. Because R1 and R2 only advertise a

Figure 7-9
Default routing to
EPGP gateway

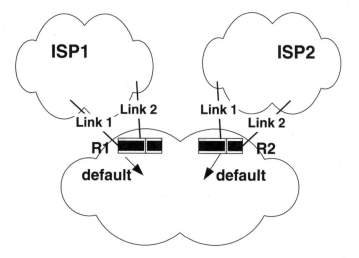

default route into the IGP domain, it is the IGP that will decide which default route has the lower metric and which ISP will be chosen. It should be decided at the design level whether it is worth running BGP on R1 and R2 purely so that they have control over the local link chosen to the ISP. The same effect could be achieved using static routes to the Internet networks in question.

BGP Path Selection and Manipulation

BGP Attributes

Until now, the ability of BGP to implement "routing policies" has been referred to a number of times. However, it has yet to be discussed how BGP performs this routing function. In order to explain this, the concept of BGP *attributes* must be introduced.

Most IGPs perform path selection using a particular type of routing metric. BGP does not use a single metric parameter; instead, it has multiple parameters that have different degrees of significance as well as differences in how they are distributed within BGP. These metric parameters are called *path attributes*. The ability to manipulate these attributes significantly empowers the network administrator in influencing BGP path selection and implementing routing policies.

BGP attributes describe key features of the BGP protocol, and in particular how it performs path selection. Before discussing the main BGP attributes, the categories into which these attributes are divided must be described.

■ Well-known or Optional

A well-known attribute is one that is described in an RFC standard and must be recognized by all BGP implementations. Well-known attributes are propagated among BGP neighbors.

An optional attribute is one that may be part of a non-standard or proprietary BGP implementation. Therefore, not all BGP implementations necessarily support or understand it. Certain supported optional attributes are propagated to BGP neighbors depending on the meaning of the attribute.

■ Mandatory or Discretionary

Well-known attributes are further classified as being mandatory or discretionary.

A mandatory attribute must be included as part of the BGP routing update.

A discretionary attribute does not necessarily have to appear as part of the route description in the update packet.

■ Transitive or Non-transitive

Optional attributes are classified as being transitive or non-transitive.

An optional transitive attribute is one that can be transparently passed on by a BGP router that does not recognize it.

A router that does not support or recognize it must delete an optional non-transitive attribute.

The main BGP attributes will now be described in terms of their operational and functional significance. The type or category that each attribute is described by will also be clarified. The relative significance of each of these attributes in influencing path selection will then be explained.

AS-path As a BGP update passes through an AS, that AS number gets appended to the update. Consider the case where a router receives an update that originated from a distant AS, and the update has traversed through a number of ASs before reaching the router in question.

That router will have path information associated with the route, which tracks each of the intermediate ASs. This is best illustrated by an example. In Figure 7-10, each of the routers advertises the network shown into BGP. The path information that Router B would have to get to 130.1.0.0 would be (10 30), to get to 180.11.0.0 the path is (10). Similarly, for Router C the path to 120.0.0.0 is (10 20), and to reach 180.11.0.0 the path is (10). What path information should Router A have for the routes to 120.0.0.0 and to the 130.1.0.0 network?

The AS-path attribute is a well-known mandatory attribute. It therefore must be included as part of the route descriptor in a BGP update and will be recognized by all BGP implementations.

Figure 7-10
BGP AS-path example

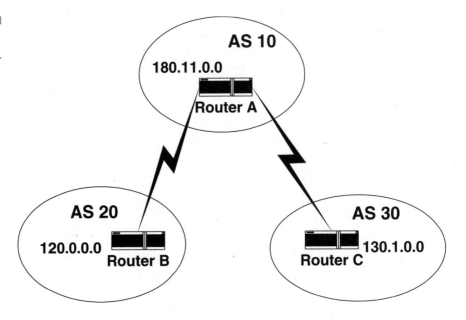

This attribute is central to BGP's loop free operation. A BGP router will not accept a route that includes its own AS within the AS-path attribute. Such an instance would mean that the route has already traversed that AS and may therefore create a routing loop.

To ensure loop free EBGP routing, a BGP router will not accept a route whose AS-path attribute includes its own AS number.

Origin The origin attribute is also categorized as a well-known and mandatory attribute. It is included in all BGP routing updates and its purpose is to indicate the origin of the path information. It can have one of three values:

- IGP: This indicates that the network was redistributed from an IGP into BGP.

- EGP: The origin is EGP. EGP is the near-obsolete predecessor to BGP. Therefore, this origin is unlikely to be encountered on most modern networks.

- INCOMPLETE: The origin is unknown. This can happen when a static route is redistributed into BGP.

Next-hop The next-hop attribute is a well-known mandatory attribute that has already been discussed in the context of IBGP. It is the IP address of the next hop associated with a BGP update. The fact that IBGP advertises the same next hop that it learns from EBGP can potentially cause problems with a downstream IBGP neighbor if that neighbor has no route to the next hop. This issue with the next-hop attribute was illustrated earlier in the example of the network shown in Figure 7-4.

Weight Weight is an optional attribute originally adopted by Cisco Systems; however, the BGP implementation of other vendors such as Juniper Networks also recognizes this attribute. It influences path selection from a router when more than one route to the destination network is present. It is configurable on a per-neighbor basis but has no significance outside of that router. Weights with higher numerical values are preferred. In Figure 7-11, R1 has two possible paths to 140.1.0.0. It will chose the path via R3 because the weight associated with this path is higher. The value of the weight attribute can be set on a per-neighbor basis or can be applied to a particular AS-path. For example on R1, the weight could be set to 30 for all updates received from R3, or alternatively, this weight value might just be applied to routes that originated in AS670. How the router is configured depends on the policy that is to be implemented.

The default weight on a Cisco router for a route that is originated by the local router is 32,768, and it is zero for all other routes. The weight attribute is never propagated between BGP neighbors.

Local Preference The local preference attribute is distributed between routers in the same AS. It is designed to influence the choice of a preferred

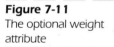

Figure 7-11
The optional weight
attribute

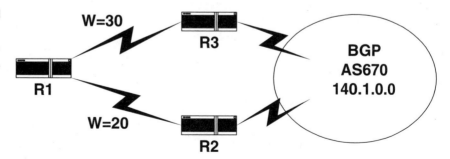

exit point from the AS. A higher value for this attribute is preferred—a typical default value is 100. As always, vendor documentation should be carefully checked to verify the default values of BGP attributes. The local preference is not distributed to EBGP neighbors. Local preference is a well-known discretionary attribute.

In Figure 7-12, R2 will be the preferred exit point from AS5000 because it has applied a local preference of 200 to all updates it receives from its EBGP neighbor in AS700. This value is higher than R1's local preference for routes to this network, so R1 will send its traffic that is destined for AS700 to R2. Each router will know of the other's local preference value because this attribute is distributed among IBGP neighbors.

The local preference can be manipulated with a certain degree of discrimination. Its value can be altered for certain routes that have a particular entry in their AS-path attribute. For example, a certain local preference value could be applied to all routes that originated in AS200 or have tra-

Figure 7-12
The local preference attribute

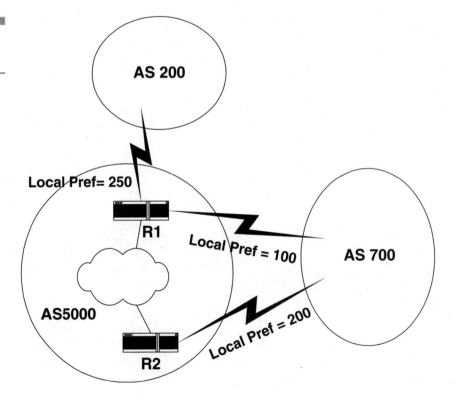

versed AS300. Returning to Figure 7-12, a policy such as this might be applied in order to make R1 the preferred exit point from AS5000 if the traffic is destined for AS200. This is because R1 is closer to AS200 than R2, and it becomes the exit point if AS200 is the destination. Therefore, a policy is on the network whereby R2 is the preferred exit point for traffic destined for AS700, and R1 is the exit point for traffic to AS200. This manipulation is achieved by appropriate router configuration. On the Cisco router, a feature known as route-maps is employed. Another example is with Juniper routers where the corresponding feature is called the Policy Language.

The manipulation of the local preference attribute can clearly be used to ensure that the optimal path to the next hop is chosen (of course, there is not necessarily any control over routing decisions after that next-hop has been reached). Apart from optimized routing, local preference manipulation can be applied to achieve load balancing. If two equal cost exit points from the AS exist, then certain destinations can be given a higher local preference for the first path and other destinations could have a higher local preference for the second path. This gives the network administrator more control over the manner in which load balancing is performed on traffic exiting the AS.

Remember:
- The local preference can be manipulated such that different AS exit points can be chosen from particular destinations. This can be used to provide optimized routing to the next hop. It can also be used for load balancing.

Metric The metric attribute (also known as the *Multi Exit Discriminator* or MED) is an optional non-transitive attribute. It is advertised to EBGP neighbors, and its purpose is to influence the path selection for entering the AS from another AS. A lower metric value is preferred. The metric attribute is distributed within an AS in order to decide on the best path into the AS from which it was received. The metric is not propagated on to a third AS; instead, it is reset to its default value of zero. This is different to most IGPs where the metric increments with the updates as they propagate throughout the entire routing domain.

In the network shown in Figure 7-13, R1 receives updates about the 152.16.0.0 network from two sources in AS 20 and from one source in AS 40. R1 will choose R2 as the next hop to 152.16.0.0 because R2 advertised the route with a lower metric than R3.

Generally, neighboring EBGP routers will only compare metrics associated with a particular route if the updates come from the same AS. This is because the metric attribute is most fundamentally intended to set the best entry point into a particular AS. Sometimes in order to execute certain routing policies, it may be desirable to have a router compare metrics for a route that it learns about from more than one AS. This can be achieved through appropriate router configuration.

In Figure 7-13, if R1 were configured to compare metrics for a route regardless of the AS it received the update from, it would choose R4 as the next hop to 152.16.0.0. Without enabling this command, R1 could not compare the metric advertised by R4 to that of R2. It could only choose R4 as the next hop to 152.16.0.0 if another attribute (such as local preference) overrode the metric attribute. The hierarchy of the relative importance of BGP attributes is outlined in the next section of this chapter.

Community The community attribute is a means of grouping a set of destinations so that a common policy can be applied to them. It is an optional transitive attribute. Therefore, if a router receives this attribute in an update and does not understand communities, it will simply pass it on transparently in its own update. The community attribute is mainly, but not exclusively, used by ISPs in order to set routing policies.

Outbound or inbound updates can be tagged as being part of a particular community. One or more other BGP routers can then be configured to recognize this community label and to implement a subsequent routing policy. All updates to or from a particular neighbor can be tagged as being part

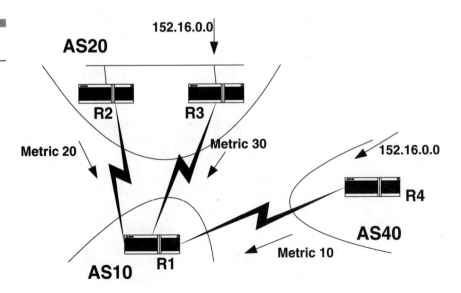

Figure 7-13
The metric attribute

of a community or, as is frequently the case, just selected destinations can be placed in a community. This attribute does not necessarily have any physical boundaries and is not restricted to one network or to a single AS.

The following are three predefined communities, which can be set in BGP routing updates in order to implement a particular policy:

- No-export: A route that is in this community should not be advertised to EBGP peers, that is, it should not be exported beyond the AS.

- No-advertise: Marking a route as being in this community prevents it from being advertised further to any BGP peers (internal or external).

- Internet: Every router belongs to the Internet community. Therefore, this community places no restraints on an advertised route.

Consider Figure 7-14 and assume that the following policy must be implemented. The 131.7.0.0 network is to be advertised from AS200 to AS300 where it is to be distributed among IBGP peers, but it is to be filtered from AS400. A number of methods to implement this policy exists, one of which is the use of BGP communities.

R2 could be configured to tag its updates to R3 about 131.7.0.0 as being part of the "no-export" community. When R3 receives updates about 131.7.0.0 from R2, it will not propagate the destination to EBGP peers; however, it will be distributed to IBGP peers. If it were required to prevent R3 from advertising the 131.7.0.0 network within AS300, R2 would be configured to set this destination as part of the "no-advertise" community in its updates to R3. Another example of BGP community filtering will be given later in this chapter when case studies of attribute manipulation are discussed.

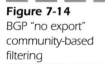

Figure 7-14
BGP "no export" community-based filtering

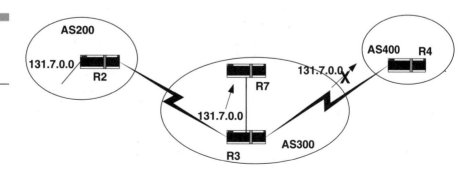

BGP Route Selection

The BGP protocol by default chooses one best path to a destination and propagates that path to its neighbors. BGP routers can also be configured to forward packets over more than one path in a load-balancing manner.

Unlike other routing protocols, a number of different parameters or attributes that BGP can use when deciding route selection exists. The following is a hierarchical list of the attributes that BGP uses for path selection beginning with the most important attributes:

- The path is ignored if the next hop is inaccessible.
- Highest weight is preferred (if this optional proprietary attribute is in use on the router).
- Highest local preference is preferred.
- Prefer a route that has originated from the router that is advertising it.
- Shortest AS path.

    This literally means the path with the least number of AS entries in it. For example, (20 30) is a shorter path to AS 30 than (10 20 30).

- Lowest Origin Code (IGP > EGP > INCOMPLETE).
- Lowest Metric or MED value.
- External path is preferred to Internal. The administrative distance for an EBGP route is 20 and 200 for an IBGP route.
- If only internal paths exist and IGP synchronization is turned off, the path through the closest IGP neighbor is preferred.
- Choose the path through the router with the *lowest* BGP router ID.

    The BGP router ID is calculated the same as an OSPF router ID, that is, the highest active IP address on the router with a loopback interface overriding physical interfaces.

BGP Filtering

All routers within the industry support a powerful range of BGP filtering techniques. These can be divided into two categories: route filtering and AS-path filtering.

Route Filtering By default, a BGP router will advertise all routes in its BGP table to each of its EBGP peers. All routes will also be advertised to IBGP peers if they were not learned via another IBGP peer or if the router is acting as a route-reflector.

It is often undesirable to advertise all routes to each neighbor. For example, a customer connecting to an ISP may only want to receive partial routes from the ISP and use a default route to connect to the remainder of the Internet. The routes advertised by the ISP could be destinations to which the customer frequently connects. This route filtering saves on router resources and BGP routing overhead.

Route filters take on different formats and are called different names depending on the router vendor; however, they all perform the same fundamental tasks. The filters are configured on a per-neighbor basis and can be used to filter inbound or outbound updates.

Refer to the example of Figure 7-14, where it was required to prevent the 131.7.0.0 network from being advertised into AS400. The same policy could be implemented using route filters. R3 could apply an outbound route filter against its neighbor definition for R4. This filter would block 131.7.0.0 and allow all other networks through. The same result could be achieved by configuring the same filter inbound on R4 in relation to its neighbor definition of R3. This is less favorable because it means that the 131.7.0.0 update would unnecessarily cross the WAN link before being blocked.

AS-path Filtering AS-path filtering enables a filtering policy to be put in place based on the characteristics of the AS-path the route has traversed. The filtering criteria are compared against the AS-path attribute in the BGP update.

As with route filtering, the conditions can be applied against inbound or outbound updates on a per-neighbor basis. AS-path filtering can potentially be based on the following criteria:

- The first AS in the AS-path attribute

  In relation to the network displayed in Figure 7-14, assume that the policy to be implemented is that no EBGP routes should be accepted into AS400. The AS-path that R4 sees to AS300 is (300), and the path to AS200 is (300 200). Therefore, this policy could be implemented by configuring R4 with an inbound filter that blocks any route whose AS-path begins with 300.

■ The last AS in the AS-path attribute

The last AS in the AS-path attribute associated with a route is the AS in which the route originated. Hence, AS-path filtering can be used to accept or deny routes that originate in a particular AS. Now consider the case where a different policy must be implemented on the network in Figure 7-14. It is required to block any routes that originated in AS200 from being advertised into AS400. This could be accomplished with an inbound filter on R4 that blocks any AS-path whose last entry is 200. Alternatively (and preferably), an outbound filter could be configured on R3 that prevents any route originating in AS200 from being advertised to R4.

■ Any AS that appears in the AS-path attribute

If a route to a destination traverses a particular AS, then that AS will appear in the AS-path attribute for that route. This can also be used as a filtering condition. A BGP router can be configured to forward or filter any routes that include a particular AS within the AS-path attribute.

Returning to Figure 7-14 and the original policy requirement to block any EBGP routes from being distributed into AS400. AS400 receives all of its EBGP routes from AS300. Therefore, a filter could be configured on R4 that does not accept any routes that include AS300 in the AS-path attribute; this, of course, covers all EBGP routes that R4 learns.

Simpler and more realistic ways to achieve this policy exist, such as simply configuring R3 to not propagate any BGP information to R4. However, this example illustrates the use of AS-path filtering based on a single AS number included in that attribute. This is a powerful filtering technique that has many potential applications. For example, it could be used to hide a path via a particular AS in the interests of optimal routing or security.

■ Routes that are local to the AS

A BGP router can also make forwarding or filtering decisions for all routes that are local to its own AS. This has an application when a customer is multi-homing to two ISPs for redundancy as shown in Figure 7-15. If BGP is run on the connection to each ISP, then a possibility exists that the ISPs may transit traffic through the customer's public AS when communicating with other routes in the

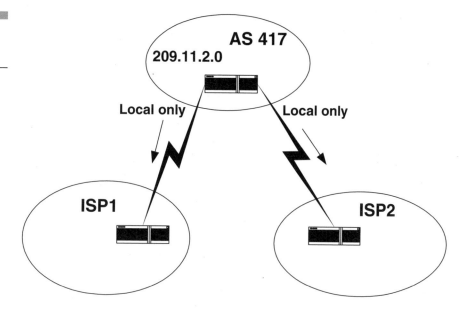

Figure 7-15
ISP multi-homing without transitting

Internet. This phenomenon can be safeguarded against if the customer's AS (AS417 in this example) only advertises routes that originate in its own AS to each of the ISP peers. All other routes are filtered; therefore, neither ISP can use AS417 as a transit to other networks because the ISPs will only see AS417 as the next hop to the customer's local network 209.11.2.0.

Attribute Manipulation and Policy-Based Routing

In the last section, some applications of route filtering and path filtering were discussed. BGP not only incorporates powerful filtering techniques but also a capability to manipulate attributes in order to influence routing decisions and implement network policies. Again, the exact manner in which this is done varies with the different platforms, but the principle and effect do not. On Cisco routers, route-maps have the power to manipulate attributes. The equivalent feature on Juniper devices is Policy Language.

Attributes can be manipulated based on source address as well as destination address. For example in Figure 7-16, R1 could be configured to send traffic from 1.1.1.0 destined for 150.10.0.0 over Path A. Likewise, traffic sourced from 2.2.2.0 could be sent with a next hop of Path B.

Figure 7-16
Policy-based routing
scenario

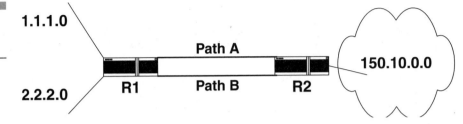

Policy-based routing provides the capability to make routing decisions based on source address as well as destination address.

Although BGP undoubtedly has a powerful capability to support policy-based routing, it is very important to remember that these policies can only be strictly implemented on a hop-by-hop basis. Beyond influencing path selection on a hop-by-hop basis, a routing policy can be potentially implemented within an entire AS, because one administration has, by definition, control over the AS. Policies can only be extended beyond the AS through agreement between the corresponding administrations. It is appropriate to illustrate this point with an example.

Policy Based Routing Examples

MED and Local Preference   Consider the network in Figure 7-17. AS300 wants to influence the path that AS200 takes when sending traffic between the two ASs. Routes that are advertised over the T-3 to R21 are given a MED value of 1, which is therefore preferable to the T-1 path MED value of 10. This policy can however be overridden at the next hop particularly because the next hop is in another AS and hence under different administrative control.

The administrator in AS200 could decide to send all inter-AS traffic over the T-1 link. The policy could be implemented by tagging all routes received from R30 with a higher local preference than those received from R31. This will override the policy set by AS300 because local preference is more significant than metric in the BGP path selection attribute hierarchy.

Clearly, it is not a good idea to send all traffic between AS200 and AS300 over the T-1 link; however, it may be prudent to utilize this link to some

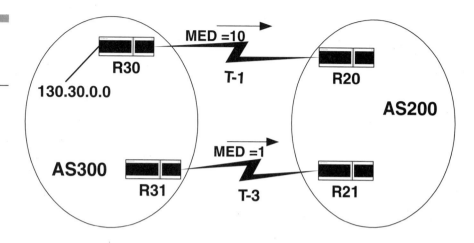

Figure 7-17
MED and local
preference
manipulation

extent. If the T-3 were the exclusive preferred link, then it would carry all traffic with the T-1 being idle. During periods of heavy traffic, the T-3 may experience congestion and a better quality of service would be experienced on the T-1 link, to implement a policy such as this, cooperation between the two administrations is required. The AS200 administrator could, for example, give a higher local preference to the 130.30.0.0 networks that is received over the T-1. Hence, the T-1 will be chosen to route to this network only.

The principle of routing certain traffic over the higher cost path in order to avoid congestion is an important principle in Internet routing. New technologies such as *MultiProtocol Label Switching* (MPLS) are also capable of employing this technique. A discussion on MPLS is beyond the charter of this book and would represent a digression; however, a section on this subject is included on the author's Web page. The appropriate URL is `http://www.cormaclong.com/intec.html`. Another possible reason why specific traffic may be sent over the higher cost path is to avoid a particular instance of sub-optimal routing. For example, the T-1 path may happen to represent the shortest path to the 130.30.0.0 network from AS200.

Remember:
- Attributes can only be manipulated on a hop-by-hop basis. For example, you cannot necessarily control how to remote AS routes to your AS.
- Specific traffic can be routed over a higher cost path in order to avoid congestion or a specific case of sub-optimal routing.

AS-path Manipulation   Dummy AS entries can be inserted in the AS-path attribute that is part of the BGP routing update. Consider again the example where it is required to use the T-1 path to 130.30.0.0 from AS200 without manipulating local preference. R21 could be configured to prepend a "dummy" AS onto the AS-path attribute received from R31 for the 130.30.0.0 network. If the value 650 were prepended, then the path to 130.30.0.0 via the T-3 would appear as (300 650), while the path via the T-1 remains as (300). The shorter AS path would then be preferred. Note that a shorter AS path will override a favorable metric, but it will not take precedence over the local preference attribute. This is in line with the BGP attribute route selection hierarchy.

AS entries can be stripped from the AS-path attribute as well as being added to the beginning or end of the AS path. The main application of this is to strip private AS numbers before they propagate through an ISP.

The AS-path manipulation features just described are supported to varying degrees with different router vendors as the techniques have yet to be fully standardized.

Community-based Filtering   BGP communities present a powerful tool for implementing policy-based routing, as the attribute is transitive and can potentially be passed transparently across multiple ASs.

Notice the network displayed in Figure 7-18. Within AS500, the group of destinations that make up the 150.50.0.0 network could be tagged as being part of a particular community. The updates relating to 150.50.0.0 could be tagged as community COM1 when advertised by R55 to R60. This community could be acted on in AS600, or alternatively, it could be transparently passed through depending on the policy requirement. Assume that the 150.50.0.0 network is advertised in AS600 but no policy action is taken on

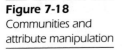

Figure 7-18
Communities and attribute manipulation

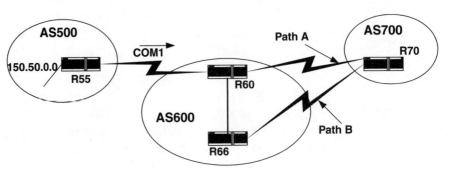

the COM1 community. This update is sent into AS700 over two paths, A and B. Within AS700, a policy is configured for COM1. Router R70 could be configured to check for the community COM1 and take a particular action. For example, destinations learned over Path A could be assigned a higher local preference if they are members of the COM1 community. Essentially this means that the 150.50.0.0 network will be accessed over Path A from AS700.

BGP communities provide a lot of flexibility in terms of where the community is defined and what routers manipulate attributes for that community. Note however that the same issue of another AS being capable of overriding the community polices again holds true.

BGP Resilience and Redundancy

Some enterprise networks connect to multiple ISPs to obtain Internet access. This is called multi-homing and is usually done for two reasons:

- Redundancy and Resilience
- Optimized routing—certain destinations should be accessed using one ISP instead of another because it represents a shorter path. This might be a requirement if the Internet gateways are geographically dispersed on the organization's network.

The manner of the logical design of a multi-homed network can be divided into three basic categories:

- The use of default routes to each provider
- A combination of BGP-derived routes and default routes
- Exclusive use of BGP-derived route to all ISPs

Each of these approaches will be discussed in more detail.

Default Routes to Each ISP

Consider the network displayed in Figure 7-19. The customer network connects to ISP1 and ISP2 but does not itself use BGP. Instead, it receives a default route from each ISP that is redistributed into the customer's IGP. The customer network administrator has an option here. The two default routes could be redistributed into IGP and each router on the customer net-

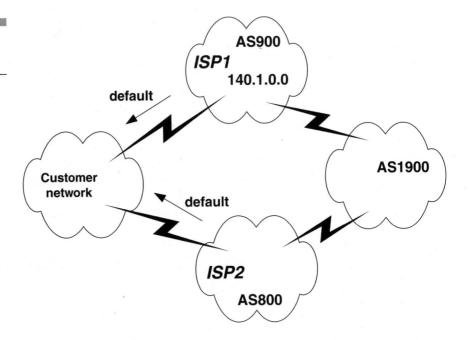

work would use the default route that it sees with the lower IGP metric. Thus, some routers in the customer's network would see ISP1 as the least cost path while others would use ISP2. This is a resilient implementation where each path is equally likely to be used.

The other alternative is to weigh one default route ahead of the other at the two points of redistribution into the IGP. This could be achieved by manipulating the administrative distance. This would mean that the entire customer network would use one ISP ahead of the other, and the backup ISP would only be used in the event of a loss of IP connectivity to the primary ISP.

Regardless of whether the default routes are weighted or equal cost, this approach presents similar pros and cons. The main advantage is the reduced CPU utilization and memory requirements on the customer routers because BGP is not being availed of. Routing overhead is also reduced on the links to the two ISPs. Technical simplicity is also an operational advantage that is not to be underestimated.

The disadvantages of using default routes include the possibility for suboptimal routing and also the loss of control in policy implementation. To expand on the latter point first, because the customer is not using BGP attribute, manipulation cannot be used to select a particular ISP for a particular destination. A possible workaround for this is the use of static routes for those specific destinations. These static routes could then be redistributed into the IGP, and they will take preference over the default routes because they represent specific routes to the destinations in question.

The other issue is the potential for sub-optimal routing. For example, routers within the customer network that see the default route from ISP2 with a better IGP metric will choose this as the path to 140.1.0.0 even though this destination relates to an *application service provider* (ASP) that is local to ISP1.

In some cases, a corporation homes to multiple ISPs that are located in different countries. If the company's worldwide enterprise network is divided into multiple regions that have a certain degree of autonomy, then it is likely that default routes to the Internet would suffice and produce few instances of sub-optimal routing.

Note that the path that other networks in the Internet take back to the customer is decided by the BGP routing between the different ISPs on the Internet.

Remember:

■ The use of default routes to multiple ISPs may result in sub-optimal rouing. This is less likely to be a problem in instances where the ISPs are located in different countries.

Default Routes in Tandem with BGP

Another method of implementing multi-homing is for the customer to run BGP, but not only accept a limited set of Internet routes from the ISPs. The route filtering should take place at the ISP in order to reduce routing overhead on the WAN links. The networks that the customer accepts might typically be ones that are frequently accessed for business reasons.

Because only a limited set of routes are accepted into the customer's BGP AS, the potential adverse effects on router memory requirements and CPU utilization are reduced to moderate levels. The customer can manipulate BGP attributes in order to select the appropriate ISP for specific destinations. For example in Figure 7-20, the update received for the 140.1.0.0 network from ISP1 can be given a higher local preference to ensure optimized routing to this destination. If attributes such as local preference are not manipulated, the exit path from the customer's AS is usually the shortest AS-path to that destination.

If the customer is going to use BGP, then an important point centers around the choice between a public or a private AS number. This is particularly significant if the customer is planning to multi-home to more than

Figure 7-20
Multi-homing with
BGP and route
filtering

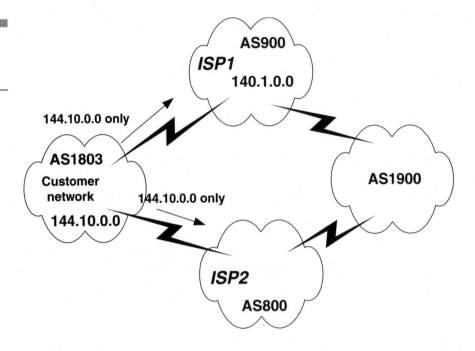

Figure 7-20
Multi-homing with
BGP and route
filtering

one ISP. If a private AS number is used, an agreement can be made with the ISP to literally strip or translate the private AS number that it receives from the customer. However with multi-homing, each ISP must deal with the private AS number in the same manner which can require some coordination between each of the relevant parties.

Remember:
■ The use of a private AS number can require a lot of coordination when multi-homing.

Although a public AS number may be desirable for the reason just mentioned, it does result in the potential for the customer's network to become a transit AS. In the context of Figure 7-20, a possibility exists that ISP1 and ISP2 could route through AS1803 (that is, the customer's AS) when accessing other networks on the Internet. This would significantly increase the BGP-related overhead within the customer's AS, along with consuming much of its bandwidth. For example, ISP2 could potentially send traffic destined for the 140.1.0.0 network via AS1803. This issue can be averted by configuring the EBGP routers in AS1803 to only advertise local networks, that is, ones that have originated in AS1803. For the network in Figure 7-20, the customer BGP routers are configured to only advertise the local registered Class B 144.10.0.0 for this exact reason.

Remember:

■ When using a public AS number in a multi-homed topology, the possibility of becoming a transit network can be averted by only advertising local routes to each of the ISPs.

Receiving Full BGP Routes

By receiving a full BGP routing table from each ISP, optimized routing is effected for all Internet destinations. This is usually the shortest AS path to each destination. This can be overridden by altering the local preference for certain destinations. The price paid for optimized routing is the extensive router CPU and memory resources that are required to support a full Internet routing table. Routing overhead on the WAN links to the ISPs is also maximized due to the fact that a full routing table is being exchanged.

It is important to be clear about what "optimized" routing means in this context. The customer's AS can choose the best exit path to each destination. This is usually the shortest AS path, but the customer can override this path choice by implementing an alternate policy.

The path choice that the customer can control is from its local AS only. Control is purely on a hop-by-hop basis. Therefore, one possibility is that other policies may be implemented on one or more interim ASs along the path to the destination. It is of course unlikely that these policies would deliberately promote sub-optimal routing.

The other issue may seem obvious but it is worth mentioning. The customer still has no control over the path that destination networks take back to its own AS. This is determined by the normal BGP routing attributes in the Internet. No guarantee exists that traffic relating to a particular Web-server session will re-enter the customer's AS over the same path that it exited. This is termed *asymmetrical routing* and is not necessarily a problem in itself, although symmetrical routing is likely to produce smaller variations in delay. Symmetrical routing on a multi-homed network is more likely to occur if one link is used as primary and the other as backup, rather than the two acting in a load-sharing mode. One instance where asymmetrical routing can be a problem is if each path has a different firewall. Appropriate firewall design must be used to ensure that one firewall does not block traffic on re-entry because it did not see that same session exiting the AS. The subject of load balancing across firewalls is revisited in detail in Chapter 10, "Network Security."

Scalable AS Routing

Certain scalability issues are faced as a BGP network grows. Potential problems can be encountered as an AS grows if IBGP is being implemented. The requirement for a large number of IBGP or EBGP peer relationships places strain on the routers and the network as a whole. The routing overhead associated with receipt and distribution of a large BGP routing table also puts strain on the system. ISPs and corporations that use a full BGP implementation constantly face these issues. Some of the solutions that can be put in place to improve BGP scalability will now be described.

Route Aggregation

The problem of IP address exhaustion was the main motivation behind the development of *Classless InterDomain Routing* (CIDR). Companies that had a requirement for more than one Class C network, but who could not avail of a Class B, instead had a contiguous block of Class C networks assigned by the InterNIC. For example, 203.10.4.0 to 203.10.7.0 constitutes a contiguous block of four Class C networks. This block of networks can be summarized or aggregated into one route that is not based on Class. In this case, the aggregated route would be 203.10.4.0/22.

BGP version 4 supports CIDR and route aggregation because its updates include the prefix length along with the route. Therefore, aggregation can occur on any bit boundary and does not have to relate to Class.

The rules for implementing route aggregation in BGP are the same as for route summarization in an IGP. The benefits are also similar, but even more critical, given the size of the Internet routing table. Apart from reducing routing table sizes, route aggregation in BGP can help reduce the effect of route flapping. A BGP router that is performing aggregation will not send updates to its neighbors if a specific member of the aggregated route changes state. Hence, as with IGP route summarization, aggregation has the effect of containing the propagation of routing updates and improving the stability of the BGP domain.

CIDR is also called *supernetting* because the aggregated routes often have masks that are shorter than the equivalent Class mask. For example, the Class B networks 150.9.0.0, 150.10.0.0, and 150.56.0.0 could be summarized as 150.0.0.0/8, provided that this "over-summarization" does not create a conflict elsewhere in the domain. The term "over-summarization" refers to a summary statement that covers a greater range of routes than is contained on the network. The 150.0.0.0/8 statement covers any destination that has 150 as its first octet. The creation of such a summary route would create a problem if other destinations that had 150 as their first octet value resided elsewhere in the routing domain.

BGP routers can be configured to propagate only the summary route or alternatively, the summary route along with the specific routes. If a customer is multi-homed to the same ISP as in Figure 7-21, then he/she may want to advertise the summary route along with the specific routes so that the ISP will have an optimal path to each of its specific networks. For example, the customer may want to advertise the specific routes over Link 1 in order to make that the preferable path for inbound traffic from the ISP. If Link 1 fails, traffic will be routed over Link 2 because the summary route has been advertised over this path. Remember that BGP routes to the most specific prefix match regardless of attribute, just like an IGP. The ISP is likely to only advertise the summary route throughout the Internet in order to minimize routing overhead.

The loss of detail associated with route aggregation can create a potential for routing loops. BGP advertises the origin of an aggregated route as the AS where the route aggregation was configured. Most BGP implemen-

Figure 7-21
BGP route
aggregation

AS900

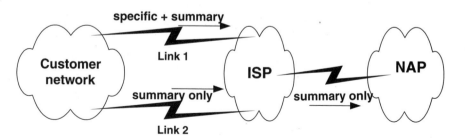

tations support the ability to carry AS-path information relating to the specific routes also. This capability should be clarified by consulting appropriate vendor documentation before configuring route aggregation.

Route Reflectors

A BGP router will not propagate a route that it learns from an IBGP neighbor onto another IBGP neighbor. This can place restraints on an administration that requires the propagation of BGP updates through the AS such as an ISP or a large enterprise network.

One possibility is to run EBGP at the edge of the AS and redistribute BGP into an IGP core. This would require mutual redistribution between BGP and IGP at each edge router, which is not advisable for stability and scalability reasons, as have already been mentioned.

Running an IBGP full-mesh is another possible solution that is not without problems. This requires alot of BGP peer statements on each router. The overhead results from the maintenance of several TCP sessions and the replication of routing traffic to each of these neighbors. This presents a fundamental scalability problem for IBGP. The number of peer relationships required to provide a full mesh for N routers within an AS can be calculated from the following formula:

`N × (N-1)/2`

For example, to provide a full-mesh for 10 routers would require 45 peer sessions within the AS, whereas 15 routers would require 105 IBGP sessions.

A more scalable solution to this problem is the concept of route reflectors. If a router is configured as a route reflector, it will pass BGP routing updates between certain IBGP peers called route reflector clients. For example in Figure 7-22, RRS is configured as a route reflector and RRC1 and RRC2 are route-reflector clients. EBGP information that RRC1 learns will be passed to RRS as in the normal course of events. However, because RRS is a route reflector, it will pass this information on to RRC2. Similarly, RRS will pass BGP updates from RRC2 to RRC1. The concept of route-reflectors enables a relaxation of the IBGP rule preventing the propagation of routing information learned from one IBGP onto a third IBGP peer. The group of routers shown in Figure 7-22 consisting of a route reflector and two clients is a called a *Cluster* and is designated with a Cluster ID.

Figure 7-22
BGP route reflector
cluster

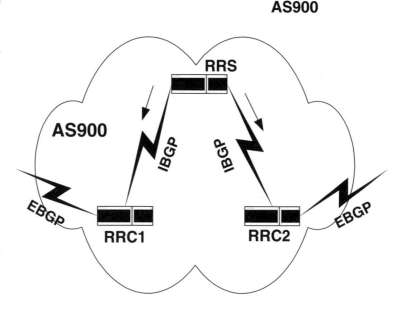

At this point, it is appropriate to dispel some popular misconceptions about route reflectors:

- Normal packet forwarding as dictated by the BGP routing attribute is not affected. Route reflectors simply modify the manner in which routing information is distributed within an AS. It should also be noted that route reflectors in no way modify the BGP attributes. For example, the IBGP next-hop attribute remains unchanged as with normal IBGP operation.

- It is possible for a router that is part of a route-reflector cluster to also have "normal" IBGP and EBGP peer relationships with other routers that do not use route reflectors.

- The normal rules of split-horizon still apply. In other words, a route-reflector server will not send routes back to the same client from which they were learned.

Within a cluster, the route reflector must be fully meshed with all route-reflector clients. The clients themselves cannot be fully meshed as it may create routing loops and would defeat the purpose of having route-reflectors.

The *Originator-ID* is an optional non-transitive attribute that identifies the originator of a route within the AS. This attribute prevents routing loops created by a poor logical or physical configuration of the cluster. A router within the cluster that receives a route containing its own router ID as the originator will discard the route.

Multiple route reflectors can be used for redundancy within the cluster as shown in Figure 7-23. In this case, a Cluster ID must be configured to prevent the unnecessary looping of routing information. The purpose of the Cluster ID is to enable route reflectors to recognize updates from other route-reflectors within the same cluster. It also enables a large AS to be divided into multiple clusters.

An AS that contains multiple clusters is shown in Figure 7-24. R1, R2, and R3 are the route-reflector servers for clusters 1, 2, and 3, respectively. They must be fully meshed in IBGP. Notice that some route-reflector servers and some clients from different clusters are also running EBGP. This in no way violates any design rules. A route-reflector server has a relationship with its clients within the cluster and also with non-clients. The

Figure 7-23
Route reflector resilience

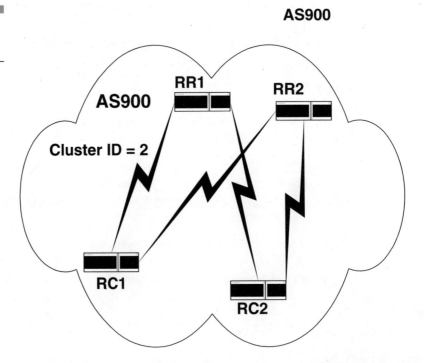

non-clients can be route reflectors in other clusters and possibly EBGP peers. If a route reflector receives an update from a client, it will reflect it to all other clients and non-clients. An update that is received from a non-client will be reflected only to the clients within the cluster. It does not have to be sent to other non-clients because a full-mesh exists between the different route-reflector servers. In the specific case of a route reflector receiving an update from an EBGP peer, it will reflect the update to all clients and its other non-clients.

The following summarizes the transfer of routing information shown in Figure 7-24:

- A route reflector receives updates from clients and non-clients (that can be other router reflectors or EBGP peers).
- Updates from clients are reflected to non-clients and clients (excluding the originator as per normal split-horizon).
- Updates from other route reflectors are propagated to clients.
- Updates from EBGP peers are propagated to clients and to other route reflectors.

Figure 7-24
Multipel route-reflector clusters

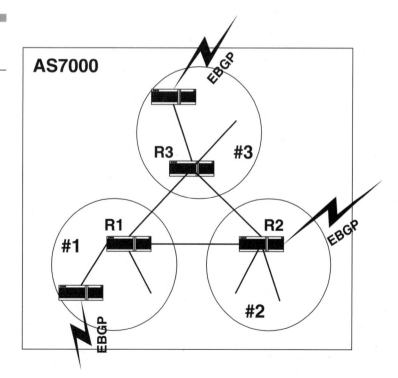

Route Reflector Design and Migration Issues

■ Ensure that adequate resources are on the route-reflector servers.
Route-reflector servers should not be over burdened with too many
clients in the cluster, because they may also have to maintain IBGP
peer relationship with other route reflectors and any other BGP
sessions that they may have. This gets back to the limiting factor
associated with too many BGP peer sessions. The route reflector must
have adequate memory and CPU resources to handle the task.

■ Follow the physical topology
All route-reflector clients should directly connect to their route-
reflector server. This type of logical configuration would be in line with
the physical topology. Otherwise, the IGP may have to be relied upon
to resolve the next hop, which is undesirable and may result in routing
loops.

■ Align physical and logical redundancy
In a cluster that has multiple route reflectors for redundancy, there
should be physical connectivity from all clients to each of the route-
reflectors. For example in Figure 7-23, if RC1 and RC2 did not *each*
have a direct connection to *both* RR1 and RR2, then there would be no
physical redundancy. This is a common mistake among administrators,
and it effectively means additional overhead on the route reflectors
without providing any real redundancy.

■ Migration rather than replacement
One of the attractions of route reflectors is that they are reasonably
straightforward to configure and roll out on the network. However as
with any significant change in a network's logical configuration,
multiple route reflectors and clusters should be implemented through
migration rather than in one big network change.

  ▪ The route-reflectors themselves should first be chosen based on the
    criteria already discussed.

  ▪ The client-server relationships within the cluster should then be
    configured, and finally, any unnecessary IBGP full-mesh peer
    connections should be removed from the cluster.

  ▪ A second route reflector can then be configured for redundancy if this
    is part of the design plan.

  ▪ This procedure is then repeated for other clusters.

BGP Confederations and Private AS

The concept of BGP confederations provides another possible method of resolving the scaling issues presented by the requirement for an IBGP full-mesh. The AS can be broken up or partitioned into multiple sub-ASs, and EBGP can be run between each sub-AS. This type of logical topology is displayed in Figure 7-25, where AS200 has been partitioned into three sub-ASs: 65000, 65010, and 65020. AS200 is then said to be a BGP confederation. These sub-AS numbers are all private, which is a typical scenario because the sub-AS numbers are not visible outside AS200. For example, R4 will be configured as an EBGP peer of AS200, *not* AS65000.

By dividing the AS into multiple sub-ASs, the requirement for full IBGP peering is eliminated. An IBGP full-mesh is only required within each sub-AS. It is important to note that although, strictly speaking, EBGP is run between the sub-ASs, IBGP attributes such as MED and next-hop are conserved within the federation just as in a normal IBGP domain.

Remember:
- Attributes such as MED and next hop are conserved across the BGP confederation just as in a normal IBGP domain.

The advantage that confederations offer over route reflectors is that no single routers have the additional overhead associated with being a route

Figure 7-25
BGP confederation

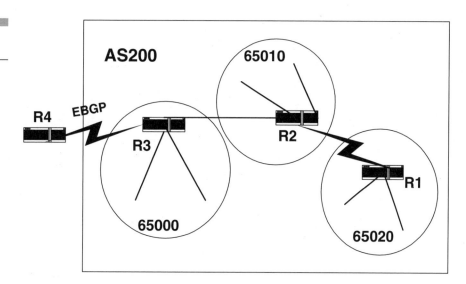

reflector. The downside of confederations is that they are more complex to configure and maintain, and this added complexity can reduce their flexibility.

Confederations also have some niche applications apart from simply eliminating the requirement for a full IBGP mesh. For the network shown in Figure 7-25, the EBGP connection to R4 could be to another ISP or the NAP because the private AS-number cannot propagate through the Internet. The use of the sub-ASs is potentially useful for segregating private networks or providing a degree of isolation between ASs.

Consider the example of a customer running BGP to its ISP. The ISP may not want to waste a public registered AS number for a small-to medium-sized client. Without using a public AS number and running EBGP to the client, three options exist:

1. Run IBGP to the customer.

2. Run EBGP to a private AS number for the client. The private AS number would have to be stripped off or translated by the ISP. This is quite possible but is not a standardized technique and can present difficulties if the client is multi-homing to multiple ISPs. Extensive coordination is required between the three parties to ensure that each ISP manipulates the private AS number in the same manner.

3. Place the customer in a private sub-AS that is part of the ISP confederation.

Option 1 is a possibility because an AS is defined as a network under a common administration, and strictly speaking, an enterprise's Internet access is administered by an ISP. The ISP may be reluctant to enable a customer to have full access to their IBGP domain so this presents another possible application of BGP confederations

To implement option 3, the customer could use a private AS number that is one of the sub-ASs in the ISPs confederation. For example referring to Figure 7-25, customers could be installed in sub-AS 65020. Because it is the confederation AS number rather than the sub-AS number that is advertised through the Internet, no requirement is needed to strip the private AS number or install a "dummy" public AS number. The added advantage for the ISP is that it can hide the remainder of the confederation from the customer apart from AS65020.

Confederation Topology   A confederation should not consist of a group of randomly distributed sub-ASs whose function is simply to reduce IBGP peering requirements. This would result in sub-ASs receiving the same updates from multiple sources. The routes would also be advertised with the same path length (because the confederation is one AS), resulting in the possibility of sub-optimal routing. Ideally, the design should entail a hierarchy with a central or core sub-AS that connects to each of the other sub-ASs. This type of logical topology is shown in Figure 7-26, where AS65000 is the core sub-AS. This structure would promote optimized and symmetrical routing within the AS.

Peer Groups Within BGP

As a network grows, so does the average number of peers per router. A large number of EBGP or IBGP peers places increased overhead on the router in maintaining the TCP sessions, as has already been discussed.

A number of router vendors support the ability to group a set of neighbors that have common outbound policies and place them in a peer group. This can significantly improve the efficiency of routing information exchange because the updates are generated once and flooded to all members of the group.

Figure 7-26
BGP confederation
hierarchy

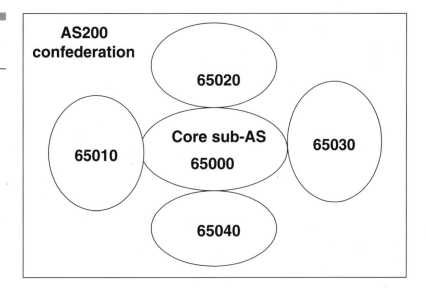

It is possible to group external neighbors within a group and also internal neighbors in a separate group. This is illustrated in Figure 7-27, where R31 has two peer groups defined. The EXTL group includes two EBGP neighbors that share the same outbound policies. The INTRNL group has two IBGP neighbors that must also have the same outbound policies as far as R31 is concerned. These policies relate to the filtering and manipulation of attributes such as MED and AS-path. On R31, the value of the attributes can be set using the peer group template rather than separately for each BGP peer. Although the use of peer groups does ease the router configuration, their real benefit lies in the consolidation of routing updates on a per-group rather than a per-neighbor basis, thus reducing routing overhead.

All members of an internal or external peer group must share common outbound policies; however, they can have different inbound policies on the router on which the peer groups are configured (R31 in this example). This is because peer groups are used to consolidate outbound updates and their attribute values. Peer groups do not presume to have control over inbound policies.

For a peer group consisting of external neighbors, a particular restriction exists that must be obeyed. The hub router must not act as a transit AS for other ASs within the group. In the case of Figure 7-27, that means that updates from R40, for example, should not be passed from R31 to R50 because the EBGP peers are in the same group. Likewise, R31 should not pass updates received from R50 on to R40 for the same reason.

Figure 7-27
BGP peer groups

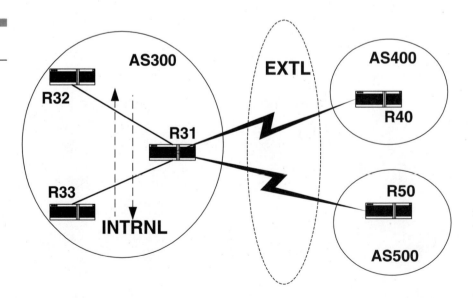

Designing the LAN I— The Campus

This is the first of two chapters relating to the design of the *local area network* (LAN). In particular, this chapter focuses on the design of large scalable LANs. For large organizations, main office LANs are extended frequently across multiple floors and multiple buildings to form a campus LAN. This chapter also addresses the design issues associated with the spread of the local area network into the campus LAN in detail.

The key factors that drive the campus network design, such as the client-server application traffic flow, will be explained. This chapter also examines the parameters by which a good campus LAN design is evaluated. Many examples in the text illustrate the different topological design models that are used to meet the design goals. We will discuss key technology issues such as the when and where of deploying routing, and layer 2 and layer 3 switching within the campus LAN.

Campus Network Design Goals

A person cannot design a network without having a clear focus on the design goals. Although it may seem obvious, this point must be emphasized. Far too often, design engineers become so preoccupied with mastering and understanding the technology that the required characteristics of the network that they should be designing are overlooked. The parameters used for judging a good campus network design are discussed next.

Performance Parameters

Applications drive all network designs; however, these applications require a certain level of performance. The main performance parameters are:

- Throughput: Throughput is measured in the same dimensions as bandwidth. A certain minimum level of throughput is required between the client and server for an application to function satisfactorily.

- Latency or delay: Some applications are more sensitive to delay or variations in delay than others. Time-sensitive data applications such as LAT or *Systems Network Architecture* (SNA) cannot tolerate a large latency between source and destination. This is also true of voice and video applications that are gaining increasing prominence on the campus LAN.

■ Packet loss: Unreliable data applications that are *user datagram protocol* (UDP)-based are the least tolerant of packet loss. Some packet loss may be permissible for voice and multimedia, provided that it does not result in significant service degradation. Reliable *transmission control protocol* (TCP)-based data applications can cope with a small percentage of packet loss by using retransmissions. However, if this percentage of packet loss becomes too large, the level of retransmissions can consume a significant portion of bandwidth, which can precipitate more packet loss and a snowballing effect.

Packet loss should not be significantly evident on a well-designed campus network that provides adequate bandwidth for the clients and applications.

Some application types are more sensitive to delay, whereas others suffer more due to packet loss. A campus infrastructure that can provide an adequate *quality of service* (QOS) for each of these application types must be put in place. This brings us conveniently to our next topic: the diversity of applications and QOS.

Diversity of Applications and QOS

Not only has the number of applications that may have to be supported on the modern network grown significantly, but an increasing diversity in their nature has also occurred. The drive toward integrated applications has attained an arguably irreversible momentum.

Loss-sensitive data applications are being integrated with delay-sensitive multimedia applications on a common network infrastructure.

Quality of service (QOS) ensures that delay-sensitive applications do not suffer as a result of this integration, particularly during periods of heavy traffic. This is a major, but not the only driving force behind the concept of QOS. Real-time applications require certain levels of consistency with respect to packet delay and bandwidth allocation. Although providing this service is a fundamental goal of QOS, it is equally important to ensure that the continuous demand for certain service parameters by real-time applications does not impinge on the data applications.

This issue of QOS design and implementation is discussed in the next chapter in the context of campus LANs. In particular, the *Resource Reservation Protocol* (RSVP) will be examined in detail because it is obtaining growing deployment within this area of application.

Effective Resilience

A high level of availability is a prerequisite of a network that supports any mission-critical applications. The requirement for resilience must be incorporated into the design of a number of network elements. Ideally, a topology change on the campus LAN should be characterized by a smooth failover to a redundant path or device without a significant degradation in service.

Redundant Resources   A redundant resource refers mainly to the applications' servers. A number of steps should be taken to ensure redundancy for this element of the network such as:

■ Storage of backup data: This is an essential component not only of campus network design, but also of the day to day administration of the network. All server data should be backed up at regular intervals and stored in a secure and separate physical location. This can be performed dynamically from each server to a backup server across the network, or alternatively, the data storage devices can be physically moved to the building that stores the backup data. Ideally, this should be done on a daily basis. This procedure is not to be confused with the company's disaster recovery plan, which is another essential element of network design and administration. Disaster recovery planning is frequently out-sourced on at least a partial basis. A typical part of the procedure is to move the backup stored data on a periodic basis from the backup site to the designated disaster recovery site, which may belong to the third-party disaster recovery specialists.

■ Redundant servers: On the campus LAN server, redundancy can be achieved by operating multiple servers in a load sharing manner, or by having one or more servers in idle standby mode. The choice between the two methods depends not only on cost, but also on the type of server platform. Listed below are some relevant questions for determining this choice.

■ Can clients dynamically discover another server if their existing server fails?

The answer to this question for most applications is something short of a clear yes. After the failure of a server, clients will typically have to reboot and issue another broadcast in an attempt to find a new server to login to. The network must be configured so this broadcast can be directed to the backup server. This solution is workable, but less than ideal as it does not produce seamless failover.

Some applications require that some information referring to the server be configured for each of the clients. They may take the form of an *Internet Protocol* (IP) address, a NetBIOS name, or the name of a Novell preferred server for example. If this is a requirement then a certain number of clients' servers would have to be reconfigured after a server failure. Servers could be operating in load sharing mode with half of the clients on the network utilizing each. After a failure, half of the clients' servers would require reconfiguration in order to point at the other server. This is an unacceptable solution. In this scenario where the clients are unable to dynamically resolve a secondary server, it is up to the servers to communicate with each other and provide the dynamic solution. This brings us to the next question:

■ Does the application support server mirroring?

Server mirroring is most likely necessary for mission-critical applications that cannot provide dynamic client-based failover. The servers operate in a primary and backup manner in which the backup server is capable of detecting the failure of the primary server. Server mirroring is normally characterized by the backup server, which assumes the IP and MAC address of the primary during failover. *Locally administered addresses* (LAAs) can be used to provide the duplicate MAC address. In the event of a failover, the LAN switches will relearn the MAC address on a different port. *The spanning tree protocol* (STP) may have to first recalculate itself if it has not been disabled on the server port.

Thus, layer 2 resolution of the backup server is reasonably straightforward. However, the handling of the failover at layer 3 does impose some design constraints. The primary and backup servers should at least be located in separate wiring closets, if not in separate buildings, as shown in Figure 8-1. However, if they are supposed to each have the same IP address while being operational, the same IP subnet will be advertised from a different location after failover. For the network in Figure 8-1, this would cause a problem if the backbone connecting the two wiring closets or buildings were routed. In other words, the two closets must be on the same IP subnet; therefore, the device connecting building A to building B must be a backbone switch rather than a router.

■ Redundant server connections: As in the case of the primary and backup servers shown in Figure 8-1, servers should have dual connections to their local LAN switch. Both of these connections could be active simultaneously using one of the proprietary channel

Figure 8-1
Redundant server
access

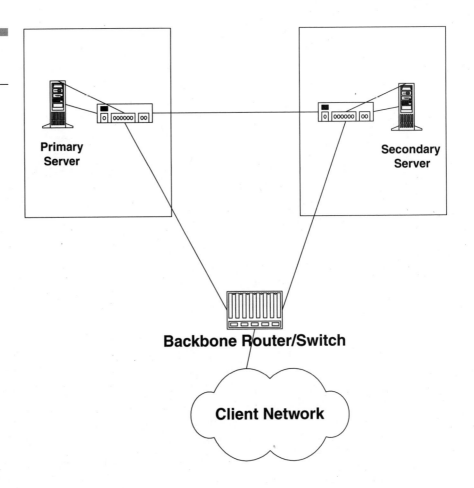

**Primary
Server**

**Secondary
Server**

Backbone Router/Switch

Client Network

aggregation protocols on the market. In this case, the failure of one link due to a *network interface card* (NIC), cable, or switch port problem results in all the traffic being carried over the other link.

Alternatively, the second link could operate in standby mode. The issue here is that when the primary server connection fails, the spanning tree protocol may take too long to recalculate and so cause a loss of service. This can be avoided by altering the STP timers (this is dangerous as discussed later). A better solution would be to disable STP entirely on this port. The second link would become active immediately and no service loss would occur. Note that it is only permissible to disable STP on ports that do not connect to other switches.

Data Path Redundancy or resilience in the physical path must exist between clients and servers. A loss of client-server connectivity should never occur due to the loss of any single connection along the data path. In this context, connection means the following:

- Server to switch
- Switch to switch
- Switch to router

Redundancy on the client to switch connection is often considered unnecessary or non-justifiable on a cost basis with the exception of certain power users.

Bandwidth utilization should not be so high on the links along the client-server data path that the failure of a single link would cause congestion on the remaining link(s) that now carry all the traffic. This could result in a significant degradation of service that may cause further congestion due to re-transmissions and eventually application timeouts. Topologies that incorporate resilience along the client-server data path will be discussed in more detail in the sample topologies later in the chapter.

NOTE: *The failure of any single connection along the client-server data path should not result in a loss of service or a significant degradation in service.*

Device Redundancy Every effort should be made within budgetary constraints to ensure that each networking device is resilient against outright failure. Routers and switches that provide critical functions should be equipped with *uninterruptable power supplies* (UPS) that ideally should be *simple network management protocol* (SNMP) manageable. Dual power supplies with redundant fans and redundant device management modules should also be part of the hardware architecture.

Even if an extensive amount of redundancy is incorporated at the device level, there is always a single point of failure that can cause a device to crash and that is the software. Therefore, apart from resilience and redundancy within the network devices themselves, a level of redundancy should also be built into the design so that the failure of any one device will not result in a significant loss of service. The key word here is *significant*. A cost-benefit decision has to be made to decide what level of service-affecting device failure can be tolerated on the network. Typically, the only device whose failure can be allowed to affect service is the local LAN switch that provides initial user connectivity to the network. With the exception of certain power users, often no resilience is present for the failure of this device.

Routers and switches that provide functions other than network access for some local users must have resilient configurations. These functions may include the aggregation of end user groups and policy implementation.

Network configurations that incorporate device resilience along the client-server data path will be demonstrated in the sample topologies later in the chapter.

Wiring Closet   No matter how much redundancy is built into the devices and the network design itself, any single physical location represents a single point of failure. A single wiring closet (or even a single building) could potentially suffer a complete power outage or a disaster scenario.

The backup policy for any key resource, such as a server, should entail the use of separate wiring closets, as shown in Figure 8-1. As we will see later in the chapter, this should ideally be true of the backup strategy, which also relates to routers and switches.

Resilience or Redundancy   Generally, resilience means the provision of a fault-tolerant network design. However, in practice the term sometimes implies that the fault tolerance is achieved through a load sharing mechanism across multiple paths and devices. Redundancy usually means that certain devices and paths remain idle in the normal steady state, and their purpose is to carry traffic only when the primary path fails. Although the two terms are often used loosely and interchangeably, it is important to be clear about the two different approaches to achieving fault tolerance.

A redundant or idle backup approach for both devices and links is likely to be the more expensive solution. The other lesser, but nonetheless potential pitfall of this approach is that idle devices and paths are untested. Therefore, they can sometimes produce unpredictable results when they are called upon. A backup solution should not only produce relatively seamless failover, but it should do so without a perceptible degradation in service.

The use of load sharing over multiple devices and paths is a potentially more cost-effective method of achieving fault tolerance on the network. The challenge is to ensure that degraded service does not result from the loss of a link or a networking device. For example, if all paths to a destination are heavily loaded, the loss of one is likely to produce significant congestion. The same can happen with device resilience if the device providing the backup does not have the processing power to do the work of two. Although the old chestnut of trading off between cost and performance is at the heart of this question, it is difficult to understand why a first rate network design has a third rate backup solution, as is frequently the case.

Speed of Convergence The speed of failover should be fast enough to avoid an interruption in client-server connectivity. The first limiting factor is the speed at which the medium detects failure, for example, the loss of Ethernet keep-alives. The second factor can cause a significant variation in convergence time as it relates to whether the section of the network is routed or switched. In the case of a routed campus backbone that consists of several different IP subnets, the routing protocol detects failure and must perform a recalculation. For a flat or switched backbone, failure is detected and resolved by the spanning tree protocol. Typically, STP converges significantly slower than a scalable IP routing protocol. This is an issue that will be debated later in the chapter when the choice of campus backbone topology is discussed.

Scalability

The campus network design must be scalable and support growth in each of the following respects:

- Application: The network must be capable of supporting the anticipated new applications that come online. Applications that arc inherently of a heterogeneous nature, such as voice and data, may also have to be provided with a specified service level.
- Bandwidth consumption: Applications can vary widely in terms of bandwidth consumption. Often the addition of a single new application can dramatically increase the bandwidth consumption on the network. The design should provide a sufficient scope so that a significant change in the bandwidth profile will not produce traffic bottlenecks and degraded performance. The key issue here is to have a clear understanding of the bandwidth consumption associated with the existing applications. A projection must also be made as to the likely future applications and their approximate bandwidth consumption. Obviously these projections will be of limited accuracy; however, this is not a reason to avoid the exercise. A network designer must have some projection about the applications that the network may be required to support throughput its lifetime; otherwise a realistic design cannot be performed.
- Users: Growth in the number of end users should be catered for by the design without any significant change in topology.

■ Physical diversification: The network design should be able to cope with the addition of new and possibly diverse physical locations for clients and servers. For example, the commissioning of a new server location should not require any significant change in campus topology.

Understanding the Campus Network

The key issues that must be understood before designing a campus network will now be examined. The importance of understanding client to server traffic flow will be explored along with the factors that influence it.

Client-Server Traffic Flow

Obtaining a detailed understanding of client-server traffic flow is arguably the greatest challenge when implementing a switched LAN design. In situations where a network is being redesigned from a shared LAN environment to a switched LAN in order to meet increased bandwidth requirements, it is possible to gather detailed quantitative information on traffic profiles. On a completely new network, this is not so easy to do prior to rollout. However, a reasonable qualitative analysis of traffic profiles should be achievable.

It is important to obtain a reasonable estimate of the following:

■ What clients are talking to what servers and for how long? How much bandwidth is being consumed now and how much will be consumed in the future?

■ What is the physical and logical location of all clients and servers? In other words, be clear about the client-server data path for each application.

■ What is the level of inter-server traffic?

To Switch or Not To Switch?

The widespread implementation of LAN switching is useful only if a high proportion of traffic is switched. For example, LAN switching provides limited benefit if a group of users are serviced by a LAN switch and must attach to their server across the WAN. In Figure 8-2, the LAN switch provides network access for local clients, but no local servers are available. The applications server is located at a different site; therefore, all client traffic to the server must be routed. In this example, the LAN switch is used to replace a hub because file transfer response times were becoming unacceptably slow as more users were added to the local LAN.

In this case, the switch will provide dedicated collision domains for each user along with the possibility for full-duplex transmission. However, this is the extent of the benefit because all client-server traffic must still cross the WAN, which at 64kbps becomes the bottleneck. This is a classic example of how LAN switching provides only a meager improvement over a shared hub due to the traffic flow pattern. In order to receive the full value of Ethernet switching, it is critical to understand application traffic flow. If the server were attached to the same local switch, the benefits would be far more extensive because all client server traffic would be switched.

The implementation of Ethernet switching instead of shared Ethernet entails the following improved operational features:

- Dedicated collision domains: Each port on a switch is in its own collision domain; therefore, a station connected to the LAN via a switch port rather than a hub port does not have to compete for access to the wire by listening for collisions before sending data. This increases the effective bandwidth on the LAN.

Figure 8-2
LAN switching of limited benefit

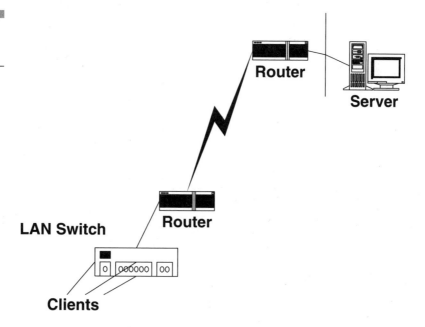

■ Traffic filtering and forwarding: A switch functions as a multiport bridge and learns the location of each station's MAC address by listening to live traffic. For each frame that it switches, it will only forward traffic to the port where the destination MAC address resides. The switch is said to filter the frame on all other ports. This reduces unnecessary traffic on the LAN significantly and improves the efficiency with which bandwidth is utilized.

■ Full-duplex transmission: Traditional shared Ethernet is half-duplex. In other words, stations cannot send and receive at the same time. As a result of the baseband nature of Ethernet, only one station can access the medium and send data at one time. Stations on a shared Ethernet medium resolve contention by listening for collisions. Full-duplex means that stations can send and receive at the same time. In Ethernet, this is accomplished by not listening for collisions. It is only valid to disable collision detection if the station is attached to its own dedicated switch port. This means that only two stations in the collision domain exist: the station itself and the switch port. Each station can then send to and receive from the other without having to listen for collisions. This is sometimes called point-to-point Ethernet. For example, in Figure 8-3, port 5 can operate in full-duplex mode because the station has a dedicated switch port. However, port 10 attaches to a shared hub and must be half-duplex because more than one station exists in the collision domain.

NOTE: *Full-duplex cannot be used on a switch port that connects to a shared hub.*

Avoid using auto-negotiation to resolve the duplex mode.

Figure 8-3
Full and half duplex connections

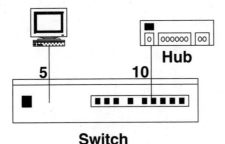

Full-duplex should be used where possible because it provides greater efficiency and bandwidth throughput. The NIC on the client or server obviously must support full-duplex operation. Auto-negotiation of duplex mode is often used between the station and the switch port. This is not recommended because the auto-negotiation protocol is poorly standardized and can result in duplex mismatches between the station and the switch. Unlike the situation of a speed mismatch where one end thinks the medium is 10Mbps and the other sees 100Mbps, a duplex mismatch will not result in a loss of line protocol. This can be even more troublesome because the network is not visibly down, but performance is degraded by a duplex mismatch. The full-duplex end will send data without listening for collisions. This may overwhelm the half-duplex end that may have to keep backing off because the full-duplex end is continuously sending data. Packets may be dropped at the half-duplex end, and this is likely to happen particularly during busy traffic conditions when it is least desirable. The network administrator should be clear as to what ports should be configured as full-duplex. All switch ports on the network should then be configured as full- or half-duplex as appropriate without relying on auto-negotiation.

One final point must be made in relation to full-duplex operation, and it relates to a particular myth that should be dispelled. Fast Ethernet is not synonymous with full-duplex operation. Baseband Ethernet is half-duplex because only one station can send data at any one time. On a dedicated switch port, a station can stop listening for collisions, and full-duplex operation is possible. Fast Ethernet is similar to 10Mbps Ethernet in terms of specification. The difference in speed bears no relationship to whether or not the medium is full-duplex or half-duplex. This point is emphasized because the incorrect assumption is made that fast Ethernet is somehow synonymous with full-duplex operation. Part of the reason for this is that fast Ethernet, like full-duplex mode, is part of the later generation of Ethernet. As a result, it is likely that fast Ethernet NICs support full-duplex, whereas this is not necessarily true of all legacy 10Mbps Ethernet cards.

NOTE: *Fast Ethernet is not necessarily synonymous with full-duplex operation.*

No review of the benefits of switched Ethernet is complete without some further words of caution regarding its limitations. The initial expectations surrounding the deployment of switched Ethernet were unrealistically high due in part to the manner in which the technology was marketed. Switch vendors claimed frequently that a 15-port Ethernet switch increased the bandwidth to 150Mbps (15x10=150). With full-duplex operation on each port, the LAN bandwidth then becomes 300Mbps! This claim is purely marketing hysteria that has no technological basis. If the maximum speed on any switch port is 10Mbps, this is the maximum throughput between any two stations attached to the switch. Full-duplex operation does mean that a station can send and receive simultaneously, but it is not normally characteristic of LAN communications for stations to continuously send and receive large amounts of data at the same time. Therefore, full-duplex operation increases throughput, but certainly does not double it.

However, exaggerations aside, Ethernet switching does provide the potential for a significant improvement in application response time and throughput. To obtain the maximum benefit of switching, as much traffic as possible along the client-server path should be switched rather than routed. It is a question of identifying the traffic bottleneck along the client-server data path and ensuring that the presence of a switch will remove this bottleneck.

When a Hub Is Preferable To a Switch   The last section illustrated an example of an Ethernet switch that provided only a limited performance improvement because all client-server traffic still had to cross a 64kbps link that was the major contributor to slow response and low throughput. Instances also occur where a switch may not result in improved performance even if the server is local. A hub might be preferable to a switch if an application relies exclusively on broadcasts, even if the server and clients are local. This is because the switch must intelligently interpret every broadcast frame and flood it out all switch ports. A hub simply repeats the frame on all ports without analyzing it. Therefore, the switch uses valuable *central processing unit* (CPU) cycles to do what the hub will do by default. The additional intelligence provided by the switch has no benefit here because the end result is the same with the broadcasts being copied to all ports. Once again, it comes down to understanding the operation of your application.

The Traditional 80/20 Rule   The 80/20 rule has been around for a long time and has spanned the worlds of voice, telecommunications, and data communications. Voice and telecommunications engineers have used it when planning traffic capacities for local and trunk central office switches and transmission. Similarly, it was adopted by data communications engineers for network planning and design. In the context of campus network design, the rule assumes that approximately 80 percent of traffic remains local to a workgroup, whereas 20 percent is directed to remote destinations.

The term *workgroup* can be used to describe a group of users attached to the same Ethernet switch or users that terminate in the same wiring closet. The term is also used in relation to clients that are on the same *Virtual Local Area Network* (VLAN) or IP subnet. Thus, the 80/20 rule suggests that a large majority of traffic remains local to the subnet, and as a rule of thumb, only about 20 percent should be routed to remote subnets.

This type of traffic profile exists where a main local server is accessed for most applications, whereas a minority of applications resides in centralized servers that are shared by all users within the enterprise. The application server topology can also be designed to ensure that the maximum amount of traffic remains local to the workgroup. Consider the example of Windows NT. It may be decided to distribute multiple *Backup Domain Controllers* (BDCs) around the network to avoid requiring users to remotely access the BDC in order to receive their profile, a procedure that can be bandwidth-intensive.

If the majority of traffic remains on the same IP subnet, most packets are switched along the client-server data path as opposed to being routed. With this type of application traffic pattern, the maximum benefits of Ethernet switching can be obtained.

The Emerging 20/80 Rule A significant change in client-server traffic patterns has occurred with the advent of new technologies. The increased deployment of more Internet-based applications and multimedia applications on the campus LAN has resulted in more servers being located centrally and shared across the enterprise. Applications such as e-mail, video-conferencing, and multimedia as well as Web-based applications are usually characterized by the centralization of shared servers that are located at the core of the campus network. The centralization of these servers arises for a number of reasons. First, it may not be cost-effective to distribute multiple servers across the enterprise. Secondly, it may be pointless because these applications often inherently require communication with resources beyond the enterprise.

These developments have resulted in a gradual shift away from the 80/20 rule, and the reverse type of profile is becoming more apt: that is, the assumption that approximately only 20 percent of the traffic remains local to the IP subnet or VLAN from which it originated. If each local workgroup is on its own exclusive VLAN, this traffic profile results in routing the majority of client-server traffic. The increased latency associated with routing serves to negate the benefits of a switched campus LAN.

This presents a potential dilemma for the campus network designer. Some key facts should be clarified. The traffic profile on modern networks is changing, and a greater proportion of traffic is not remaining local to the workgroup. This is due to the nature of the applications, and it is not going to change. The applications drive the design so this fact must be acknowledged as a starting point. The design question becomes a matter of finding the optimum design to meet these traffic flow requirements. As we will see, certain benefits are associated with implementing VLANs, such as the containment of broadcasts. The tradeoff is the latency associated with routing between the VLANs. However, this can be minimized by the use of layer 3 switching technology. Another alternative is to not use separate VLANs in each wiring closet, or to extend the VLAN all the way to the enterprise backbone to avoid the necessity for routing. However, this would significantly increase the size of the broadcast domain and could potentially slow down network and device performance at the backbone. The solution to be implemented depends on the nature of the application, in particular the extent to which it relies on broadcasts. The other issues to consider are the technological capabilities of the devices (layer 3 switching and processing power) and the level of bandwidth utilization on the network.

The Alternatives for Server Location Traffic flow is inherently influenced by the locations of the application's servers relative to the clients. Keeping clients and their corresponding servers localized to the same workgroup will usually localize traffic, and the flow of any unnecessary traffic across the campus is minimized. It is not always cost-effective to distribute servers in this manner, and in many cases servers cannot be local due to the nature of the application (for example, Web server or e-mail).

Here are the main alternatives for server location:

■ Local to the workgroup: It is certainly appropriate and prudent to locate a server local to a workgroup if that workgroup engages in a specialized application that may not be of irrelevance to the entire enterprise. For example, certain members of the company's finance department might only use a payroll application. Another example could be a legal department that operates in relative isolation to the rest of the enterprise.

It should be a goal of the campus network design to minimize the length of the client-server data path in terms of switch hops or router hops. The traffic should cross the minimum number of networking devices and network links. Thus, a well-designed network entails a minimization in device CPU utilization and network bandwidth consumption. Apart from improving network and device performance, the localization of servers may also be necessary from a security standpoint. In the example of a legal department's server, it is probably contrary to the company security policy to locate the server at the network backbone where it may be visible to the entire network.

■ Common between workgroups: As stated earlier, fewer applications on modern networks are characterized by a workgroup of clients communicating with a specialized local server. More applications are being shared by the enterprise; therefore, most client-server traffic is terminating remotely rather than locally to the workgroup.

If applications are shared between a number of workgroups or a section of the organization, but will not be accessed by the entire enterprise, it may be a good idea to choose their location with care. In line with the philosophy of shortening the client-server data path as much as possible, locating these servers in a server farm at the network backbone may not be the optimum solution. Consider the network in Figure 8-4, which can be assumed to belong to an electronics company. The engineering design department is located in building B, whereas the administrative headquarters is building A. The engineering design department is divided into two basic groups: circuit and fabrication design. Each group has its own server, but also requires access to the other group's server to satisfy cross-functional tasks. Both servers use

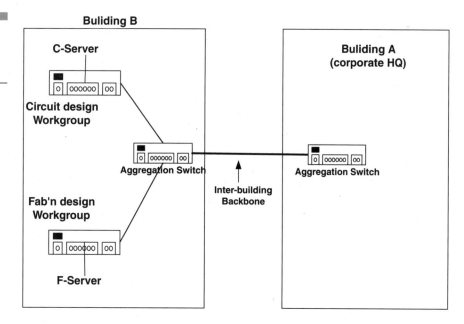

Figure 8-4

Localization of high-bandwidth application servers

bandwidth-intensive, *computer-aided design* (CAD) applications; therefore, it is not desirable to locate them at the main enterprise server farm in building A. If the servers were located in building A, the high-speed, inter-building links may become congested due to the nature of the CAD applications. This would not only affect the performance of these applications, but also of common office applications, Internet, and e-mail services used by clients in building B.

This is an example of servers that are not just of local significance to one workgroup, but are still not located in a head-office server farm. A local print server is another classic example of a resource that can be effectively located close to most of its clients.

■ Common to the enterprise: If applications are shared by the entire enterprise, it makes sense to locate the server at a centralized backbone location that is equally accessible by the entire enterprise. The growth in the number of applications that are shared by the full organization has given rise to the concept of the server farm. One or more server farms are located typically at the enterprise's headquarters. A high-speed backbone switch will provide at least switched 100Mbps for each server.

■ Centralized versus distributed: As previously mentioned, two fundamental alternative approaches to locating servers are available. They can be centralized in a server farm or distributed around the campus network.

Each approach has instances where it is more applicable. From the standpoint of centralizing the servers, a number of pros and cons are worth emphasizing.

Advantages of Centralization

■ Secure location: A centralized server farm should be located in a wiring closet that has a high security specification with controlled access for personnel.

■ Highly-specified location: Given the strategic importance of the server farm, a particular effort can be made to enhance the standard of its location. Apart from security, the specifications of the server farm location should meet a high standard with respect to each of the following availability specifications:

   ▪ Power: The location should be designed for zero power downtime. Backup power should serve the location along with each of the devices. In conjunction with dual power feeds, all devices should be equipped with *uninteruptible power supplies* (UPS), which ought to be *simple network management protocol* (SNMP) manageable to indicate when they are being used.

- Vibration: The server farm room should meet strict vibration specifications in order to lengthen device lifetime and provide for maximum availability.

- Environment: Environmental factors such as temperature and humidity should be stringently controlled within the device operating specifications.

- Clear backup strategy: If the servers are located in a single location, the backup strategy is simplified. It is easier to plan and design a backup or mirroring strategy for a single server location than for multiple locations distributed across the network.

- Administration: A centralized server farm also provides for the ease of administration because it is easier to track and document resources that reside at a single location. It is also more convenient in terms of managing the relocation of users as no resulting requirement exists to relocate servers.

- Cost: Server centralization also presents the possibility to aggregate multiple services on a single server, which is usually a more cost-effective approach.

Disadvantages of Server Centralization

- Sub-optimal data flow: The centralization of multiple servers presents the possibility of sub-optimal client-server data flow for applications that are not shared by the entire enterprise. Refer to the example of Figure 8-4. The location of the engineering CAD servers in the main office building would be sub-optimal. High-bandwidth traffic would needlessly traverse from building B to building A because that is where the server farm resides.

It should be an aspiration that the servers are located so that the average length of the client-server data path is minimized. The word aspiration is used because it is unrealistic to distribute servers at several locations around the network simply to ensure that client-server data paths are minimized. The issues preventing this, as previously stated, include cost, suitability of locations, and administration. Choosing the location of all servers on the network is a question of striking a realistic balance between all the issues that have been discussed. On most networks, the most workable solution is a certain degree of centralization coupled with some distribution of specialized servers.

Before finishing this point, one other issue deserves further clarification: how does one measure the length of the client-server data path? The actual length of the path is the number of separate network links that the data must cross. However, some consideration must also be given to traffic levels. For example, it may be more acceptable to have a larger number of network links between a client and server if the traffic levels are small. Thus, a minimal adverse effect would occur on bandwidth utilization and device processing load. With this rationale, a server should be located physically closer to the clients that generate the most bandwidth-intensive sessions. For the network shown in Figure 8-5, a small group of clients in Workgroup 2 frequently engages in bandwidth-intensive file transfers from the server FSERV. A much larger group of clients in Workgroup 3 mainly uses interactive telnet sessions to the server and consume little bandwidth. This results in the server being physically closer to Workgroup 2 because it minimizes the average length of the client-server data path when traffic levels are considered.

■ Single point of failure: Centralizing the servers can facilitate the formulation of a server backup strategy. However, it is critical that this is a good backup strategy that can cater to the simultaneous failure of multiple and diverse servers. This type of minor disaster scenario is a

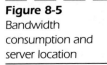

Figure 8-5
Bandwidth
consumption and
server location

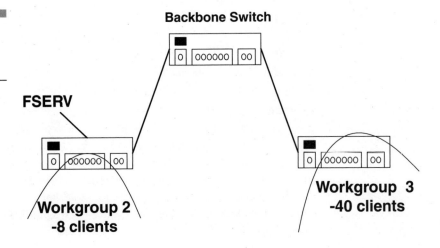

possibility that must be planned if all servers reside in the same physical location or wiring closet.

Distributing servers also eliminates the possibility of a complete loss of all major servers within the enterprise because the physical location is no longer a single point of failure.

NOTE: Ideally, servers should be located so as to minimize the distance that client-server traffic has to travel.

However, it is usually not feasible or realistic to locate servers purely on this criterion. A certain degree of server centralization is usually desirable for reasons of administration and cost.

Designing a LAN Topology

As a campus network scales, a certain degree of LAN segmentation is required. This segmentation can be provided through two different approaches: routing and switching. The LAN topology and characteristics are significantly influenced by the choice of option. In this section both approaches will be examined.

Segmentation Using Routing

One of the traditional limiting factors for the size of the LAN is the level of broadcasts. Broadcasting is still an intrinsic part of many communications protocols within the LAN. NetBIOS, *Internetwork Packet Exchange* (IPX), AppleTalk, and UDP-based applications typically use broadcasting as a primary method of resolving access to essential resources. If the size of the broadcast domain becomes too large in terms of users or traffic, two problems arise:

- Bandwidth consumption: If the level of broadcasts becomes too large on a LAN, an excessive amount of bandwidth may be consumed, resulting in a possible adverse effect on network performance. Although bandwidth consumption due to broadcasts is certainly an issue in the LAN, it generally does not have the same level of criticality as the WAN because bandwidth is more plentiful in the local area network.

- Device CPU utilization: Device CPU utilization is an even more serious issue than bandwidth consumption in relation to excessive broadcasts. Every time a station on a LAN receives a broadcast, it must process the frame because it is addressed to that station (a broadcast is addressed to every station). This means the station must interrupt its CPU upon each receipt of a broadcast even if that broadcast is of no relevance to that particular station. If the level of broadcasts received goes beyond a certain level, too much processing power is used to interpret broadcasts to the detriment of other tasks. Any type of station on the LAN can suffer from this problem: client, server, LAN switch, or router.

If the entire campus LAN were one big broadcast domain, even the simple act of a station sending an *address resolution protocol* (ARP) broadcast would cause the packet to propagate across the entire LAN, and therefore be processed by every station.

Although the issue of broadcast containment is one of the main reasons why LANs are segmented, another issue relates to the constraints imposed by Ethernet operation and also by the IP addressing plan. The *Carrier Sense Multiple Access with Collision Detection* (CSMA/CD) method of access resolution is likely to result in performance problems if more than 100 stations exist on the LAN segment. Theoretical figures suggest a greater number of stations can be supported. It depends mainly on traffic levels. This cutoff figure could be significantly less if the stations were busy and engaging in batch applications such as file transfers.

The IP addressing scheme may also place an upper limit on the size of the LAN segment. If n host bits exist for the LAN subnets, a maximum of $2^n - 2$ hosts can be supported on each subnet.

These forces, particularly the issue of broadcasts, resulted in the frequent segmentation of LANs into different routed segments in order to create multiple broadcast domains. Figure 8-6 shows a sample topology.

Segmenting the LAN using routers offers the following benefits:

- Multicast and broadcast control: Multicasts and broadcasts do not propagate beyond the routed subnet on which they originated unless the router is programmed to allow exceptions to this rule.

- Increased network intelligence: Routers have more intelligence than switches or hubs. Thus, they have the capability to gather more information on the network to which they are attached. This makes routers potentially powerful troubleshooting tools within themselves. Routers usually have more sophisticated troubleshooting and debugging capabilities than switches. In addition to the layer 2

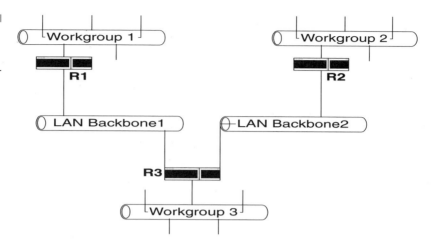

Figure 8-6
LAN segmentation
using routers

intelligence provided by the data link media that is attached, the
router also has the information provided by the IP routing protocol.

The role of the router as a network analysis and troubleshooting tool is
not to be underestimated, and is a key selling point for the placement
of routers within the network.

NOTE: *Routers are powerful network analysis tools in addition to their
function as networking devices.*

- Ability to enforce policies: Routers possess the ability to perform traffic
  filtering, management, and policy-based routing.
- Security: To implement layer 3 security in the network, some form of
  routing functionality is required. Per-packet examination and filtering
  policies can be enabled. These policies can be implemented on a per-
  address, per-port, or per-protocol basis. For example, in Figure 8-7, a
  policy could be configured on the router so that client A could not have
  a *File Transfer Protocol* (FTP) session with the server although the
  other clients could. This is a very specific policy that prohibits a single
  application to a single client. A device with layer 3 and layer 4
  awareness is required to implement such a policy.
- WAN and remote access: Routers will be required to provide WAN
  access to the campus network. Remote access to telecommuters and

mobile users also presents a requirement for routers. However, this is not a reason in itself for segmenting the LAN using routers. The LAN could be a single IP subnet with the routers providing WAN access.

■ Convergence: On medium to large networks, a scalable routing protocol such as *Open Shortest Path First* (OSPF) is normally used. This converges quickly, and even on a large campus network containing several subnets, routers will require only a few seconds to inform each other of a topology change. In Figure 8-8, if port 1 on router R1 fails as indicated, the main convergence delay is due to failure detection by the loss of Ethernet keep-alives. After the failure has been detected, the

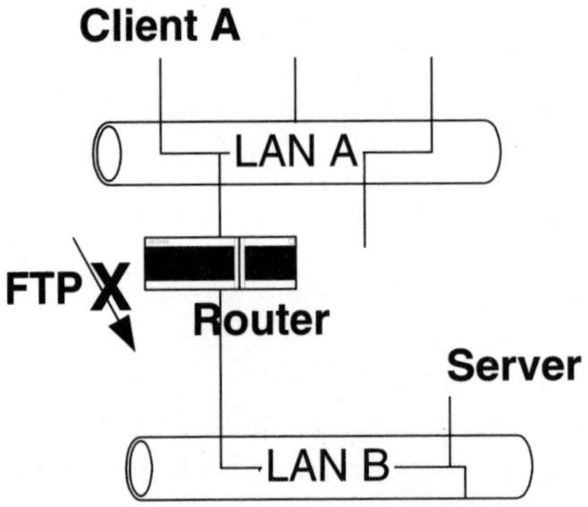

Figure 8-7
LAN segmentation using routers

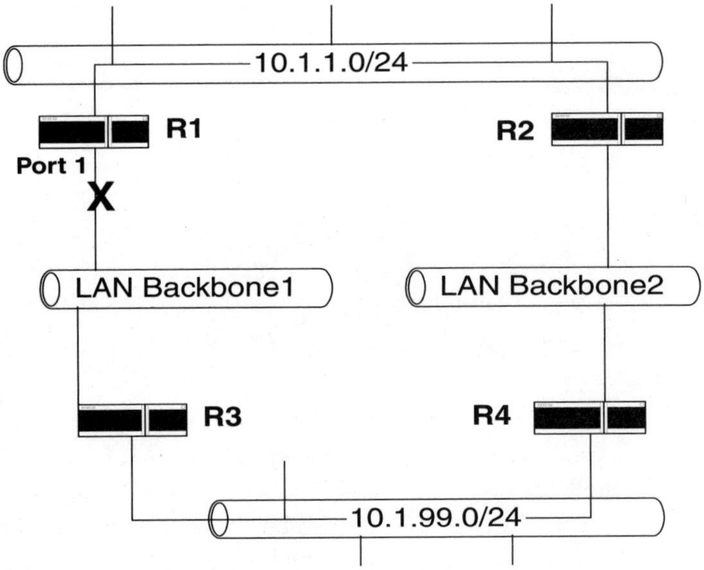

Figure 8-8
Convergence in a routed LAN environment

routing protocol will propagate this information to all routers, and an alternate path will be selected. In this example, traffic will then be routed from 10.1.99.0/24 to 10.1.1.0/24 exclusively via R2.

The speed and smoothness with which failover occurs is an important design requirement in a segmented network. Ideally, the loss of any link or device should not cause a loss of a client-server session.

Having highlighted the benefits of segmenting the LAN using routed subnets, it is now necessary to discuss the potential problems associated with this method of scaling the campus LAN.

- Latency: Routing is traditionally slower than switching. The act of a routing table lookup that was built using routing software incurs additional latency. The fact that a routing table lookup is not a one-to-one lookup can result in inefficiencies.

  The latency or delay associated with routing is compounded when multiple router hops are incurred between clients and servers.

  However, technologies such as layer 3 switching and multi-layer switching address the performance gap between packet and frame forwarding technologies.

- Cost: Router platforms are significantly more expensive than LAN switches with a much higher per-port cost. The cost-effectiveness of a router-based solution is certainly questionable if the main purpose of the router is to provide LAN segmentation.

The more negative issues associated with the use of routers as a LAN segmentation tool has helped fuel the advent of Ethernet switching as an alternative approach.

Segmentation Using Switching

Switching is basically high-speed, multi-port bridging that provides dedicated collision domains on a per-port basis. If a user station (a client or a server) is directly connected to a switch port, then by having its own collision domain, it has dedicated access to the 10Mbps or 100Mbps medium and does not have to compete with other stations for LAN access.

LAN switches segment the local area network by creating multiple collision domains as distinct from routers that go one step further and create multiple broadcast domains.

Switching in many ways becomes an ideal solution for LAN segmentation by offering the following benefits:

■ High-speed bridging: LAN switches operate as high-speed bridges with few limitations on the number of ports. Switches are faster than traditional bridges because any common functionality (such as bridging table lookup) is implemented in hardware rather than software. State of the art *Application Specific Integrated Circuits* (ASICs) are used to implement algorithms that were previously performed through software. Software is flexible, but it is not fast. For applications such as fixed functions like table caching and lookup, a hardware-based implementation provides more speed.

The bridging functionality of switches means that the location of all MAC addresses on the network is learned by listening to live traffic. This learning function enables the switch to build a switching table or MAC address table from which it will make forwarding and filtering decisions. The switch will only forward traffic on the port where the destination MAC resides, and it will filter the frame on all other ports. In other words, the switch will only forward traffic where it is needed. This is different from a hub, which is just a physical layer Ethernet repeater that copies the packet out of all ports without performing any intelligent analysis.

■ Dedicated collision domains: As a consequence of each switch port being in its own collision domain, the port can operate in full-duplex mode provided that only a single station is connecting to the port. If a hub or concentrator is connected, the switch port must be half-duplex because multiple stations are sharing the collision domain; hence, collision detect cannot be disabled in the form of full-duplex transmission.

■ Bandwidth scalability: Switches, like routers, can scale up to high speeds, but can do so in a more cost-effective manner. The ASIC technology has reduced the per-port cost of switches and improved high-speed scalability. The switched Ethernet infrastructure can scale from 10Mbps Ethernet, through 100Mbps fast Ethernet, and up to Gigabit Ethernet as bandwidth requirements dictate.

■ Low latency: Switches operate at wire speed. The switch table lookup is a one-to-one lookup for a specific MAC address and can be ASIC-based rather than software-based. The latency or delay incurred at a switch hop is therefore significantly less than at a router hop.

■ Cost: As previously mentioned, a switching platform is substantially less expensive than a routed LAN or campus backbone.

Another more debatable advantage of a switched LAN backbone is that because it is all one IP subnet, the amount of routes advertised to the rest of the network is reduced. This is shown in Figure 8-9, although it may be a more significant issue with a distance vector routing protocol such as *Routing Information Protocol* (RIP), where routing overhead is directly proportional to the number of routes contained in the updates. It is also potentially significant if floating static routes are used as a backup solution to attach to the campus headquarters. In this case, only a single static route is required on all remote routers; this points at the main campus LAN subnet. Other ways of reducing the number of HQ routes through summarization are available. This activity can be achieved using a contiguous range of HQ subnets that can be summarized by a single route. This type of configuration is illustrated in Figure 8-10, where four routed subnets exist on the campus LAN 10.1.1.0/26 to 10.1.1.192/26. Because this is a contiguous range, the campus WAN router can summarize this as a single route 10.1.1.0/24 to the rest of the network. The benefits of this type of route summarization gain significance as the number of subnets on the campus LAN grows.

The use of switching as a LAN segmentation methodology creates some problems. Some of the benefits provided by routing cannot be achieved through switching alone.

Figure 8-9
LAN segmentation
and routing protocol
overhead

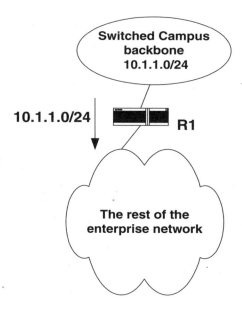

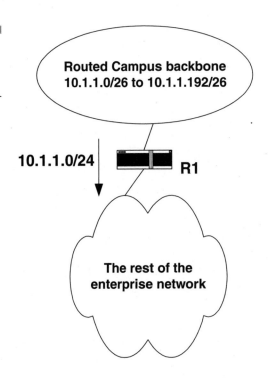

Figure 8-10
Routed campus LAN
with contiguous
subnets

The potential limitations of an exclusively switched campus LAN include:

■ Broadcast containment: A switched LAN is one big broadcast domain. The effect of this depends entirely on the level of broadcasts on the LAN. The percentage of broadcasts relative to overall traffic is determined by factors such as the nature of the application and the efficiency of the IP routing protocol. A high level of broadcasts on a switched backbone can have a severely degrading effect on performance. Consider the network of Figure 8-11, where a number of devices that issue periodic broadcasts attach to the same switched backbone. The servers issue application-related broadcasts, and the routers send periodic routing updates.

If these broadcasts are having a detrimental effect on performance by slowing down the common backbone, a number of steps can be taken.

  ▪ Curtail the source of the broadcasts: The predominant source of the broadcasts could be inhibited through redesign or reconfiguration.

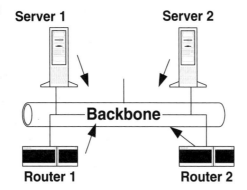

Figure 8-11
The effect of broadcasts on a common backbone

For example, the application could possibly be reconfigured to use multicasts instead of broadcasts. For this to be effective, the switch must be capable of distinguishing between multicasts and broadcasts, as we will see when multicasting is studied in the next chapter. Other potential solutions are available such as filtering application advertisements at the server or router level. These approaches are not always viable in practice and depend entirely on the application in question.

Likewise, the routing protocol could be altered, or any unnecessary updates could be filtered and prevented from propagating onto the switched backbone. Refer again to Figure 8-11. A distance vector routing protocol would periodically broadcast the entire routing table onto the LAN. The effect of these updates is multiplied by the number of routers attached to the LAN, and they all contain mainly the same information. This is unnecessary and route filters can ensure that the same route is advertised onto the LAN by no more than two routers.

▪ Configure the switch to limit the level of forwarded broadcasts: Most switch vendors support the capability to limit the percentage of bandwidth consumed by broadcasts. This may refer to the percentage of the total throughput on the switch, or it may be configured on a per-port basis.

The worrying aspect of this solution is that it may be addressing the symptom rather than the cause of the problem. By choking broadcasts without thinking further about the matter, application or network connectivity may suffer on other parts of the network.

- Implement VLANs: Multiple broadcast domains can be created using VLANs and in fact, this is typically a major driving force behind their deployment. A VLAN is usually synonymous with an IP subnet; hence, routing is required to enable inter-VLAN communication. Therefore, the use of VLANs is in many respects, moving back toward routing as a LAN segmentation strategy.

■ Switches are less intelligant than routers: As previously discussed, routers have greater intelligence and network awareness than switches. The corollary of this is that a purely switched LAN solution provides less power to implement policies and will also be characterized by an inferior network analysis capability.

■ Slow spanning tree convergence: When a topology change occurs on a link between two switches, the spanning tree protocol must detect the change and perform a recalculation to determine an alternate path.

The design issues associated with the spanning tree protocol will be discussed in an upcoming section. One of the main problems that STP can have on a large switched network is its relatively slow reaction to topology changes. It is vastly slower to converge than the more sophisticated IP routing protocols such as OSPF or *Enhanced Interior Gateway Routing Protocol* (EIGRP).

The Importance of Layer 3 Switching

Two fundamentally different approaches to LAN segmentation have been addressed so far: routing and switching. Switching provides clear improvements over traditional shared Ethernet. The creation of dedicated collision domains coupled with frame filtering and the possibility of full-duplex transmission greatly increases the efficiency with which LAN bandwidth is utilized. However, switches do not contain the propagation of broadcasts, which can be a limiting factor especially at the backbone of the campus LAN.

Routers are required to create broadcast domains, but they too have limiting factors in the form of increased packet latency and cost. From our discussion on server location, it should be evident that some degree of server centralization is almost inevitable on the modern campus LAN; hence, a likely requirement exists for routing beyond the mere containment of broadcasts.

Modern campus LANs have moved to a stage where a requirement is necessary for the speed of switching coupled with the intelligence of routing. This has led to the development of layer 3 switching, which unfortunately is a much abused and misused term in the industry.

Layer 3 switching and routing are logically equivalent because both technologies make packet forwarding decisions based on the layer 3 address. The difference is that layer 3 switching combines routing functionality with the speed and cost-effectiveness of layer 2 switching, where the forwarding decision is made based on the MAC address. One could argue that layer 3 switching could also have been called high-speed routing. So why was it not called this? In my opinion, switching is perceived in the marketplace as a more modern and cutting-edge technology than routing, so vendors made their product appear more state of the art by describing them as switches rather than routers. The router market was also perceived as more mature and difficult to gain a foothold within and so it was better to enter the marketplace with a new type of switch rather than a new type of router.

Moving on from this ranting about the mechanics of the marketplace, the benefits surrounding layer 3 switching will now be explained.

Layer 3 switching could be described as efficient hardware-based routing. It has better latency characteristics than traditional routing because it approaches the function in a different manner. The latency associated with routing is due to the inefficient manner in which routing table lookup and packet forwarding are performed. With ordinary routing, after the router receives a packet on an inbound interface, the routing table must be examined to determine the path to the destination network. This usually entails copying the packet across an internal communications bus to a multiprocessor that stores the routing table. When a match is found in the routing table for the destination network, the packet is forwarded to the appropriate outbound interface. This procedure is slow for a number of reasons. The act of copying the packet to the multi-processor incurs latency. In addition, the multi-processor that stores the routing table did not operate with optimum efficiency traditionally because it was also responsible for other device tasks. Routing table lookup also entails a delay because it is not a one-to-one lookup. The algorithm for a one-to-one lookup can be implemented in ASIC hardware and therefore, it is fast. This is why a switching table lookup for a specific destination MAC address can be performed at wire speed. With router operation, the destination IP address must be matched against the destination network. The router does not know the subnet mask of the destination IP address. Hence, the routing table is a one-to-many lookup that produces additional delay, particularly with large routing tables. After the next-hop has been resolved, the packet must be forwarded to a destination outbound interface. The exact manner of the inefficiencies associated with this procedure vary depending on the vendor platform, but can be summarized generally as follows:

- The processor that handles routing is distinct from the router interfaces, and packets have to be copied to and from this processor.

- The processor itself may be a multi-processor that is not dedicated to the routing function.

- Routing table lookup is one-to-many instead of one-to-one.

Layer 3 switching addresses the inefficiencies of routing using the following principles:

- Dedicated ASICs: The processor that handles the routing function is usually a dedicated ASIC that is free from other tasks.

- "route once, switch many": Layer 3 switching is often described as "route once, switch many." When the router receives a packet, the next-hop is resolved using normal routing table lookup. With a layer 3 switch, the processor is likely to be enhanced and dedicated; however, it is still a one-to-many lookup on a specialized processor. Before forwarding the packet out of the destination interface, the routing table forwarding entry is copied to a high-speed memory or storage facility called a cache. All future packets in the flow to that particular destination are switched using the entry in the cache and without referring to the routing table. The cache entry can be accessed faster than the routing table because it is a specific one-to-one lookup. Also, the architectural location of the cache can be closer to the router interfaces, further reducing delay.

Figure 8-12 shows a schematic representation of a layer 3 switching scenario. The router receives an initial packet with a destination address

Figure 8-12
Simple layer 3
switching illustration

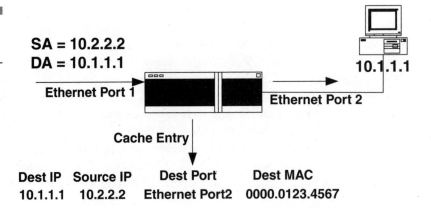

SA = 10.2.2.2
DA = 10.1.1.1
Ethernet Port 1
10.1.1.1
Ethernet Port 2

Cache Entry

Dest IP	Source IP	Dest Port	Dest MAC
10.1.1.1	10.2.2.2	Ethernet Port2	0000.0123.4567

10.1.1.1 on Ethernet port 1. The routing table resolves that the 10.1.1.0/24 subnet is directly attached on Ethernet port 2. Because the destination subnet is directly connected, the router must forward the packet directly to the destination address 10.1.1.1 on Ethernet port 1. To do this, it must resolve the destination MAC address by checking its ARP table. If no entry for 10.1.1.1 exists in the ARP table, an ARP broadcast must be issued by the router on 10.1.1.0/24. When the destination MAC address is resolved as being 0000.0123.4567, the Ethernet frame can be built and forwarded to the destination host.

The steps outlined involve all of the delay associated with routing table lookup and the resolution of the next-hop layer 2 address. By employing layer 3 switching, the routing table entry along with the appropriate destination layer 2 information is copied to the high-speed cache. This enables all subsequent packets destined for 10.1.1.1 to be forwarded to the appropriate MAC address on Ethernet port 2 after consulting the cache rather than the routing table. This is in line with the "route once, switch many" operation. The delay associated with routing table lookup and the layer 2 address resolution for the next-hop is eliminated, and the Ethernet frame can be built with a minimum latency.

In this example, the destination address resides at a directly connected network 10.1.1.0/24. For example, if the destination network were a number of router hops away, the exact same principle would be employed. The next-hop IP address would be obtained from the IP routing table for the initial packet in the flow. The layer 2 address for the next-hop would then be resolved. If the next-hop is over a LAN, it is an ARP resolution. If the next-hop to the destination were over a frame relay *Permanent Virtual Circuit* (PVC), the *Data Link Connection Identifier* (DLCI) would have to be resolved from the frame relay mapping table. In either scenario, the destination layer 2 address is stored in the cache so that subsequent packets can be forwarded to the next-hop without incurring these lookup delays.

The benefits of a hardware-based, one-to-one lookup means that layer 3 switching is comparable to layer 2 switching for speed. The main difference is that the forwarding decision is made based on the destination layer 3 address, exactly as with traditional routing. Because packets are processed at layer 3, no loss of device intelligence occurs.

Routers have two fundamental functions. The first is the routing control function that relates to the formation and maintenance of a routing table. The other function is packet switching or forwarding from an inbound interface to an outbound interface. Layer 3 switching technology has moved in the direction of separating the routing function and the packet forwarding function. A consequence of this, apart from reducing device latency, is reduced cost without a loss of functionality. The processor that handles the routing and control functions can supply the device intelligence to be shared by a larger number of ports, reducing per-port cost over a traditional router.

Building on the principle of layer 3 switching is a term that has gained much attention in the industry in recent years: layer 4 switching. Vendors who wish to gain a marketing edge have also overtly touted this term. Layer 4 switching entails the capability to make forwarding decisions based on layer 4 parameters such as TCP or UDP port numbers. The architectural implementation is the same as layer 3 switching in that the first packet in the flow is routed, and subsequent packets are switched using the high-speed cache. The difference is that a greater level of detail exists in the cache because the entry also includes layer 4 information. Traditional routers are capable of making forwarding decisions based on layer 4 information. For example, router A shown in Figure 8-13 could use filters and policy-based routing techniques to forward telnet traffic to 172.16.2.2 over port 1 and send FTP traffic to the same host over port 2. This is an example of layer 4 switching. The problem with its implementation on conventional router platforms is that each packet must be compared against the filtering criteria, which can introduce significant latency to the data flow. Hardware-based layer 4 switching that employs the same cache as layer 3 switching minimizes this latency.

Layer 4 switching is an efficient method of implementing different policies based on application-related information. This can include helping to satisfy certain quality of service parameters for specific applications. One potential issue with layer 4 switching is that it may cause the cache to grow in size because a different entry is required for each application flow to each IP destination. Most vendors support reasonably simple methods of man-

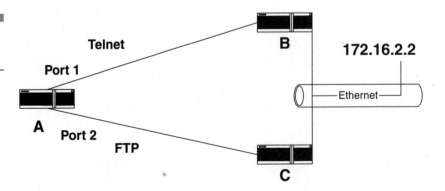

Figure 8-13
Illustration of layer 4 switching

aging the size of the cache. The entry timeout parameters can be varied, and it should also be possible configure a shorter timeout value for entries that are associated with short-lived flows such as a small *Trivial File Transfer Protocol* (TFTP) session or a *Domain Name System* (DNS) resolution. This usually operates by clearing an entry from the cache if no packets are switched relating to that flow within a configurable time interval.

NOTE: *Layer 3 switching is basically high-speed, hardware-based routing.*

Layer 4 switching incorporates the additional capability to consider layer 4 information when making forwarding decisions.

Layer 3 switching provides routing functionality in the campus LAN without the additional overhead and latency associated with routing. Because traffic patterns dictate that a certain amount of routing is necessary on most campus LANs, the efficiency of layer 3 switching can make an important contribution to improving network performance. Although layer 3 and layer 4 switching are much abused terms, they do relate to technology that has a purpose. The exact manner in which the technology is implemented varies on the different industry vendor platforms due to different approaches to hardware architecture and software features. The most important issue for the network administrator to know is the understanding of what exactly the technology entails and why it is of practical importance.

Campus Hierarchical Design

In this section, the different functional elements of a campus network will be presented in the form of a three-layered model. Each layer in the model relates to a section of the network and the functions associated with it. Although the use of such a model can greatly facilitate the engineer in conceptualizing the network, it should be emphasized that this is only a model and not something that should be followed exactly. It is important to be able to sub-divide the network in terms of the different functionality that will enable the design goals to be satisfied. However, as the case always is with network design, each network is different and must be designed on its own merits, to its own requirements, and within its own constraints. The three-layered model presented here is an extremely useful starting point, but it must be remembered that it is only a starting point. For example, some smaller networks may only have a two-layered hierarchy. The most important principle to understand is the functionality associated with each layer in the design model and how it relates to the design requirements.

Access Layer

The point at which end users attach to the network is commonly referred to as the access layer. The device that provides a first point of contact for the user is usually either a shared hub or as is more frequently the case on modern networks, a LAN switch. The relative merits of switched Ethernet over a shared medium have already been discussed along with one or two potential drawbacks. These issues determine whether the access device is a hub or a switch.

In a switched deployment, the VLAN that each user belongs to is determined by the configuration of the access layer switch. Each access layer device can have ports or stations in a single VLAN or in multiple VLANs. The planning issues surrounding VLAN deployment will be discussed later in this section.

The access device must be capable of supporting the aggregated throughput of all attached devices. In a switched Ethernet environment, a switched 10Mbps port is typically supplied to each desktop device. Fast Ethernet is also frequently deployed to the desktop for high-bandwidth users that use CAD or multimedia applications. Auto-sensing of speed and duplex is possible at the access layer. However, it is not recommended for the reasons already given: namely that auto-negotiation is a poorly standardized protocol for both speed and duplex and therefore, is unreliable. The network administrator should have a clear picture of what speed and duplex type is required and can be supported on which stations, and the port configurations should be set accordingly.

The access layer is one of the most vulnerable points on the network for malicious intrusion. Security features should be implemented on access layer devices as part of implementing the corporation's security policy. All means by which the LAN switches can be accessed such as console port, auxiliary port, or telnet should be password protected. It is a popular aspiration of organizations to tie the switch port to a particular MAC address in order to achieve intrusion prevention. All major LAN switch vendors support a mechanism whereby the switch can be configured to learn one MAC address on each port for security reasons. If that station is unplugged and another station attempts to access the LAN, the switch port is automatically disabled. This is an aspiration because although many companies find this level of security desirable (as indeed they should), an administrative overhead is associated with it. Also, scenarios occur where switch ports are swapped while troubleshooting, resulting in further outage on a second port. The entire subject of access layer security will be addressed rigorously in the final chapter of this book.

The access layer is probably one of the most neglected regions of the network when designing for resilience. Typically, most workstations have one connection to the switch without any resilience. A failure on the workstation, the connection to the switch, the switch port, or indeed the switch itself, results in a total loss of network connectivity. At the other end of the scale, high-availability requirements could be met by installing two NIC cards in each workstation and dual-homing to two switches.

Scalability at the access layer should entail the accommodation of growth in the number of network users as well as supporting growth in bandwidth requirements without requiring a radical change in topology. Scalability for growth in the number of projected users can be easily achieved using stackable or chassis and card-based switches. In terms of throughput, an estimate must be made of the maximum likely throughput requirements over the network lifetime, as dictated by the applications. Ideally, the access switches should be capable of accommodating an increase in throughput requirements up to this level without a significant change in hardware platform.

Intermediate Layer

The most fundamental function of what will be termed the intermediate layer is to provide an efficient point of aggregation for access devices. By connecting multiple access layer switches to intermediate layer switches via high-speed up-links, a reduced requirement exists for ports at the backbone of the campus network. Beyond device and connection aggregation, the introduction of an intermediate layer between the access layer and campus backbone presents the possibility to localize a significant amount of network functionality and offload it from the backbone.

A typical topology can entail a group of access switches connecting to two intermediate layer switches for redundancy, as shown in Figure 8-14. This configuration can be termed an intermediate switch block. The switch block can be an aggregated group of users within the same wiring closet or within

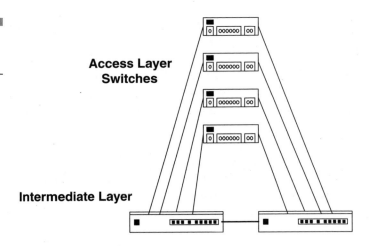

Figure 8-14
Typical intermediate
layer switch block

**Access Layer
Switches**

Intermediate Layer

the same building. We will discuss the issues that pertain to sizing the switch block soon.

The functionality that can be supplied by the intermediate layer includes the following:

- Logical and physical aggregation: The intermediate layer must provide an adequate point of aggregation for the access layer both in terms of connection and bandwidth capacity. The potential traffic bottlenecks at the intermediate layer are the links from the access devices and the throughput capability of the intermediate devices. Capacity planning should be performed to ensure that these parameters satisfy current and future requirements.

  A potential point for logical aggregation is also presented by the inclusion of an intermediate layer. The IP addressing structure will relate in part to whether routing is implemented at this layer or not. If routing is implemented and the intermediate switch block contains multiple subnets, a contiguous subnet address range should be chosen in order to facilitate route summarization.

- Workgroup localization: The topology presented by the existence of an intermediate layer can facilitate cases where logical workgroups are also in close working proximity to each other. Servers can be localized and the workgroup traffic can be kept off the backbone of the network. This can provide significant performance benefits when it is a high-bandwidth application, as in the earlier example of the engineering design department.

■ VLAN termination: The creation of VLANs is also facilitated. The VLANs can terminate at the intermediate layer in which case they are said to be local VLANs. Alternatively, the VLANs can span throughout the network, grouping users and servers that are in physically diverse locations. These VLANs are usually termed end-to-end VLANs.

As we shall see in the upcoming discussion on VLANs, local VLANs are becoming more common than end-to-end VLANs due to the increasing trend to centralize resources. Local VLANs terminate at the intermediate layer, meaning that this layer must incorporate routing functionality. The main benefit of these VLANs is the reduction in the size of the broadcast domains.

■ Inter-VLAN routing: A possible downside to the implementation of local VLANs is the routing latency that is incurred along the client-server path, which further emphasizes the need for efficient routing or layer 3 switching at the intermediate layer. A sample logical topology for local VLANs is shown in Figure 8-15. Communication between any of the VLANs shown or from these VLANs to centralized resources will involve routing.

The routing functionality at the intermediate layer can be implemented using an external router that connects to the intermediate layer switches or via a routing card that sits in the intermediate layer chassis. The pricing and performance issues related to the vendor in question will determine the option chosen.

Figure 8-15
VLAN implementation
with routing at
intermediate layer

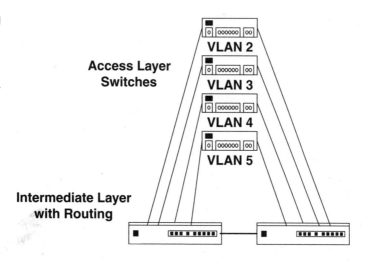

Routing may be employed at the intermediate layer in order to curtail the propagation of any unnecessary broadcasts onto the backbone. This can help restrict the traffic traversing the backbone to that related to centralized resources.

■ Spanning tree termination: A single instance of the spanning tree protocol that relates to all VLANs on the network can be implemented. This is usually synonymous with the use of 802.1q VLAN trunking. Most vendors also support the capability to implement a separate instance of spanning tree for each VLAN. In such a scenario, the spanning tree domain terminates at the VLAN boundary. Hence, the spanning tree domain would terminate at the intermediate layer device when implementing local VLANs. With smaller domains, the frequency of layer 2 topology changes and the regularity with which the spanning tree must be recalculated are reduced. A second benefit of a smaller domain is the reduction of the spanning tree convergence time following a topology change. Given that the STP convergence time is a likely limiting factor to the scalability of switched networks, this is a potentially significant benefit.

■ Policy implementation: The inclusion of routing functionality at the intermediate layer increases network intelligence at that point in the network. This is allied with the capability to implement various network policies such as security, filtering, and QOS. The intermediate layer devices will also have increased network analysis and management capability as a result of their layer 3 awareness.

A point is worth noting in relation to the implementation of QOS policies at the intermediate layer. Some commentators cite this as a major advantage of having routing functionality at this layer. However, it is more accurate to say that routing functionality further facilitates QOS because QOS should ultimately be implemented end-to-end between the end devices rather than simply at one point along the data path.

■ Media translation: Media translation is required at some point in networks that incorporate multiple media types. The distribution layer is a typical point in the network for translating between fast Ethernet and gigabit Ethernet or *Asynchronous Transfer Mode* (ATM).

■ Redundancy and resilience: The intermediate layer should have redundant physical connections to both the access layer and the backbone. Layer 2 redundancy is incorporated using the spanning tree protocol, and layer 3 resilience is provided in a routed network by the routing protocol. Ideally, the failover convergence time should not interrupt the existing client-server sessions, and the backup paths should not result in degraded service due to reduced bandwidth capacity.

Resilience should be incorporated with respect to devices as well as links. Link aggregation provides resilience in the event of the failure of a single link; however, it does not protect against device failure. A sample redundant topology within an intermediate layer switch block is shown in Figure 8-16. Each access switch is dual-homed to a separate intermediate layer switch. The intermediate switches have resilient connections to the campus backbone. This topology incorporates resilience in the devices as well as the links.

Scaling the Intermediate Layer The intermediate layer should be scaled by widening the network rather than by introducing a further layer. Introducing another intermediate layer device that provides direct access to

Figure 8-16
Resilient campus
topology

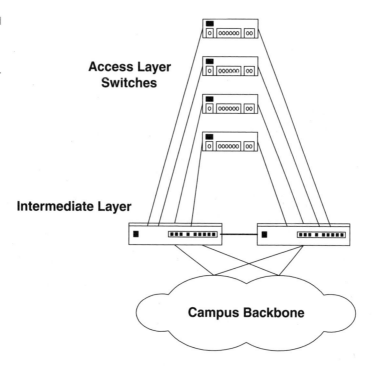

the backbone should accommodate a growth in the number or physical dispersion of access layer devices. The temptation to use quick fixes to accommodate growth should be avoided if they compromise the consistency of the network topology. As the case always is in network design, a compromise in the original design causes a loss of predictability in performance often to the point where the original design has been eroded into non-existence.

Adequate capacity planning should be performed to support the throughput and performance requirements of current and projected future applications. The aggregation of all access layer traffic should be catered for and should include a scope for growth. The capacity parameters in question include the bandwidth on links between the access and intermediate layers, and also the speed of the intermediate links to the campus backbone. The intermediate layer devices must also have adequate processing power to meet current and future throughput specifications.

When scaling the network at the intermediate layer, it is important to have some estimate of the maximum acceptable size of the intermediate layer switch block. This is the point at which it will be deemed necessary to begin the construction of a new switch block rather than expanding an existing one. This growth must be estimated both in terms of the number of users as well as traffic. It is difficult and not necessarily essential to have precise figures for these parameters; however, an understanding of the issues that determine the maximum size of the intermediate switch block is important. The following issues shape that determination:

- Number of users: This determines the number of access switches and hence, the number of switch ports required at the intermediate layer. The maximum number of switch ports available on the intermediate layer switch is likely to place an upper limit on the number of users within the block. A large number of users within an intermediate block is not necessarily a problem in itself because the more relevant parameter is the traffic profile associated with these users. However, it is not bad practice as a rule of thumb to place the upper limit on the number of allowed users in a block because on average, more users mean more traffic.

- Traffic level and profile: The importance of this parameter in sizing the intermediate switch block cannot be overstated. The switch block should be dimensioned by the amount of traffic going through the intermediate layer devices rather than by the number of users in the block. If clients are engaging in bandwidth-intensive applications, this should reduce the maximum allowable number of users per block. In the case where local VLANs are implemented, a high percentage of inter-VLAN traffic places greater route processing demands on the intermediate layer devices. Hence, if the traffic profile is such that most of it terminates remotely rather than locally to its VLAN, a further limiting factor is placed on the size of the intermediate block. The opposite is true in cases where most of the traffic remains within the VLAN.

■ Sizing the broadcast domains: A specific question related to traffic profiles is the level of broadcasts that will be observed within the intermediate block. The key benefit of local VLANs is the manner in which the size of the broadcast domains is reduced. The number of end stations within a broadcast domain is determined by the level of broadcasts associated with the applications within the domain. If all users within the intermediate switch block are in the same VLAN (and hence, the same broadcast domain), the level of broadcasts associated with the applications will place a limit on the number of users within the block. A high percentage of broadcasts also limits the size of the intermediate block in cases where the broadcasts are contained using multiple VLANs. This is true because the intermediate layer device must still process the broadcasts on each VLAN. More VLANs also mean that more routing must be performed at the intermediate layer, which can increase the CPU processing strain on devices at this layer.

■ Sizing the spanning tree domain: Spanning tree convergence issues place an upper limit on the size of the spanning tree domain even when a separate instance of STP occurs for each VLAN. This can limit the size of each VLAN as well as the size of the intermediate switch block. Without good design and some fine-tuning, STP convergence can result in a network outage of the order of minutes following each layer 2 topology change. Containing the size of the STP domain is one way of reducing this effect. The next chapter will discuss some steps that can be taken to improve spanning tree convergence and hence, its scalability.

Campus Backbone

The campus backbone provides two simple yet critical functions. First, it is used to establish interconnectivity between intermediate layer switch blocks. Secondly, it provides high-speed access to all resources that are shared by parts of the enterprise.

Given its criticality, the campus backbone must be characterized by high throughput and high availability. If the backbone is slow or congested, the entire network's access to common resources is slow. By the same token, an outage on the backbone affects the entire network underlying the requirement for resilience and high availability.

The requirement for high throughput at the backbone should be satisfied as follows:

- Bandwidth aggregation: The links between the intermediate layer devices and the backbone devices should cater to the total current and projected aggregated traffic from each intermediate switch block. The typical speeds deployed at the backbone are multiples of fast Ethernet, gigabit Ethernet, or ATM.

- Minimal policy implementation: Network policies should not be implemented on the backbone devices if possible. The configuration of access filters' security features and special policy-based configurations usually have the result of increasing device overhead and CPU utilization. The backbone is the least desirable place on the network to incur additional overhead. Networking polices should be implemented on access and intermediate layer devices where possible, allowing the backbone to remain lean and mean.

- Elimination of unnecessary traffic: As a general rule, only traffic that is essential to client-server connectivity should traverse the backbone. Any unnecessary traffic should be filtered from the backbone at the intermediate layer. For example, broadcasts relating to the applications or the routing protocol that are sent onto the backbone from multiple sources can be filtered appropriately.

Implementing the following steps can satisfy the high availability requirements of the backbone:

- Resilient connections: Each intermediate layer device should have dual connectivity to each backbone device.

- Device resilience: The simplest type of backbone configuration is a direct connection between two intermediate switch blocks. This is also called a collapsed backbone and is a topic that will be revisited shortly. For all other backbone topologies, at least two backbone devices should be deployed for resilience. Each intermediate layer device should be dual-homed with the two backbone devices, as shown in Figure 8-17.

- Fast convergence: The provision of resilient connections and dual-homed devices ensures that resilience exists along the physical data

Figure 8-17
Resilient campus topology

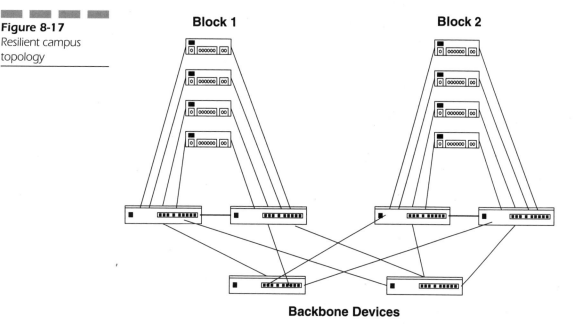

path through the backbone. In order to gain the full benefits of a resilient topology, the convergence to a backup path must be fast to avoid application failure. Layer 2 convergence is determined by the spanning tree protocol, whereas convergence at layer 3 depends on the routing protocol., The issue of convergence is a key element to the decision of whether or not layer 3 functionality should be incorporated at the backbone.

Gigabit Ethernet   Ethernet has become the dominant technology in campus LAN environments due not only to the simplicity and maturity of the technology, but also because it is now available at different speeds. Fast Ethernet or 100Mbps Ethernet is identical in specification to 10Mbps. It can be deployed directly to the desktop for power users, and it is a popular choice for server NICs. Fast Ethernet to the client desktop is still the exception rather than the rule. A more typical configuration is switched 10Mbps to the desktop with fast Ethernet connections between the access layer and intermediate layer switches. Aggregated fast Ethernet links are used frequently to provide the bandwidth between the intermediate layer and the backbone. These connections must provide sufficient bandwidth to cater to the total aggregated throughput of all intermediate blocks. This bandwidth requirement has provided the most popular niche for the deployment of gigabit Ethernet. It is not the only point where gigabit Ethernet is being rolled out on modern networks. In cases where the demand for bandwidth is high, gigabit Ethernet can be deployed between the access and intermediate layers. Gigabit Ethernet NICs can be used in high performance UNIX-based and multimedia servers that have the capability of creating congestion on fast Ethernet connections.

Gigabit Ethernet is described by the 802.3z standard and is similar to 10/100 Ethernet at the data link layer. The main difference is that the minimum frame size has been increased to 512 bytes in order to enable collision detection on such a high-speed medium where frames are sent onto the wire quickly. Another slight deviation from traditional Ethernet is the addition of extension bits between successive frames. This enables frame bursting where a station is able to send several successive frames without losing access to the wire.

Despite these minor alterations to the data link standard, gigabit Ethernet is fully compatible with legacy Ethernet and does not require any frame translation in a switched Ethernet environment.

The physical layer is significantly different in order to achieve the 1Gbps speed. The 802.3 Ethernet standard is amalgamated with the ANSI X3T11 fiber channel standard in order to produce the physical layer specification for 802.3z.

Although the primary physical specification relates to a fiber medium, implementations of gigabit Ethernet over copper also are available; however, they are currently characterized by short distance limitations. Table 8-1 summarizes the various physical implementations of 1Gbps Ethernet along with the corresponding distance limitations.

Table 8-1

Physical Implementations of Gigabit Ethernet

Technology	Transmission category	Distance limitation
1000BaseCX	Copper shielded twisted pair (STP)	25 meters
1000BaseT	Copper category 5 UTP (uses 4 pairs)	100 meters
1000BaseSX	Multi-mode fiber cable (using 780nm short wavelength laser sources)	250 meters
1000BaseLX	Single-mode fiber cable (using 1300-1500nm long wavelength laser sources)	3km - 10km (some vendor platforms support a higher specification than the 1000BaseLX standard)

The advent of gigabit Ethernet has in many ways rolled back the development and deployment of ATM as a LAN technology. The single greatest driving force behind ATM was bandwidth and that issue has now been resolved in the form of gigabit Ethernet. Unlike ATM, gigabit Ethernet does not directly incorporate any *quality of service* (QOS) features. However, the implementation of specific QOS policies can be delegated to other protocols such as *Resource Reservation Setup Protocol* (RSVP) (as we will discuss). An argument can also be made that if bandwidth is sufficiently plentiful, then ensuring a certain QOS for particular applications is less of an issue.

Gigabit Ethernet also holds other important advantages over ATM. Namely it exhibits simplicity and is based on a mature technology with which technical support staff is already familiar. This reduces the cost of deployment and more importantly, support. Of course gigabit Ethernet still has room for improvement on the development cycle. Cost will come down and distance limitation figures will improve. At the moment, these are the issues that can still give ATM some advantage as a backbone technology for a large and geographically dispersed campus.

Scaling the Backbone   The campus backbone must support aggregation of all network traffic as well as accommodating future projected growth. The network must be capable of supporting a growth in network users and application traffic without radically altering the backbone configuration or topology.

Increasing the number of intermediate layer switch blocks, which in turn increases the connectivity requirements at the backbone, should ideally scale a campus network. It is important to understand that it is the increased user and application requirements experienced in each intermediate switch block that fuels the growth of the backbone rather than the other way around. After all, the function of the backbone is to provide high-speed connectivity between the intermediate blocks and also to enterprise resources. The backbone scales as necessary in order to continue satisfying these functions.

As the throughput requirements of an intermediate block grows, more links may be added for connecting to the backbone. As more switch blocks are added, more backbone devices may also be commissioned to accommodate this growth. The key issues that relate to scaling the backbone are intrinsically linked to whether the backbone is exclusively flat (in other words layer 2 switched) or whether it incorporates routing functionality. The question of scalability is central to the upcoming discussion on the relative merits of a layer 2 switched or a layer 3 routed backbone.

Collapsed Backbone versus Distributed

Before progressing to a discussion of the different alternatives for a logical backbone configuration, the two fundamental types of physical backbone implementations will be explained.

A collapsed backbone uses the minimum amount of equipment to facilitate the interconnection of the intermediate layer blocks. In the case of just two intermediate blocks, a collapsed backbone could be implemented by directly connecting the two blocks, as shown in Figure 8-18. If a larger number of blocks is present or if it is required to plan for possible growth, interblock connectivity could be achieved by using a single backbone switch, as displayed in Figure 8-19. The advantage of a collapsed backbone is simplicity, and the fact that a minimum amount of equipment is used. The disadvantage is that it may represent a single point of failure.

The capability of providing redundant connections from each switch block is often the reason why a distributed backbone topology is implemented. A distributed backbone consists of multiple devices that usually provide resilient connectivity to each intermediate switch block. Figure 8-20 illustrates a network diagram that represents a distributed backbone consisting of two devices. For a larger number of switch blocks, more backbone devices could be added. In general, a collapsed backbone is a realistic choice

Figure 8-18
Collapsed backbone topology

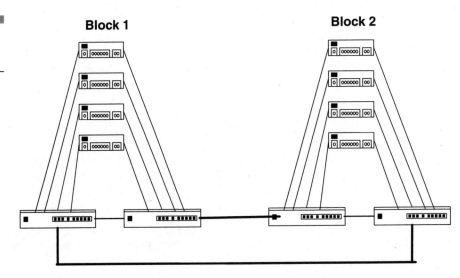

Block 1

Block 2

Figure 8-19
Backbone collapsed
into a single device

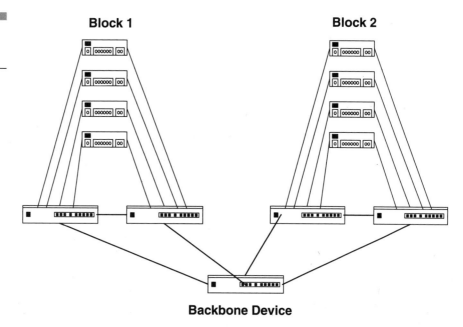

Block 1   Block 2

Backbone Device

Figure 8-20
Distributed campus
backbone

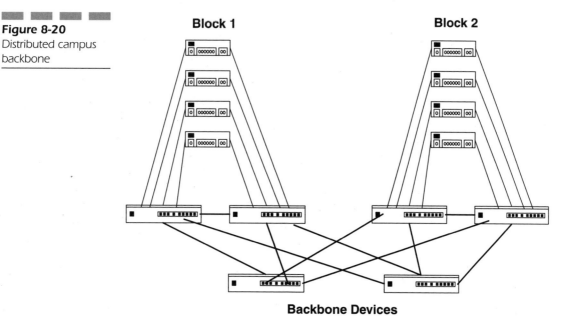

Block 1   Block 2

Backbone Devices

on a small campus, perhaps where only two intermediate blocks exist. For larger campus networks, a distributed backbone is more likely to be implemented due to its greater resilience and scalability.

Having discussed the different physical implementations of the backbone, we will now address the issue of its logical configuration, and in particular whether it should consist of layer 2 or layer 3 devices.

NOTE: *A collapsed backbone uses a minimum amount of equipment.*
A distributed backbone is more resilient and scalable, making it preferable for larger campus networks.

Routed Backbone versus Switched

As we have already seen, some routing functionality is deployed at the intermediate layer on many large campus networks in order to create isolated broadcast domains and to terminate the spanning tree domains. Part of the motivation behind the use of routing at the intermediate layer is to offload processor-intensive functions, such as policy implementation, from the backbone devices. Thus, it may seem reasonable to assume that if routing is employed at the intermediate layer, then it is not required at the backbone itself. An exclusively layer 2 switched backbone is indeed a viable and prudent alternative for many networks. We will discuss this approach now along with its benefits. However, it does present some limitations on very large campuses that will also be highlighted, which will lead to a discussion on the merits of a layer 3 routed backbone.

High throughput and high availability must characterize the campus backbone. With regard to the network shown in Figure 8-20, the resilient connections and devices are intended to ensure high availability. Routing is implemented at the intermediate layer devices with the intention of eliminating the need for routing at the backbone. Let us examine the functionality of this network on the assumption that the backbone only has layer 2 awareness.

The logical configuration of the backbone is presented in Figure 8-21, where the two backbone subnets are both dually attached to each of the intermediate layer routers. If this is a purely switched backbone, it may be valid to ask why do two subnets exist instead of just one? The reason that the backbone switches are not interconnected is to avoid bringing spanning tree into the equation. If the backbone switches were connected, the STP would have to block one of the ports in order to prevent bridging loops. STP is slow to converge, and so although no loss of redundancy would occur, the

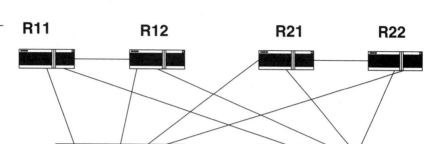

Figure 8-21
Logical representation
of intermediate layer
routing

network would be slow to react to topology changes, possibly resulting in
network downtime while STP is recalculating itself.

NOTE: *Backbone switches should not be connected to each other in order
to avoid using the spanning tree protocol and having the resulting
convergence issues.*

A second reason also exists, which suggests that it is better to not interconnect the backbone devices. If the backbone consisted of just one IP subnet, dual connections could not be made from each discrete intermediate
layer router to the backbone. This is because the same subnet cannot connect at more than one point to the same router.

This example shows two equal cost paths, but what if three or four equal
cost paths were required in order to achieve the necessary throughput
across the backbone? If three equal cost paths were required, three subnets
with the corresponding backbone switches would be necessary. For four
equal cost paths, four backbone devices would have to be deployed and so
on. Any other solution would mean that a one-to-one correspondence would
not exist between logical and physical redundancy.

Generally for the topology that we are dealing with here, if n equal cost
paths are required, then n backbone devices are necessary to support this.
Ultimately, the maximum number of equal cost paths is dictated by the
routing protocol. Most IP routing protocols can typically support up to four
equal cost paths, and some can be configured to support six. Thus, an upper
limit is placed on the number of backbone switches that can provide equal

cost paths. If a greater number of backbone devices were available than the maximum number of equal cost paths supported by the routing protocol, the remaining devices would have to be interconnected to maintain a resilient topology.

It may seem reasonable to assume that on most networks, four high-end backbone switches would provide the necessary connectivity requirements for the intermediate layer blocks. This is where another issue comes in to play, and it relates again to the routing protocol.

Return again to a consideration of the topology shown in Figure 8-21. In terms of layer 3 redundancy, each intermediate layer router has two equal cost paths to the backbone and to the other switch block. For example, R11 has two equal cost paths: one via each of the backbone subnets. It will also learn a path via R12, but this will have a higher cost, and hence, will not be placed in its routing table. The use of equal cost paths can be desirable because it means that the loss of one path does not require any convergence time. If one path is lost, this path will be removed from the routing table, and all traffic will traverse the second path instead of being load-shared. In earlier chapters, caution was voiced in relation to load sharing. With layer 3 switching, the load sharing is likely to be on a per-destination basis. The network administrator should check that the load sharing is well balanced and the busiest destinations are not mainly cached against one path. A second word of warning relates to the tolerance that the applications have for packets arriving out of sequence. TCP-based applications can overcome this, but UDP-based applications would require some intelligence in the higher layers to correct out of sequence packets. A final point to note in relation to load sharing over equal cost paths is that sufficient under-subscription of the bandwidth utilization should exist so that the failure of one link will not overload the remaining link(s).

NOTE: *The use of equal cost paths eliminates convergence issues.*
Exercise caution with equal cost load balancing. Understand in particular traffic distribution on links and application tolerance for out of sequence packets. Links should also be less than fully utilized to avoid overloading in a fault scenario.

This example shows two equal cost paths but what if three or four equal cost paths were required in order to achieve the necessary throughput across the backbone? If three equal cost paths were required then three subnets with the corresponding backbone switches would be necessary. For four equal cost paths, four backbone devices would have to be deployed and so on. Any other solution would mean that there would not be a one to one correspondence between logical redundancy and physical redundancy.

Generally for the topology that we are dealing with here, if n equal cost paths are required, then n backbone deviced are necessary to support this. Ultimately the maximum number of equal cost paths is dictated by the routing protocol. Most IP routing protocols can typically support up to four equal cost paths and some can be configured to support six. Thus an upper limit is placed on the number of backbone switches that can provide equal cost paths. If there were a greater number of backbone devices, than the maximum number of equal cost paths supported by the routing protocol the remaining devices would have to be inter-connected to maintain a resilient topology.

It may seem reasonable to assume that on most networks four high-end backbone switches would provide the necessary connectivity requirements for the immediate layer blocks. This is where another issue comes in to play and it relates again to the routing protocol.

If a non-scalable distance vector routing protocol is employed, an excessive amount would route overhead traffic on the backbone devices. Periodic routing updates would be broadcast from every intermediate layer router that attaches to the particular backbone switch. With this level of broadcast replication, an upper limit is placed on the number of intermediate layer router devices that can attach to any backbone device. For this type of network, a scalable routing protocol such as OSPF is far more likely to be employed given the size and scalability requirements of the network. However, scalable protocols such as OSPF and EIGRP rely on neighbor formation, which presents its own limiting factor. In the earlier chapters on IP routing protocols, we learned that an upper limit was placed on the number of neighbors that these protocols could support. This limitation is more pronounced for EIGRP than for OSPF. This is because EIGRP routers maintain a copy of their neighbor's routing table, and a large number of neighbors means excessive memory consumption and also the possibility of convergence problems given the operation of EIGRP. To be fair to EIGRP, convergence problems are less likely if the neighbor formation is predominantly over high-bandwidth LAN links as opposed to heavily utilized WAN links. However, this does not excuse the fact that an upper limit is placed on the number of possible neighbors as is the case with OSPF. With a switched backbone, each intermediate layer router will form a neighbor with every other intermediate router. Thus, if 10 intermediate blocks exist with dual-homed connections to two backbone switches, each intermediate router will form 38 neighbor relationships (two from each of the other routers).

It is loathsome to quote upper limits on the number of neighbors that can be supported by each protocol. It is essential to understand the operation of the protocol within one's own network as explained in earlier chapters. A lot depends on how busy the backbone links are, particularly in the case of EIGRP. Because people like to have a ballpark figure, it will be provided in Table 8-2 as a crude guideline. The figures quoted should be supported by each protocol. It may well be possible to support a greater number of neighbors, but that depends on the network topology, traffic conditions, and the processor and memory resources available on the routers.

If the maximum neighbor limit is reached on a switched backbone, it is likely that more backbone switches would have to be introduced to accommodate a growth in the number of intermediate layer blocks. Each intermediate block would connect to two of these backbone switches, and the backbone switches would have to be interconnected to maintain resilience. Then we would be back facing the spanning tree issue of slow convergence. This is a compelling argument for incorporating routing functionality at the backbone.

A logical representation of a routed backbone is displayed in Figure 8-22. By employing routing at the backbone, the issue regarding the maximum number of neighbors is eliminated. This is because each intermediate router forms a neighbor relationship with the backbone routers only.

A routed backbone also means that the backbone routers can be interconnected without having to rely on spanning tree. Thus, the interconnection of backbone devices is an option that does not carry with it the cost of slow convergence.

Advantages of a Layer 3 Campus Backbone   We will now summarize the reasons why layer 3 functionality might be introduced at the backbone. The common thread of these reasons is that they apply to very large campus networks. Basically, a layer 3 backbone has better scalability than an exclusively switched backbone.

Table 8-2

Routing Protocol
Neighbor
Limitations

IP Routing Protocol	Maximum number neighbors	Number of links from each intermediate block	Maximum number of intermediate blocks
OSPF	45	2	22
RIP	25	2	12
EIGRP	35	2	17

Figure 8-22

Logical representation
of a routed backbone

Block 1

Block 2

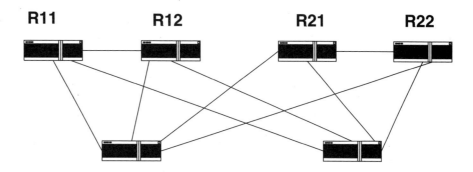

R11

R12

R21

R22

Backbone Routers

- Routing protocol and application overhead: A distance vector routing protocol has the potential to saturate a switched backbone with periodic routing updates.

  A switched backbone also means a larger broadcast domain that can be susceptible to other types of broadcasts such as those relating to applications. Routing at the intermediate layer curtails the propagation of many application broadcasts; however, instances occur (for example, IPX) where the intermediate routers store application information and broadcast it periodically.

- Routing protocol neighbor limitations: Scalable routing protocols such as OSPF and EIGRP rely on neighbor formation. A practical upper limit is placed on the number of neighbor relationships that can exist on each intermediate layer router. Therefore, as the number of intermediate layer devices grows, a point will come where more backbone devices must be added. The maximum number of equal cost paths that can be supported by the routing protocol dictates the maximum number of subnets at the backbone. Hence, a point may come where no new subnets can be added, and the existing backbone subnets cannot be expanded without incurring more routing protocol neighbors. Also, if new backbone devices are added that do not represent new subnets, not only does a problem arise with the number of routing protocol neighbors, but the spanning tree protocol must be used between the switches.

- Speed of convergence: On a layer 2 switched backbone, the backbone devices cannot be connected to each other without using the spanning tree protocol. On a very large network, it may be necessary to interconnect the backbone devices. The convergence time associated with the spanning tree protocol is significantly slower than a scalable IP routing protocol, and a topology change will often result in a temporary loss of client-server connectivity.

- Load balancing: Load balancing can take the form of equal cost paths, as seen by the intermediate layer routers. This has the advantage of not incurring any convergence time in the event of link failure. If the number of backbone devices exceeds the number of equal cost paths supported by the routing protocol, the backbone switches must be interconnected to maintain resilience. This means that the load balancing is dictated by the spanning tree protocol rather than the IP routing protocol. This has two disadvantages. First, converging STP is significantly slower. Secondly, load balancing at layer 2 is more complex to configure and administer. Particular switch ports must be configured to forward for some VLANs and block for others. On a routed backbone, the load balancing is always handled by the IP routing protocol because the spanning tree protocol is not required.

NOTE: *On very large campus networks, arguments can be made for implementing routing at the backbone.*

Advantages of a Layer 2 Backbone

- Cost: Routing is always more expensive than switching. Cost always has input into network design policy decisions.

- Elimination of router latency: A problem with implementing routing functionality at both the intermediate layer and backbone is that the campus network becomes logically more like a routed network than a switched network. The majority of packets along the client-server data path are routed with resulting overhead and increased latency. However, with the advent of layer 3 switching, this overhead can be minimized. Also, the issue of layer 3 switching and load balancing arises . It is important to ensure that the busiest destinations are not cached against the same path producing a distorted traffic profile with possible congestion. This is an issue for the routers at the intermediate layer as well.

It may seem that the implementation of routing at the backbone has brought matters full circle and is a throwback to legacy routed networks. Certainly an element of truth rests in this. The fundamental explanation for this trend is that traffic patterns are changing with a greater move toward centralization. Also, with the advent of layer 3 switching, the performance penalty associated with layer 3 functionality has been reduced. However, bear in mind that layer 3 functionality is only likely to be necessary at the backbone of very large campus networks. The limiting factors that we discussed for a layer 2 backbone are essentially related to scalability limits that are unlikely to be exceeded on most campus LANs. In this context, it is not so surprising because in networking, as networks grow, so does the requirement for more layer 3 processing generally.

Increased routing generally means increased cost and at least the possibility of a performance penalty. Other options can be explored to reduce the amount of routing on the campus LAN.

■ Switching at the intermediate layer: Figure 8-23 shows a topology where each intermediate block consists purely of layer 2 switches that may also have VLANs configured. The backbone routers are required in order to communicate between the VLANs. Thus, routing is confined exclusively to the backbone.

The first problem here is that the broadcast domains extend down to the backbone, which is at odds with the principle of keeping unnecessary traffic off the backbone.

Another issue relates to the fact that in the physical topology, each intermediate layer switch connects to each of the backbone routers. However, each backbone router can only implement the same VLAN on one interface. This means that each intermediate switch can only trunk for half of the VLANs in that block and must enable the other switch to trunk for the remaining VLANs. Figure 8-23 shows a schematic diagram of such a configuration.

■ Implement trunking on the servers: NICs on the market support 802.1q as well as some of the proprietary VLAN trunking protocols. A network configuration could be implemented whereby the servers do the trunking between the VLANs at the backbone of the network. With this topology, routing would be required at the intermediate layers;

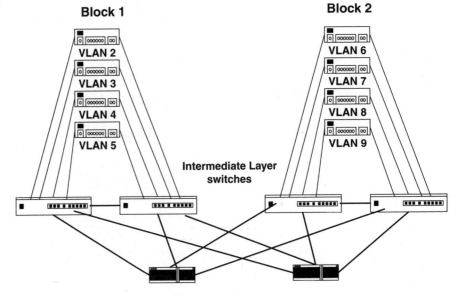

Figure 8-23
Inter-VLAN routing at
the backbone

otherwise the broadcast domains would be too large and would most
likely slow down the servers. This leads to the main disadvantage of
such an approach: the processing overhead placed on the server that
must trunk between all or certainly multiple VLANs.

Sample Campus Topology

Having discussed the pros and cons of the various approaches to designing
a campus LAN, it is appropriate to give an example of a typical topology for
a medium to large campus.

The topology displayed in Figure 8-24 incorporates full device and link
redundancy. On most networks, a cost versus availability tradeoff may exist
so a certain level of resilience may have to be sacrificed. This design
assumes under-subscription of bandwidth during normal operation; thus,
guaranteeing that no overload will be present on the remaining active links
during a fault condition.

The access layer is layer 2 switched. Each port is in its own collision
domain, and full-duplex Ethernet can be implemented to the desktop. Each
access switch is in a separate VLAN in order to locally contain broadcasts.

Figure 8-24
Sample of resilient
campus technology

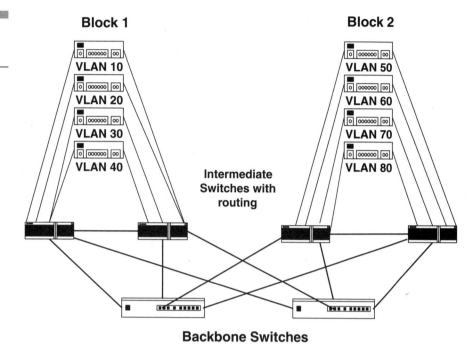

Block 1

VLAN 10
VLAN 20
VLAN 30
VLAN 40

Block 2

VLAN 50
VLAN 60
VLAN 70
VLAN 80

**Intermediate
Switches with
routing**

Backbone Switches

Redundant fast Ethernet links are available from each access switch to the two intermediate layer switches that also incorporate routing functionality. Spanning tree blocks one fast Ethernet link on each switch. The spanning priority parameters have been manipulated to ensure that each intermediate switch has an approximately equal number of ports forwarding traffic.

The routing functionality at the intermediate layer can be implemented using discrete routers or modular cards that form part of the switch chassis. This is a decision that relates to the vendor platform. The intermediate layer devices perform inter-VLAN routing and are dual-homed to each of the backbone switches. There are a total of five intermediate switch blocks, one of which contains most of the centralized servers. Therefore, each intermediate layer router will see 18 routing protocol neighbors on the backbone interface, which is within the neighbor limitations.

A mechanism should also be in place to provide the end stations with a redundant IP default gateway. Each station has an active connection to one intermediate switch, as dictated by the STP. A path exists to each intermediate layer router; hence, each station can have either of these routers as its default gateway regardless of what fast Ethernet link is in a forwarding state. Ideally, a dynamic failover mechanism should be in place in the event of a fault on the active default gateway. This issue will be returned to later as a number of standardized and proprietary solutions are available for implementing redundant default gateways.

The backbone switches are not connected in order to avoid any spanning tree issues. Two equal cost paths are presented by the backbone to each router for the purpose of connecting to other intermediate blocks.

Designing the LAN II— VLANs, Multicasting, and QoS

This is the second chapter dealing with the campus *local area network* (LAN). Here, some of the issues already discussed in relation to campus network design will be expanded upon and new topics will also be explored. Specifically, the question of *virtual local area networks* (VLANs) will be discussed in more detail. The rationale behind the deployment of VLANs will also be explained. The key issues that must be understood before VLANs can be implemented will also be discussed, as will the techniques for optimizing a network that employs VLAN technology.

The design issues associated with the *spanning tree protocol* (STP) are also studied in this chapter. A key element of this discussion is the method used to optimize spanning tree operation and convergence on any switched network.

The switched campus LAN is supporting more bandwidth-intensive and diverse applications than ever before. This trend is very much in tandem with the development of IP multicasting technology that can efficiently support high-bandwidth real-time applications. Allied to the greater diversity in the nature of network applications is the need for *quality of service* (QoS) technology that can enable these applications to efficiently coexist on the same network. For this reason, the last two sections of the chapter will deal with IP multicasting and QoS techniques with a particular emphasis on the *Resource Reservation Setup Protocol* (RSVP).

VLAN Planning

The motivations behind the deployment of VLANs are described in this section. The key issues to be considered in realtion to the design, implementation and management of VLANs are also examined.

Why Implement VLANs?

The following is a summary of the main driving forces behind the implementation of virtual LANs:

- *Broadcast containment*: Each port on a switch represents a separate collision domain; however, all ports on a switched network are in the same broadcast domain. The adverse effects of the unnecessary propagation of broadcasts have already been well documented in this book. Any broadcast that is issued by any station on the campus LAN would have to be processed by every station on that LAN on a completely flat-switched network. The interruption of each device's *central processing unit* (CPU) is probably a more serious issue than the bandwidth consumption associated with broadcasts in a LAN environment.

VLANs provide a mechanism for creating multiple broadcast domains in a switched network. A broadcast issued by a particular station will then only propagate to stations that are on the same VLAN. A router is required to enable communication between VLANs just as one is required for communication between physical LANs. This can be easily understood by noting that a VLAN is synonymous with an IP subnet. In a switched environment, if two stations are on the same VLAN, then they must also be on the same IP subnet.

NOTE: *A VLAN is synonymous with an IP subnet. For this reason, a device with routing functionality is required to enable communication between VLANs.*

- *Security*: By filtering broadcasts, VLANs impose a certain level of security similar to that normally associated with routed subnets. Consider the case of a network analyzer that is plugged into a particular switch port. If this port is assigned to a particular VLAN, then the analyzer will only detect broadcasts associated with that VLAN rather than for the entire LAN. Security policies can also be configured on the router that controls the inter-VLAN communication just as for conventional LAN segments.

- *IP address plan*: The IP address plan may also in part dictate the VLAN strategy. For example, if a 26-bit mask is being used for LAN subnets, then the maximum number of hosts per subnet is 60. This means that the entire LAN cannot simply remain flat with 60 hosts. If a large number of hosts exists on the switched LAN, VLANs must be created with a maximum of 60 hosts per VLAN.

  The reverse of this is also true, of course. If VLANs are created on a campus LAN, then they must each correspond to a particular IP subnet. For example, 20 VLANs require 20 LAN subnets and the IP address plan must be designed accordingly.

- *Flexibility*: VLANs go towards combining the intelligence of a routed network with the flexibility of a switched LAN. For example, a user that is on a particular VLAN can remain on that VLAN after moving to a different physical location within the campus. All that is required is a change in the relevant switch configurations. No need exists for a hardware change or a repatching of cables. This flexibility is further facilitated by the fact that VLANs can be extended across multiple switching using a VLAN trunking protocol. Generally, VLANs have helped simplify the administration and management of moves, adds, and changes in a LAN environment that uses layer 3 processing.

■ *Problem localization*: VLANs impose some hierarchy on the campus LAN. Network problems such as broadcast storms are localized to the VLAN on which they originated rather than affecting the entire switched network.

Bear in mind one issue in relation to the use of VLANs (or indeed normal routed LANs) to contain broadcast storms. The broadcast storm obviously affects every station on the VLAN in question, and in theory, it should not affect any other VLAN. This is true up to a point. Other VLANs should not be directly affected; however, inter-VLAN communication may well be inhibited because the local router's CPU utilization is likely to overload due to the level of broadcasts that it must process. Consider the configuration shown in Figure 9-1. If most of the traffic generated on VLAN 3 is remotely accessing services on VLAN 10, then a broadcast storm on VLAN 4 will affect the connectivity of users on VLAN 3. This is due to the overload experienced by the router.

Figure 9-1
VLANs and broadcast storms

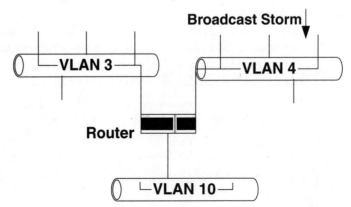

NOTE: *The effect of a broadcast storm can be felt beyond its own VLAN due the processor overload experienced by the router.*

The Physical Scope of VLANs

There are two fundamentally different approaches to implementing VLANs. They can be localized to the wiring closet or workgroup or alternatively each VLAN can potentially span the campus network. In this section the two approaches are examined.

End-to-End VLANs VLANs can be extended across multiple switches courtesy of trunking. Thus, users can be physically distributed across the campus and still be members of the same VLAN. The extension of VLAN membership across the LAN environment is termed the creation of end-to-end VLANs.

The classic example of this type of VLAN configuration is where members of the same workgroup might be distributed across several floors of the same building or across multiple buildings. However, as we have seen from the discussion on the changing traffic patterns within the corporate LAN environment, a move has begun towards centralizing an increased proportion of enterprise resources. These changing traffic patterns have gone some way towards rolling back the implementation of end-to-end VLANs.

End-to-end VLANs span the organization; therefore, the inter-VLAN routing must occur at the backbone of the network, as shown in Figure 9-2. In this particular example, VLANs 10 and 20 span across multiple switch blocks (in other words, switches exist in more than one block that have stations in VLANs 10 and 20). The routing functionality that is required for communication between these VLANs takes place on the campus backbone devices. This VLAN configuration thus places constraints on the network's logical topology. Apart from using a router, an arguably more cumbersome solution would be to implement the trunking on the servers. The main problem with this is the level of processing strain that would be placed on the servers as a result of processing traffic and broadcasts for multiple VLANs.

Local VLANs Bearing in mind the changing campus LAN traffic patterns where resources are increasingly being centralized rather than localized in workgroups, end-to-end VLANs are to some extent losing their

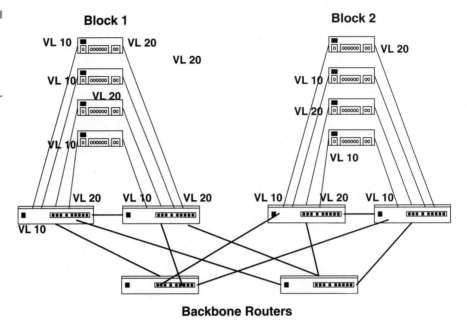

Figure 9-2

End-to-end VLANs
distributed across the
campus—routed at
the backbone

significance. VLANs are now more frequently allocated by geographic location rather than by workgroup function. This type of VLAN configuration is termed local VLANs or geographic VLANs.

Returning to our layered campus network model, local VLANs terminate at the intermediate layer. In fact, they are often local to the wiring closet. One of the reasons for implementing local VLANs is that if resources are centralized, routing will have to be employed in any case. So, it is arguably better to perform this routing at the intermediate layer rather than at the backbone. Another reason that is at least as significant is the ease of administration, management, and troubleshooting that is synonymous with local VLANs.

Local VLANs ensure that the broadcast domains and spanning tree domains terminate at the intermediate layer. The effect of broadcast storms is also contained within the intermediate switch block.

Although the predominant benefit of local VLANs is broadcast containment, they should be fully exploited where possible through the intelligent location of servers. For example, a print server that is accessed exclusively by clients in a particular VLAN should be placed within that VLAN to avoid having to route traffic unnecessarily.

VLAN Management

The two different approaches to VLAN configuration are discussed in this section. This is followed by a study of the factors that influence the sizing of VLANs.

VLAN Assignment and Configuration   VLANs can be assigned on a switched network in a static or dynamic manner. Static assignment entails configuring specific switch ports to be in predefined VLANs. Therefore, this type of assignment is said to be performed on a per-port basis.

The alternative is to assign VLANs dynamically by pointing each switch on the network to a VLAN database server. This server contains a database of VLANs against *media access control* (MAC) addresses. Hence, dynamic assignment is driven by the station's MAC address rather than by the switch port numbers. The main advantage offered by dynamic VLAN assignment is in a scenario where stations are regularly moved around the campus network. For example, employees are moving and taking their workstation with them or are using laptop PCs. Thus, no reconfiguration is required because their VLAN membership is tied to the MAC address.

Dynamic assignment is, however, difficult to administer. For example, if a station changes its *Network Interface Card* (NIC), then a new entry must be created in the VLAN database. The difficulty with conceptualizing and troubleshooting dynamic VLANs is one reason why static VLAN assignment is predominant within the industry. Also, another reason that is equally compelling is performance. The VLAN-to-port mapping can be implemented in hardware using an *Application-Specific Integrated Circuit* (ASIC). The hardware-based mapping and VLAN lookup offers superior performance over the interrogation of a software-based database.

NOTE: *VLANs can be assigned statically on a per-port basis or dynamically using an external server that allocates VLAN membership on a per-MAC address basis.*

Static assignment is predominant in the industry due to easier administration and improved performance in the execution of VLAN membership lookups.

Sizing the VLANs   The sizing of VLANs is obviously an essential part of VLAN planning. When deciding how many VLANs should be employed on the network and how many users they should contain, the following issues must be considered:

■ *Traffic profiles*: The client-server application traffic flows should be understood before attempting to implement VLANs. If servers are mainly located within specific workgroups, then it may be feasible to arrange VLANs by workgroup. For example, a marketing department, although dispersed throughout the campus, exclusively uses their own server that will not be accessed by other groups. Otherwise, it is more likely that VLANs will be implemented on a geographic basis.

The bandwidth-intensity of the applications and also the degree to which they rely on broadcasts will provide an estimate of how many users should be in each VLAN.

■ *Number of users per VLAN*: It is good practice to have an estimated maximum number of users per VLAN. This does not necessarily have to be consistent throughout the enterprise. For example, VLANs containing clients that utilize a high bandwidth application should have a lower number of users. The IP addressing plan may also present a limiting factor to the amount of hosts on each subnet and hence on each VLAN.

■ *Number of VLANs*: Avoid creating VLANs for the sake of it. The network designer should be clear on the benefit that will accrue as a result of implementing VLANs. With this in mind, the number of VLANs to be used can be decided upon. This decision can be made independently of the IP addressing plan where the number of LAN subnets will correlate to the number of VLANs deployed.

■ *Size of the spanning tree domain*: For implementations where a separate instance of STP can be found on each VLAN, the VLAN terminates the STP domain. By limiting or localizing the size of the VLAN, the size of the STP domain is also reduced with the result of improved spanning tree convergence and stability.

VLAN Trunking

Trunking enables VLANs to be extended across the campus switch fabric and it facilitates VLAN membership on multiple switches. A VLAN trunking protocol such as 802.1q or a proprietary trunking protocol is usually configured on switch ports that attach to other switches. The trunk port may or may not already reside in its own particular VLAN, but as a trunk it is capable of carrying traffic relating to all VLANs. For this reason, trunk ports are sometimes conceptually thought of as residing in all configured VLANs.

With regard to Figure 9-3, consider the case where a broadcast originates in VLAN 4. This broadcast floods to all stations on switch A that are in VLAN 4. However, switch A will have learned via trunking that VLAN 4 also resides on switch B, so it will propagate the broadcast on its trunk link to switch B. It must indicate that the frame originated in VLAN 4 by tagging it appropriately. Switch B will then read the tag and forward the broadcast on all ports within VLAN 4.

The example in Figure 9-3 only relates to two switches, but the principle of trunking enables VLAN information to propagate across multiple switches and throughout the entire switched network.

The exact method of tagging the VLAN information onto the frame varies depending on the trunking protocol. With IEEE 802.1q, an additional four bytes are inserted into the Ethernet frame. This process is called *internal tagging* and the most important part of the tag is the VLAN ID.

Other trunking protocols such as Cisco's proprietary *Inter-Switch Link* (ISL) use *external tagging* or encapsulation to append the VLAN information to the frame. With ISL, the sending switch encapsulates the frame with a 26-byte header that includes the VLAN ID. The receiving switch strips off this header before deciding on which ports to forward the frame.

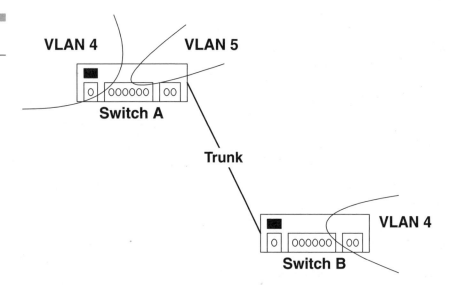

Figure 9-3
VLAN trunking

The choice of trunking protocol is determined by the media type on the network (Ethernet, Fast Ethernet, Gigabit Ethernet, *Asynchronous Transfer Mode* (ATM), *and Fiber Distributed Data Interface* (FDDI)) and it also depends on whether it is a single or multi-vendor switched network. It is often dictated by the fact that some lower-end switches only support a single trunk protocol such as 802.1q or indeed a proprietary protocol.

Controlling Trunk Advertisements   Generally, a trunk link will carry VLAN information for all VLANs configured within the switched domain. This is not always desirable because it can lead to the propagation of unnecessary traffic, particularly broadcasts that may consume excessive bandwidth on the trunk links.

Return to Figure 9-3 and assume that VLAN 5 is only implemented on switch A. Because this VLAN is not in use on switch B or any other switch that is downstream from switch B, it does not have to be advertised by switch A.

In this example, switch A could be configured *not* to advertise VLAN 5 on its trunk link to switch B. This has two positive effects. First, any broadcasts originating in VLAN 5 is not advertised on the trunk link between switches A and B. Secondly, if a topology change takes place in VLAN 5, the rest of the network is not needlessly informed about it.

NOTE: *Switches should not advertise VLANs over their trunk links into areas of the network where those VLANs are not used in order to eliminate unnecessary bandwidth consumption and processing overhead.*

VLAN Gateways and Resilience

Consider the network shown in Figure 9-4. The workstation in question is on the VLAN associated with the 172.16.10.0/24 subnet. Two routers are shown schematically and they provide redundant access off this VLAN. These routers could take the form of a routing module that is internal to each switch or alternatively they could be discrete routers attached, as shown in the diagram. Just one VLAN is referred to here, but either router implementation could support routing between multiple VLANs. In the case of a discrete router, a VLAN trunking protocol would be configured on the LAN interface to facilitate inter-VLAN routing.

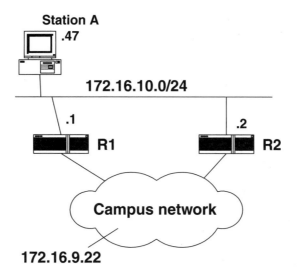

Figure 9-4
Resilient VLAN
gateway routers

Station A

Station A .47

172.16.10.0/24

.1

R1

.2

R2

Campus network

172.16.9.22

These routers provide redundant inbound and outbound connections for each VLAN. The choice as to which router is used for inbound traffic is determined by the IP routing protocol. With regard to outbound traffic, however, some mechanism must be employed to make full use of the additional router in a dynamic manner.

In the example being studied here, two gateway addresses are available, 172.16.10.1 and 172.16.10.2. It is possible to configure approximately half of the clients on the LAN with the first address as their default gateway and the other half with the second address as a gateway. The problem with this is that if, for example, the 172.16.10.1 router failed, then all of the clients using this as their gateway would have to be reconfigured. Clearly, a dynamic failover mechanism must be in place to fully exploit redundant gateways without incurring significant application downtime. A number of alternatives are available:

■ *Proxy Address Resolution Protocol* (ARP): Proxy ARP can be used if the workstation is not configured with a subnet mask. Say, for example, station A has an IP address of 172.16.10.47. If no mask is configured, the station assumes that no subnetting is taking place. Therefore, a default class B mask of 255.255.0.0 is assumed. Now consider the following scenario. The actual subnet mask being used is 255.255.255.0, as in the previous example. Therefore, if the station needs to communicate with station B at 172.16.9.22, it must go through its local router. However, the station thinks that the destination is on its own network, because it belongs to the same class B network. Hence, station A will do an ARP broadcast for 172.16.9.22. If proxy ARP is not enabled on the router, then station A will receive no response because the router will drop the ARP broadcast. Proxy ARP, on the other hand, enables the router to respond to the ARP broadcast with its own MAC address. The router will only respond to ARP broadcasts for IP addresses that are on different subnets to the one on which the ARP originated. This prevents the router from interfering in the normal ARP process on a given LAN subnet. The router will also check its routing table for a route to 172.16.9.22 before responding in order to avoid any possibility of having to drop the packet it receives from the workstation. Thus, station A is fooled into thinking that station B is on its own subnet with a MAC address of the local router's interface.

In terms of configuring proxy ARP with UNIX and Windows NT™ hosts, the gateway address is set to be the same as the workstation address. Other platforms may require changing the mask back to the default mask for that class of address.

Two problems must be highlighted in relation to proxy ARP. First, a problem will occur when communicating to destinations that are not on the same major network as the local host, because no ARP broadcast will be issued by the host for a destination that could not be on the same network as itself.

The second issue relates to the manner in which proxy ARP deals with redundant gateways. Returning to Figure 9-4, consider the case where R1 answered the ARP request for 172.16.9.22 with its own MAC address. Hence, R1 becomes the default gateway for the host in question. If R1 then experiences a problem, the host continues sending traffic to it until its own ARP table times out or the station is rebooted. Thus, even with redundant gateways in place, the use of proxy ARP results in a loss of application connectivity during the failover period.

■ *Routing Information Protocol* (RIP) or *Open Shortest Path First* (OSPF): Some hosts such as UNIX-based stations may support RIP. The use of a dynamic routing protocol does provide an automatic failover mechanism, but RIP is relatively slow to converge with lost routes not being flushed out for almost four minutes.

Also, other potential problems may occur with running RIP on the workstations. First of all, not all platforms support it. Secondly, RIP is not a scalable routing protocol for large networks. Therefore, it is often likely that a second protocol is required on the main network and mutual redistribution must then be configured between the two protocols. This adds complexity to the network design and configuration solely for the purpose of providing dynamic redundant gateways on the LAN. The final issue with RIP is overhead. The stations are required to maintain routing tables that may sometimes be large. The level of broadcasts will be increased significantly on a LAN when a large number of stations are running RIP.

OSPF is also supported on platforms such as UNIX. This sophisticated protocol is supported on fewer platforms than RIP. If OSPF is implemented on the LAN, then it is also likely to be the main *wide area network* (WAN) routing protocol. Hence, a single protocol caters to the network, eliminating the need for protocol redistribution. The biggest downside to running OSPF on end-stations is the memory requirements and processing overhead associated with this protocol. Another issue is that if each LAN station is running OSPF, more links will be created on the network, significantly increasing the size of the link state database.

- *ICMP Router Discovery Protocol* (IRDP): IRDP is a standardized gateway discovery protocol. It uses periodic multicast messages to discover the gateway router. The problem with the use of IRDP is twofold. First, despite the fact that it is a standard described by RFC 1256, not all host platforms support the protocol. The second issue is a familiar one: convergence. Updates are processed every seven to 10 minutes and the default lifetime for a gateway is 30 minutes. Hence, the use of IRDP and redundant gateways results in network downtime during the failover period.

- Cisco's *Hot Standby Routing Protocol* (HSRP): A number of proprietary solutions are available on the market that, in my opinion, address the issue of redundant gateways better than the standardized solutions. Recent versions of Windows NT™ support the capability to configure multiple default gateways and toggle between them in a dynamic manner.

Cisco's HSRP is another method of providing dynamic failover. HSRP takes an alternative approach as it is configured on the routers rather than on the workstations. The redundant gateway routers share a single virtual IP address that is configured on each router's LAN interface.

In the context of the earlier example where the two physical LAN addresses on the routers were 172.16.10.1 and 172.16.10.2, the virtual HSRP address could be 172.16.10.3, for example, as shown in Figure 9-5. HSRP uses multicast messages exchanged between the routers to elect one router to an active state and the other to a standby state. The active router seizes the HSRP address (172.16.10.3 in this example) and will receive traffic destined for that address.

Each workstation on the LAN is configured with the 172.16.10.3 address as its default gateway. The active router is the actual default gateway router. Assume that R1 is the active router in this example. Thus, all traffic from the 172.16.10.0 segment is being forwarded via R1. A failure on R1 will be detected by R2 after a number of HSRP multicast hello packets have been missed (this is called the *holdtime* and is 10 seconds by default). R2 then becomes the active router and receives traffic destined for 172.16.10.3. Therefore, a dynamic failover has occurred in just over 10 seconds. This holdtime is configurable and instances have occurred in which it had to be reduced to three seconds in order to avoid timeouts on time-sensitive *Systems Network Architecture* (SNA) sessions.

The active router is the one with the highest HSRP priority, a parameter that has a default value of 100. In Figure 9-5, R1 seizes the active state because it was configured with a higher priority of 200. The router with the highest IP address will become active if the priority parameter is left at the default values. This is not desirable

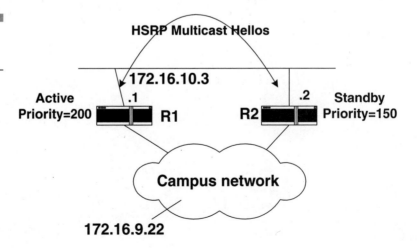

Figure 9-5
Hot standby routing protocol

because it is better to instill a level of control and predictability over which router becomes active.

The following is the relevant configuration for enabling HSRP on R1 and R2:

```
R1#

interface ethernet0
ip address 172.16.10.1 255.255.255.0
standby 1 ip 172.16.10.3
standby 1 priority 200
standby 1 timers 2 6
standby 1 preempt
standby 1 track serial0 60


R2#

interface ethernet0
ip address 172.16.10.2 255.255.255.0
standby 1 ip 172.16.10.3
standby 1 priority 150
standby 1 timers 2 6
standby 1 preempt
standby 1 track serial1 60
```

This configuration contains some elements that have not been explained yet:

■ *HSRP groups*: The use of HSRP groups enables load sharing for outbound traffic. For this example, a single group (namely group 1) has been configured. If a significant amount of bandwidth-intensive outbound traffic exists, then it may be appropriate to configure multiple groups. For example, consider Figure 9-6. Two HSRP groups are configured. Group 1 has a particular HSRP address associated with it, 172.16.10.3, and this group is configured such that R1 is the active router. HSRP group 2 uses the virtual address 172.16.10.4, and it is biased so that R2 is the active router. Approximately half of the workstations on the LAN have 172.16.10.3 as their default gateway and the other half use 172.16.10.4. Thus, load sharing of the outbound traffic takes place between R1 and R2. If either of these routers fails, the other router becomes active for both groups and no loss of service results.

■ *Preempt*: The preempt command is used to ensure that the router with the highest priority is always the active one. This is important in providing predictability in relation to the active router. With this configuration, if the router with the highest priority has not failed, then

Figure 9-6
HSRP groups with
load sharing

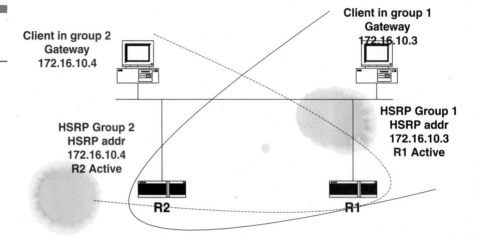

it is certain to be the active router. This becomes relevant, for example, in Figure 9-5 if R1 failed and R2 assumed the responsibility of being the active router. After R1 comes back up, it will seize the active state if the preempt option has been configured, as in this example.

■ *Interface tracking*: Consider the case where a certain router is in the active state but its main WAN interface has just failed. The HSRP hello packets simply track the state of the LAN interface so that packets will still be forwarded to this active router that is no longer capable of accessing the WAN. This will result in dropped packets and the loss of application connectivity.

The resolution to this problem is to configure the HSRP process on each router to track its WAN interfaces and reduce the priority accordingly, if the line protocol is lost on the interface being tracked. In this example, R1 is the active router, but HSRP tracks its serial interface and reduces the priority on R1 by 60 if the line protocol is lost on the serial 0 interface. This would reduce the HSRP priority on R1 to 140, which is less than R2. Therefore, R2 would take over as the active router in the event of a failure on R1's serial interface.

In situations where the routers each attach to multiple LANs or VLANs, as is the case with a typical intermediate layer router, it is better to stagger the HSRP priority values so that each router is the active router for approximately half of the VLANs. This is illustrated in Figure 9-7 and it avoids putting undue load on a single router.

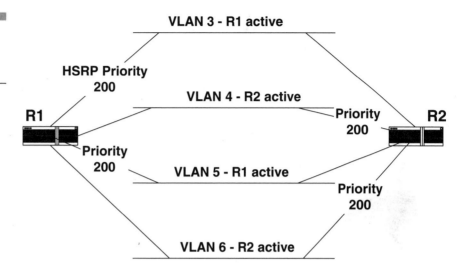

Figure 9-7
Alternating HSRP priorities for multiple VLANs

Finally, it is worth emphasizing some points in relation to HSRP that have created confusion in practice:

■ *HSRP relates to outbound traffic only*: People think that the standby HSRP router is simply doing nothing but waiting for a failure on the active router. The standby router may be processing a lot of inbound traffic to that LAN segment. The router that deals with inbound traffic is determined by the IP routing protocol, which has nothing to do with HSRP.

■ *HSRP relates only to IP traffic*: Confusion can arise in multiprotocol environments where it is assumed that the active HSRP router is an outbound forwarding router for all protocol traffic. HSRP relates only to IP and traffic that is encapsulated within IP *while it is still on the LAN*. It is important to be clear, especially in the heat of a troubleshooting situation, that HSRP bears no relationship to other protocols such as AppleTalk and Novell.

Note that Cabletron's *Virtual Router Routing Protocol* (VRRP) is a very similar proprietary solution to HSRP. VRRP works very well in a Cabletron environment. The reason HSRP has been described in detail rather than VRRP is simply due to the greater current penetration of Cisco technology within the industry.

Spanning Tree Protocol (STP)

The spanning tree protocol will now be discussed in more detail from a design viewpoint. In particular, techniques for optimizing the operation and convergence of STP on a large switched environment will be explored. The different approaches to treating spanning tree in a VLAN topology will also be studied.

Spanning Tree Refresher

Switched networks could not support redundant topologies without using STP. Broadcast storms and bridging loops would occur as a consequence of the fact that switches forward broadcasts. Bridging loops can also occur when a switch must flood a frame out all ports when it has not yet learned where the destination MAC address resides. The problem occurs when a redundant topology is used, as shown in Figure 9-8. A broadcast that is forwarded by switch A will also be forwarded by switch B. It will again be received by switch A and will be forwarded again. This cycle will continue indefinitely, resulting in a broadcast storm. The original broadcast may have been a broadcast relating to an application or routing protocol. Alternatively, it may have been a frame flooded by switch A in order to learn the location of a particular destination MAC address as part of its learning function.

STP prevents bridging loops by placing a sufficient number of ports into a blocking state in order to break the loop. In the context of Figure 9-9, the bridging loop is broken by placing a single port in blocking mode, as displayed. A port in blocking mode cannot send or receive live data traffic.

Figure 9-8
A broadcast-related bridging loop

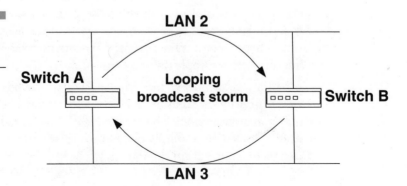

Figure 9-9
*Basic spanning tree
topology*

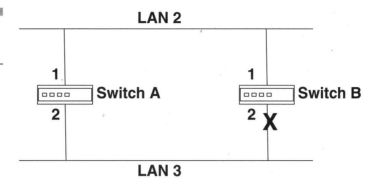

At first sight, it might appear that spanning tree prevents bridging loops, but it also eliminates the redundancy, which was the point of the exercise to begin with. This is not true, however, because a port in blocking may not send or receive live traffic, but it does continue to process *Bridge Protocol Data Units* (BPDU), which are the messages used by STP. Each switch port that has spanning tree enabled sends and receives BPDUs every two seconds by default. This is the BPDU *hello interval*.

In the context of Figure 9-9, these BPDUs would enable switch B to detect a failure on switch A, and port 2 on switch B would then move to a forwarding state whereby it can send and receive live traffic. Thus, the use of spanning tree does not eliminate the redundancy provided by a second switch. If switch B misses 10 consecutive BPDUs from switch A on its port 2 (the port that is in blocking mode), it will assume that the switch port on switch A is down and spanning tree will begin recalculating itself.

The time interval corresponding to 10 BPDU hello packets is 20 seconds by default. This is called the MAXAGE time, as it is the time interval after which STP information is aged out.

When switch B detects a failure on switch A after the MAXAGE timer expires, it cannot simply bring port 2 out of blocking immediately because it has no way of knowing that this action would not create another bridging loop. STP is thus quite rudimentary and unsophisticated. The switches running spanning tree do not maintain detailed topological information about the network. Hence, when a topology change takes place, the spanning tree information must be recalculated before any ports can be taken out of blocking mode. This means that a spanning tree topology change, which could entail the loss or addition of a switch, is usually synonymous with a convergence delay before the network regains a steady state.

For this reason, spanning tree is often thought of as "redundancy at a price." To start with, spanning tree will not even acknowledge the topology change until the MAXAGE timer expires, which is 20 seconds by default. It must then calculate a new loop-free topology and decide which port, if any, can be taken out of blocking. This convergence time usually takes minutes rather than seconds particularly on a large network, which means that application connectivity can be affected during a topology change on a switched network. Later in this section, we will explore methods for reducing the spanning tree convergence time, which is extremely important, particularly on medium to large networks.

Before going any further, however, it is appropriate to do a high-level recap on how spanning tree decides which ports to put in blocking mode. In the further discussions on spanning tree, the terms bridge and switch will be used interchangeably due to their functional similarity and the fact that STP was originally developed for bridges.

STP engages in two fundamental steps when calculating a loop-free topology:

- *Root election*: The first action performed by spanning tree is the election of a root bridge. This bridge becomes the main reference point of the spanning tree, and when the spanning tree process converges, the root bridge has all of its ports forwarding. Root election is performed through the exchange of BPDUs. The structure of a BPDU message is shown in Figure 9-10. Initially, all bridges begin by assuming that they are the root bridge. Hence, the bridge ID and the root ID are initially the same. Eventually, when spanning tree has converged, it is the bridge with the lowest ID that becomes the root. It is usually a good idea to avoid allowing the root election to be a random matter of bridge ID. Later in this section, the design issues relating to the root election will be discussed in more detail.

- *Root association*: After electing the root bridge, every other bridge on the network performs root association. A designated port for each LAN segment is calculated. This represents the least cost path from that segment to the root-bridge. Each switch then calculates a root port, which is their least cost path back to the root. If there are multiple paths to the root, then all ports leading to the root that are not designated or root ports are put in blocking mode.

  Each port on a bridge or switch has a default cost associated with it. This cost is, predictably enough, inversely proportional to the

Bytes	Field
2	Protocol ID
1	Version
1	Message Type
1	Flags
8	Root ID
4	Path Cost
8	Bridge ID
2	Port ID
2	Message Age
2	Maximum Age Time (MAXAGE)
2	Hello Time
2	Forward Delay Timer

Figure 9-10

The structure of a BPDU message

bandwidth or speed of the port. It is important to be clear that two standard methods of deriving the cost value from the bandwidth exist. The traditional IEEE specification uses this formula:

$$Cost = 10^9/Bandwidth$$

This formula results in an Ethernet port with a cost of 100 and a Fast Ethernet port with a cost of 10. The problem with this method is that Gigabit Ethernet has a cost of 1, and speeds beyond this will have a cost lower than unity. It is not advisable to use figures less than 1 in computing because the calculations are prone to rounding errors and also present the possibility of number tending to infinity. Those of you with a mathematical background will appreciate these issues. For this reason, the IEEE reratified the specification for the spanning tree cost calculation method and simply assigned costs to different speeds rather than using a formula.

The following mini-table shows the different cost values versus the corresponding port speeds for the two IEEE specifications. Some switches in the marketplace use the old specification, while some rely on the reratified method. Even on different models within the same vendor product line, different methods may be in use; it is important to be clear on which standard is being applied for the cost calculations of each switch platform on your network.

Port Speed	Old IEEE Cost	Cost per Reratified Specification
10 Mbps	100	100
100 Mbps	10	19
1 Gbps	1	4
10 Gbps	1	2

The root path cost is the total cost from a switch in question back to the root switch. This is simply the sum of the costs associated with each link along the path, as shown in Figure 9-11. The port that accesses the path with the minimum root path cost becomes the root port and assumes a forwarding state. This means that it can send and receive live traffic. All other ports that lead to the root switch are put in blocking mode.

The path cost value is also carried within the BPDUs (refer again to Figure 9-10). In the event of root path costs being equal, the port ID becomes a tie-breaker in deciding the root port on the switch. The port ID is a two-byte priority value and the port with the lowest priority or ID becomes the root port. All ports have an equal priority by default. However, this can be manipulated by configuring the switch in order to make one port preferable

Figure 9-11
Root path cost
calculation

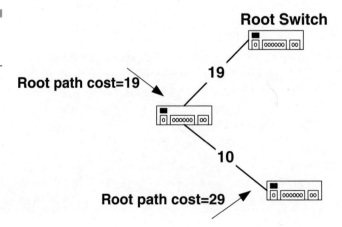

over another. In the event of the path costs and port priorities being equal, the port with the numerically lower MAC address is chosen as the root port. The upshot of root election and root association is that each switch only has one active path back to the root, which ensures a loop-free topology.

NOTE: *Spanning tree first elects a root bridge based on the lowest bridge ID. All other switches then calculate their least-cost path to the root switch. All other ports that lead to the root are put in blocking mode. This ensures a loop-free topology.*

Spanning tree has a potentially significant convergence delay following a topology change as it calculates a new loop-free topology.

Fundamental Design Issues

STP is enabled by default on most switches on the market. Hence, the "plug and play" term is often used in relation to STP, but we'll now discuss the reasons why spanning tree requires some degree of thought in relation to the design of the spanning tree domain. As a result of this, switches frequently require a reconfiguration of some of their spanning tree parameters.

Root Election   The root bridge triggers the spanning tree BPDU messages that propagate throughout the switched network every two seconds. This is one of the reasons why the root bridge should be located at a central point close to the backbone of the network. This ensures that all downstream switches will experience similar delays in receiving and hence processing BPDU messages, which enhances the stability of the spanning tree calculation. The role of the root bridge in triggering BPDUs is illustrated in Figure 9-12.

More particularly, the root bridge should be located close to the center of the spanning tree domain. If only one spanning tree process is running on the switched network, then this coincides with a central point within the switched network. However, it is also possible to run a separate instance of spanning tree for each VLAN on the network. In this situation, a separate root switch may be available for each VLAN and that switch should be located at a pivotal point in the VLAN rather than at its periphery. The pros and cons of running a single instance or multiple instances of the spanning tree protocol will be studied later in this section.

The root switch should not be an access-layer device for reasons even apart from the unsuitability of that device's location on the network. The

Figure 9-12
BPDUs are triggered
by the root switch

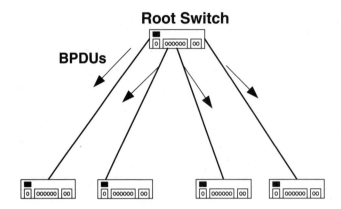

device that becomes root should ideally be of reasonable processing power and memory resources because it will have all ports in a forwarding state and will process more traffic than any other switch on the network. The root switch should therefore be an intermediate or backbone-layer device.

The root should be located close to the center of the spanning tree domain for another reason. When a topology change does not necessarily directly affect the root, such as a link failing elsewhere in the domain, all switches must then recalculate their shortest path to the root. The level of STP recalculation is minimized if the root is located close to the center of the domain, thus reducing the convergence time. If the topology does directly affect the root switch such as the failure of a directly attached link to the root or indeed the failure of the root itself, the STP recalculation is also minimized. The reason is that a central location for the root switch means that all other switches will hear about a failure on the root at similar time intervals. This facilitates a more efficient and faster spanning tree recalculation than if the root was at the network periphery and some switches learned of its failure faster than others simply because they were closer to the root.

We have now discussed some reasons why the root switch should be located close to the center of the spanning tree domain and should be one of the more powerful switches on the network. From a design perspective, the root switch should be chosen prior to rolling out the network. In order to control the root switch election, the bridge ID parameter must be manipulated. The switch with the lowest bridge ID always becomes the root of the spanning tree. The bridge ID is an eight-byte parameter held within the BPDU. The six least significant bytes constitute the lowest MAC address on the switch, as shown in Figure 9-13.

Figure 9-13
The Bridge ID
parameter

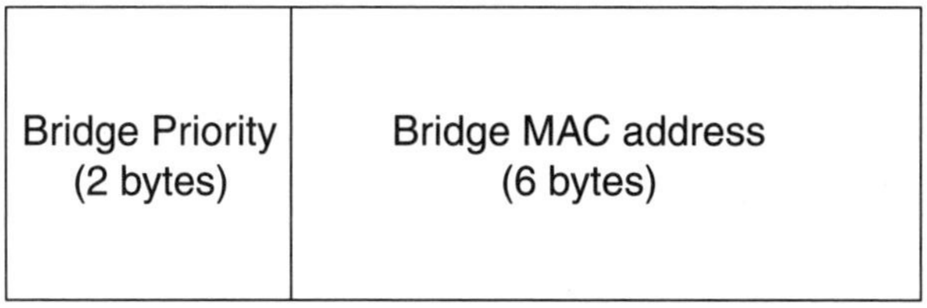

Bridge Priority (2 bytes)	Bridge MAC address (6 bytes)

The lowest MAC address on the switch may be a physical MAC address or a pre-assigned virtual MAC address, depending on the switch vendor and model. The two most significant bytes constitute the bridge priority. If a switch has the lowest bridge priority on the network, then it will become the root switch because this will override the MAC address and result in a lower bridge ID. However, all switches on the network are likely to have the bridge priority set at the manufacturer's default value. Hence, unless some configuration is performed, the root election comes down to a lottery of the lowest MAC address. Clearly, this is undesirable, as it gives no control over the root switch election.

The switch that is designated to become the root switch should be given a bridge priority of 0, which absolutely ensures that it will become the root switch. It is also important to pre-assign the switch that will take over as root switch in the event of a failure on the root switch. This device should be assigned a priority value of 1, as shown in Figure 9-14. In this particular example, switch A is elected as root switch because it has a priority of 0. In the event of a failure on switch A, switch B will become root switch because it has been configured with a priority equal to 1. This is important because the new root switch should be of requisite processing power and also close to the center of the domain. The STP recalculation time is also reduced following a failure on the root switch with this configuration in place.

The importance of choosing an appropriate root switch and ensuring that it becomes root switch through relevant device configuration cannot be overstated. The author saw an instance on a switched network once where a new switch was being commissioned. No users were to attach to it immediately, so it was decided to commission the switch during normal office hours. The problem was that the new switch had a lower base MAC address (and hence a lower bridge ID) than the root switch. Spanning tree began recalculating itself because the BPDUs detected a new root candidate.

This presented a very serious problem for two reasons. First, the network crashed for approximately an hour because the spanning tree domain was large and the convergence was slow. Secondly, the new root was now at the

Figure 9-14
Bridge priority
manipulation for root
and "backup" root
switch

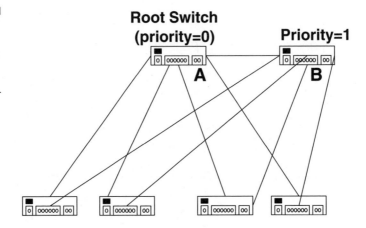

edge of the network and did in no way meet the criteria for a root switch. Needless to say, the career prospects of the network administrator were not enhanced by this episode! The entire problem would have been avoided if the original root switch had been configured with a lower priority.

Controlling Root Association Each non-root switch elects a root port, which connects to the least-cost path back to the root. This port sends and receives live traffic, while any other ports on the switch that lead on a path to the root are put in blocking mode. As explained earlier, the spanning tree cost is calculated from port speed. Therefore, it is likely that the fastest path back to the root switch should become the root port by default. If this is not happening or if, for whatever reason, it is desired to make a slower path to the root path, then appropriate parameters can be manipulated. The spanning tree cost parameter can be reconfigured to a different value. If path costs are equal back the root switch, then the tie-breaker parameter for deciding the root port is the port with the lowest port priority. Thus, port priority is another spanning tree parameter that can be manipulated in order to influence the shape of the root association tree.

Spanning Tree and VLANs For a switched network that does not implement VLANs, a single instance of spanning tree is available. However, if VLANs are being employed, running a separate instance of spanning tree for each VLAN can be employed. This fundamental and important decision as to how spanning tree should be treated in relation to the VLANs is determined by the choice of VLAN trunking protocol. The IEEE 802.1q treatment is to use a single instance of spanning tree or a *Common Spanning Tree* (CST). The BPDU messages are passed using VLAN 1, the default VLAN. A number of proprietary trunking protocols such as Cisco's ISL employ a separate instance of spanning tree for each VLAN.

Each approach has validity. A single instance of spanning tree might seem intuitive on a switched network. However, a similar argument can be made for multiple instances of STP. STP is required because it switches forward broadcasts, resulting in bridging loops where redundant topologies exist. However, VLANs contain broadcasts so it can easily be argued that the spanning tree process is only of local significance within each VLAN, just as on a routed network.

One of the key differences between these two approaches is the nature of the root switch election. If multiple instances of spanning tree are run, then a different root switch is located on each VLAN. Thus, in relation to our model for campus network design, the root switch for each VLAN is likely to be an intermediate layer switch servicing that particular VLAN (assuming that the VLANs terminate at the intermediate layer).

On the other hand, if CST is employed, just one root switch will be used for the entire network. In this case, it would be prudent to ensure that, in the case of a distributed backbone, one of the backbone switches becomes the root switch. This is in keeping with the principle that the root switch should be located close to the center of the network.

Each approach has pros and cons that are summarized as follows:

- *Reduced BPDU traffic*: With a single instance of spanning tree, just one root switch triggers BPDU messages for the entire switched network. This reduces the bandwidth consumption associated with BPDUs.

- *Less spanning tree overhead*: If fewer BPDUs are propagating throughout the network, the switches have to interrupt their CPU less frequently in order to process these messages. Thus, the processing overhead as a result of spanning tree on each device is minimized.

The advantages of running multiple instances of spanning tree are now summarized and they coincide with the disadvantages of a common spanning tree topology.

- *Optimum root election*: A separate instance of spanning tree on each VLAN means that a separate root switch election occurs on each VLAN. Thus, the optimum root switch can be selected for each VLAN.

An optimized root switch selection does not always take place in a CST implementation, particularly in a non-hierarchical network. Consider Figure 9-15 where CST is being employed with a single root switch, as indicated. This root is an optimal choice for users in VLAN 20, but this is certainly not true of VLAN 30.

■ *Smaller spanning tree domains*: The use of a separate instance of STP for each VLAN has the effect of reducing the size of the spanning tree domains. This in turn reduces the convergence time after a topology change, which is a big issue for spanning tree. A smaller spanning tree domain also means that, on average, topology changes will occur less frequently and therefore STP recalculations have to be performed with less regularity. Multiple instances of spanning tree can thus improve the stability of the switched network.

CST is also more likely to result in sub-optimal forwarding paths as a consequence of the larger spanning tree domain. The root path is the optimum path from each LAN segment to the root, but it is not necessarily the optimum path between given pairs of LAN segments. This likelihood of sub-optimal paths occurring increases in proportion with the size of the spanning tree domain.

■ *Load balancing*: A particular application can be tailored because a separate instance of spanning tree is in use on each VLAN, and that is load balancing. With a single instance of spanning tree, certain ports

Figure 9-15
Common spanning tree with a single switch

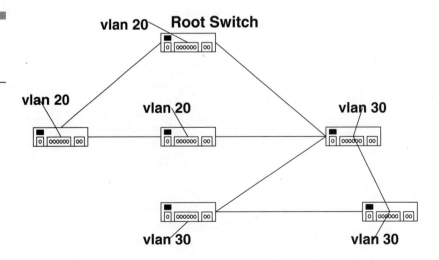

are in blocking mode as decided by the root association tree. These ports cannot send or receive live traffic and are redundant pending a failure on the link that is forwarding traffic. If a separate instance of spanning tree is employed for each VLAN, then the STP parameters can be manipulated such that one link is forwarding for a given set of VLANs and another link can forward for the remaining VLANs. This principle is illustrated in Figure 9-16. The two switches A and B each have ports in the 10 VLANs numbered 1 through 10. A parallel path exists between the two switches. With CST, one of these paths would be blocked and could not forward any traffic. Running a separate spanning tree for each VLAN enables one port to forward and one to be blocked *for that particular VLAN*. The forwarding ports can be alternated to achieve a load-balancing effect. The paths in this example are equal cost and the manipulation is performed by altering the port priorities. Path 1 forwards traffic for each of the odd numbered VLANs and path 2 is forwarding for the even numbered VLANs.

Figure 9-17 displays the same principle in action but in relation to the model of an intermediate layer switch block. The VLANs and spanning tree domains terminate at the intermediate layer switch. Switch 1 forwards traffic for all odd VLANs, and switch 2 forwards traffic for all even VLANs. Apart from manipulating costs or port priorities, this effect could be achieved by designating switch 1 as the root switch for all odd VLANs and having switch 2 the root for all even VLANs. In any case, when using multiple instances of spanning tree, it is good practice

Figure 9-16
Load sharing with multiple instances of STP

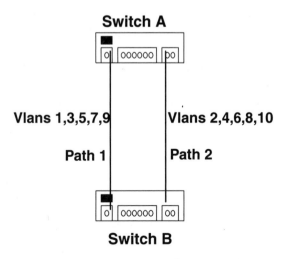

Figure 9-17
Load sharing on a
per-VLAN basis within
a switch block

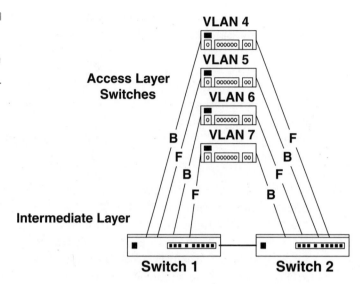

to avoid allowing the same switch to become root for all VLANs, unless of course no other switch is suitable for the task. If the same switch is root for all VLANs and it fails, then a maximum amount of traffic disruption takes place, as every VLAN must elect a new root switch.

NOTE: *When implementing multiple instances of STP, if possible, avoid having the same switch as root for all VLANs.*

Optimizing STP

The question of optimizing STP operation will now be addressed. The steps that can be taken to reduce the spanning tree convergence time in order to minimize session loss following a topology change will be examined in particular.

Improving Convergence Spanning tree is potentially very slow to converge after a topology change. This can be a particular problem on large networks where not only is the convergence time greater, but a higher occurrence of topology changes take place.

We have already seen that switches will wait until the MAXAGE timer expires before aging out old protocol information and reacting to a topology change. However, this is just the first delay as spanning tree begins to recalculate itself.

To counteract the effect of propagation delay within the switched network, spanning tree uses timers that protect against looping effects during network transitions. Some of these timers have already been discussed.

■ *Hello interval*: This is the frequency at which BPDUs are triggered by the root switch. It has a value of two seconds by default.

■ *Max Age time*: The Max Age time is the time interval after which spanning protocol information is aged out and a topology change is detected. It has a default value of 20 seconds. Thus, after 10 BPDUs have been missed, a topology change is detected and spanning tree can commence recalculation.

■ *Forward delay time*: The forward delay timer has a default value of 15 seconds. Before explaining exactly what it means, it is appropriate to discuss the different spanning tree states that a port transitions through from the beginning of the spanning tree convergence process.

■ *Blocking*: All switch ports start in a blocking state. In this state, they do not process BPDUs or live traffic. Ports stay in the blocking state for the duration of the MAXAGE timer (20 seconds by default). The port will remain in the blocking state if the spanning tree protocol determines that by taking this port out of blocking, a loop would be created on the network.

■ *Listening*: If spanning tree determines that a port will not create a loop, the port will transition from blocking to the listening state. In this state, the port can process BPDUs but cannot process live traffic. The purpose of this state is to protect against loops in case some BPDUs have not yet been received by the switch due to network propagation delay. These BPDU(s) may serve to indicate that the port would create a loop; hence, STP adopts a wait-and-see approach before allowing the port to process live traffic. The port stays in the listening state for the duration of the forward delay timer, which is 15 seconds by default.

■ *Learning*: The port then transitions from listening to the learning state. In the learning state, the port can also monitor live traffic and learn the destination of the observed MAC addresses. Hence, in this state, the port can contribute to building the switch's MAC address table. It cannot, however, forward live traffic while in the learning state. The purpose of this state is to enable a particular time interval that is dedicated to learning the location of MAC addresses in order to reduce the amount of traffic flooding when the port goes live. The port stays in the learning state for the duration of the forward delay timer.

■ *Forwarding*: The port finally transitions from learning to the forwarding state. In this state, the port is capable of sending and receiving live traffic.

The time taken for the port to move to a forwarding state is the MAX-AGE time plus twice the forward delay time. For a default IEEE spanning tree implementation, this totals 50 seconds (20 + 15 + 15). This should give you an idea of the convergence delays associated with the spanning tree protocol. Obviously, these delays add up on even a medium-sized network. We will now examine some methods of improving spanning tree convergence.

Some fundamental design principles have already been discussed in relation to the location of the root switch that can help reduce the spanning tree convergence time. At the configuration level, the most obvious approach to improving convergence time might be to reduce the value of the timers: hello, MAXAGE, and forward delay. These timers would have to be changed on the root switch because it is responsible for generating the BPDUs and hence the root switch sets these parameter values within the spanning tree domain. It is quite dangerous to change the value of these timers because by reducing them the network stability may be compromised.

The default timer values that have been discussed are calculated based on a network diameter of seven or fewer switches. The network diameter is the maximum number of switches between any two end users on the network. If the root switch were configured with a lower network diameter, then the values of these timers would automatically be reduced because the propagation delay would be lower with fewer switches. It is more sensible to reduce these timers by reducing the configured network diameter than by directly altering the configured timer values. The configured network diameter should never be less than the actual network diameter in the interests of protecting network stability. Most of the major switch vendors in the market incorporate features that can be configured in order to improve spanning tree convergence time.

Access switches can be configured to quickly bring their standby uplink to a forwarding state in the event of a failure on the primary uplink. Normally following a failure on the primary uplink, the access switch would have to wait for the backup link to go through the normal spanning tree states before moving to a forwarding state.

Most switch vendors support the capability to configure an access switch such that the backup uplink can bypass the MAXAGE and forward delay timers and move to a forwarding state with minimal delay. This fast track to the forwarding state can only occur if a failure takes place on the primary link. Thus, applications would not be interrupted by a transition. This type of feature should only be configured on access switches; otherwise, you have no guarantee that moving the backup link to a forwarding state will not create a loop. This is one example of the type of feature that is available to speed up spanning tree convergence. Before attempting to deploy any of these techniques, it is important to have a clear understanding of the vendor's software features and how exactly the use of them will impact your network.

We will now move on to discuss a feature that is supported on all major switch platforms in order to improve workstation and server access to the network.

Disabling STP   The delay before a switch port starts forwarding is normally of the order of 50 seconds with default spanning tree timer values in place. This delay can cause applications to fail at the outset. A typical symptom of this type of problem is if an application initially fails after the client's PC is powered on, but eventually the application works. This is due to the delay imposed by spanning tree after powering up the station and providing an Ethernet line protocol to the port. Another classic example is of mobile employees that use laptop PCs to access corporate services. The initial attempt to logon to the server might fail for the same reason. Another scenario can cause a loss of connectivity at the server level. A server might contain two NICs for redundancy with one backing up the other on the same subnet. If the primary NIC fails, a 50-second delay occurs before the second NIC can begin processing live data, which will result in the disruption of service.

The solution is to disable spanning tree on the ports that exhibit this problem. Different switch vendors have different names for the feature, enabling the disabling of STP on a per-port basis. Most describe it as the capability to almost immediately move the port to the forwarding state and bypass the other states. This effectively amounts to turning off the STP on that port. If this type of feature is to be employed, it is imperative that it is only used on switch ports that connect to client or server stations. Spanning tree cannot be disabled on ports that connect to other switches as it may result in bridging loops.

NOTE: *Spanning tree can be disabled on ports that connect to client or server stations in order to eliminate problems associated with the forwarding delay.*

Never disable spanning tree on ports that connect to other switches!

STP and Port Aggregation

A number of proprietary solutions exist that enable inter-switch links to be aggregated in order to provide high-speed backbone connections. This type of topology is shown in Figure 9-18. The aggregation of four Fast Ethernet links would thus provide a 400Mbps pipe between the two switches, as shown. This is a relatively simple principle that usually requires the following of stringent configuration guidelines. In terms of configuring whatever method of link aggregation is used, the vendor's manual should be consulted with care.

An evolving standard, 802.3ad, is moving towards the standardization of a link aggregation specification. At layer 2, the 802.3ad standard presents a single logical MAC address to other protocols in the stack. It utilizes the *Link Aggregation Control Protocol* (LACP), a new physical layer protocol

Figure 9-18

Port aggregation on inter-switch links

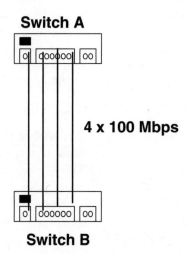

that is responsible for managing the separate but grouped physical connections. Under LACP, aggregation involves two distinct layer 2 tiers or sublayers. One tier deals with the physical ports on a switch, while the other tier maps physical ports to an aggregate port, where users are grouped by multiplexing.

Pending the full ratification of 802.3ad, only proprietary solutions are in place. These solutions vary slightly in how they achieve the same end result. An evaluation of the subtle differences between these implementations will not be covered here for a number of reasons. First, this book is intended to deal with design principles rather than configuration. Secondly, vendor-specific information is easily obtained and is continuously changing in any case.

The aggregated links form a single logical link for the purposes of STP. This must be the case; otherwise, bridging loops would occur. If the port aggregation facility is ever disabled, then caution must be exercised to ensure that spanning tree is enabled on all ports that had formed the aggregated block.

Proprietary methods of link aggregation can also be performed between a switch and a high-performance server in order to supply more bandwidth with a view to improving application response times. This leads on to a more general issue about port aggregation. The links that are aggregated can be trunk links but do not necessarily have to be. The links could be native to a particular VLAN and be aggregated for the purpose of providing a high level of inter-switch bandwidth for users in that VLAN.

If the aggregated links are trunks, then key configuration parameters are usually required to match at each end of the links. These parameters include the exact type of trunking and the trunk mode (is autonegotiation being used?). The range of VLANs that are advertised across the trunks must also match; otherwise, traffic may or may not get forwarded for a VLAN, depending on the physical link chosen. Security parameters must also be disabled on aggregated ports in order to avoid the possibility of traffic being dropped because it is from a disallowed MAC address for a given physical port that is a member of the aggregated group. For implementations where the aggregated links are part of a particular native VLAN, all aggregated ports must be in the same VLAN and security features should also be disabled.

One final point in relation to link aggregation relates to the manner in which the load sharing is performed. Two basic methods are used:

(i) The first is round-robin load sharing where packets are alternatively sent over the different physical links. This is like dealing cards and is done on a per-packet basis.

(ii) The switch can also perform a Boolean XOR operation on the last bit of the source and destination MAC addresses. The answer will be 0 or 1, which is the port that will be used for forwarding when just two ports are aggregated. If four ports are aggregated, the XOR operation is performed on the last two bits of the source and the destination MAC address combination. In this case, the answer will be one of four possible values, 00, 01, 10, and 11, which will denote the port used for forwarding.

The many implementations of port aggregation give the network administrator the choice of which load sharing method to select and configure.

NOTE: *Link aggregation can be used on trunk links or on links that are native to a particular VLAN.*

Check with the vendor documentation regarding the configuration parameters that must match between each port and at each end of the aggregated links.

IP Multicasting

The advent and increased integration of heterogeneous applications such as voice, video, and multimedia on IP-based networks has helped fuel the development of multicasting technology. In this section, an overview of the principles and practices of multicasting will be provided both in relation to the corporate campus and the enterprise network as a whole. Particular attention will be paid to the design challenges surrounding the support of multicast applications on the campus network and beyond.

The Significance of Multicasting

Consider the network shown in Figure 9-19. A multimedia server is required to propagate information to a particular group of relevant clients as indicated. This data transfer can take place through a number of different methods:

■ *Unicasting*: The server could issue a unicast to each of the clients. This solution does not scale well for a number of reasons:

- As the number of clients grows, so does the processing power required by the server to replicate the packets to each of the clients.

- A multimedia application is likely to be reasonably bandwidth-intensive. Assume for this application that the average client-server data flow is in the region of 1.5Mbps. Thus, for 50 clients, the corresponding bandwidth consumption on the server end of the network would be 75Mbps. This bandwidth consumption would gradually reduce as packets reached their destination clients. However, this is an extremely inefficient use of bandwidth that may be prohibitive with regard to network performance. The inefficiency of this approach is underscored by the fact that this level of bandwidth consumption is associated with just a single application.

- The fact that several copies of the same packet are propagating from the server means that an additional processing strain is placed on networking devices such as LAN switches and routers that reside along the server-to-client path. This is another factor that presents a scaling limitation to multicasting.

- An increased number of clients leads to a greater variation in delay or jitter associated with a very large number of unicasts of the same stream. Jitter creates a particular problem for real-time applications such as voice and video, which are intolerant of a large variation in delay.

- *Broadcasting*: Most of the problems just described could be resolved through the use of broadcasting. The server issues a single broadcast packet that propagates throughout the switched IP subnet. If it is required to send the transmission across multiple subnets, then the campus routers can be configured appropriately to direct the broadcast packets.

  The use of broadcasting reduces bandwidth consumption and resolves the server and device CPU utilization issues because only a single copy of each transmission packet is required. The problem with broadcasting is that it is difficult to exercise control over their propagation. On a switched network, the broadcast floods everywhere, although a routed network confines the broadcast to the local subnet. In order to bend these rules, a lot of potentially high-maintenance router configuration is required.

  In Figure 9-19, all devices are on a flat, switched network and therefore the same IP subnet. Thus, all devices receive the broadcast including

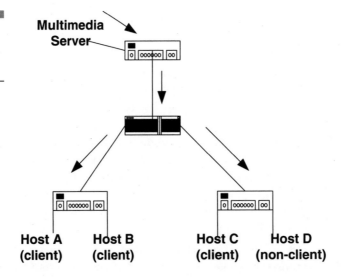

Figure 9-19
Multimedia Server to
Client data
propagation

host D, which is not running the multimedia application. If a large
proportion of users on a switched network are not interested in the
multimedia application, then broadcasting becomes increasingly
inefficient.

■ *Multicasting*: Multicasting, like broadcasting, entails the issuing of a
single packet addressed to multiple clients. Unlike a broadcast, the
multicast packet is not addressed to everybody. Instead, it is addressed
to a defined membership of a multicast group. We have already
encountered several examples of multicasting in this book. For
example, routers running OSPF use multicasts to communicate with
each other. A router wanting to send a routing advertisement to all
OSPF routers sends an advertisement to the address 224.0.0.5, which
is the multicast IP address reserved for this particular group. Any
router that is configured to run OSPF will become a member of this
group and therefore will process packets that it receives with this
destination address.

Returning to the example of Figure 9-19, all clients that want to receive
the multimedia transmission from the server could join the same
multicast group as the server. This could be performed by associating
the multimedia application with the same multicast group address on
the server and all of the appropriate clients. Now when the server

transmits, it sends the packets to the multicast IP address that each member of the group will listen to.

Later we will discuss what must be in place to ensure that packets sent to the multicast address by the server will be received by all group members. For the moment we will just assume that this is the case. For the network in Figure 9-19, clients A, B, and C use the application and therefore are members of the group. Host D does not avail of the application and hence is not a group member and will not have to process packets that are destined for this multicast address. This resolves the problem presented by broadcast packets being addressed to and therefore processed by all stations regardless of their relevance to that station. The network in Figure 9-19 is simple for the purposes of illustration, so this might not seem like a great benefit in this context. However, consider the efficiency improvement where over 100 hosts on the campus LAN are not utilizing this application. If the benefit of multicasting had to be summarized in one sentence, it would be that it makes applications more scalable, particularly if they are of the high-bandwidth or delay-sensitive variety.

NOTE: *Multicasting improves the scalability of applications particularly high-bandwidth or delay-sensitive applications.*

An Overview of IP Multicasting

Before discussing the topic of IP multicasting in more detail, it is first appropriate to summarize some of its operational characteristics:

■ A multicast group typically, but not necessarily, consists of a server and a number of clients. The server sends a single copy of each data unit to the multicast group address. This transmission will be received by all other hosts within the group. Although a typical application of multicasting entails a server using a destination multicast address to communicate with all group members, any host within the group can send data to this same address and hence to the entire group.

■ The multicast group can be local or spread across geographically diverse locations. Multicasting can thus be confined to the local LAN, or it can be performed over the Internet depending on the application and communication requirement.

■ Members can dynamically join and leave groups courtesy of the *Internet Group Management Protocol* (IGMP), which we are just about to discuss.

■ Members can also belong to more than one group. A classic and simple example of this is an application that uses one multicast group address for video and another for audio. For example, 226.1.1.10 could be used for video and 226.1.1.11 for audio. All members receiving the application would have to belong to both groups.

■ To receive traffic from a group, a host must be a member of that group. However, a station can send traffic to a multicast group without being a member of that group.

■ Applications that use multicasting are transported using *User Datagram Protocol* (UDP) best-effort delivery. This makes sense because multicasting is most frequently used for real-time applications such as audio and video. In this scenario, maintaining a reasonably constant delay is more important that guaranteeing delivery. The reliability and retransmissions provided by TCP is of little use to real-time applications. Not having reliability will, of course, increase the likelihood of packet loss, which, if occurring to a significant degree, will degrade service. This is where the area of *Quality of Service* (QoS) comes in. The methods that can be used to guarantee a certain QoS level to real-time and multicast applications are discussed in detail later in this chapter.

Components of a Multicast Network   For a multicast application to work end to end, the following functionality must be in place on the network:

■ *Multicast application*: Obviously, the application that supports multicasting must be loaded on the server(s) and clients. These applications are typically real-time and often bandwidth-intensive applications. They may place particular demands for system resources such as CPU processing power, memory, and also a requirement for specialized NICs.

The following mini-table lists some sample applications that are well suited to using multicasting along with approximate values for the corresponding bandwidth utilization.

Application	Typical Bandwidth Requirement
Uncompressed audio	64 kbps
Application sharing (collaborative computing, desktop conferencing)	100–120 kbps
Video conferencing	128k–1 Mbps (depending on required quality)
MPEG video	1.5–2.0 Mbps
Imaging applications	8 Mbps–100 Mbps
Virtual reality	100 Mbps and upwards depending on the nature of the application

■ *IP stack that supports multicasting*: The IP stack on the server(s) and clients must be multicast-aware. In other words, it must be capable of processing Class D IP addresses. RFC 1112 is the relevant standard that should be supported by all stations.

■ *Multicast-capable NICs*: The NIC cards on the server(s) and clients must be capable of monitoring and processing multicast packets in addition to conventional unicast and broadcast packets. Some multicast applications may have special requirements such as graphics accelerators and other types of specialized network drivers. Also, NICs on the market incorporate the capability to filter out traffic destined for multicast groups of which the host is not a member. It is an economic decision if the additional cost is worth the benefit of avoiding any unnecessary interruption in the host's CPU due to the receipt of unwanted multicast packets. This is only an issue on a LAN that includes members of a number of different multicast groups.

■ *Multicast-capable networking devices*: In a normal scenario, every networking device along the path between multicast senders and receivers must be multicast-aware. Routers must be aware of which interfaces lead to members of each specified multicast group on the network. The routers must be able to communicate with each other in order to establish a logical path that will connect senders with receivers within a multicast group, as shown in Figure 9-20. Multicast routers are responsible for constructing a distribution tree within the network for this purpose. The area of multicasting routing will be discussed in detail in the upcoming section because it poses some

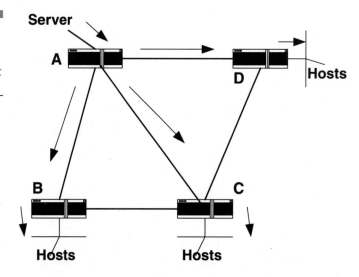

Figure 9-20

Multicating routing
and the construction
of logical server-client
paths

different challenges compared to conventional unicast routing. The
LAN switches on the network must also be multicast-aware for reasons
that likewise will be discussed.

Earlier it was mentioned that in a normal scenario each networking
device along the sender-to-receiver path must be multicast-capable.
The exception to this is the use of tunneling, which can be used to
enable communication between multicast group members that happen
to be dispersed on either side of a network region that does not support
multicasting. The multicast packets are encapsulated in conventional
IP unicast packets and routed accordingly, as displayed in Figure 9-21.
This is the same principle as the tunneling of IPX or AppleTalk packets
within IP across a region that does not support these protocols.

Multicast Addressing   Class A IP addresses are in the range of 1 to 126
in the first octet (127 is reserved). This range is obtained from the rule that
the first bit of the first octet in a Class A address must be zero.

Class B addresses are identified by the range 128 to 191. This range is
likewise obtained from the rule that for Class B the first bit must equal 1
and the second bit must equal 0. The variation in the remaining six bits provides the range 128 to 191.

Similarly, Class C addresses require that the first two bits are equal to 1 and the third bit must equal 0. The variation in the five lower-order bits of the first octet gives a range of 192 to 223.

Now we finally get to Class D, which relates to multicast addresses. The rule here is that the first three bits must each equal 1 and the fourth bit must equal 0. This results in the following range:

11100000 to **1110**1111

Expressed in decimal, this is the range 224 to 239. This means that the layer 3 IP multicast address for any multicast group must fall in the range of 224.0.0.0 to 239.255.255.255.

The corresponding layer 2 multicast is derived directly from the layer 3 address. The first three bytes of a layer 2 multicast MAC address are always denoted by 01-00-5E. The first bit of the fourth byte is always set to 0. This leaves 23 bits to be resolved, and they are mapped directly from the 23 lower-order bits of the layer 3 address. An example of this is shown in Figure 9-22 for the IP multicast address 226.9.10.14. The corresponding layer 2 address is 01-00-5E-09-0A-0E.

What would be the multicast MAC address corresponding to 226.137.10.14? If you perform the calculation, you will see that this is a loaded question. It works out to have the same layer 2 address. This is anti-intuitive, but it is a simple consequence of the fact that both layer 3 addresses have the same 23 lower-order bits and hence have the same layer 2 address. This demonstrates that no one-to-one correspondence takes place between layer 3 and layer 2 multicast addresses. The first four bits in an IP multicast address are reserved for identification purposes. This leaves 28 bits; however, only the lower-order 23 bits map to the MAC address. Hence, 32 possible multicast IP

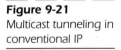

Figure 9-21

Multicast tunneling in conventional IP

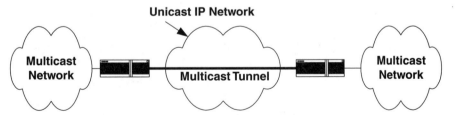

Unicast IP Network

Multicast Network — Multicast Tunnel — Multicast Network

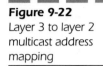

Figure 9-22
Layer 3 to layer 2
multicast address
mapping

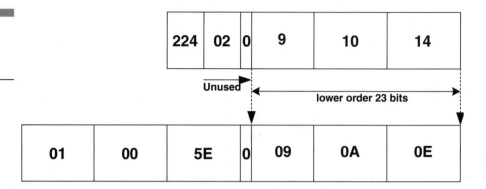

addresses exist for every multicast MAC address. This would only cause a problem if two multicast groups that were identified by the same MAC address had members residing on the same LAN. Members of each group might have to process traffic for the other group. Both multicast applications should continue to work okay, but unnecessary processing would take place between the groups, which partly defeats the purpose of using multicasting.

NOTE: *Multicast IP addresses are identified by a first octet address in the range 224 to 239 inclusive. Multicast MAC addresses take the form **01-00-5E-0xxxxxxx-XX-XX**. The first three bytes have the values shown, and the first bit of the fourth byte is 0. The remaining 23 lower-order bits are mapped directly from the 23 lower-order bits of the multicast IP address.*

The range of addresses 224.0.0.0 to 224.0.0.255 is reserved for designated, well-known networking applications such as routing protocols as well as topology discovery and network maintenance protocols. Routers that run a multicast routing protocol should not forward packets that have destination addresses within this range. The following mini-table is a summary of some of the most frequently used well-known multicast addresses. All of the addresses in this table refer to RFC standardized protocols (with the exception of Cisco's *Enhanced Interior Gateway Routing Protocol* [EIGRP]). Also, a large multiplicity of well-known multicast addresses in the 224.0.0.X range have been allocated to proprietary protocols.

Reserved Multicast IP Addresses	Use
224.0.0.1	All hosts on a subnet
224.0.0.2	All routers on a subnet
224.0.0.4	All *Distance Vector Multicast Routing Protocol* (DVMRP) routers
224.0.0.5	All OSPF routers
224.0.0.6	All OSPF-designated routers
224.0.0.9	All RIP v2 routers
224.0.0.10	All EIGRP routers
224.0.0.12	DHCP server/relay agent
224.0.0.13	All *Protocol Independent Multicast* (PIM) routers
224.0.0.14	RSVP-encapsulation

Notice that many of the reserved addresses listed here relate to IP unicast routing protocols. It is not a coincidence that all of the more recent or more sophisticated IP routing protocols use multicasts rather than broadcasts to exchange routing information. This means that on a shared medium such as a LAN, devices that are not routers do not get subjected to unnecessary broadcasts.

IGMP　The *Internet Group Management Protocol* (IGMP) is a standard described by RFC 1112 and is responsible for managing multicast group membership on a local basis. It relies on the processing of Class D addresses to create and maintain multicast groups. It can be thought of as a multicast protocol that is run between hosts and the local router on a LAN. The local router uses IGMP to discover multicast group members on the local LAN. If at least one member of a multicast group is discovered on an attached LAN segment, the router then forwards packets destined for that group address onto the LAN in question.

IGMP supports two fundamental message types:

- *Query messages* are used to discover which devices belong to a particular multicast group.

- *Report messages* are used by hosts in response to queries to inform the querying device that it is a group member.

Typically, it is the local router that issues query messages, and LAN hosts respond with a report message. In Figure 9-23, three clients exist on the local LAN. Two of the clients C1 and C2 are members of the group 229.1.2.3. The remaining client C3 is not a member. A typical sequence of events and messages that would be exchanged between the router and the hosts is as follows:

1. When each client joined the group (namely, C1 and C2), they issued an IGMP join message or *report* to the well-known address 224.0.0.2, which is the all-routers reserved address.

2. This message enables the router to learn that members of 229.1.2.3 are located on LAN 1. Therefore, if it receives a packet from a remote sender destined for this address, it forwards a single copy onto the LAN 1 segment. This packet will be processed by C1 and C2, but not C3 as it is not a group member.

3. Periodically, the router will send a query message to the all-hosts reserved address 224.0.0.1 in order to check that group members are still present on this LAN segment. This IGMP query interval is 60 seconds by default.

4. C1 and C2 will receive this query message but will not respond immediately. Instead, they each begin to decrement a random timer. The station that reaches zero first responds to the query with a report that confirms its group membership. The other station suppresses its report in order to conserve bandwidth. This is perfectly valid because the router is only interested in confirming that at least one host is a group member on that LAN. In the example of Figure 9-23, C2 is the host that issues the report, while C1 suppresses its report. If one member or more is on the LAN, then the router forwards multicast

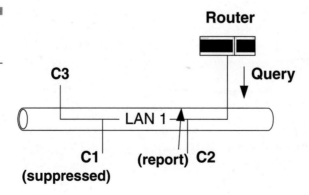

Figure 9-23
IGMP queries and reports

traffic destined for 229.1.2.3 onto LAN 1. If no members are on LAN 1, then it no longer forwards this traffic.

5. With IGMP version 1, if a host leaves the group, it does so "silently." In other words, it does not send any message. The router only notices a difference when the last member of 229.1.2.3 (staying with our example) leaves on LAN 1. When this happens, the router detects that no members are remaining on LAN 1 when no reply is made to its next periodic IGMP query. At this point, the group times out on this interface and the router no longer forwards traffic destined for 229.1.2.3 on LAN 1.

IGMP Version 2   IGMP version 2 offers a number of enhancements over its predecessor, namely:

■ *Leave reports*: Hosts that use IGMP version 2 do not leave the group silently; instead, they issue a group leave report. When an IGMP version 2 router receives a leave report, it immediately issues a query (rather than waiting for the next periodic query). If no more hosts are group members, no report will be received and the group will time out. Thus, IGMP version 2 groups time out faster when the last member leaves.

Many of these additional features in IGMP and IGMP v2 might seem like niceties, but when you are dealing with bandwidth-intensive applications, any bandwidth-conserving feature is worthwhile.

■ *Group-specific queries*: With IGMP v1, the router must query all multicast groups, and if multiple groups are on a LAN segment, the router will receive multiple simultaneous reports. IGMP v2 enables group-specific queries as well as general all-hosts queries. This is another feature intended not only to conserve bandwidth, but also router CPU processing by eliminating any unnecessary messages.

■ *Designated routers*: On a LAN that has more than one router, for reasons of redundancy or otherwise, an IGMP v1 implementation will have all multicast routers issuing queries to the hosts on the LAN. This results in unnecessary traffic.

IGMP v2 alleviates this issue by performing a designated router election on the LAN. The designated router is responsible for querying the hosts in order to verify group membership. The criteria by which a designated router election is resolved can vary depending on the vendor model and platform. Instances can occur where the router with the highest active IP address becomes the designated router and other cases where the router with the lowest IP address becomes the querying router. As ever, it is a question of checking your documentation.

Note that the author does not know of any router vendors that currently support the auto-detection of the IGMP version. The two versions are *not* compatible, so it is important to verify that all hosts and routers on the same LAN are using the same IGMP version.

NOTE: *IGMP versions 1 and 2 are not compatible, so it is important to ensure that all devices (routers and hosts) on the LAN are using the same version.*

So we have seen how IGMP enables a station to inform the network that it is a member of a specific group. The manner in which IGMP enables routers to periodically verify group membership on its attached segments has also been discussed. The router thus assumes an IGMP group management role on each local LAN. It forwards traffic only on segments where it sees group members.

We'll now discuss how the router communicates with remote subnets in order to enable multicast groups to have a membership that is dispersed across the internetwork. This is similar in principle to the role of a router in enabling unicast communication between remote networks using a unicast routing protocol and it leads into the area of multicast routing.

Multicast Routing Multicast transmission is based on the idea of one-to-many or many-to-many communication. This implies that it poses a greater networking challenge than the traditional one-to-one communications that are facilitated by unicast routing protocols. Conventional routing protocols were commissioned with the task of providing the optimum path between two networks. A multicast routing protocol must provide the optimum path between a sender's network and several receiver networks.

It is therefore not surprising that multicast routing entails the use of some additional principles above and beyond traditional unicast routing techniques. A logical path must be established between each sender and the corresponding receivers in the multicast group.

Distribution Trees A distribution tree is used to construct a logical transmission path between all members of a multicast group. The routers on the network build distribution trees that chart paths from each multicast sender to all receivers. Two fundamentally different approaches to building distribution trees are available:

- Source-based distribution trees
- Shared distribution trees

Source-Based Distribution Trees A source-based tree structure consists of a separate distribution tree for each sender on the network. The branches of the tree are the shortest paths from the sender to each receiver. Figure 9-24 illustrates a source-based distribution tree where multicast packets for the group in question are forwarded along the shortest path between the sender and each receiver. The construction of these paths is achieved using the principle of *reverse path forwarding* (RPF).

RPF employs two operational principles:

- With RPF, a router floods a packet out all interfaces except the one it received the packet on, provided that the packet was received on the interface that represents the shortest path back to the source. A packet that is received on paths that do not represent the shortest path back to the source will be dropped. Figure 9-25 demonstrates this RPF principle. Router C forwards the packet received from router A but not the one received from router B. Router C is said to build a branch of the tree that leads back to the source via router A, and it prunes (or eliminates) the path via router B.

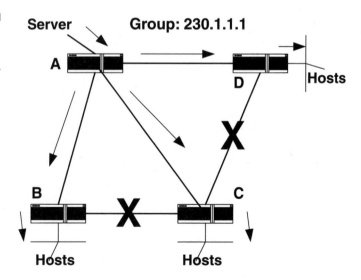

Figure 9-24
Source-based
distribution tree

Server   Group: 230.1.1.1

Figure 9-25
Reverse path
forwarding

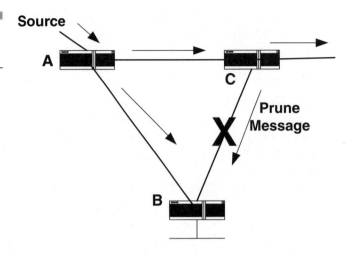

The shortest path in this context is the path with the lowest metric, as indicated by the unicast IP routing protocol. Hence, this is the first example that we encounter of the multicast routing protocol using information obtained from the unicast routing protocol to construct a distribution path.

■ Routers employing RPF will only forward a packet to a destination or receiver on the shortest path to that receiver. This again is dictated by the unicast routing metric.

Consider again the network shown in Figure 9-24. A single source or server is used, so therefore the branches of the tree consist of the shortest path between this source and each of the three receiver networks. Reverse path forwarding constructs the tree branches by dictating that traffic should only be forwarded on the shortest path from the sender to each of the receivers. Therefore, no multicast traffic for this group is forwarded on the direct link between router B and router C or on the link between router C and router D.

If a second server is added to the network, then RPF would calculate the shortest path between this new source and each of the receiver networks. If, for example, the second source is placed on router D's LAN, then multicast traffic would be forwarded on the direct link between router C and router D because it would present the shortest path from the new source to router C's LAN hosts.

RPF therefore facilitates the construction of a distribution tree that is optimized with respect to each source, hence the term source-based distribution tree. In the event of a second sender being added to the network, a further tree would have to be constructed for this sender also. The branches in each tree represent the shortest path from a particular sender to each receiver.

Clearly, source-based distribution trees facilitate optimized routing for every possible sender-receiver combination. The disadvantage of this type of approach is that a multicast routing protocol employing source-based principles would inevitably entail a significant amount of routing overhead that may be prohibitive for certain scenarios. This fact creates a niche for an alternative approach to the construction of distribution trees.

Shared Distribution Trees With a shared distribution tree, a single tree is constructed for the entire multicast group regardless of how many senders exist within that group. The tree contains a core router that is the logical center of the tree. This is analogous to the root bridge in spanning tree. In fact, the principle of shared distribution trees is quite similar to spanning tree in a bridged or switched environment.

Figure 9-26 displays a network that uses a shared distribution tree. The core router is B, and the arrows indicate the path that the traffic takes from each source. If this were a source-based distribution topology, a tree would be rooted at each source. Instead, just one shared distribution tree is used with B as its root. The tree is built by first deciding on a core router and then the shortest path from the core to each sender and receiver is calculated. As we shall see when multicast routing protocols that use a shared tree approach are discussed, hosts must first issue explicit IGMP join mes-

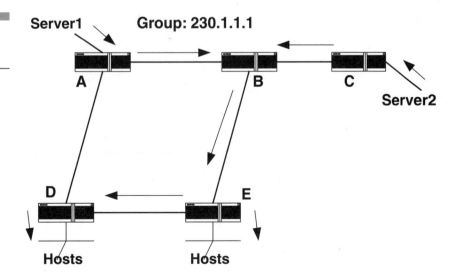

Figure 9-26
Shared distribution tree

sages before they can add a branch to the tree. The tree shown in Figure 9-26 is optimized for the overall group, but unlike a source-based tree, it is not optimized for each sender/receiver pair. For example, group members on LAN D receive data over the optimal path for server 2, but the path from server 1 is sub-optimal. This is the tradeoff with shared distribution trees. They entail less routing overhead than source-based trees, but they can also result in sub-optimal path selection.

It is worth emphasizing that although each multicast group has only one shared distribution tree regardless of the number of senders, different trees can exist for different multicast groups.

Multicasting Routing Protocols   IP multicasting routing protocols are grouped into two categories that loosely relate to the two different mechanisms for building distribution trees. *Dense mode* protocols relate to source-based trees and *sparse mode* routing protocols use a shared distribution tree.

Dense Mode Routing Protocols   The term *dense mode* refers to the manner in which the receivers are distributed around the network. A dense mode protocol should be used if the receivers are densely distributed. In other words, this type of protocol is appropriate if many receivers are in close proximity to each other such as being on the same campus LAN.

IP PIM Dense Mode   The first dense mode multicast routing protocol that we will discuss is the *Protocol Independent Multicast* (PIM) dense mode. This protocol uses reverse path forwarding to build source-based distribution trees. The reverse path-forwarding algorithm constructs the tree by considering the shortest path between senders and receivers. PIM derives its name from the fact that any IP unicast routing protocol can be used to provide the metric to calculate the shortest paths. In other words, it does not rely on any particular unicast routing protocol.

Dense mode routers make two assumptions:

- Bandwidth is plentiful on the network, so it is appropriate to initially flood multicast traffic on all interfaces except the one on which the packet was received.

- Most routers on the network forward multicast traffic either to directly attached hosts or to downstream hosts. This is another reason why dense mode routers initially flood traffic.

Figure 9-27 displays a network that uses PIM dense mode. Initially, traffic from the server is flooded by every router *on each interface that has PIM dense mode configured*. Remember that multicast routing must be explicitly configured on each router. Therefore, a single copy of the data transmission from the server is flooded throughout the multicast network. A distribution tree is built for each sender with that sender as the root of the tree. In this example, only one sender is used and hence only one tree. The branches in the distribution tree are the shortest paths from the sender to each receiver, as dictated by the reverse path-forwarding algorithm. Although the initial packets are flooded on all links, subsequent packets only get forwarded over the shortest path between sender and receiver.

If a PIM dense mode router receives multicast traffic for a group that it has no knowledge of, it sends a *prune* message back to the source and that branch of the tree will be removed. For example, in Figure 9-27, router D knows that it has no attached hosts belonging to 230.1.1.1 because it received no answer to its queries for that group. It also has not received a PIM dense mode update about this group from a downstream router and hence knows that it has no need to forward traffic for 230.1.1.1. It therefore

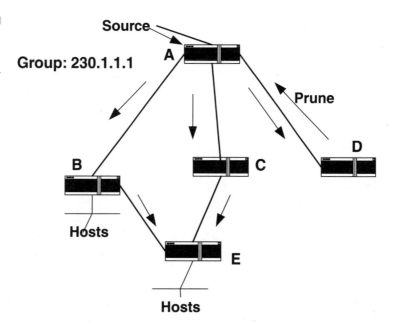

Figure 9-27

PIM DM flooding and pruning

sends a prune message back to the source, and router D is then removed from the distribution tree for that group.

Periodically, PIM dense mode initiates a reflooding in order to verify that no additional branches must be added to the tree due to new members joining.

To summarize PIM dense mode:

- Initially, traffic is flooded throughout the network.

- Routers prune on the non-shortest path back to each source, thus removing non-optimal paths from the distribution tree.

- Routers also prune branches that contain no group members.

- PIM dense mode periodically refloods.

- In the steady state, every sender has a distribution tree. The branches in each tree relate to the shortest path from the sender to each receiver. The shortest path is dictated by the metric used by the unicast IP routing protocol employed by the routers.

The operational behavior of PIM dense mode makes it suitable for an implementation where the senders and receivers are in close proximity to one another such as on the same campus LAN. Dense mode protocols also assume that bandwidth is plentiful and so the use of flooding is an appropriate method of initially building a distribution tree. This assumption is also more valid in a LAN or campus environment. The fact that a separate distribution tree exists for every sender implies that the routing overhead associated with dense mode protocols may become excessive if alot of senders are active. Dense mode routing is generally more appropriate when there are few senders and many receivers.

From an application standpoint, the generous approach to bandwidth utilization that is a characteristic of dense mode protocols makes them suited to applications that create a heavy and consistent volume of traffic. In this type of scenario, the bandwidth consumption associated with the dense mode routing protocol would be less in percentage terms relative to the overall bandwidth consumption.

Some of the typical applications that use dense mode multicast routing include LAN TV, corporate broadcasts, or financial broadcasts.

NOTE: *A dense mode multicasting routing protocol is appropriate when*
- *Bandwidth is plentiful.*
- *Senders and receivers are in close proximity to each other.*
- *Few senders but many receivers are active.*

DVMRP   The *Distance Vector Multicast Routing Protocol* (DVMRP) is also a dense mode protocol. It is described by RFC 1075 and came to early prominence in the world of multicasting by being widely used on the *Internet Multicast Backbone* (MBONE). Despite early and ubiquitous use in sections of the industry, DVMRP is far from being an ideal multicast routing solution.

As it is a dense mode routing protocol, it employs the same techniques as PIM dense mode. A source-based tree is constructed and rooted at each sender. Traffic from a source is flooded throughout the network initially. The principle of reverse path forwarding is used to prune the non-shortest paths between the sender and receivers. Areas of the network that contain no members are also pruned back. Periodic reflooding is also a feature of DVMRP.

However, as stated earlier, dense mode protocols are more suitable for groups where the members are in close proximity to each other. Bandwidth is also assumed to be plentiful for dense mode operation. Neither of these conditions holds true for the Internet MBONE.

The scalability of DVMRP also is an issue because of the unicast protocol on which it relies. DVMRP uses its own unicast routing protocol, which is very similar to RIP. The metric it employs, like RIP, is hop count. Therefore, if the main unicast routing protocol on the enterprise is anything other than RIP (which on a large network is very likely to be the case), then it is quite possible that unicast and multicast traffic may take separate paths. In addition to this, the crudeness of this DVMRP unicast routing protocol places a scalability limitation on its deployment. This limitation must often be circumvented through the use of DVMRP tunnels that connect senders to receivers while incurring the minimum number of hops. For this reason, DVMRP tunnels are frequently configured for multicast Internet access. An ISP may suggest that you create a DVMRP tunnel to them in order to gain access to the multicast backbone on the Internet.

MOSPF   *Multicast OSPF* (MOSPF) is described by RFC 1584 and is really an optional extension to OSPF that enables the support of multicasting. To use MOSPF, the unicast routing protocol on the network must be OSPF. MOSPF is a dense mode protocol that constructs source-based distribution trees for each sender/group pair in a similar fashion as the other dense mode protocols already discussed.

MOSPF relies on OSPF for two functions:

- It uses the OSPF administrative cost metric to calculate the shortest path back to each source and hence to construct the trees.
- MOSPF includes multicast information in OSPF link state advertisements. In other words, it uses OSPF as its transport mechanism.

A multicast routing protocol that is closely tied to OSPF might seem like a logical choice for scalability. However, MOSPF is not without its potential drawbacks, some of which relate to the inherent difference between unicast and multicast environments. The first issue is that when routes time out of the MOSPF routing table, the tree must be recalculated for that group. This issue is not so serious because timers can be configured to set the timeout to a relatively high value. The second issue is that trees must be recalculated every time a change occurs to a link state topology. This is a potential problem on an unstable network.

Apart from requiring a stable network, MOSPF is unsuitable (like most dense mode protocols) on a multicast network that features many senders. In this case, a large number of trees would have to be calculated, resulting in heavy router memory consumption and CPU utilization.

Sparse Mode Routing Protocols   Sparse mode multicast routing protocols take the alternative approach to dense mode and rely on a common shared distribution tree for each multicast group. Sparse mode multicast routing derives its name from the fact that it is optimized for communication within multicast groups that feature sparsely distributed receivers. The most prevalent sparse mode routing protocol in use in the industry is PIM sparse mode.

IP PIM Sparse Mode   Spare mode routing assumes that the multicast group members are physically scattered at different locations across the internetwork. This type of routing is also designed to consolidate bandwidth. In essence, this approach is very much the opposite of dense mode routing and is optimized for a WAN rather than a LAN environment. PIM sparse mode (like its PIM dense mode counterpart) derives its name from the fact that it can utilize whatever unicast IP routing protocol is in use on the network.

Sparse mode PIM builds a single shared distribution tree for each multicast group. The tree is rooted at a core router or *rendezvous point* (RP). Although certain proprietary implementations enable the RP to be dynamically discovered, the RP must usually be statically configured on the other routers in the network. A sample implementation of PIM sparse mode is shown in Figure 9-28, where router B is the RP.

In a sparse mode implementation, initially no branches are used in the distribution tree. Branches only get added after an explicit IGMP join message is issued by a host. For example, the branch from the RP to router C was only added when the host C1 issued an IGMP join report to router C, which then updated the RP router. This leads to some of the operational functions of the RP that must be described:

■ If a host wants to receive data from the group, then it must join the group, as is the case with any IP multicast implementation. On a sparse mode network, receivers must also register with the RP in order to receive remote information from senders within that group. Hosts register with the RP by issuing an IGMP join message to their local router. This router, which is also known as a *leaf router*, forwards the message to the RP, which in turn sends the join message to the source router. A leaf router on a sparse mode network is simply any multicast router that is not an RP. Leaf routers are configured with the IP address of the RP, enabling them to appropriately forward registration messages.

Figure 9-28
PIM sparse mode

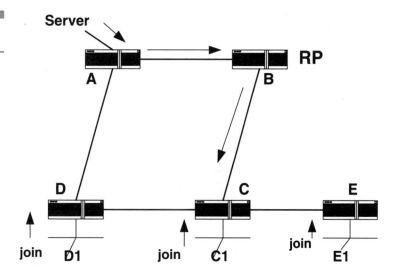

■ When a multicast source wants to send data to the group, it initially sends to the RP via its local router. In the example of Figure 9-28, the transmission path between the server and the host on router C's LAN would then be via routers A-B-C. This happens to coincide with the optimum path between sender and receiver. If a host on LAN D joins the group, it must register with the RP, and a branch of the distribution tree is added between C and D. Initially, the traffic from the sender to LAN D will take the path via the RP, namely A-B-C-D, which is sub-optimal. PIM sparse mode, however, incorporates the capability to direct subsequent traffic from sender to receiver along the optimal path, which in this case is A through D. This capability to optimize the sender-receiver path by eliminating any unnecessary hops is a significant feature of PIM sparse mode.

Having described sparse mode operation and the role of the RP, some design issues are worth discussing in relation to the RP:

■ Choose the RP with care. The sparse mode core router or RP can be thought of as being analogous to the root bridge in spanning tree. Like the selection of the root bridge, the choice of an RP should not be performed by random selection. The RP is likely to process more multicast traffic than any other sparse mode router and therefore should have adequate memory and CPU processing resources to match the task. In terms of location, the RP should approximately mirror the physical topology of the network and be located close to the core. This increases the likelihood that more routers will have optimal paths to the RP.

■ A router can be an RP for more than one multicast group. This is practically sensible if, for example, separate group addresses were used for audio and video that related to the same application. If the RPs were different for the two groups, then it is possible that audio and video traffic would take a different path through the network. The potential for a variation in delay between the two streams is certainly not desirable for time-sensitive applications.

■ A multicast group can have more than one RP. It is good practice to have a second RP configured on the leaf routers for redundancy. In a single RP environment, a failure on the RP does not necessarily render the sparse mode environment inoperable. Instead, the packets may be flooded in a dense mode manner and be pruned back on branches that contain no members. However, sparse mode operation would have been configured for a reason and it is likely that the advent of packet flooding is undesirable for reasons such as bandwidth consumption and routing overhead.

Sparse mode is clearly a different philosophy to dense mode and is a routing method designed and optimized for a different networking environment. With this type of routing protocol, no hosts receive data until they issue an explicit join message (or at least some host on the same LAN issues a IGMP join report). Hence, sparse mode operates on the assumption that most LANs on the internetwork do *not* contain receiver hosts for this group.

The branches in the distribution tree are pruned back if a local router detects through IGMP that group members are no longer active on its local LAN. This feature, apart from the obvious benefit of bandwidth conservation, is intended to make sparse mode applicable in environments where the multicast traffic profile is intermittent. Unlike dense mode operations, no periodic reflooding is used to verify the distribution of group members. Sparse mode is therefore extremely conservative in its use of bandwidth, making it a suitable implementation for a group that has its membership scattered across a WAN where bandwidth is expensive and less than plentiful.

At this point, it is appropriate to summarize the types of environments where sparse mode routing is most applicable:

- Bandwidth is limited.
- Relatively few receivers may be scattered across the WAN.
- The multicast traffic is intermittent.

Some of the typical applications that use sparse mode multicast routing include desktop conferencing and collaborative computing across a WAN. Multicasting can also be used by e-mail platforms to simultaneously update multiple e-mail servers. PIM sparse mode could be used to perform this task across a large organization. If the Internet is used to provide the inter-server communication, then DVMRP is likely to be the multicast routing protocol.

Multicasting and LAN Switching   Excessive Ethernet collisions can degrade the service experienced by real-time multimedia traffic. A shared LAN is only likely to prove adequate for most low-bandwidth audio applications. For real-time applications that consume even medium levels of bandwidth, a switched LAN environment is required.

LAN switches treat multicasts much the same as broadcasts and flood them to all ports except the one on which the multicast was received. Thus, on a large switched LAN, the key differentiating benefit of multicasts over broadcasts is lost. Switches must be made multicast-aware in order to restore these benefits. Rather than flooding multicast frames, switches need a mechanism for learning the location of multicast group members and only forwarding the group traffic on the relevant ports.

This issue has a number of possible solutions:

- *IGMP snooping*: IGMP snooping is a standardized solution that enables the switch to learn the location of IGMP group members. With IGMP snooping enabled, the switch listens to or snoops IGMP query and report messages in order to learn the port location of group members. Because the switch is now tracking the multicast group, it only forwards multicast frames for that group on ports where it has observed join reports. The switch's group membership awareness can be updated dynamically by listening to query, report, and leave messages in the case of IGMP v2.

  The downside of IGMP snooping is that every multicast packet must be snooped in order to track the location of group members. This results in increased CPU processing cycles that may adversely affect the switch's capability to forward frames with low latency, particularly during high-traffic conditions.

- *Generic Attribute Registration Protocol (IEEE 802.1p):* The IEEE 802.1p protocol was designed for use between end-system hosts and the LAN switches. Running this protocol on the hosts and the switch enables the hosts to communicate directly with the switch in order to join an 802.1p group that corresponds to a multicast group. This approach makes the switch, rather than the router, the main fulcrum of responsibility for managing local multicast group membership. In fact, this scheme has alot of validity on a large and mainly flat switched LAN.

- *Proprietary solutions such as Cisco's CGMP*: Most switch vendors have their own method of communicating multicast information to their LAN switches. Let us consider *Cisco's Group Management Protocol* (CGMP), which is arguably one of the better solutions.

The CGMP protocol is run between a Cisco router and a Cisco switch. The switch acts as a CGMP client with the router being the CGMP server. Figure 9-29 illustrates CGMP operation between a router and a switch.

Note that although IGMP is employed between the hosts and the router, CGMP is run between the switch and the router.

Consider the case where a host station issues an IGMP join report, which is received by the router (recalling that IGMP is run between hosts and the local router). The switch transparently passes on this IGMP message. If the router and switch are each configured to run CGMP, then the router sends a CGMP join message back to the switch. This message is sent to a well-known reserved address that is listened to by all CGMP-enabled devices. The CGMP message sent by the router includes the layer 2 multicast group address along with the MAC address of the host that just joined this group. The switch knows from its MAC address table the location of this host. Hence, when it receives traffic for the particular layer 2 multicast address, the switch forwards it out the port where this station resides. If multiple stations are group members, the switch forwards traffic on all of the corresponding ports.

In the case of IGMP v2 being employed between the hosts and the router, CGMP can be configured to process leave messages. This enables CGMP to dynamically update the switch on group membership both in terms of hosts joining and leaving.

Without the use of a protocol such as CGMP, the switch would flood multicast traffic out all of its ports, hence negating the benefit of multicasting in the LAN.

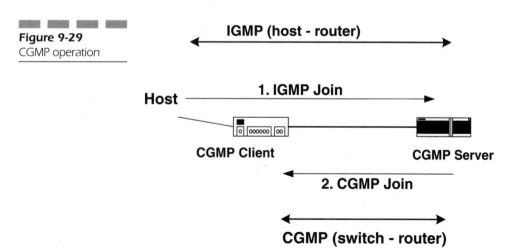

Figure 9-29
CGMP operation

QoS and RSVP

We have already seen that modern networks are required to support an increasingly diverse range of applications. Loss-sensitive data applications are being integrated with delay-sensitive multimedia applications on a common network infrastructure.

One of the main goals of providing a specific class or QoS is to ensure that delay-sensitive applications do not suffer as a result of this integration, particularly during periods of heavy traffic. However, that is not the only driving force behind the concept of QoS. Real-time applications require certain levels of consistency with respect to delay and bandwidth allocation. Although providing this service is a fundamental goal of QoS, it is equally important to ensure that the continuous demand for certain service parameters by real-time applications does not impinge on the data applications. Thus, it is important to provide a certain QoS for data traffic, particularly that small packet-size transactions should not be excessively delayed behind large packets. The ultimate goal of QoS is to strike an effective balance to ensure a satisfactory level of service for the multiple heterogeneous applications on the network.

To achieve this goal, applications must be associated with an appropriate level of service with regard to parameters such as delay, delay variation, and bandwidth throughput. This desired QoS must then be communicated to all devices along the traffic path. The possible methods for accomplishing these two steps include IP precedence, the *Real Time Protocol* (RTP), and what we are about to discuss in detail, RSVP. Each of these methods were mentioned in Chapter 3, "Choosing the WAN Technology," when discussing QoS in the WAN. It is appropriate to give a more rigorous treatment of RSVP at this point, as it is a QoS technique that is gaining increasing deployment in the campus LAN and beyond.

A protocol such as RSVP can attempt to allocate resources and service levels to particular applications that then are communicated to all relevant devices. This, however, is not sufficient to achieve the required service level for these applications. A mechanism must be in place to ensure that the network and each relevant device along the path can counteract the sources of delay and deliver the requisite QoS. Adequate bandwidth and a device-processing capability must first be available. With enough bandwidth, sophisticated QoS protocols would rarely be required, but this is a luxury that few networks can afford to possess. Queuing and fragmentation techniques must be supported on the network devices to ensure that high-priority packets are switched with a minimum delay (these issues were also dealt with in Chapter 3). Therefore, it is important to be clear that a protocol like RSVP does not replace QoS-related queuing techniques; rather, it must work in conjunction with them.

NOTE: *The ultimate goal of QoS is to provide adequate service levels for certain heterogeneous applications without reducing the service experienced by other applications.*

RSVP works in conjunction with interface-queuing techniques in order to deliver specified QoS levels.

RSVP Overview

RSVP is a standardized protocol that was developed with the aim of providing end-to-end service levels for heterogeneous IP applications.

RSVP supports three different traffic types:

- *Best effort delivery*: This is similar to traditional IP data delivery where the responsibility for guaranteed delivery is delegated to the higher layers if at all. Applications were also assumed not to be particularly delay-sensitive.

- *Rate-sensitive*: This traffic category characterizes applications that require a guaranteed bit rate possibly at the cost of additional delay.

- *Delay-sensitive*: This traffic type relates to applications that require minimized and consistent delay but may not necessarily entail very large bandwidth consumption. A potential example is MPEG video, which has two basic types of frames. One relates to the picture (key frames) and the other relates to changes in the picture (delta frames). All frames, despite widely varying sizes, must be delivered within a particular delay specification for the MPEG protocol to work. Delta frames are usually substantially smaller than keys and require a special priority to avoid being delayed behind the larger frames.

For RSVP to operate, all devices along the path between the source and destination must be RSVP-capable including the end-stations. The protocol is designed to work in a multicast or unicast environment. Obviously, for a multicast application, the sending station must first issue an IGMP join message to join the multicast group. It then sends an RSVP message to the destination. This message is routed using a unicast or multicast routing protocol as appropriate. The destination or receiver returns an RSVP resource reservation message to the sender. The request specifics the QoS level required by the application along the data path in question. If each RSVP device along the path between sender and receiver can support the desired QoS, then the request will be accepted. Otherwise, the reservation will be rejected and the application may have to proceed on a best-effort basis.

RSVP Operation

RSVP traffic flows are usually characterized by sessions that share a common destination IP unicast or multicast group address. A session in RSVP terms is a set of data flows that has a common destination. The session may also include a number of separate data flows from various senders.

Although it is possible to tunnel RSVP across the Internet, campus implementations require that all devices along the path are RSVP-capable. Hosts use RSVP to request certain QoS levels from local routers and switches. The router and switch devices use RSVP to request the corresponding QoS level as far as the next adjacent router or switch. This intercommunication between all devices along the data path ensures that an attempt is made to allocate the required resources along the entire path between sender and receiver.

In the case of a tunnel, no control can be exerted over the QoS level within the tunnel because the section of the network that is being tunneled through does not support RSVP. Hence, although RSVP is implemented on the edges of the tunnel, you have no guarantee of the end-to-end QoS experienced by the application.

An RSVP session starts when the sender issues an *RSVP path message* to the destination IP address (that can be unicast or multicast). A path message is used to store the path state at each node.

After receiving the path state message, the receiver sends an *RSVP reservation request message* back to the sender. The reservation request specifies the QoS parameter values required by the application along the data path. This message is routed back to the sender using the information obtained from the path message and the IP routing protocol. Figure 9-30 shows a summary of the RSVP message sequence.

Each node along the reverse path back to the source must look at the reservation request and decide if the user has permission to request the reservation and secondly if sufficient resources are available to secure this reservation. To make the resource reservation at a router node, the RSVP daemon communicates with two local modules: admission control and policy control. The admission control decision module determines whether

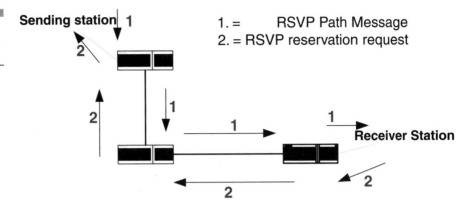

Figure 9-30
RSVP session startup
messages

Sending station 1

1. =   RSVP Path Message
2. = RSVP reservation request

Receiver Station

the node has sufficient resources to satisfy the QoS request. The policy control module verifies that the user has permission to request this reservation. If either of these checks fail, the reservation request is denied and an appropriate error message is sent back to the application that originated the request. If both checks succeed, the RSVP daemon communicates with two other modules, the packet classifier and packet scheduler, in order to prepare the packet for transmission with the desired QoS. This procedure is illustrated graphically in Figure 9-31.

The packet classifier determines the route and QoS for each packet. The packet scheduler allocates the requisite resources for transmission on the data link medium. If the interface over which the packet is to be sent already has its own QoS configuration, the packet scheduler negotiates in order to secure the requested QoS. This procedure is repeated at each router node in its attempts to secure the requested QoS for the end-to-end application stream. The low-latency queuing and prioritization techniques on the routers are ultimately the tools used in attempting to satisfy each resource request.

RSVP reacts to route and topology changes within the network. Resource reservations quickly time out after a route is lost. It reroutes traffic and reservations along new paths, as indicated by the IP multicast or unicast routing protocol.

RSVP Reservation Types   Two types of dynamic reservations can be made with RSVP:

■ Controlled load
■ Guaranteed services

Figure 9-31

Decision modules at
RSVP node

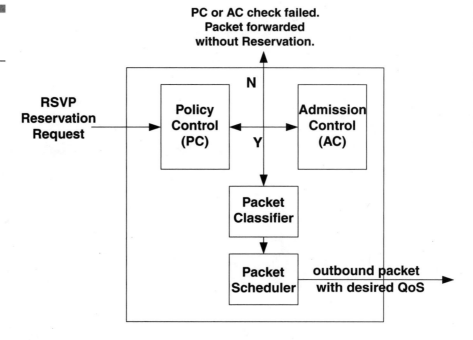

The difference between the two relates to the level of QoS reservation specification that is guaranteed.

To quote from the RSVP RFC, the *controlled load service* provides end-to-end behavior that "tightly approximates the behavior visible to applications that receive best effort service under unloaded conditions, or conditions not heavily loaded or congested."

The specification goes on to state that with a controlled load service it may be assumed that

- A very high percentage of transmitted packets will be successfully delivered by the network to receiving nodes.

- The transit delay experienced by a very high percentage of the delivered packets will not greatly exceed the minimum delay experienced by any successfully delivered packet. In other words, delay will not be significantly greater than the delay due to the limiting factors of the network, namely the propagation delay on the link and the device processing time.

To ensure that these conditions are met, clients that request a controlled-load service issue an estimation of the data traffic that they will generate.

This is known as the *TSpec.* The controlled load service allocates resources adequate to ensuring the desired throughput, and delay characteristics are met, provided the TSpec is not exceeded.

As can be observed from the RFC, although a controlled-load service endeavors to provide high-quality results that would be experienced under unloaded conditions, it does not make any absolute guarantees. A service that provides such guarantees is the aptly named *guaranteed service.*

The end-to-end service provided by a series of network elements conforming to a guaranteed service is an assured level of bandwidth and a delay-bounded service with no queuing loss for conforming datagrams. Guaranteed service controls the maximum queuing delay that is experienced beyond the minimum delay of the medium itself. It must therefore work in conjunction with the low-latency queuing and prioritization techniques implemented by different vendors.

A guaranteed service is also subject to admission control at each node in order to verify that resources are available to guarantee the provision of such a request.

What has just been discussed relates to two fundamental types of service that are differentiated by the level of guaranteed service that they provide. RSVP also defines two types of reservation that are distinguished by the nature of the flow and manner in which the reservation is allocated:

- *Distinct reservation:* A classic example of distinct reservation is a video stream where a sender emits its own distinct data stream. The flow from each sender therefore requires its own resource reservation in order to ensure a certain QoS for the application. A distinct reservation is defined by a *fixed filter* (FF) mask that provides a separate resource reservation for each sender or source-destination flow.

- *Shared reservation:* A shared reservation applies a single RSVP resource allocation that is shared between all flows to a particular destination. The shared reservation for the session is the largest of the resource requests made by all receivers within the pipe or session. An example of a shared flow is an audio application where each sender emits a distinct data stream. However, a limited number of senders is actually transmitting at any given time. A *wildcard filter* (WF) is used to define a shared reservation among a list of sender or source addresses carried in the reservation message.

In a multicast environment, a shared allocation effectively means that multiple senders to a particular multicast group share the same resource reservation.

RSVP Message and Packet Structure In this section the different types of RSVP messages are summarized and described. The RSVP packet structure is also examined.

RSVP Message Types The different types of RSVP packets are now summarized, some of which have already been discussed:

- *Resource reservation messages:* This message is sent by receivers towards senders. Its purpose is to inform the sending host and all network elements along the reverse path of the required QoS and resource allocation for the application.

- *Path messages:* The path message is emitted by the sender when initiating the RSVP session. It is sent along the path dictated by the IP routing protocol and it enables the receiver to route reservation request messages in the reverse direction.

- *Error and confirmation messages:* Three RSVP error and confirmation messages are used:

  - *Path error messages* result from path messages and are routed back towards senders.

  - *Reservation-request error messages* are routed towards senders when an admission control failure occurs or resources are unavailable to satisfy the reservation request.

  - *Reservation-request acknowledgment messages* are forwarded to the receiver confirming the details of the reservation.

- *Teardown messages*: RSVP teardown messages delete the path state and/or reservation state at each node. These messages can be generated by the end station application or by a router detecting a state timeout or topology change.

RSVP Packet Structure The RSVP packet structure is displayed in Figure 9-32. An analysis of the packet format can be subdivided into the header fields and the object fields.

RSVP Message Header Fields RSVP message header fields consist of the following fields:

- *Version*: Indicates the protocol version number (currently version 1).

- *Flags*: Reserved for future use. No flags are currently defined.

- *Type*: This eight-bit field denotes the type of RSVP message and can have the values shown in the following mini-table along with the corresponding message type.

Figure 9-32

RSVP packet format

RSVP Message Header Fields

Version (4 bits)	Flags (4)	Type (8)	Check-sum (16)	length (16)	reserved (8)	Send TTL (8)	Message ID (32)	Re-served (15)	MF (1)	Frag Offset (16)

RSVP Object Fields

Length (16)	Class -Num (8)	C-Type (8)	Object Contents (variable)

Value	Message Type
11	Path
22	Reservation-request
33	Path-error
44	Reservation-request error
55	Path-teardown
66	Reservation-teardown
77	Reservation-request acknowledgment

■ *Checksum*: This represents a standard TCP/UDP checksum over the contents of the RSVP message, with the checksum field replaced by zero.

■ *Length*: This is the length of the RSVP packet in bytes, including the common header and the variable-length objects that follow. If the *More Fragments* (MF) flag is set or the fragment-offset field is non-zero, this is the length of the current fragment of a larger message.

■ *Send TTL*: This indicates the IP *time-to-live* (TTL) value with which the message was sent.

- *Message ID*: This identifies different fragments of the same message.
- *MF Flag*: Low-order bit of a one-byte word with the other seven high-order bits specified as reserved. MF is set on for all but the last fragment of a message.
- *Fragment Offset*: The byte offset of the fragment in the message.

RSVP Object Fields   The RSVP object fields consist of the following:

- *Length*: The total object length in bytes (must always be a multiple of four and be at least four).
- *Class-Num*: This identifies the object class. Each object class has a name. The high-order bit of the Class-Num determines which action a node should take if it does not recognize the Class-Num of an object. The object class describes the QOS specification and its characteristics. The different objective classes are summarized in the table below.
- *C-Type*: This is the object type, unique within Class-Num. The Class-Num and C-Type fields (together with the flag bit) can be used together as a 16-bit number to define a unique type for each object.
- *Object Contents*: The Length, Class-Num, and C-Type fields specify the form of the object content.

Object Class	Description
Null	Contains a Class-Num of zero, and its C-Type is ignored. Its length must be at least four but can be any multiple of four. A null object can appear anywhere in a sequence of objects, and its contents will be ignored by the receiver.
Session	Contains the IP destination address and possibly a generalized destination port to define a specific session for the other objects that follow.
RSVP Hop	Carries the IP address of the RSVP-capable node that sent this message.
Time Values	Can contain values for the refresh period and the state TTL to override the default values.
Style	Defines the reservation style and style-specific information that is not a flow-specification or filter-specification object (included in a reservation-request message).
Flow Specification	Defines a desired QoS (included in a reservation-request message).
Filter Specification	Defines a subset of session-data packets that should receive the desired QoS (specified by a flow-specification object within a reservation-request message).

Object Class	Description
Sender Template	Contains a sender IP address (included in a path message).
Sender TSPEC	Defines the traffic characteristics of a sender's data stream (included in a path message).
Adspec	Carries advertising data in the path message.
Error Specification	Specifies an error (included in a path-error or reservation-request error message).
Policy Data	Carries information that will enable a local policy module to decide whether an associated reservation is permitted (included in a path or reservation-request message).
Integrity	Contains cryptographic data for authentication purposes.
Scope	An explicit specification of the scope for forwarding a reservation-request message.
Reservation	Carries the IP address of a receiver that requested a confirmation.

Design and Implementation Considerations

The planning of a QoS strategy is important on modern networks that have anything less than an abundance of bandwidth. A number of standardized protocols such as RSVP were developed for this purpose. Each router and switch vendor has low-latency queuing and prioritization techniques that can be used to enforce the QoS policies. The tools are unquestionably available in the marketplace; however, it is vital to put some planning into a QoS strategy without diving in and implementing a set of features simply because you can.

Too often have QoS been configured on the network devices without any real benefit to the performance of applications. This is almost always because a headless chicken approach was used rather than the implementation of a planned strategy. For this reason, some fundamental steps will be outlined that should be followed before implementing any form of QoS, and we'll also examine the specific steps that relate to the use of RSVP:

■ *Understand the applications*: Without an adequate understanding of the network applications, a QoS strategy cannot be implemented successfully. The level of bandwidth consumed by each application on a per-client basismust be understood. The application throughput requirements and time-sensitivity must also be known, along with the distribution of clients around the network. In other words, client-server traffic patterns must be understood both qualitatively and quantitatively. Any special application characteristics such as sensitivity to packet loss, delay, and delay variation should be quantified.

■ *Establish the QoS requirements*: From the information gathered in the first step and a knowledge of the network topology and traffic, it should be possible to identify potential traffic bottlenecks. These are points in the network that will require a special device configuration in order to assure the service level requirements that were established.

■ *Decide on the QoS tools*: QoS methodologies typically consist of two components. The first is to identify traffic that has specific requirements in terms of bandwidth allocation, delay, and variations in these two parameters. These requirements must be communicated to all devices within the data path. Techniques used to do this include IP precedence, RTP, and RSVP.

The second component of QoS consists of the queuing, prioritization, and fragmentation techniques used to ensure that these requirements are met along the data path. These techniques are often proprietary to the router or switch vendor, and their operation must be clearly understood before being used.

The two components should be chosen if it is understood that they will do the best job of ensuring the service level requirements of particular applications without hindering the operation of the more robust applications. It is not good enough to choose a technique by default. For example, RSVP should be chosen to work in conjunction with a certain type of low-latency queuing only if it is clearly understood how these two techniques can work together to meet the application QoS requirements.

■ *Plan details of RSVP implementation*: This section has been discussing the specifics of RSVP, so we will continue by examining the salient considerations that must be made in planning its implementation.

  ▪ All devices along the data path must be RSVP-capable (including end stations). An exception to this is RSVP tunneling that is frequently used on the Internet. Problems, however, can ensue with RSVP tunnels if a traffic bottleneck exists in the non-RSVP tunnel area.

- RSVP messages must be communicated between the router and the LAN switch. This is to give prioritization to traffic within the switch fabric. This, in a way, is just a special instance of the previous point.

- Decide how much interface bandwidth needs to be reserved on each networking device for RSVP. These figures should have been derived from your application's QoS audit.

- Assess how much interface bandwidth *can* be reserved for RSVP. On a network that is characterized by high percentages of bandwidth utilization, it may not be possible to meet the optimum resource allocation requirements for all applications at every point in the network. It is the old cost versus performance tradeoff and a decision has to be made as to which applications and/or clients should tolerate less than ideal performance guarantees.

- This assessment is also particularly important when real-time and non real-time applications are being used. End-to-end transport control for data applications tends to dynamically avoid congestion, such as the behavior of TCP window negotiation. This is not true of real-time applications that may continuously seize resources that are allocated to them. It is therefore important that a certain level of bandwidth is allocated to bursty data applications to avoid them being overwhelmed as a result of an RSVP allocation that is too large for real-time applications.

- Having decided on interface resource allocations, determine the maximum allocation for any individual flow. For example, a router interface within the campus may have a total RSVP allocation of 300kbps and may be configured so that no individual end-user flow has more than 30kbps reserved. The choice of these parameter values again requires a good understanding of the applications. The individual allocation limit may be higher relative to the total RSVP allocation if the interface predominantly services shared reservation applications such as audio. The opposite would be true if distinct reservations were predominant.

Network
Security

This chapter is intended to be a starting point that indicates how security should be incorporated into the design and management of *Internet protocol* (IP) networks. The term starting point is used because security is not only an area that requires a tremendous breadth of expertise, but it is also continuously changing. New technologies bring with them new threats, which require new solutions.

The chapter opens by explaining the approach that is necessary for developing an adequate security strategy. The different security tools available for protecting IP networks will then be discussed. These include packet filtering, device hardening, encryption, and virtual private networks. The specific role of the firewall will also be examined in detail.

Design and implementation procedures for protecting network devices and the network itself will then be studied. Finally, some of the more common IP threats will be discussed along with techniques for counteracting them.

Developing a Security Strategy

We'll begin by outlining the questions that must be addressed and the points to focus on before developing a security policy for an organization.

Productivity Versus Protection

One of the most fundamental high-level goals of an effective security strategy is to balance information protection with productivity in the most cost-effective manner. The budget that is available to ensure information protection, like any budget, it is not without a limit. If excessive resources are funneled into information protection, it may be to the detriment of the productivity achieved from the network. Even aside from budgetary resources, if too stringent a focus is placed on security, the effectiveness of the network may be impaired. For example, the excessive use of security filters may increase the *central processing unit* (CPU) processing overhead on the network devices, resulting in degraded performance. Another example is in an extreme case where information is protected to such a degree that those who require the information cannot access it in a timely manner.

Information protection and security is a critical area, but it is equally important that the implementation of a security strategy does not impinge on productivity.

Elements of Information Protection

Information protection has three basic components: confidentiality, integrity, and availability. These qualities of information must be preserved. They are the cornerstones of good information protection.

Confidentiality The unauthorized disclosure of information must be prevented. Encryption is the best method for ensuring information confidentiality.

Confidential information is normally sealed and marked accordingly when transferred in manual hard copy form. However, when this type of information is transmitted electronically, it is often completely unprotected due to the misguided assumption that the transmission network is secure.

Encryption is intended to protect the confidentiality of sensitive information. Data should be encrypted if a paper copy of that same information would be marked as classified or confidential and sealed. If paper copies of sensitive information would be stored in a locked desk or filing cabinet, then that information, when transferred electronically, should be encrypted. The concept of confidentiality relates to the control of who gets to view sensitive information.

NOTE: *The concept of confidentiality relates to the control of who gets to view sensitive information.*

Integrity Information must be protected to ensure that no unauthorized changes are made to its contents. It must be ensured that the information is reliable and accurate.

The concept of information integrity relates to the control of who gets to manipulate valuable information. It is important to remember that information can be manipulated or destroyed without actually viewing it.

Integrity can be protected using tools that include access controls, secure backups, the separation of duties, virus protection, and so on. These tools will be described in detail during the course of this chapter.

NOTE: *The concept of integrity relates to the control of who gets to manipulate sensitive information.*

Availability Information must be available when required. Accurate, confidential information that is not available in a timely manner has reduced value. This concept relates back to the principle of balancing protection with productivity. The security steps taken to ensure the confidentiality and integrity of data should not reduce productivity by making the information very difficult for authorized parties to access.

Information availability can be protected using the same security tools that are used to protect data integrity. In addition, a good resilient network design and practical security practices promote information availability.

The cost-effective balancing of information confidentiality and integrity with a high level of appropriate availability is characteristic of a good security strategy.

Risk and Vulnerability Assessment

Prior to the development of a security policy, a risk and vulnerability assessment should be performed. This pertains to two key elements that will become the reason for forming a security policy:

1. The information that is to be protected must be identified and assessed. The effect of a compromise of this information must also be evaluated. This defines what the organization risks losing without a security policy and strategy. The result of this risk analysis varies significantly depending on the nature of the business.

2. An analysis of all threats that could potentially compromise this information must then be performed. These threats are both internal and external to the organization and tend to be of a similar nature for most businesses. For this reason, an overview of typical internal and external threats to the protection of information has been included in this section.

The nature of the threat can relate to the theft or destruction of valuable and sensitive information. Threats can also culminate in sabotage or a denial of service. In this case, no information is stolen or manipulated, but the network service is degraded or rendered inoperable for a period of time.

When analyzing security threats, it is important to concentrate on the information under threat rather than the networking environment. By remaining focused on the information rather than the environment, the most appropriate security tools can be implemented at different points of the network when you get to that level of detail.

Internal Threats   Most security threats reside on the inside of an organization. As we shall see, threats do not have to be synonymous with malicious intent. The following is list of internal threats that is not intended to be exhaustive:

- Physical security or the lack of it is a major threat. Systems and networks cannot be considered secure without controls to physical access.

- Physical security systems and networks cannot be considered secure without controls to physical access.

- Incompetent employees threaten network and resource availability. This is an example of a threat that does not relate to malicious intent.

- Disgruntled employees or former employees are a massive internal threat. They can sell sensitive information to competitors. Information also can be manipulated or destroyed, or sabotage can be performed on networking devices.

- Business competitors that are unscrupulous most often attack from the inside by approaching an employee. This highlights the need to limit the availability of information or the capability to effect information or its availability.

- Poor administration is another potential problem. This would be defined as a network design that does not incorporate security or an administration that has gradually compromised the secure design.

- Hot desks and laptop PCs are major risks. When information is decentralized at unsecured locations, other security measures must be taken. Sophisticated authentication technology should be used with laptops to verify the identity of person using the laptop PC.

- Avoid complacency. Managers and engineers might adopt the attitude that they have a policy in writing, so that's enough. The security policy is not good if it isn't obeyed. The security policy is no good if it is not obeyed.

- To protect against internal malice or incompetence, the access to all network devices and network analyzers should be limited to the appropriate personnel.

External Threats   This section outlines some major external threats:

- As ever, physical security is probably the single most basic threat. This is particularly relevant if non-employees are allowed into the building.

- Malicious competitors can initiate an attack on the confidentiality, integrity, or availability of your information.

- Former employees or business partners are another potential threat.

- A third party that network administration might be outsourced to. This threat relates both to the potential for malice or incompetence on the part of the third-party employees.

- Corporate vandalism or hackers.

- The Internet.

- The corporate network itself, elements of which are particularly vulnerable, such as the *Integrated Services Digital Network* (ISDN) and the *Public Switched Telephone Network* (PSTN).

- Social engineering, where the attacker might gather sensitive information by socially contacting employees by visiting or by making a telephone call.

- On-site third parties.

Developing a Security Policy

The ultimate goal of the security policy is to ensure the confidentiality, integrity, and availability of information while balancing productivity with performance in a cost-effective manner. To achieve this goal, the security policy must address the following issues:

- Establish information protection as a management priority. This must then filter to every level within the organization. A security policy will not be fully implemented until the organization is "thinking secure."

- Identify information resources and determine threats and potential losses. This relates to the risk and vulnerability analysis.

- Select and implement controls to reduce potential losses.

- Put in place a procedure to audit and monitor the results of an implemented security plan. Security is a complex business and nobody gets everything right at the first attempt. It is also in a continuous state of flux as new threats emerge. Some details of the security policy will require frequent periodic refinements and modifications.

Security: A Work in Progress   The entire area of security is very much a work in progress. The job of the security group is never complete. It is critically important to keep up to date by subscribing to relevant newsgroups.

The latest threats require the latest patches; however, it is equally important to ensure that the patches can be trusted. Patched software should always be tested for bugs by working closely with the manufacturer or reseller.

The importance of developing a security consciousness at every level of the organization cannot be overstated. Security is not the responsibility of the security group or the IT group; it is the responsibility of everyone. Although the networking professional, along with management, is responsible for developing a security policy, it is the responsibility of all employees to ensure that the policy is implemented.

Many companies have no formal security policy. Instead, they simply have some rules that lack any proper benchmark. The lack of a systematic and methodical approach to security should be thought of as a crime that is waiting to be punished.

If a security policy is in place, then practices that compromise this policy for the sake of a quick fix should not be tolerated. If the security policy (just like any plan) is compromised on even a small number of occasions, then it is invalidated and effectively no longer exists. A security policy, by definition, does not allow for exceptions. The making of exceptions to the policy amounts to the creation of potential security holes. It is better not to have any security policy in place rather than one that is not strictly adhered to. A company without a security policy should be under no illusions that they have yet to get their house in order from a security standpoint. However, a corporation that has a policy in name only may suffer from additional complacency simply because a paper document outlines a security strategy that is not being followed.

NOTE: *There is no point in having a security policy if it is not strictly adhered to. Making exceptions only creates security holes.*

Security Tools

This section examines some generic security tools that can be employed on IP networks. This will lead up to a discussion on firewall technology, which relates to the specific application of many of these tools.

Packet Filtering

Packet filtering is frequently employed on routers to implement security policies. The most sophisticated router platforms are capable of inspecting and filtering packets sent from the router and can also filter inbound updates.

Some or all of the following criteria can be used to filter inbound or outbound packets:

- Source IP address (or a range of addresses)
- Destination IP address (or a range of destinations)
- Source and destination ports numbers used by the *Transmission Control Protocol* (TCP) and the *User Datagram Protocol* (UDP)
- Random port numbers assigned by applications (greater than 1,023)
- IP protocols that do not use TCP or UDP transports, such as OSPF (protocol #89) or *Internet Control Message Protocol* (ICMP) (protocol #1). Specific ICMP services can also be passed or filtered.

Figure 10-1 is used to demonstrate traditional router-based packet filtering. A router is used to connect two networks that are at different levels of trust. A packet filter is configured to inspect inbound packets on the untrusted side of the router. The filter is designed to implement the following security policies:

- *Domain Name System* (DNS) requests are allowed from any host on the 197.10.10.0 network, provided that the destination IP address is that of the DNS server (namely, 150.10.1.10). This ensures that for a DNS request to be successful the requesting station must know the IP address of the DNS server. The router will drop a DNS broadcast by default.

- ICMP echo requests are not allowed in this interface from the untrusted network, but echo-replies are allowed. This prevents devices on the untrusted network from sending pings to the trusted *local area network* (LAN). However, stations on the trusted LAN can ping stations on the untrusted network.

This is just one example of the types of security policies that can be implemented using router-based packet filtering. It is important to note that not all router vendors support inbound packet filtering. In many cases, the same policy can be implemented as an outbound filter on another interface. However, for the more stringent security policies, this is not always the

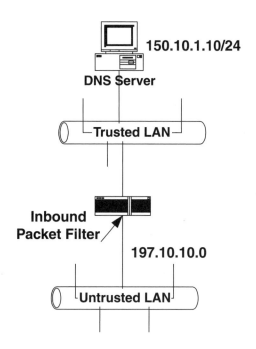

Figure 10-1
Router-based packet
filtering

150.10.1.10/24

DNS Server

Trusted LAN

**Inbound
Packet Filter**

197.10.10.0

Untrusted LAN

case. Also, inbound packet filtering is usually preferable for security applications because it is better to deny unwanted services before the router processes the packet. The use of outbound packet filters can make it easier for a hacker to gain access to the router itself. This would provide a very threatening jumping-off point for the intruder. Apart from the possibility of sabotaging the router configuration, the hacker could also use the router as an information-gathering tool. Therefore, it is generally better practice to use inbound filters on the router.

The Limitations of Static Packet Filtering   Traditional packet filtering at the router might at first seem like a powerful troubleshooting tool. It is not without a number of significant limitations, however, and these limitations combine to render traditional routers unsuitable for high-specification security requirements.

Stateless Inspection   The packet filtering on a router is usually performed on a static basis with each packet that traverses the router interface being inspected as a standalone entity. Referring back to the previous section, each packet that comes into the router interface from the untrusted network is compared to the filtering criteria. If it is a DNS request to 150.10.1.10 or an ICMP echo-reply, the packet is forwarded; otherwise, it is dropped.

Because each packet is inspected in isolation, you have no way of confirming whether or not it is part of an existing conversation. This is termed *stateless inspection*. There is no way to ascertain that the echo-replies are actually in response to echo requests that originated on the trusted network. ICMP echo-reply packets could be spoofed from the untrusted network and passed into the trusted network by the route filter. A computer program on the untrusted network could generate a constant output of these echo-replies. The packets could have a destination address of 150.10.X.Y and thus be directed to the trusted network. If sufficiently large and constant, this could be used as a crude technique to waste CPU cycles on the router and fill its interface buffers. Although the ICMP echo-reply packets will not enable the hacker to access any network resources, they could facilitate a *denial-of-service* (DoS) attack where the network functionality is impaired by the hacker. Later in this chapter, we will see more serious and threatening examples of DoS attacks.

A frequent security requirement is to disallow unspecified inbound traffic into the trusted network unless it is in reply to corresponding outbound traffic. In other words, the client-server session must have been initiated from the inside. For TCP-based applications, a crude means of achieving this policy can be done with router packet filters. Before describing the technique, the TCP three-way handshake that coincides with the initiation of a TCP session will be briefly summarized.

The client sends an initial Synchronize or SYN message to the server, as indicated in Figure 10-2. The server replies with a Synchronize, Acknowledge message or SYN ACK. The SYN ACK message has the ACK bit set in the TCP header. At this point in the sequence, the TCP session is said to be *established*. In fact, the only time a TCP session is not in the established state is when the initial SYN packet is sent. The final message in the three-way handshake is a further Acknowledgement or ACK sent from the client to the server.

TCP uses sequence and acknowledgement numbers to track the session. The setup messages therefore must also have sequence and acknowledgement numbers that verify that the packets are in the correct sequence and also that the remote client that sent the original SYN is the same one that sends the final ACK to initiate the session. After the session is initiated, data can flow between server and client. When one party wants to terminate the session, it sends a TCP FIN message, the response to which is a FIN ACK.

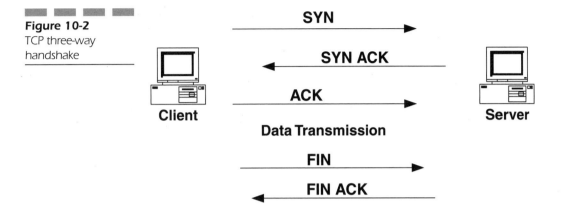

Figure 10-2
TCP three-way
handshake

SYN

SYN ACK

ACK

Data Transmission

FIN

FIN ACK

Client   Server

   Traditional packet filters can be used to only enable inbound, established TCP sessions onto the trusted network. TCP packets would only be allowed in if the ACK bit were set. This means that TCP sessions cannot be initiated from the outside network. This policy would, for example, deny Telnet access (Telnet uses TCP port 23) from the outside to the trusted network. However, users on the trusted network could Telnet to the outside network. Although this might seem a secure policy, it is quite easy for a hacker to circumvent it if traditional packet filters are used. Code is available that emulates TCP packets that have the ACK bit set. The fact that you are also placing your trust in the status of a single bit in the TCP header might also suggest that this filtering technique could be easily compromised.

   In relation to UDP-based applications, no concept of a session being established exists because UDP is a connectionless protocol. Therefore, the protection provided by packet filters against unwanted inbound UDP traffic is even more easily compromised. The best practice with packet filters in this case is to implicitly deny all inbound UDP-based services unless explicitly defined. The allowed services should also be defined as specifically as possible. For example, returning to the filter in Figure 10-1, the policy should be to allow inbound UDP port 53 (DNS) with a destination address 150.10.1.10 (the DNS server). The range of allowed source IP addresses should also be restricted to those clients that use this DNS server.

   The filtering techniques that have been described in relation to TCP and UDP applications are good practice, but they are by no means foolproof. IP addresses, IP application services, and the status of IP packets can be spoofed by hackers. This exposes the limitation of filtering each packet as a standalone entity. To protect against even moderately sophisticated attacks, it is essential that the filtering device maintain information on the state of the connection. This verification that each packet is part of an existing conversation is often referred to as *stateful* inspection. Before discussing stateful inspection, some further limitations of traditional packet filters will be highlighted.

NOTE: *Traditional router-based packet filtering has a very limited capability for inspecting state information on the connection.*

Only established TCP sessions should be allowed inbound to a trusted network. This filtering policy can, however, be easily compromised.

UDP services provide no means of extracting state information. Allowed inbound services should be defined as specifically as possible.

Multi-Channel Protocols Conventional packet filters also have a limited capability to inspect and filter protocols that use more than one port number. Consider the example of the *File Transfer Protocol* (FTP). The FTP connection sequence is displayed in Figure 10-3. FTP uses TCP port 21 in order to set up the connection. Thus, when a client wants to initiate an FTP session with an FTP server, it sends a TCP packet with a destination port 21 and a randomly assigned source port above 1023. Port 21 is used for the exchange of an FTP command that enables the connection setup. Once the connection is set up, a separate port number (namely, TCP port 20) is used for the data transfer. This requires a separate TCP session that *is initiated by the server*. It is therefore very important to remember that FTP is not only characterized by two separate TCP sessions, but these sessions are initiated in different directions.

Figure 10-3
FTP session set-up

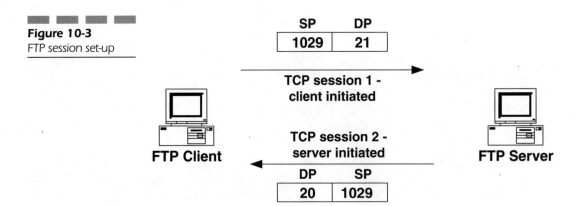

It might be a typical policy requirement to allow FTP sessions to be initiated from the trusted network outbound but to disallow the initiation of inbound FTP sessions. With conventional packet filters, this can only be achieved by allowing inbound established TCP sessions and by blocking all other inbound TCP connection attempts. This would cause a problem with FTP because the initiation of an FTP session from the trusted network outbound would then be followed by the server initiating an inbound session to TCP port 20, which would be blocked by the filter. The filter would, for example, prevent local clients from performing an FTP download from the Internet. In order to allow FTP to work in this scenario, new TCP connections with a destination port number of 20 would have to be allowed through the packet filter. This relaxation of the filtering rules compromises the original policy of only allowing established TCP sessions inbound to the trusted network. It also leaves the network exposed to the potential risk of a hacker opening inbound TCP sessions to port 20 in order to perform a DoS attack.

The added complexity of multi-channel protocols such as FTP fueled a fundamental requirement for a more sophisticated method of packet inspection and filtering. It became evident that state-based information must be stored and examined in relation to each connection passing through the filter.

NOTE: *Multi-channel protocols such as FTP force a relaxation of the filtering rules for conventional packet filters that do not maintain state information on each connection.*

Stateful Packet Filtering A stateful packet filter is capable of maintaining information on the state of each connection that attempts to cross the filtering device. The source and destination layer 4 port numbers can be inspected and stored in a state table that can then be consulted by the filtering software. The initial packet in a data flow that crosses a filtering device can be inspected up to and including the layer 4 information. A stateless packet filter would simply make a forward or block decision after comparing this information to the filtering criteria. A stateful filter will also do this, but it also stores the layer 3 and layer 4 state information in its state table. Subsequent packets in the flow are not only checked against the filtering criteria, but they are also compared against the state table in order to verify that they are part of an existing conversation.

The capability to verify that the data flow has source and destination port numbers corresponding to an existing conversation provides the following significant benefits over stateless filters:

- So-called back connections can be securely allowed to facilitate multi-channel applications. For example, an FTP back connection to port 20 from an untrusted server can be allowed through the filter if the source port matches the source port from the original trusted outbound connection to port 21. This is shown schematically in Figure 10-4.

- Established TCP sessions are securely allowed inbound. By consulting state tables, all inbound TCP traffic can be verified as being part of an existing conversation that was initiated from the trusted network. This is vastly more secure than relying on the ACK bit being set in the TCP header.

- UDP-based connections can be securely allowed inbound if they are in response to outbound packets that initiated the conversation in question. This can likewise be verified from the state table.

Applications Using Changing or Random Port Numbers Applications that use random TCP or UDP port numbers can pose additional challenges even for stateful packet filters. Many multimedia applications are characterized by random port numbers, or port numbers that change during the course of the session. Even sophisticated filtering tools have difficulty tracking the connection and verifying that each packet is part of an existing conversation if the port numbers do not remain consistent.

Figure 10-4
FTP packet filtering

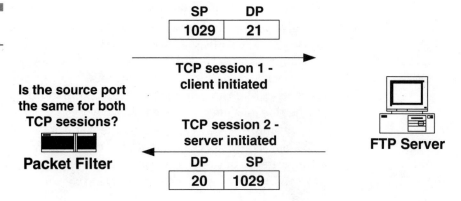

Most firewalls will be required to potentially pass several Web-based multimedia applications that use random port numbers. Many of these applications are also multi-channel with the external untrusted server, creating a back-connection similar to the operation of FTP. The vendor that develops the filtering or firewall platform must understand these applications in detail from a networking point of view. The possible range of port numbers should be known, along with operational information such as the number of TCP or UDP connections and the directions in which they are initiated.

If the behavior of the application is understood in sufficient detail, then the firewall rules can be applied specifically to enable the application through. Otherwise, the filtering rules might have to be relaxed to an excessive degree to get the application working. This would result in potential security holes as a result of a loose firewall policy.

NOTE: *Multimedia applications frequently use multiple connections with random or changing port assignments. It is important to verify that the firewall platform can support these applications without too great a compromise of the filtering rules.*

Encryption

Confidential information is normally sealed and marked accordingly when transferred in manual paper form. However, when this type of information is transmitted electronically, it is often completely unprotected due to the misguided assumption that the transmission medium is secure.

Two fundamental encryption technologies are available: *single key encryption* (SKE) and *dual key encryption* (DKE). The former is more susceptible to compromise than the latter. It is a question of deciding from the results of your risk and vulnerability analysis which method is required to provide the level of confidentiality necessary to satisfy your corporate security policy.

Single key encryption performs a mathematical coding algorithm on the data before transmitting between two points on a communications network. The key is the bitstream used to encode the data. In an SKE implementation, the key must be copied and securely transferred to the other party on the receiving end of the transmission. The receiver uses the key to decrypt the data.

Several SKE methods are in use nowadays, one of the most ubiquitous of which is the *Data Encryption Standard* (DES). This algorithm is based on a 56-bit key and encodes files in 64-bit blocks. Until recently, DES had been considered to be very secure with 2^{56} possible keys. However, with the advent of very high-speed processing and supercomputing, it is possible to test for all of these combinations within a few hours.

DES has enhancements where the key is more difficult to crack. Triple DES uses 112-bit keys and a three-step process to encrypt data more securely than its predecessor does. One of the latest SKE methods is the *International Data Encryption Algorithm* (IDEA). This scheme employs a 128-bit key and a very complex, eight-stage encryption algorithm. A schematic illustration of a SKE operation is shown in Figure 10-5.

Figure 10-5
The single-key encryption and decryption process

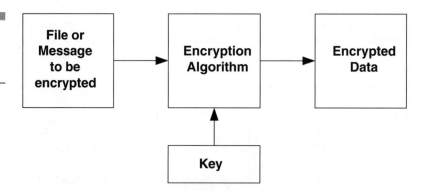

Encryption by sender

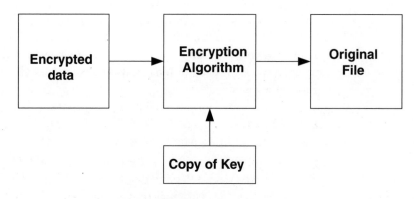

Decryption by receiver

Apart from the possibility of cracking the key combination, one of the security drawbacks of SKE is that both parties at each end of the communications link must share the key. It becomes difficult to protect the key if it is shared between multiple parties. SKE is really only practical when each end of the encryption tunnel is part of the same trusted network. This could work, for example, when two sites on the same corporate network communicate sensitive data across a public *wide area network* (WAN) carrier. However, it is not feasible for applications where the far end of the encryption tunnel cannot be trusted. The best example of this is the Internet. This second issue in particular provides a motivation for using a second type of encryption technology and that is DKE.

With DKE, the parties at both ends of the encrypted link each have two keys. One is used to encrypt data and the other is used to decrypt data. Either key can be used for the purpose of encryption or decryption, but both must be used. For example, if key X is used to encode data, then key Y must be used to decode it at the other end of the encrypted link. In actual implementations, one key is kept secret by the user (called the secret or private key) and the other key is publicly available (the public key).

Consider the example of DKE displayed schematically in Figure 10-6. If Cormac is sending confidential information to Sarah, Cormac encrypts the data with Sarah's public key. At the receiving end, Sarah's private key is the only one that can decrypt the information.

DKE can also be used to verify the integrity of the information and that it actually came from the source that it appeared to come from. For example, if Sarah sends Cormac data that has been encrypted with Sarah's private key, Cormac can only decrypt it with Sarah's public key. This ensures that Sarah must have sent the data. In fact, this technique is effectively a secure digital signature.

A typical DKE algorithm generates the keys by multiplying two very large prime numbers. The keys in question are usually large and may be of the order of 1,024 bits. To crack the keys, the original prime factors used to generate them must be decoded. This task is considered beyond even the processing power of supercomputers.

Although DKE provides an extremely secure level of data confidentiality, it does place overhead constraints on the end devices. A large file that is encrypted with a large key is likely to be transmitted and processed at a rate that is noticeably slower than unencrypted messages.

It is important to be clear that devices that will perform encryption on a firewall system or at each end of a *Virtual Private Network* (VPN) link support dual key encryption if that is the required level of guaranteed confidentiality. The vendor should also clarify the overhead associated with DKE implementation on these devices.

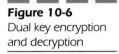

Figure 10-6
Dual key encryption
and decryption

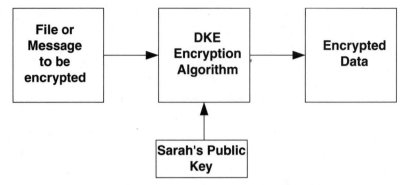

Encryption on Cormac's endstation

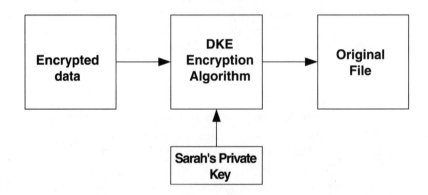

Decryption on Sarah's endstation

NOTE: *DKE provides greater data confidentiality than single key implementations because a common key does not have to be shared at each end of the link. DKE can also be used to provide secure digital signatures, but it does, however, result in greater overhead and latency than SKE.*

A final point about encryption should be made and that is in relation to the interaction of encryption and compression algorithms. Data that is encrypted is frequently sent across WAN links that are part of an untrusted environment such as a public carrier's network or the Internet. Data compression may sometimes be utilized on low-speed WAN links in order to improve throughput efficiency, as discussed in Chapter 3. However, potential complications can result from the co-existence of compression and encryption across the same link.

Compression is a layer 2 operation, while encryption is typically performed at layer 3. Therefore, the data is encrypted at the sending device before the compression algorithm is performed at the data link layer. However, when the compression engine receives the encrypted data, which by definition has not repeated patterns, it will expand rather than compress. The compression engine will compare the two data images before and after compression, and will always send the smaller one. In this case, the smaller image will be the uncompressed data. Ultimately, this means that the combination of data encryption with a layer 2 compression algorithm renders the compression algorithm ineffective.

━━ ━━ ━━ ━━ ━━ ━━ ━━ ━━ ━━ ━━ ━━ ━━ ━━ ━━ ━━ ━━ ━━ ━━ ━━

NOTE: *Encrypted data cannot be compressed at the data link layer.*

Virtual Private Networks (VPNs)

A VPN is an encrypted connection between two devices that facilitates secure communication between two trusted networks across an untrusted domain. The connection or VPN tunnel traverses an untrusted network such as the Internet, resulting in the need for encrypting confidential information. A schematic diagram of a simple VPN between two firewall devices is shown in Figure 10-7.

Figure 10-7
Virtual private
network from firewall
to firewall

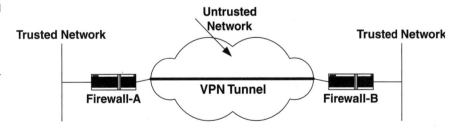

The VPN is a logical point-to-point connection and the end point devices could be of the following combinations:

- Host to host
- Gateway to gateway
- Host to gateway

The hosts in question could be clients or servers and the gateway devices could be routers, firewalls, or intelligent servers.

The VPN is usually considered a security tool, and its use is considered adequate in helping to secure communication between two networks. But all a VPN does is ensure that a communications link can be established with the communications link itself being reasonably secure. The end points are critical. For example, if the VPN has been established with a business partner, the actual degree of security depends on the security practices at the business partner's site. When using a VPN to connect to another network that does not have the same level of trust as your own network, as is the case with a business partner's network, it is important to ascertain the following information:

- Does your business partner or remote office engage in secure ongoing practices? For example, do they keep updated on new threats and the corresponding patches or solutions?
- Does your business partner have a security policy in place? How well is it being implemented? What aspects of the policy relate to the communication to and from your own network?

NOTE: *A VPN can secure the actual communications path between two networks. However, the overall security of the information exchanged relates to the level of security practiced on the two end-point networks.*

Intrusion Detection Systems (IDSs)

A secure network should not only prevent malicious attacks or intrusions; it should also be capable of detecting an intrusion attempt. Intrusion detection or attack recognition techniques fall into two fundamental categories:

■ *Pattern recognition*: Pattern recognition techniques usually use intrusion detection software to identify a specific bit pattern, packet type, byte sequence, or keyword that is associated with a known method of attack. This *Intrusion Detection System* (IDS) software may run on the firewall host or alternatively it could be distributed across multiple hosts on the network. A number of maintenance issues are associated with pattern recognition techniques. The software must regularly be upgraded with new patches as new attacking patterns are discovered and documented. Another limitation is that a sophisticated hacker may alter the pattern that is being checked for and hence bypass the IDS system.

Intrusion detection can also be performed by manually inspecting the firewall logs. Any unusual traffic patterns may be indicative of a hacker at work. Knowledge of the common IP attacks that are outlined in this chapter would tell the security engineer what are the first signs to check for. For example, packets attempting to enter the secure network that have source IP addresses matching those found on the secure network itself indicates attempted IP address spoofing. A large number of TCP SYN packets that time out is an obvious indication of a DoS attack.

■ *Effect recognition*: Effect recognition examines the effect of an attack. This might also be ascertained from log file entries. It is important to be capable to distinguish between a network event that occurred due to a network failure and one that was the result of an attack. If a networking device reboots, it is important to have an audit trail to identify if the device was accessed either locally or remotely prior to the reboot. The auditing technique should also be capable of identifying the user in question. We will discuss network auditing in the upcoming section.

Another example of effect recognition is when a LAN switch port fails suddenly. The network management system must be capable of indicating whether the failure was due to a loss of line protocol or due to a security violation. In other words, the port should change to a particular disabled status that indicates a physical intrusion attempt. The software running on the device itself determines this capability.

Any intrusion detection technique should include as much identifying information about the attack as possible. All information should be time-stamped and the source IP addresses of the attacking device or the identity of the malicious user should be revealed.

The firewall should log all traffic passing through it. Any packets that violate the firewall filtering rules and hence get dropped should have prioritized entries against them in the log. The more sophisticated firewall platforms engage in a proactive reaction and can page a manager when a break-in attempt occurs. This further underlines the need for very specific policy rules in the firewall configuration.

Finally, intrusion detection, like so many aspects of network security, is a continuous ongoing task that must be performed by proactive monitoring.

Password Management

The compromise of passwords is arguably the greatest network security threat to most organizations. Security consultants that perform network vulnerability assessments often seek to exploit weak and poorly managed passwords as the first weak link into an organization. For a company with poor security practices, the good news is that this is one of the easiest and most effective tools that can be quickly addressed.

The following points on password management may seem obvious, but they are worth emphasizing because they are rarely followed. The result is a major chink in the company's security amour.

- Passwords should be difficult to guess or break. They should not consist of a particular word. This could be broken using some software that scrolls through an entire dictionary in order to guess a password. Ideally, the password should consist of a mixture of letters and numbers along with one or more punctuation marks. For example, instead of "hansolo," use "han_s010."

- Passwords should be changed at regular intervals. The maximum tolerable interval should be no more than 90 days.

- For a high-security specification, the use of one-time passwords is recommended. A classic example of a one-time password system is the SecureID™ product developed by Security Dynamics. With this system, each user must carry a card with a *liquid crystal display* (LCD) of a numeric password that changes every 60 seconds. To authenticate, the user must enter this one-time password along with a second static password. The LCD display cards are synchronized with the SecureID application server that the users get authenticated on. Users get authenticated in this manner by configuring the network devices to refer to the SecureID server to authenticate login attempts.

■ The placing of passwords or password-related information in areas where they can be found represents a violation of security policy. All employees should be reminded of this and held accountable for breaches. Hackers often initiate a visit to a corporation and find passwords near wallcharts and under keyboards that can then be used for network access.

■ Laptop computers represent a significant security hazard not only for their capability to provide network access, but also for the information and data that might be contained on the PC itself. Laptops should be configured to automatically log out the user from the operating system after a certain period of keyboard inactivity. A one-time password system should be used to obtain network access from the laptop. Access to the operating system prior to logging on the network should also be tightly secured, as device access may represent a serious threat even without network access. New laptops on the market support features such as the use of a physical key to enable them prior to bootup. An even more sophisticated approach is the use of fingerprint recognition technology for user authentication.

Security Servers

Specific servers can be used to provide authentication, authorization, and accounting services to the network. These terms are sometimes used interchangeably so it is important to exactly clarify their meaning.

Authentication is the process of validating the identity of the host at the remote end of the connection. *Authorization* is the process of ascertaining which services that host can use. *Accounting* is used for ascertaining who did what and for how long. All three of these services are typically implemented on a *Remote Access Dial-In User Service* (RADIUS) or a *Terminal Access Controller Access Control System* (TACACS) server.

Any access to a client or server station should be authenticated. All forms of access to networking devices such as routers and switches should likewise be authenticated. As stated in the previous section, the most secure form of authentication uses one-time passwords. All devices on the network (hosts, servers, routers, switches, and so on) can be configured to point to an authentication server in order to validate the identity of the user requesting access.

The process of authentication typically uses a username and password combination. The username relates to a user that is entitled to a certain level of network or device access. This parameter is fixed and is used to identify each user that can access a given resource or a networking device. However, the password should vary by being changed at regular intervals if it is not indeed a one-time password application.

Each username should have an authorization profile that is contained on the security server. This is a list of privileges that the user has. For example, a user may have access to the network server drives that relate to the Engineering department but not to the Sales department. Another example is of a user accessing a network device such as a router where they are authorized to issue basic monitoring commands, but they are not authorized to alter the router configuration. In this case, if they attempt to change the configuration, they will receive an error notification.

The combined use of usernames, logging facilities on each device, and time-stamping enables an accounting application to be run on the security server. This provides a useful audit trail of network access and activity. The audit trail can be used for the accounting of the inter-departmental use of shared resources for budgetary purposes. Essentially, it indicates who used what resources and for how long. It is also a significant tool for security and troubleshooting. It can be used to ascertain which users accessed a network resource or device at a particular time and what tasks they performed.

IPv6 and IPSec

IP version 4 (IPv4) was designed for implementation across networks that were presumed secure. Hence, security was not integral to its design, but a number of security patch protocols can be incorporated with IPv4. One such protocol is IPsec.

With IPv4, IPsec is optional and each end of a connection must ask its peer if the peer supports IPsec or not. With IPv6, IPsec support is mandatory. By mandating IPsec, it can be assumed that your IP communication can be secured whenever you talk to IPv6 devices. The addressing structure of IPv6 uses 128 bits, but IPv4 addresses have forward compatibility where the 32 bits are mapped as the least significant bits of the IPv6 address with the higher order bits having a constant predefined value.

The IP security protocol, IPSec, is a set of open standards that provides data confidentiality through encryption, information integrity, and authentication between participating peers. IPSec provides these services at layer 3. The *Internet Key Exchange* (IKE) protocol is used to manage peer negotiation. IKE also generates the encryption and authentication keys that are used by IPSec.

IPSec negotiates secure tunnels between two peers and in this respect it is similar to the implementation of VPNs. These peers are usually two routers or firewall devices. These end-point devices must be configured to denote which packets are considered sensitive and should be sent through the secure tunnels. Specifying the encryption and authentication parameters for the tunnel also configures the protection for the tunnels. This protection can be specified through manual configuration or through IKE negotiation between the peers. When so-called sensitive data is exchanged between IPSec peers, the IP packets are encapsulated in IPSec packets that contain the security parameters.

Figure 10-8 shows a schematic representation of an IPSec peer relationship that uses authentication and encryption to protect the data in the IPSec tunnel. In this example, the IPSec peers are configured to set up a secure tunnel when they receive packets that are exchanged in either direction between 47.10.10.10 and 131.2.2.10. All other traffic passes between the peers without encryption or authentication.

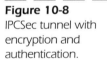

Figure 10-8
IPCSec tunnel with encryption and authentication.

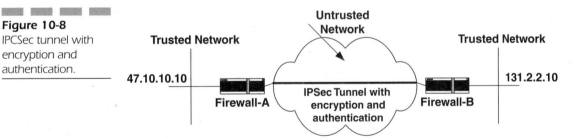

The following is a summary of the security services provided by IPSec:

- *Data authentication*: The data authentication can include two separate concepts:

  - *Data integrity*: The integrity of the data must be verified to confirm that it has not been altered. This is a mandatory element of data authentication.

  - *Origin authentication*: Additional data origin authentication may be performed. This is intended to verify that the data was actually sent by the claimed sender.

- *Data confidentiality*: Encrypting all traffic that passes between the IPSec peers protects data confidentiality. The encryption parameters such as the keys are either statically configured or established via the IKE protocol.

- *Anti-replay*: This service enables a receiver to reject old or duplicate packets in order to protect itself against replay attacks. The persistent resending of duplicate packets is often characteristic of a DoS attack.

A number of issues or restrictions must be considered before implementing IPSec. At the time of writing, the *Internet Engineering Task Force* (IETF) has only ratified standards for unicast IPSec traffic. No standards have as yet been developed for multicast or broadcast traffic.

Some interoperability issues must be addressed in regard to *Network Address Translation* (NAT). Generally, static translations should be used to ensure that no random allocation of external global addresses takes place. Also, the NAT translation should occur before the IP packet is encapsulated in IPSec. This guarantees that IPSec is used with global addresses.

A significant overhead and CPU utilization is associated with IPSec. An additional encapsulation step must be done along with authentication and encryption processes. This can increase latency and also place additional processing requirements on the routers at each end of the secure tunnels.

The act of encapsulating the IP packets in IPSec can potentially cause the packet to exceed the *maximum transmission unit* (MTU) of the transmission medium and hence require fragmentation. The reassembly process incurs additional overhead and further slows down the communication. Also, you must be mindful of a further issue in relation to fragmentation. Some firewalls may be configured to perform additional checks to drop fragmented packets because they are often used for DoS attacks. If problems are encountered passing IPSec traffic to a destination firewall, this is an issue that should be checked for.

IPSec uses IP protocol numbers 50 and 51, and IKE uses protocol 17 with UDP port 500. These protocols and ports must be allowed by firewalls and packet filters along the secured path.

Firewalls

The firewall is the main point of restriction and control that borders a trusted environment with a non-trusted environment. The non-trusted environment can be external or internal to the corporate network in question. Firewalls are usually thought of in the context of protecting and controlling the point at which a company connects to the Internet. However, firewalls are also frequently deployed as an access control mechanism between different internal segments of the corporate network. For example, a firewall may be used to provide secure isolation for a legal department that resides within the main corporate network.

Firewall Functions

The following is a summary of the security services that should be provided by the firewall system. As will be emphasized, the firewall should be treated as a multi-component system rather than a single host. The functions that are about to be listed are functions of the firewall system and all of them are not necessarily implemented on the host that runs the firewall application software.

Enhanced Packet Filtering   The importance of stateful packet filtering has already been discussed and this is a mandatory feature on any high-specification firewall system. State information should be stored on each connection that passes through the firewall in order to verify that each packet is part of an existing conversation.

The packet filtering technology should also be capable of securely inspecting multi-channel protocols such as FTP along with protocols that use random or changing port numbers, as is the case with many multimedia applications.

Encryption and VPN   The firewall should enable the creation of VPNs by supporting encryption. As we have seen from our discussion on encryption, DKE provides a higher level of security over SKE.

A VPN can obviously be created between two firewall devices, but it may be required to extend the secure connection end to end between the host devices. In order to support VPNs on remote client-to-server connections, the firewall must also be capable of creating VPNs with end-system hosts.

Authentication The firewall system is used to validate the identity of hosts that send traffic through it from the untrusted side of the network. This entails the process of authentication. As we shall see, authentication should be performed using a high-specification password system such as one-time passwords. The passwords should also be encrypted as passwords that traverse the network in clear text can easily be picked up using a network analyzer or a debugging facility on a network device. The firewall can be configured to only pass traffic that it can authenticate itself.

The use of firewall authentication can sometimes be employed by hackers to initiate a DoS attack. A hacker may flood the firewall with authentication attempts that will never be validated. This has the effect of consuming firewall resources and impairing its capability to perform other tasks. It is important to ensure that the firewall platform that is chosen for your network incorporates a protection against this threat. An intelligent firewall should limit the amount of system resources that can be consumed by authentication requests.

NOTE: *The firewall host should be capable of limiting the amount of system resources consumed by authentication requests. This protects against DoS attacks relating to authentication flooding.*

Network Address Translation (NAT) An increasing trend is taking place within the industry to use private addressing on the corporate network and then translate to a registered address when accessing the Internet. The main motivation behind this is scalability and the exhaustion of registered IP address space.

Consider, for example, a corporation that has multiple registered Class C addresses or one that may even have a registered Class B address. If the network is reasonably large, then it is unlikely that the registered IP address space is sufficient for the corporate network. The use of a private Class A address or multiple private Class B addresses would provide adequate IP address space, but each host would have to connect to the Internet via a NAT gateway.

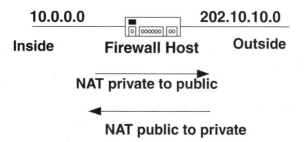

Figure 10-9
NAT implemented on
the firewall host

10.0.0.0   202.10.10.0

Inside   **Firewall Host**   **Outside**

NAT private to public

NAT public to private

Figure 10-9 illustrates a case where the firewall host translates between private Class A addresses and registered Class C addresses that are advertised to the outside network (which in this case is the Internet). The fact that NAT enables the inside trusted network to be hidden from the outside domain provides an additional security benefit.

Logging   The log on the firewall host should be written at regular intervals to a Syslog server. The logs should be routinely audited to check for any unusual traffic patterns that may signify a potential hacker at work. The firewall host should also incorporate a mechanism for protecting itself from a DoS attack due to the log overflowing as a result of spurious repeated traffic.

Alarm Generation and Notification   Each time a firewall security rule is violated, such as a packet being blocked by one of the filters, an alarm should notify the *Network Management System* (NMS) station or network administrator. The alarm or *Simple Network Management Protocol* (SNMP) trap should include identifying information (such as the IP address and layer 4 port number) of the attacking host.

Proxy Services   A proxy service can be used as a secure intermediary between an untrusted and a trusted network. The proxy server is located in a particular part of the firewall system known as the *Demilitarized Zone* (DMZ) located between the inside and outside network. The server intercepts and examines requests for a particular application made from the outside network. The requests are answered or passed on to the inside trusted network if they meet predefined security criteria. Examples of such proxy services include FTP proxy and Telnet proxy.

Firewall Architecture

It is frequently assumed that a firewall is merely a single device that provides sophisticated packet filtering used to implement a security policy on the border of two environments that have different trust levels. This may be true of some companies that have a less than stringent approach to security management. However, for any company that is serious about security or has a rigorous security policy, then the firewall must be thought of as a multi-component system rather than a single device.

A high-specification firewall system should incorporate the following components, as illustrated in Figure 10-10:

- *Outside router*: The so-called outside router connects the firewall system to the untrusted network or the network that has the lower level of trust. Its main function is to perform the task that routers do best and that is route packets that are exchanged between the trusted network and untrusted networks. Like each element of the firewall system, it must be a fully security hardened device (exactly what that entails will be described later). As we will see, it may also perform some of the more rudimentary tasks of the firewall system. These include elementary packet filtering and possibly NAT. In the diagram of Figure 10-10, the firewall host performs the NAT function between the private Class A addresses and the public registered addresses.

  In some scaled down implementations, the outside router functionality may be performed on the firewall host itself without the use of an additional discrete router. To meet a stringent specification, this approach would not be recommended for a number of reasons. First of all, the outside router is the point at which the untrusted environment connects to your network. If this should be compromised, then it is

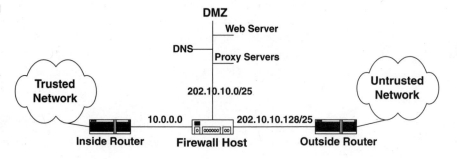

Figure 10-10

Typical architecture of a multi-component firewall system

important that a further line of defense be used in the form of the firewall host. Even if it is the firewall host that performs the more sophisticated context-based filtering, the outside router should be a hardened router device.

The second reason for the use of a discrete router to connect to the untrusted environment is that, aside from security, packets must be routed to and from the untrusted network. The device that performs this task most efficiently is a router supplied by a mainstream router manufacturer. Although firewall hosts are certainly capable of performing routing, this function is not their forte and can result in added latency and reduced throughput over the secure connection. This point relates back to the principle that security is not just about protection; it must be balanced against productivity and the question of availability.

- *The DMZ*: The DMZ is the dead zone between the inside router and the outside router. The DMZ effectively bridges the gap between the trusted and non-trusted networks. The firewall host resides in the DMZ or can even be thought of as creating the DMZ, as shown in Figure 10-10.

Any servers that are mainly accessed from untrusted networks should be located in the DMZ. These include mail servers, the Web, DNS, and FTP. A separate authentication server such as RADIUS or TACACS may also be located in the DMZ if the firewall host does not provide the authentication function itself. This is illustrated in Figure 10-11.

It is good practice to have the DMZ addressed using public registered addresses in the case where the firewall system is connecting to the

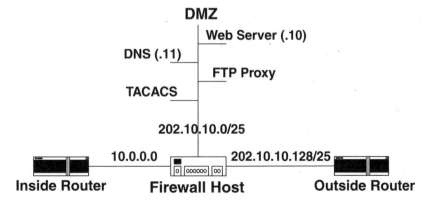

Figure 10-11
The DMZ featuring a public address and all public servers or proxy servers

Internet. This is the network address that is advertised by the outside router, while the internal network addresses remain hidden. In Figure 10-10, the DMZ has a public registered Class C address for the public servers, while the internal corporate network uses a private Class A address. In this case, it is the responsibility of the firewall host to perform the NAT function because it has interfaces that belong to the registered and unregistered domains.

■ *The firewall host*: The firewall host is responsible for implementing stateful packet inspection and filtering based on the rules that are configured on it. Traffic that enters the firewall from the untrusted side of the network is examined using what is termed the outside filter. The inside filter examines traffic that is exchanged between the firewall host and the trusted side of the network.

Although the exact manner in which the filtering is implemented on the firewall host can vary with the vendor platform, it is important that two basic traffic flows must be inspected: traffic that the firewall host exchanges with the untrusted network and traffic exchanged with the trusted network. The logical location of these filters is illustrated in Figure 10-12 where they are applied to the so-called outside and inside interfaces of the firewall host.

Aside from filtering, the firewall host may also implement the following functions: encryption and VPN, authentication, NAT, logging, and alarm generation and notification.

■ *Inside router*: The inside router is a hardened device that provides a routed connection between the internal trusted network and the firewall host.

Figure 10-12
The firewall filter for inbound and outbound traffic

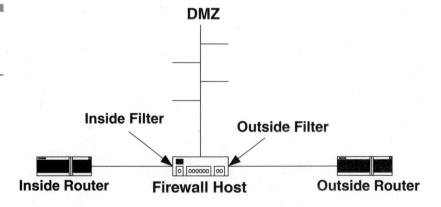

Firewall Policies

This section summarizes the policies that should be implemented on the firewall system. These policies relate to two fundamental issues:

- Firewall policies that relate to the firewall system's role in implementing network security.
- Policies that ensure the security of the firewall system components themselves. This is emphasized separately because the compromise of the firewall system itself is often the first step to the compromise of the network and the information contained on it.

The following list of policies is intended to protect the network and the firewall components. It is by no means exhaustive as the threats and hence the remedies are in a constant state of flux.

In relation to the firewall system itself, any software used on the routers or the firewall host should be well tested and in widespread deployment within the industry. The firewall system is the last part of the network that should be exposed to risk. Anything less than mature software may contain bugs, which not only threaten network availability, but they also provide potential security holes.

This in turn leads to a second principle that, while applicable to any aspect of network design, it is of particular relevance to security. That is the KISS principle: Keep It Simple and Stupid. Any additional complexity in hardware or particularly software configuration leads to an additional scope for errors or bugs and the resulting security holes.

▬ ▬

NOTE: *Only utilize mature software on any device within the firewall system. Bugs can create security holes. Also keep configurations as simple as possible.*

All devices within the firewall system should be hardened from a security point of view. The process of device hardening entails strictly controlling any local or remote access to the device. Any services or protocols that the device supports should be disabled by default. Services that are required by the network should only be allowed in a limited and well-defined manner to control which hosts can use these services. In the next section, many of the services listed that provide potential security holes relate to the issue of device hardening as well as protecting the network.

The parameters that specifically relate to hardening devices include the following:

■ *Limit physical port access*: Physical terminal access to any firewall should be strictly controlled with a one-time password system or an equally secure access protection method. This protection should be enabled on the console port and any auxiliary ports the device might have.

Of course, it is of equal importance that the location of the firewall devices is secure. Most firewall hosts on the market such as Checkpoint, Eagle Raptor, or Cisco PIX are secure out of the box and cannot be easily broken into. This is not true of the inside and outside router devices. For example, Cisco publishes the break-in techniques on their Web site. Hence, if you are in the same room as a Cisco router, then you can break into it!

■ *Limit remote access*: The IP address of hosts that are allowed to Telnet into the firewall devices should be specified in a Telnet access filter on each device. Other techniques can be used where the remote host must specify a line number when doing a Telnet to the secure device. The secure host will only accept a Telnet to a particular line number, such as Telnet 202.10.10.2 3004.

It is also critical to control the Telnet facilities outbound from the firewall devices. Telnet sessions from the firewall devices should only be allowed to specific hosts and should undergo one-time password authentication before being established. This ensures that the firewall devices cannot be used as a jumping-off point for hackers, whereby they can infiltrate the trusted network after one of the firewall devices has been compromised.

■ *Limit SNMP access*: SNMP, as we shall see later in this chapter, is a protocol with security vulnerabilities. It should not be possible to perform any configuration on firewall devices via SNMP. In other words, they should belong to the read-only community. Even with this protection in place, SNMP can provide an abundance of information valuable to a malicious party. Hence, SNMP access should only be permitted to the specified NMS IP addresses. The SNMP interactions should be protected by a read-only community string that is *difficult to guess* (and has not been left at the default setting).

■ *Control the configuration downloads*: *Trivial File Transfer Protocol* (TFTP) configuration downloads are not recommended on the firewall devices. They may be used on other devices throughout the trusted domain. On each device within the trusted network, TFTP access should only be allowed from specific IP addresses within the trusted network.

■ *Disable any unnecessary services*: Any service or protocol that may reveal information about the device or network should be disallowed by default. If it is absolutely necessary, then it may be allowed for specific and well-defined services. The upcoming section discusses the protocols and services that can represent security holes. For example, ICMP services must be strictly controlled. Proprietary troubleshooting and management protocols such as the *Cisco Discovery Protocol* (CDP) should be disabled on any Cisco routers in the firewall system.

NOTE: *All devices in the firewall system should be hardened to an even stricter specification than devices on the trusted network. It is imperative that the firewall devices reside in a physically secure location.*

Controlling Access from the Outside Network   This filter is usually implemented against traffic that enters the firewall host from the outside router and hence the untrusted network. Some of the more elementary filtering may be performed on the outside router itself. The more sophisticated inspection and policies are implemented on the firewall host.

The filtering and policies that are implemented on the outside filter should include, but not necessarily be limited to, the following:

■ *Static routing only*: With the exception of very large enterprises, static routing is generally used to connect to the Internet. The internal network typically uses a default route to access the Internet. The local ISP then must have a static route pointing back to the corporation's registered IP network.

A significant overhead is associated with the use of the *Border Gateway Protocol* (BGP) on the connection to the ISP and in many cases it does not provide a benefit over the use of default routes. Purely from a security standpoint, static routing is preferable to using a dynamic routing protocol over secure connections. A dynamic routing protocol has the potential to advertise routing information about the secure environment. The use of route filtering and the authentication of routing updates on the outside router can reduce the probability of this occurrence. However, if the outside router is compromised, then the dynamic routing protocol may help the hacker to obtain information about the internal subnets.

■ *Deny all inbound connections by default*: All inbound traffic from the outside untrusted network should be implicitly blocked by default. The only inbound traffic that should be allowed is the following:

▪ Traffic that is part of an existing conversation that was initiated from the inside network. The firewall's state table during the inspection of each inbound packet verifies this.

▪ Any inbound traffic initiated from the outside network that is to be allowed must be explicitly and *specifically* listed. For example, in the case of Figure 10-11, the firewall is configured to allow Web traffic with a specific destination address of 202.10.10.10 and DNS requests are only allowed if they have a destination address 202.10.10.11. For each public service located in the DMZ, the outside network must know the IP address of the server and cannot simply perform a sweep to find a server. With this philosophy, the firewall blocks all inbound traffic by default and is only opened up for very specific and well-defined services.

NOTE: *By default, you should only allow inbound traffic that is in response to a session initiated on the inside network.*
   Any inbound sessions allowed that are initiated on the outside network must be precisely defined while all other traffic is blocked.

■ *Strict ICMP control*: The manner in which the different ICMP services are treated on each component of the firewall system is of critical importance to network and device security. ICMP is a protocol that provides useful troubleshooting information. For the same reason, however, it represents a potential security hole that can be used to compromise your network. ICMP unreachable messages are sent back to the source when a router does not have a path to the destination or if a filter is blocking the access. This unreachable message has a source IP address from the DMZ or trusted network. The hacker can then attempt to Telnet to this address or alternatively "swamp" it with ICMP echo packets to initiate a DoS attack. ICMP redirects that are sent to the untrusted network also reveal information about the inside network. The following approach to ICMP on the firewall is recommended:

Figure 10-13
Possible ICMP control
policy

Outbound ICMP Policy (from trusted to untrusted network)	1. Allow echo-requests with inside source addresses 2. Block all other ICMP traffic
Inbound ICMP Policy (from untrusted network)	1. Allow echo-replies 2. Allow time-exceeded messages 3. Block all other ICMP traffic

- All ICMP services should be blocked inbound or outbound from the firewall by default. Specific ICMP services can be allowed in a secure manner, as they are required.

- It may be desired to ping the Internet from the trusted network and likewise do route traces. In this case, ICMP echo-reply packets that are in response to outbound ICMP echo-requests can be allowed inbound from the outside network. To allow route traces, inbound ICMP time-exceeded messages can be allowed. This ICMP policy is illustrated in Figure 10-13.

■ *Disable IP route caching*: Fast switching technologies that cache destinations based on live traffic that was routed represent a potential loophole. If the inside or outside router is compromised by a hacker, the contents of the layer 3 cache could provide information on destinations on the inside network. The attacker could then spoof these destination addresses.

■ *Disable Telnet access to or from the firewall system devices*: The only device on the DMZ that should support inbound Telnets is the Telnet server itself. This should be specified in the firewall rules. All other inbound Telnets should be blocked. This includes the outside router, the inside router, the firewall host, and all other DMZ servers.

Telnet attempts should likewise be blocked from entering the trusted network *regardless of their origin*. Don't allow Telnets inbound from the firewall itself because a compromise of the firewall host would then represent a dangerous jumping-off point for hackers.

■ *Prevent TFTP services*: TFTP is a protocol that is quite devoid of security features. A number of well-documented hacking techniques utilize TFTP. For this reason, TFTP services should be disallowed by default and any exceptions must be well justified and precisely defined.

■ *Disable Proxy ARP*: With Proxy ARP enabled, a router may answer ARP requests for IP addresses pertaining to remote subnets. The router answers the ARP request with its own Ethernet MAC address. Any service that provides information about the inside network or the devices that make up the firewall system should be disabled.

■ *Disable directed broadcasts*: A broadcast address for a particular subnet can sometimes be routed to that subnet as a unicast packet. This is sometimes termed a *directed broadcast*. For example, 172.16.10.255 could be routed to the 172.16.10.0/24 destination. If this were a persistently repeated broadcast, it could initiate a DoS attack on that subnet in the form of a broadcast storm. If the packets were ICMP echo-requests that were not blocked, then the broadcast could be used to obtain the IP addresses of the devices on that subnet.

■ *Decide on a secure FTP implementation*: As already discussed, FTP is a multi-channel protocol with the sessions being initiated in different directions. FTP can be used to access sensitive data and also to initiate DoS attacks by performing large downloads to saturate the WAN or Internet links. This causes a potential security risk that requires stateful packet inspection and filtering at a minimum. An alternative is to run *passive FTP* (PFTP). This requires special PFTP client software and the server daemon must support the passive open command PASV. With this implementation of FTP, which is described in RFC 1579, no active back connection is initiated from the untrusted network.

FTP is also poorly secured in terms of authentication, whereby passwords are sent in clear text and can easily be picked up by network analyzers. The security extensions that are being added for strong authentication, integrity, and confidentiality with FTP sessions are described in RFC 2228.

■ *Disable Finger service*: The Finger service should be disabled on the routers within the firewall system. It is used to obtain information about a user account on a remote host, which must be running the Finger service in order to respond. This Finger command (which requests information about a user account on a remote system) causes a network connection to be formed between the local host, which happens to be *vala*, and the remote system, *godot*, a UNIX system elsewhere in the network. The Finger service uses the TCP transport protocol (number 6) and port 79.

■ *Disable source routing*: A router on the outside network that extracts routing information about the subnets on the trusted network could use source routing. For this reason, it must be ensured that the feature is disabled on the outside router, inside router, and the firewall host itself.

■ *Prevent MOP services*: The MOP server supports the request ID message, periodic system ID messages, and the remote console carrier functions. The MOP server periodically multicasts a system ID message, which is used by DEC's Ethernet configurator to determine which stations are present in an Ethernet network. The periodic system's ID messages are sent to the multicast address *AB00.0002.0000*. MOP is designed to be used for the basic management of network components. It is a special-purpose protocol that does not support many of the features supported by other protocols. MOP can only be used between systems connected to the same LAN or between systems connected by transparent bridging. It cannot be routed, because it does not have a network layer. Because it is a service that broadcasts system information, it must be blocked on routers within the firewall system.

DMZ Policies   As stated earlier, the DMZ is the dead zone between the inside router and the outside router. The DMZ effectively bridges the gap between the trusted and non-trusted networks. If a separate firewall host is distinct from the inside and outside routers, then this host can be thought of as being part of the DMZ. Alternatively, the firewall host can be thought of as being connected to the DMZ as well as to the inside and outside routers, as shown in Figure 10-10. For this reason, a firewall host should support a minimum of three LAN interfaces in order to create an appropriate DMZ.

NOTE: *The firewall host should have a minimum of three LAN interfaces in order to create an appropriate DMZ.*

All public servers should be placed in the DMZ LAN. These include services such as Web access, Anonymous FTP, Telnet, DNS, and Mail. These servers should not be allowed to initiate communication with any hosts or servers on the internal trusted network. There should not be any reason for them to attempt to initiate such as a session. Therefore, it must be assumed that such communication cannot be trusted. This is also true of the firewall host itself. The stations on the DMZ must not be trusted on the internal network because they could present a convenient jumping-off point for hackers, should any of these stations become compromised. For this reason, Telnet traffic from any of these DMZ servers, including the firewall host, should be blocked from entering the trusted network.

Ideally, each of the public applications resident in the DMZ should be implemented on a separate box. This is a worthwhile additional cost when weighted against the following security benefits:

- *Specific policy control*: The outside router or firewall host should be configured to only enable specific applications to specific hosts. For example, the only traffic allowed to the Web server should have a destination TCP port number of 80 for WWW. The only traffic allowed to the DNS servers should have a destination port number of 53 and so on.

  Effectively, each server in the DMZ is only allowed to respond to requests for the specific application that it provides. Thus, a very stringent form of access control is created.

- *Intrusion detection*: The stringent access control to each specific server/application combination also means that a potential hacker must know the IP address along with the application associated with a particular server. Hence, explicit attempts to connect to a particular server that request the incorrect application can be logged by the firewall for intrusion detection purposes.

- *Reduced vulnerability*: If server platforms on the DMZ run multiple applications, then their operational complexity is increased. Increased complexity is usually synonymous with increased vulnerability in network security terms. This is a principle that has its foundation for a number of reasons. Administrative and configuration errors are more likely on a complex system. Also, as a platform becomes more complex, it is also more susceptible to bugs, which are always potential security holes.

NOTE: *All public servers (WWW, DNS, FTP, Mail, and so on) should be located in the DMZ. These servers should be kept as simple as possible and each application should be implemented on a separate box.*

One final point must be made in relation to the servers present on the DMZ and that relates to their maintenance. It is of critical importance that these servers are kept up to date with the latest security patches. This is in line with the philosophy that security is very much a dynamic task where the threats and challenges are continuously changing.

The Inside Filter   The main function of the inside filter is to block the initiation of any communication from the DMZ servers or firewall host to the internal network. It is important to be very clear that the firewall components and DMZ servers are not actually part of the trusted network and must be treated accordingly. This principle offers a further line of defense of the trusted network in the event of the firewall being compromised. The inside filter function should be implemented on the firewall host itself and also on the inside router as a second line of defense.

Load Balancing with Firewalls   The failure of the firewall host would result in the loss of all service to or from the outside network if no redundancy were incorporated in the design. The redundancy can take two forms. The firewalls can operate in a load-sharing manner, as shown in Figure 10-14, which results in the most efficient use of firewall resources, but it is also the most complex method of providing redundant gateways to untrusted networks. The two firewall hosts must run a protocol that enables them to be immediately updated on which traffic has passed through the other fire-

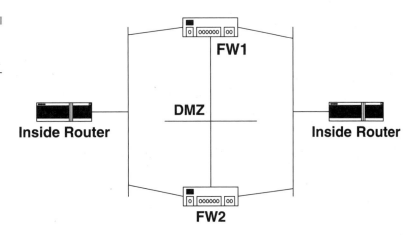

Figure 10-14
Firewalls operating in load-sharing mode

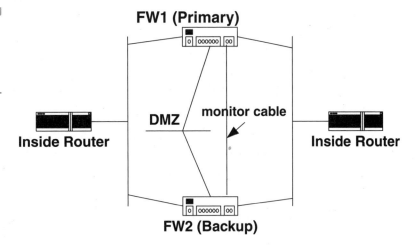

Figure 10-15
Firewalls operating in primary and redundant backup mode

wall. Otherwise, their state tables will be different, resulting in sessions being incorrectly dropped. For example, in Figure 10-14, established inbound TCP traffic could be dropped by FW2 if the initial outbound connection passes through FW1. FW2 would have to be updated about this session so that it could create a corresponding entry in its state table, enabling it to recognize the return traffic as being part of an existing conversation. Such solutions are available on the market, such as Checkpoint's Stonebeat™ protocol.

A less sophisticated solution would be to have a second firewall operating in a purely redundant mode. This is shown in Figure 10-15, where a backup firewall monitors the primary firewall and only begins to process traffic when the primary device fails.

Security Design and Implementation

Device Security

All networking devices such as routers and switches should be hardened against malicious access. This is a concept that was already discussed in the context of the firewall devices. The principle is equally applicable to all network devices.

Device hardening should entail the implementation of the following procedures:

- *Secured physical and remote access*: Physical terminal access to any network device should be strictly controlled with a one-time password system or an equally secure access protection method. This protection should be enabled on the console port and any auxiliary ports the device might have.

  The location of the wiring closet must also be secure. Physical access to the device means that it can be powered down to deny service and possibly be broken into after power-up.

  Remote virtual terminal access should be protected with one-time passwords also. Each device should only accept Telnet connections from specific IP addresses, such as from stations residing on the network management LAN. Outbound Telnet connections should also be controlled from each device. This prevents a hacker from hopping around the network after one device is compromised.

Different authorization levels should be defined for experienced technical support personnel and these levels are likewise password-protected. This would prevent inexperienced personnel altering the device configuration in error.

The network devices should be configured so that all passwords appear in encrypted form when the configuration is viewed. This prevents hard copies of the device configurations from revealing password information.

- *SNMP*: SNMP access should be limited to the IP addresses of the network management stations. Both the read-only and read-write community strings must be altered from the default settings of public and private respectively. Only NMS stations with read-write capabilities should be allowed write access to the devices.

- *TFTP*: The devices on the network should be configured to only exchange TFTP to or from stations on the NMS LAN. This prevents the malicious download of a flawed configuration. By controlling TFTP uploads from the devices, configuration information cannot be gathered by inappropriate parties.

- *Disable any unnecessary services*: Any service or protocol that reveals information about the device or network should be disabled unless it is specifically required. The section on firewalls discussed many such services such as ICMP, Proxy ARP, Finger, and so on. The policies on the network devices will be different because many of these services are important monitoring tools on a trusted network. However, the administrator should remain mindful of the security risks and if some of these services are not being used, then they should be manually disabled.

Network Security

Security can sometimes be a parameter that influences network design choices in relation to the physical and logical topologies and also to the type of networking devices that are deployed. For example, VLANs might be implemented on a switched LAN in order to prevent local broadcasts from being detected by any LAN analyzer on the campus. Here we will look at some network design and implementation practices appropriate for a secure network.

Securing Routing Information The most secure type of routing protocol that can be used on the border between a trusted network and one that is of a lesser trust level is static routing. Without a dynamic routing protocol, information about the subnets within the trusted domain will not be advertised.

In some cases, static routes may entail excessive administrative overhead and coordination between the two organizations, resulting in the use of a dynamic routing protocol. In this case, the following practices should be followed:

- *Route filtering*: Route filtering should be employed on the bordering routers such that the only subnets advertised into the untrusted network are destinations that the outside domain must attach to.

- *Authentication*: It is good practice to implement the authentication of routing updates even within the trusted domain. Protocols such as RIP v2 and OSPF support both clear text and *Message Digest 5* (MD5) authentication. MD5-encrypted passwords are the only worthwhile option due to the security hazards of clear text.

  When connecting to an untrusted domain, an encrypted authentication of routing information should also be employed. However, for obvious reasons, the key and password parameters should not match those used within the trusted domain.

- *The option of NAT*: NAT can also be used when connecting to an untrusted environment. This hides the internal addresses of the trusted network. Some applications such as *Network Basic Input/Output System* (NetBIOS) do not work well with NAT, so possible caveats should be checked carefully before implementing NAT.

Preventing Malicious Intrusion Most LAN switches support security features that can be used to prevent intrusion onto the LAN. A particular MAC address can be specified against each switch port or the switch can possibly be configured to only learn one MAC address against each port. The port is automatically disabled if any other station plugs into that port. An SNMP trap is generated, indicating a security violation on the port rather than a loss of line protocol. These features are intended for ports that connect to end-stations rather than to other switches.

The downside of this type of feature is the administrative overhead and also the potential to make troubleshooting more complicated, as ports cannot simply be swapped for test purposes.

Physical Network Security and the Role of Fiber   Fiber, as opposed to copper cabling, provides better immunity to *Electo-Magnetic Interference* (EMI). This means that fiber has improved noise characteristics over copper. The increased immunity to EMI also makes fiber a more secure transmission medium that cannot be easily tapped by closely adjacent cables.

Networks that have a high-security requirement are likely to deploy fiber beyond the campus backbone and out to the edges of the network. In some cases within the defense industry, fiber is used all the way to the desktop for security reasons. It is a question of balancing cost with the security specification.

Security on the Public WAN   Dial-up public WAN services such as the PSTN or ISDN are serious security holes. Anybody with these services in their home is a potential hacker.

In the case of ISDN, the *Point-to-Point Protocol* (PPP) is by far the most appropriate layer 2 transport protocol, mainly because of its authentication capabilities. PPP supports the *Password Authentication Protocol* (PAP) and the *Challenge Handshake Authentication Protocol* (CHAP) authentication. Both protocols are easy to configure, but CHAP encrypts the passwords, meaning that it is the only viable option for a public network.

For PSTN, dial-in secure modems should be used ideally with one-time passwords on the device ports that present the modems. Callback is often thought of as a secure mechanism for accepting dial-in connections. However, it is no substitute for a rigorous authentication procedure. In fact, callback is used more for cost-cutting purposes than for security.

Protection Against Common IP Threats

IP Address Spoofing   Hosts that are used on an untrusted network to impersonate the IP addresses of hosts on the trusted network can use IP address spoofing. Unsophisticated packet filters may pass certain traffic because the source address matches a host on the trusted network.

An untrusted host could, for example, generate a TCP SYN message that may be passed by the firewall because of its trusted source address. The server that receives the SYN will reply with a SYN ACK message that will be directed to the legitimate host that is being impersonated. In order for the malicious station to complete the three-way handshake, it must correctly guess the TCP sequence number used in the SYN ACK. Although this may sound difficult, software programs are designed for this task.

Even if TCP sessions cannot be completed, IP address spoofing can be used for DoS attacks such as SYN flooding (which we are about to discuss). Hence, it is important to protect against spoofing at layer 3. A patch called address verification checks for spoofed source addresses. When a packet is received, the source address of the packet can be compared to the route to that address. If the route doesn't exist, or would pass through a different interface than the packet was received from, the packet contains a spoofed source address.

Stateful packet inspection, when combined with address verification, can be an effective tool to combat address spoofing. Basically, inbound packets should be dropped if their source address matches the inside network.

NOTE: *To protect against IP address spoofing, use stateful inspection and block any inbound traffic that has a source address matching the inside network.*

SYN Flooding   SYN flooding entails the generation of persistent TCP SYN messages that may have spoofed source IP addresses and hence are not dropped by a poorly configured firewall. The SYN messages may not even be directed at a valid inside host address. But this is not relevant, as the goal of SYN flooding is DoS. The idea is to overwhelm the firewall with half-open TCP (or indeed UDP can be used for the same purpose) connections that must time out before being closed. If these connections are persistently being opened, then the firewall's capability to process valid traffic may be inhibited.

Appropriate stateful inspection on the firewall that protects against spoofed addresses and only enables inbound traffic that is part of an existing conversation is often adequate protection against SYN flooding. However, additional steps should be taken to protect the network in the event of these filters being compromised.

The firewall should be capable of monitoring half-open TCP and UDP connections. The firewall can be configured to limit the number of simultaneous TCP or UDP sessions supported that are awaiting bidirectional flow.

Any server that can be reached from an untrusted network is likely to be vulnerable to this attack if it has not been patched. Increasing queue lengths while reducing the TCP timeout values are further steps that at least limit the damage.

One kernel patch adds an overflow queue, so when the queue becomes full, new connection requests can go into an overflow queue. The overflow queue is kept as a hashed list for quick lookup, and only the minimum amount of state information is stored, keeping memory requirements lower.

NOTE: *The number of simultaneous half-open TCP or UDP sessions should be controlled at the firewall.*

SNMP   The security issues associated with SNMP have already been referred to. Here we will examine the topic in some more detail. SNMP presents the capability to poll network devices and monitor data on the host. This management protocol is also capable of altering the configurations on the host, allowing the complete remote management of the network device. The protocol uses a community string for authentication from the SNMP client to the SNMP agent on the managed device. The default community string that provides the monitoring or read capability is often public, while the default management or write community string is often private. An attacker can take advantage of these default community strings to gain information about a device using the read community string public, and the attacker can change a systems configuration using the write community string private. This vulnerability is augmented by the fact that the SNMP agent is often installed on a system by default without the administrator's knowledge.

SNMP *Management Information Bases* (MIBs) provide so-called soft information such as the system name, location, contacts, and sometimes even phone numbers. This information can be very useful in social engineering. An attacker could call an organization and use this contact information to obtain a password from an unsuspecting user.

SNMP information also provides a great deal of hard technical information about the system. An MIB could provide the system description that reveals the operating system software version that the host is using. This can be matched against known vulnerabilities in this version that would enable the attacker to gain further access into the host. SNMP data also provides interface descriptions, types, and other device and protocol configuration information. This device information can be gathered from more that one system to enable an attacker to compile a network topology map.

On devices that must be managed using SNMP, the community strings should be set at their maximum length and include a combination of letters, numbers, and special characters to avoid a brute force attack. All network devices on the network should be scanned using an SNMP vulnerability scanner to ensure that they do not use the default community strings.

SNMP access should also be limited to only the devices that require SNMP for monitoring. This can be accomplished by allowing only authorized clients to access UDP port 161. All access to UDP port 161 should be denied from external networks.

The latest of SNMP (version 3) has superior security because it does not use community strings. Users can retain them for backward compatibility to SNMPv1 and v2, but version 3 uses a cryptographic technique to secure data.

Ideally, SNMP should be disabled on all routers that are part of the firewall system. The firewall host itself should not enable the generation of or response to SMNP messages. As a rule, SNMP access should not be available from outside the trusted network. The hosts within the DMZ likewise should not have SNMP enabled.

The Teardrop Attack   A program called Teardrop has been written that enables a malicious user to crash Windows 95 and Windows NT machines that are connected to a network. This program has also been shown to be able to crash Linux machines. This attack exploits an overlapping IP fragment bug present in Windows 95 and Windows NT. When a Windows machine receives this attack, it is unable to handle the data and can exhibit behavior ranging from a lost Internet connection to the so-called blue screen of death. This bug has not been shown to cause any significant damage to systems, and a station reboot will clear the problem. However, though non-destructive, this bug could result in the loss of any unsaved data in an open application on the attacked station.

Because of this and other attacks based on IP fragmentation, most firewalls are capable of monitoring the number of fragmented packets passed. The throughput rate of fragmented packets can be limited to a certain number of packets per second.

INDEX

Symbols

20/80 rule, LANs, 315
80/20 rule, LANs, 314

A

AAL (ATM Adaptation Layer), 95
ABR (Available Bit Rate), ATM WANs, 95
ABRs (Area Border Routers), OSPF Summary LSAs, 157, 181–182
access layer, hierarchical LANs, 336
accounting
 network design management, 6
 security, 457
Ack packets, EIGRP, 210
Active state, EIGRP, 218
active timeout parameter, EIGRP, 221
addresses, IP. *See* IP addresses.
adjacencies, OSPF, 160
administrative costs, OSPF metrics, 133
administrative distances, EIGRP
 adjusting to avoid floating static routes, 242
 adjusting to avoid sub-optimal routing, 241
 differences from metric, 242
 migration issues, 245
 route determination, 240
advantages
 centralized LAN servers, 318–319
 flat WANs, 23
 LAN segmentation, 322
 layer 2 LAN backbone, 356–357
 layer 3 LAN backbone, 355
 OSPF, 152
  stub areas, 189
 private ATM WANs, 97
 route summarization, 138
 static routes, 143–144
advertised distances, EIGRP, 216
aggregating leased lines, hierarchical WANs, 32–35
alarms, firewalls, 463

applications, network design issues, 3, 9
architecture of the Internet, 256
areas, OSPF
 Area 0, 178
 alleviating scalability problems, 173
 backbone, 174, 178
 discontiguous, 196
 guidelines for usage, 174–176
 IP addresses, 180
 route summarization, 173
 scaling limits, 179
 virtual links, 193–194
AS path filtering, BGP, 279–280
AS-Path attribute, BGP, 271, 283
ASBRs (Autonomous System Boundary Routers), OSPF, 157, 178, 183–184, 187
ASs (Autonomous Systems), BGP routing, 254–256
asymmetrical routing, BGP, 289
ATM WANs
 ABR (Available Bit Rate), 95
 bandwidth, 89
 broadcasts, 90
 CBR (Constant Bit Rate), 94
 CDV (Cell Delay Variation), 94
 cell tax, 91
 CLR (Cell Loss Ratio), 94
 CTD (Cell Transfer Delay), 94
 EIGRP over NBMA, bandwidth, 234
 increased hop counts, 92
 LANE (Lan Emulation), 88
 latency, hop counts, 92
 OAM, troubleshooting, 93
 overhead, 91
 PCR (Peak Cell Rate), 93
 private, 97–98
 PVCs, 90
 QoS, 94–96
 redundancy, 92
 SAR (Segmentation And Reassembly), 91
 SCR (Sustainable Cell Rate), 93
 subinterfaces, 89
 UBR (Unspecified Bit Rate), 95
 VBR (Variable Bit Rate), 95

VCs, 89
VoIP, 100–101
ATM MANs, Tier-1 site connections, 49
attributes, BGP
  AS-Path, 271
  Community, 276–277
  discretionary, 271
  editing, 281–283
  Local Preference, 274–275
  mandatory, 271
  MED, 275
  Next-Hop, 273
  non-transitive, 271
  optional, 270
  Origin, 272
  Originator-ID, 293
  path, 270
  transitive, 271
  Weight, 273
  well-known, 270
authentication, 142, 457
  CHAP, 86
  firewalls, 462
  IPSec, 460
  PAP, 86
  PPP WANs, 86
authorization, 457
automatic route summarization, EIGRP, 229
automatic throttling, Frame Relay traffic
    shaping, 77
availability of applications, network design, 3
availability of data, security, 438

B

backbone
  campus, typical components, 48–49
  hierarchical WANs, 47–49
  LANs
    collapsed, 348
    distributed, 348
    layer 2, 356–357
    layer 3, 355
    resilience, 344
    routed, 350–354
    scalability, 347

    switched, 350–354
    throughput, 344
backbone areas, OSPF, 174, 178
backbone routers, OSPF, 181
backbone sites, hierarchical WANs, 31
backup redundancy, Frame Relay WANs, 82
balancing load. *See* load balancing.
bandwidth
  ATM WANs, 88–89
  dynamic routing over Frame Relay WANs,
    consumption issues, 72
  EIGRP, 214
  hierarchical WANs
    leased line/PVC aggregation, 33–34
    reduced leased line distance, 34
    reduction in core router ports, 35
    Tier-1, 51
  OSPF, routing metric, 162
  periodic updates, flat WANs, 26
  point-to-multipoint subinterfaces, EIGRP over
    NBMA, 235
  point-to-point subinterfaces, EIGRP over
    NBMA, 234
  private ATM WANs, costs, 98
  PVCs, EIGRP over NBMA, 234
  serial links, 60
  WAN design, 53–54
Bandwidth parameter, EIGRP, 221
bandwidth top-up, ISDN WANs, 62
BDCs (Backup Domain Controllers), LANs, 315
BDRs (Backup Designated Routers), OSPF, 160
BECNs (Backward Explicit Congestion
    Notifications), Frame Relay WANs, 76
best path determination, metrics, 133
best paths, OSPF, routing table calculations, 155
BGP (Border Gateway Protocol), 254
  AS-Path attribute, 271
    editing, 283
  asymmetrical routing, 289
  attributes, editing, 281–282
  CIDR (Classless InterDomain Routing), 290
  Community attribute, 276–277
  community based filtering, 284
  confederations, 297–298
  CPU overutilization, 263
  default routes, ISPs, 285–288
  discretionary attributes, 271
  EBGP, 259

filtering
  AS paths, 279–280
  routes, 278–279
half lives, 264
IBGP, 260
IGP redistribution, 265–266
  enterprise networks, 267–268
Keepalives, 255
Local Preference attribute, 274–275
  editing, 282–283
mandatory attributes, 271
MED attribute, 275
  editing, 282–283
multi-homing, 285
Next-Hop attribute, 273
non-transitive attributes, 271
Notifications, 255
occasions to use, 257–258
Open messages, 255
optimized routing, 289
optional attributes, 270
Origin attribute, 272
Originator-ID attribute, 293
path attributes, 270
peer groups, 299–300
peers, 255
policy based routing, 282–283
private ASs, 297
receiving full Internet routing tables, 289
redundancy, 285
resilience, 285
reuse limits, 264
route aggregation, 290
route dampening, 263
route processing, 263
route reflectors, 292, 296
  clusters, 292–294
route selection, 278
router memory, 263
scalable AS routing, 290
security, 142
sessions, resetting, 264
soft reconfiguration, 265
supernetting, 290
suppress limits, 264
synchronization, 261–262
transitive attributes, 271
Updates, 255

Weight attribute, 273
well-known attributes, 270
bit boundaries, IP address route
    summarization, 120–121
boundary LSAs, OSPF, 157
bounding EIGRP queries
  via distribute lists, 223
  via route summarization, 224
broadcast control, hierarchical WANs, 37
broadcast domains, flat WANs, potential
    problems, 29
broadcast networks, OSPF, 165
  DR election, 166–167
  LSA flooding, 165
  multicast groups, 166
broadcast queuing, Frame Relay WANs, 78
broadcast replication
  Frame Relay flat WANs, 29
  Frame Relay WANs, 64
broadcasts
  ATM WANs, 90
  flat WANs, reducing, 30

C

calculating
  paths, EIGRP neighbors, 220
  routing metrics
    dynamic routing over Frame Relay WANs, 74
    OSPF, 161
  routing tables, OSPF, 161
  summary masks, IP addresses, 118-119
campus backbones, typical components, 48-49
campus networks. *See* LANs.
capacity planning
  serial links, 61
  Tier-2 traffic, hierarchical WANs, 46
case studies, EIGRP migration issues, 246, 248
CBR (Constant Bit Rate), ATM WANs, 94
CDV (Cell Delay Variation), ATM WANs, 94
cell tax, ATM WANs, 91
centralized LAN servers, 318-319
CHAP (Challenged Handshake Authentication
    Protocol), 86
choosing Tier-2 sites, hierarchical WANs, 45
CIDR (Classless Inter-Domain Routing), 146, 290

CIR (Committed Information Rate), Frame
    Relay WANs, 76
classful routing protocols
    discontiguous networks, 135
    route summarization, 124-125
classless routing protocols, 111-112, 123
client-server traffic flow, LANs, 310
CLR (Cell Loss Ratio), ATM WANs, 94
clusters, BGP route reflection, 292, 294
collapsed backbone, LANs, 348
community attribute, BGP, 276-277
community-based filtering, BGP, 284
complexity of OSPF, 248
compression
    encryption conflicts, 452
    PPP WANs, 86
    serial link WANs, 62-63
confederations, BGP, 297-298
confidentiality, security, 437
configuration management, network design, 6
conflicts between encryption and
    compression, 452
connections
    ATM MAN Tier-1 sites, 49
    flat WANs, resilience, 22
    hierarchical WANs, Tier-3 resilience, 47
    LANs, redundancy, 307
contiguous IP address blocks, 116
convergence, 131
    dynamic routing over Frame Relay WANs, 74
    EIGRP
        DUAL, 218
        neighbors, 212
        potential problems, 220
        route summarization, 137, 231
    failure detection, 131
    improved time via route summarization, 137
    LANs, 309
    medium influences on resolution, 133
    OSPF, 152, 163–164, 249
    RIP, 147
    update mechanisms, 131
core sites, hierarchical WANs, 31, 47
cost issues, network design, 7–8, 37, 52
    bandwidth utilization, 33
    leased lines, 24
    OSPF routing metric, 161
    telecom carriers, 53

count to infinity, 128
CPUs, overutilization, BGP, 263
CTD (Cell Transfer Delay), ATM WANs, 94

D

data authentication, IPSec, 460
data link layer protocols, serial links, 61
data sequencing, Multilink PPP WANs, 87
databases, link state. *See* link state database.
DDPs (Database Description Packets), OSPF, 158
default bandwidth, EIGRP, 214
default routes, BGP, 285–288
delay, EIGRP metrics, 213
delay-sensitive applications, LANs, 303
demand circuits, OSPF, 202
designing
    LANs, 302
    networks
        applications, 9
        costs, 7–8
        disaster recovery, 7
        downtime costs, 10
        fundamental design principles, 13–16
        growth planning, 5
        investment protection, 8
        management, 6
        performance parameters, 2-3
        predictability, 12–13
        proof of concept tests, 10–12
        protocols, 9
        redundancy, 4
        resilience, 4
        scalability, 5
        security, 7
        support costs, 8
    WANs, 18
        bandwidth, 53–54
        cost issues, 52
        flat topology, 18
        hierarchical topology, 20, 46
        ISDN, 79
        latency, 54
        redundancy, 55–57
        resilience, 55–57
        serial links, 60–62

telecom carrier costs, 53
VoIP, 101
device hardening, security, 476–477
device redundancy, LANs, 307
dial backup, ISDN WANs, 83–84
dial plans, video/VoIP, 103–105
dialup connections, static routes, 144
Dijkstra algorithm, calculating routing table,
    OSPF, 161
disadvantages
  centralized LAN servers, 319
  flat WANs, 25
  OSPF, 153
    stub areas, 189
  private ATM WANs, 98
  routing metrics, 134
disaster recovery
  hierarchical WANs, 37
  network design, 7
Discard Eligible packets, Frame Relay
    WANs, 76–77
discontiguous areas, OSPF, 196
discontiguous networks
  EIGRP migration issues, 245
  subnet addresses, 135
discretionary attributes, BGP, 271
distance vector routing protocols, 122
  convergence, medium influences on
    resolution, 133
  count to infinity, 128
  flat WANs, 26
  hold down timers, 131
  ISDN WANs, 81
  route calculation algorithms, 132
  safeguards against routing loops, 129
  stability tradeoff, 129
distribute lists, EIGRP, bounding queries, 223
distributed backbone, LANs, 348
DKE (dual key encryption), 449–452
DMZ (Demilitarized Zone), firewalls,
    463–465, 473
DNS (Domain Name System), security
    filtering, 442
DoS attacks (Denial of Service), 444
downtime costs, network design, 10
DRs (Designated Routers), OSPF, 160, 166–167
DUAL (Diffusing Update Algorithm), 209, 218
dual homing, flat WANs, 22

dual partial mesh Frame Relay WANs, 69
duplex modes, LANs, 312
dynamic routing
  Frame Relay WANs
    bandwidth consumption, 72
    convergence, 74
    metric calculation, 74
    router overhead, 73
    split horizon, 75
  ISDN WANs, 80

E

EBGP (External BGP)
  next hop addresses, 260
  peers, 255, 259
editing BGP attributes, 281–283
effect recognition, security intrusion
    detection, 455
EGPs (Exterior Gateway Protocols), 254
EIGRP (Enhanced Interior Gateway Routing
    Protocol), 208
  active state, 218
  active timeout parameter, 221
  backbone router neighbor number
    recommendations, 27
  bandwidth, 214, 221
  convergence
    DUAL, 218
    potential problems, 220
  distribute lists, bounding queries, 223
  DUAL (Diffusing Update Algorithm), 209
  ease of configuration, 249
  feasible successors, 215
  flexibility of network design, 248
  floating static routes, adjusting administrative
    distances, 242
  Hello intervals, 210
  Hello packets, 211
  hold times, 211
  load balancing, 225–226
  metrics
    advertised distances, 216
    delay, 213
    differences from administrative
      distances, 242

feasible distances, 216
k values, 213
minimum bandwidth, 213
MTU, 213
migration, 243–244
    administrative distances, 245
    case study, 246–248
    discontiguous networks, 245
    VLSM, 245
multiprotocol networks, 236–238
mutual redistribution, 238
NBMA networks, 233–235
neighbors
    convergence problems, 212
    formation process, 210–211
    limiting number, 221
    memory issues, 212
    path calculation, 220
operations, 208–209
packets, 210
path selection
    administrative distances, 240
    prefix lengths, 239
    route determination, 239
policy-based routing, 226
potential problems, increasing number of router
        neighbors, 27
protocol redistribution, 237–238
queries, limiting propagation, 222
route filters, 239
route maps, 239
route summarization, 232–233, 250
    automatic, 229
    bounding queries, 224
    improved convergence time, 137
    manual, 230–231
routing loops, 239
SIA (stuck in active), 220
sub-optimal routing, adjusting administrative
        distances, 241
successors, 215
summary routes, 240
topology table, 214–215
VLSM, 227
EIR (Enhanced Information Rate), Frame
        Relay WANs, 76

encryption, 142, 449
    compression conflicts, 452
    firewalls, 461
    SKE, 450
    VPNs, 453
enhanced packet filtering, firewalls, 461
enterprise networks, BGP redistribution to
        IGP, 267–268
enterprise services, flat WANs, 20
equal cost load balancing, 142, 225–226
error detection, PPP WANs, 86
Ethernet switching, LANs, 311–312
exchanging routing data, OSPF, 155
external attribute LSAs, OSPF, 158
external costs, OSPF, 186
external LSAs, OSPF, 157
external routes, OSPF, 178, 202
external threats to security, 439

F

failure detection, convergence, 131
Fast Ethernet, LANs, 313
fault management, network design, 6
feasible distances, EIGRP, 216
feasible successors, EIGRP, 215
FECNs (Forward Explicit Congestion
        Notifications), Frame Relay WANs, 76
filtering
    BGP
        AS paths, 279–280
        community-based, 284
        routes, 278–279
    EIGRP routes, 239
    hierarchical WANs, 42
    OPSF, 185
        route redistribution, ASBRs, 187
    security option, 442
firewalls, 461–462
    alarm generation, 463
    DMZ, 463–465
    hosts, 466
    inside routers, 466
    logging, 463
    NAT, 462–463

operations, 461
outside routers, 464
policies, 467
  disabling services, 471–472
  DMZ, 473
  FTP, 472
  ICMP, 470
  inside filters, 475
  load balancing, 476
  outside filters, 469–470
  physical port access, 468
  remote access, 468
  SNMP access, 468
  TFTP downloads, 469
proxies, 463
flat WANs, 18–20
  advantages, 23
  broadcast domains, potential problems, 29
  broadcasts, reducing, 30
  collapsed back to central site, 23
  disadvantages, 25
  dual homing, 22
  enterprise services, 20
  factors behind leased line costs, 24
  fewer PVCs, 24
  fewer subnets, 24
  Frame Relay. *See* Frame Relay flat WANs, 29
  increased router overhead, 26
  IP routing table, minimizing size, 28
  minimal router hops, 23
  periodic update bandwidth consumption, 26
  potential problems, 26-27
  resilient connections, 22
  route summarization, OSPF areas, 28
  scalable distance vector routing protocols, 26
  VLSM (Variable Length Subnet Masking), 24
floating static routes
  EIGRP, adjusting administrative distances, 242
  ISDN WANs, 82
flooding LSAs, OSPF, 163
flowcharts for network design, 10
Frame Relay
  EIGRP over NBMA, bandwidth, 234
  WANs
    BECNs (Backward Explicit Congestion
        Notifications), 76
    broadcast queuing, 78
    broadcast replication, 64

CIR (Committed Information Rate), 76
Discard Eligible packets, 76–77
dual partial mesh, 69
dynamic routing, 72–75
EIR (Enhanced Information Rate), 76
FECNs (Forward Explicit Congestion
    Notifications), 76–77
full mesh, 71
hub and spoke, 68
packet replication, 30
partial mesh, 69
private implementations, 78
PVCs, 67–68
QoS, 77
PVCs, replicating broadcasts, 29
split horizon, disabling, 65
subinterfaces, 65
traffic management, 76
traffic shaping, 76
VoIP, 99
FTP (File Transfer Protocol)
  firewall policies, 472
  multi-channel protocol security, 446-447
full data compression, serial link WANs, 62
full duplex mode, LANs, 313
full mesh Frame Relay WANs, 71
full meshing, BGP, 262
fundamental network design principles, 13-16

G

Gigabit Ethernet, LANs, 345–347
growth planning, network design, 5
guidelines
  OSPF area usage, 174–176, 188
  passwords, 456

H

half lives, BGP, 264
hardening devices, security, 476–477
HDLC, serial link WANs, 61
header compression, serial link WANs, 63
Hello intervals, EIGRP, 210

Hello packets
  EIGRP, 210–211
  OSPF, 158
hierarchical LANs, 335
  access layer, 336
  intermediate layer, 337–343
hierarchical WANs, 20
  broadcast control, 37
  cost issues, 37–38
  disaster recovery, 37
  IP route summarization, 35–36
  Layer-3 switching, 40
  leased line aggregation, 32–34
  leased line distance reduction , 34
  NAT (Network Address Translation), 44
  PVCs
    aggregation, 33–34
    reduced leased line distance, 34
    reduction in core router ports, 35
  reduction in routing protocol neighbors , 35
  route filtering, 42
  security policies, 42
  static routes, 41
  Tier-1 sites, 31, 47–49
    bandwidth, 51
    minimizing overhead, 50
    policies, 51
    resilience, 52
  Tier-2 sites, 31
    designing, 46
    functions, 44
    local users, 45
    resources, 45
    site selection, 45
    tech support, 45
    Tier-3 network connectivity resilience, 47
    Tier-3 site support, 46
    Tier-3 to Tier-1 resilience, 47
    traffic capacity planning, 46
  Tier-3 sites, 31
    networking functions and policies, 41
    preventing Tier-4 sites, 43
hold down timers, 129–131
hold times, EIGRP, 211
hop counts, ATM WANs, 92
hosts, firewalls, 466
hub and spoke Frame Relay WANs, 68
hubs, LANs, 314

I

IANA (Internet Assigned Numbers Authority), AS
    number assignments, 256
IBGP (Internal BGP)
  full meshing, 262
  next hop addresses, 260
  peers, 255, 260
  route reflectors, 260
ICMP (Internet Control Message Protocol),
    firewall policies, 470
IDEA (International Data Encryption Algorithm),
    450
IDSs (Intrusion Detection Systems), 454–455
IGP (Interior Gateway Protocols), 254
  BGP redistribution, 265–268
  BGP synchronization, 261–262
IGRP (Interior Gateway Routing Protocol), 208
  EIGRP migration, 244
    administrative distances, 245
    case study, 246–248
    discontiguous networks, 245
    VLSM, 245
IKE (Internet Key Exchange), IPSec security, 458
information protection
  availability of data, 438
  confidentiality, 437
  integrity of data, 437
  risk/vulnerability assessments, 438
  See also security.
inside filters, firewall policies, 475
inside routers, firewalls, 466
integrity of data, security, 437
inter-area routes, OSPF, 174, 177, 199–201
interesting traffic, ISDN WANs, 82
intermediate layer, hierarchical LANs, 337–343
internal routers, OSPF, 181
internal threats to security, 439
Internet, fundamental architecture, 256
Internet community, BGP, 277
InterNIC, private IP address ranges, 108
intra-area routes, OSPF, 177
investment protection, network design, 8
IP (Internet Protocol), routing protocols, 122–123
IP addresses
  contiguous address blocks, 116
  OSPF areas, 180

overloading, 108
private address ranges, 108–109
route summarization, 35–36, 114–115
   bit boundaries, 120–121
   over-summarization, 117
   stringency in summarization, 117
   summary masks, 118–119
spoofing, 480
subnet masks, 110–113
subnet planning, 109–110
VLSM, 113
   classless routing protocols, 111–112
IP over ATM WANs. *See* ATM WANs.
IP over Frame Relay WANs
   broadcast replication, 64
   dual partial mesh, 69
   full mesh, 71
   hub and spoke, 68
   partial mesh, 69
   PVCs
      meshing, 68
      multipoint, 68
      point-to-point, 67
   subinterfaces, 65
IP routing
   flat WANs, minimizing size, 28
   ISDN, 79
   OSPF, 152
IP Unnumbered feature, serial link WANs, 63
IPSec, 458–460
IPv6 security, 458
ISDN (integrated Services Digital Networks)
   connections, flat WANs, resilience, 22
   OSPF
      configurations, 203
      problems, 202
   security, 479
ISDN WANs, 79
   bandwidth top-up, 62
   dial backup, 83
   distance vector routing protocols, 81
   dynamic routes, 80
   floating static routes, 82
   Frame Relay backup redundancy, 82
   interesting traffic, 82
   link state routing protocols, 81
   static routes, 79

ISPs (Internet Service Providers)
   BGP
      default routes, 285–288
      redistribution to IGP, 266–268
   Internet architecture, 256

K–L

k values, EIGRP metrics, 213
Keepalives, BGP, 255
lab testing network designs, 10–12
LANE (Lan Emulation), ATM WANs, 88
LANs (Local Area Networks)
   20/80 rule, 315
   80/20 rule, 314
   backbone
      resilience, 344
      scalability, 347
      throughput, 344
   backup storage, 304
   BDCs (Backup Domain Controllers), 315
   centralized servers, 318–319
   client-server traffic flow, 310
   collapsed backbone, 348
   connections, redundancy, 307
   convergence, 309
   delay-sensitive applications, 303
   device redundancy, 307
   distributed backbone, 348
   duplex modes, 312
   Ethernet switching, 311–312
   Fast Ethernet, 313
   full duplex mode, 313
   Gigabit Ethernet, 345–347
   hierarchical, 335
      access layer, 336
      intermediate layer, 337–343
   hubs, 314
   layer 2 backbone, 356–357
   layer 3
      backbone, 355
      switching, 330–333
   layer 4 switching, 334
   performance parameters, 302–303
   QoS, 303
   redundant resources, 304

redundant servers, 304
    server connections, 305
resilience, 308
routed backbone, 350–354
routing segmentation, 321–324
scalability, 309
servers
    locating, 316–318
    mirroring, 305
switched backbone, 350–354
switching, segmentation, 325–329
topologies, 358–60
wiring closets, 308
latency, WAN design, 54, 92
layer 2 backbone, LANs, 356–357
layer 3 backbone, LANs, 355
layer 3 switching
    hierarchical WANs, 40
    LANs, 330–333
    load balancing, 141
layer 4 switching, LANs, 334
LCP (Link Control Protocol), 86
leased lines
    flat WANs, factors driving cost, 24
    hierarchical WANs, 32–35
limitations of flat WANs, 25
limiting access, firewall policies, 468
limiting number of EIGRP neighbors, 221
limiting propagation of EIGRP queries, 222
line state changes, dial backup, ISDN WANs, 84
link compression, serial link WANs, 62
link state database, OSPF
    composing, 155
    exchange process, 160
    scalability problems, 172
link state routing protocols, 81, 123
load balancing, 141
    EIGRP, 225–226
    firewall policies, 476
    OSPF, 162
    RIP metrics, 133
    serial link WANs, 62
    unequal cost, 142
Local Preference attribute, BGP, 274–275,
        282–283
local users, hierarchical WANs, 45
locating LAN servers, 316–318
logging, firewalls, 463

longest prefix rule, route summarization, 139
loops, routing, 127
LSAcks (Link State Acknowledgements),
        OSPF, 158
LSAs (Link State Advertisements), OSPF, 155
    delay, route calculation, 132
    flooding, 163–165, 172
LSRs (Link State Requests), OSPF, 158
LSUs (Link State Updates), OSPF, 158

                                    M

malicious attacks, network security, 478
management, network design, 6
managing WAN traffic. *See* traffic management.
mandatory attributes, BGP, 271
MANs (Metropolitan Area Networks), 31
manual route summarization, EIGRP, 230–231
maximum metrics, routing protocols, 129
maximum network diameter, routing protocol
        performance, 126
MED attribute (Multi-Exit Discriminator), BGP,
        275, 282–283
memory
    EIGRP neighbor issues, 212
    routers, BGP issues, 263
meshing PVCs, Frame Relay WANs, 68
metrics
    best path determination, 133
    dynamic routing over Frame Relay WANs, 74
    EIGRP
        advertised distances, 216
        delay, 213
        differences from administrative
                distances, 242
        feasible distances, 216
        k values, 213
        minimum bandwidth, 213
        MTU, 213
    limitations, 134
    OSPF, 185
        administrative costs, 133
        calculating, 161
    RIP, load balancing, 133
MIBs, SNMP security, 481
migration, EIGRP, 243–248

minimum bandwidth, EIGRP metrics, 213
minimun of router hops, flat WANs, 23
mirroring servers, LANs, 305
MOSPF (Multicast OSPF), Type 6 LSAs, 157
MPLS (MultiProtocol Label Switching), 89, 283
MTU (Maximum Transmission Unit), EIGRP
    metric, 213
multi-channel protocol security, 446–447
multi-homing, BGP, 285
multicast groups, broadcast OSPF networks, 166
multilink PPP WANs, data sequencing, 87
multiple ABRs, OSPF, 182
multipoint interfaces
    EIGRP over NBMA, bandwidth, 235
    Frame Relay, OSPF NBMA networks, 170–171
multipoint PVCs, Frame Relay WANs, 68
multiprotocol networks, EIGRP, 236–238
mutual redistribution
    EIGRP, 238
    EIGRP over NBMA, 237
    OSPF, 184

N

NAPs (Network Access Points), Internet
    architecture, 256
NAT (Network Address Translation)
    firewalls, 462–463
    hierarchical WANs, 44
    IP address translation, 108
NBMA networks (Non-Broadcast Multi-Access),
    168
    EIGRP, 233
        point-to-multipoint, 235
        point-to-point, 234
        PVC bandwidth, 234
    OSPF, 168
        multipointFrame Relay
            subinterfaces, 170–171
        neighbors, 168
        point-to-multipoint, 171–172
        point-to-point subinterfaces, 170
NCPs (Network Control Protocols), 86
neighbors
    backbone routers, 27
    dynamic routing over Frame Relay WANs, 72

EIGRP
    convergence problems, 212
    formation process, 210–211
    limiting number, 221
    memory issues, 212
    path calculation, 220
OSPF
    formation process, 159
    formation states, 160
    NBMA networks, 168
networks
    designing
        applications, 9
        costs, 7–8
        disaster recovery, 7
        downtime costs, 10
        fundamental design principles, 13–16
        growth planning, 5
        investment protection, 8
        management, 6
        pedictability, 12–13
        performance parameters, 2–3
        proof of concept tests, 10–12
        protocols, 9
        redundancye, 4
        resilience, 4
        scalability, 5
        security, 7
        support costs, 8
    multiprotocol EIGRP, 236–238
    OSPF
        links, 156
        NBMA, 168
        types, 165
    security
        fiberoptics, 479
        malicious attacks, 478
        routing data, 478
    stabilizing via route summarization, 136
next hop addresses, BGP, 260
Next Hop attribute, BGP, 273
no-advertise community, BGP, 277
no-export community, BGP, 277
non-transitive attributes, BGP, 271
notifications, BGP, 255
NSSAs (Not So Stubby Areas), OSPF, 157,
    191–192
numbers, ASs, 256

O

OAM (Operation and Maintenance), ATM
    WANs, 93
Open messages, BGP, 255
OPSF
optimized routing, BGP, 289
optional attributes, BGP, 270
Origin attribute, BGP, 272
origin authentication, IPSec, 460
Originator-ID attribute, BGP, 293
OSPF (Open Shortest Path First)
    ABRs, 157, 181–182
    adjacencies, 160
    advantages, 152
    areas, 178
        alleviating scalability problems, 173
        guidelines for usage, 174–176
        IP addresses, 180
        route summarization, 173
        scaling limitations, 179
    ASBRs, 157, 178, 183–184, 187
    backbone areas, 174, 178
    backbone router, 27, 181
    BDRs, 160
    boundary LSAs, 157
    broadcast networks, 165–167
    complexity, 248
    convergence, 152, 163–164, 249
    DDPs, 158
    demand circuits, 202–203
    design restrictions, 248
    disadvantages, 153
    DRs, 160
    external attribute LSAs, 158
    external costs, 186
    external LSAs, 157
    external routes, 178
    flat WANs, route summarization, 28
    Hello packets, 158
    hierarchical structure, 152
    inter-area routes, 174, 177
    internal routers, 181
    intra-area routes, 177
    ISDN configurations, 203
    ISDN problems, 202
    link state database, 155
        composing, 155
        exchange process, 160
        scalability problems, 172
    load balancing, 162
    LSAcks, 158
    LSAs, 155
        delay, route calculation, 132
        flooding, 163, 172
        types, 156–157
    LSRs, 158
    LSUs, 158
    metrics
        administrative costs, 133
        types, 185
    mutual redistribution, 184
    NBMA networks, 168
        multipoint Frame Relay subinterfaces,
            170–171
        neighbors, 168
        point-to-multipoint, 171–172
        point-to-point subinterfaces, 170
    neighbors, 159
    network links, 156
    NSSAs, 157, 191–192
    point-to-point networks, 168
    potential problems, 27
    redistribution loops, 187
    route filtering, 185
    route maps, 185
    route redistribution, 186
    route summarization, 153, 198–202
    router links, 156
    router memory requirements, 154
    routing metrics, 161
    routing tables, 155
    scalability, 152, 173, 249
    security, 142
    SPF algorithm, 154, 161
    spf-delay time, 163
    states, 160
    stub areas, 188–189
    Summary LSAs, 157
    Totally Stubby Areas, 190
    Type 6 LSAs, 157
    Type 7 LSAs, 157
    virtual links, 193–196
    VLSM, 197
outside filters, firewall policies, 469–470

outside routers, firewalls, 464
over-summarization, IP addresses, 117
overhead
    ATM WANs, 91
    Tier-1 hierarchical WANs, 50
overloading IP addresses, 108

                            P

packet filtering
    firewalls, 461
    security, 442
        stateful inspection, 446
        stateless inspection, 443
        TCP three way handshake, 444
        UDP, 445
    stateful
        random/changing port numbers, 448–449
        security options, 447
packets
    EIGRP, 210
    Frame Relay WANs, 76
    OSPF, 158
    replication, 30
PAP (Password Authentication Protocol), 86
parameters, EIGRP, 221
partial mesh Frame Relay WANs, 69
passwords, security, 456
path attributes, BGP, 270
path calculation, EIGRP neighbors, 220
path selection, EIGRP, 239
pattern recognition, security intrusion
        detection, 454
payload compression, serial link WANs, 63
PCR (Peak Cell Rate), ATM WANs, 93
peer groups, BGP, 299-300
peers
    BGP, 255
    EBGP, 259
    IBGP, 260
per packet load balancing, 142
performance, network design, 2-3
performance parameters
    LANs, 302-303
    routing protocols, 125–127
periodic updates, flat WANs, 26

planning hierarchical WANs, 46
point-to-multipoint Frame Relay flat WANs, 30
point-to-multipoint OSPF NBMA networks,
        171-172
point-to-multipoint subinterfaces
    ATM WANs, 90
    EIGRP over NBMA, 235
point-to-point Frame Relay flat WANs, packet
        replication, 30
point-to-point networks, OSPF, 168
point-to-point PVCs, Frame Relay WANs, 67
point-to-point subinterfaces
    ATM WANs, 90
    bandwidth, EIGRP over NBMA, 234
    OSPF NBMA networks, 170
poison reverse, 129
policies
    EIGRP route filters, 239
    firewalls, 467
        disabling services, 471-472
        DMZ, 473
        FTP, 472
        ICMP, 470
        inside filters, 475
        limiting physical port access, 468
        limiting SNMP access, 468
        limiting TFTP downloads, 469
        limitingremote access, 468
        load balancing, 476
        outside filters, 469-470
    hierarchical WANs, 51
    Tier-3, hierarchical WANs, 41
policies for security, 440
policy based routing
    BGP, 282
    EIGRP, 226
POPs (Points of Presence), Internet
        architecture, 256
potential problems, flat WANs, 26-27
PPP (Point-to-Point protocol), 61, 86
PPP WANs, 86
predictability, network design, 12-13
predictor compression, PPP WANs, 86
prefix lengths, EIGRP route determination, 239
preventing routing loops, EIGRP, 239
principles of network design, 13-16
priorities, DR election process, OSPF, 166
prioritizing traffic. See traffic prioritization.

private ASs, BGP, 297
private ATM WANs, 97–98
private Frame Relay WANs, 78
private IP address ranges, 108-109
process switching, load balancing, 141
proof of concept tests, network design, 10, 12
protocols
  BGP, 254
  distance vector routing, 122
    scalability in flat WANs, 26
    See also distance vector routing protocols.
  EIGRP, 208
    redistribution, 237-238HDLC
    serial link WANs, 61
  IGRP, 208
  IPSec, 458
  LCP, 86
  NCP, 86
  network design, 9
  PPP, 61, 86
  RIP, 145
  RIPv2, 146
proxies, firewalls, 463
PSTNs (Public Switched Telephone Networks),
    security, 479
PVCs (Private Virtual Circuits)
  ATM WANs, 90
  bandwidth, EIGRP over NBMA, 234
  flat WANs, 24
  Frame Relay WANs
    broadcast replication, 29
    meshing, 68
    multipoint, 68
    point-to-point, 67
  hierarchical WANs
    aggregation, 33-34
    reduced leased line distance, 34
    reduction in core router ports, 35

Q

QoS (Quality of Service)
  ATM WANs, 94–96
  Frame Relay WANs, 77
  LANs, 303
  video WANs, 101–102
  VoIP, 101–102

queries, EIGRP, 210
  bounding
    via distribute lists, 223
    via route summarization, 224
  limiting propagation, 222
queuing
  Frame Relay WANs, 77–78
  video, 102
  VoIP, 102

R

RADIUS servers (Remote Access Dial-In User
    Service), 457
rate enforcement, Frame Relay traffic shaping, 77
redistributing
  BGP routes into IGP, 266
  IGP routes to BGP, 265
  multiple protocols, EIGRP, 237–238
  routes. *See also* route redistribution.
redistribution loops, OSPF, 187
redundancy
  ATM WANs, 92
  BGP, 285
  Frame Relay WANs, 82
  network design, 4
  OSPF, 195
  resources, LANs, 304
  serial link WANs, 61
  server connections, LANs, 305
  WAN design, 55–57
relationships, OSPF neighbors, 159
replicating unicast broadcasts, Frame Relay
    WANs, 64
replies, EIGRP, 210
resetting BGP sessions, 264
resilience
  BGP, 285
  flat WAN connections, 22
  hierarchical WANs, 52
  LANs, 308
    backbone, 344
  network design, 4
  WAN design, 55, 57
resource redundancy, LANs, 304
resources, hierarchical WANs, 45
reuse limits, BGP, 264

RIP (Routing Information Protocol), 145
  convergence, 147
  metrics, load balancing, 133
RIPv1, 145
RIPv2, 146
risk assessments, security policy
      development, 438
route aggregation, BGP, 290
route calculation algorithms, distance vector
      routing protocols, 132
route dampening, BGP, 263
route filtering
  BGP, 278-279
  hierarchical WANs, 42
  OSPF, 185
route maps
  EIGRP, 239
  OSPF, 185
route poisoning, 129
route processing, BGP, 263
route redistribution, OSPF, 186
route reflectors
  BGP, 292, 296
    clusters, 292–294
  IBGP, 260
route selection, BGP, 278
route summarization
  advantages, 138
  classful routing protocols, 124–125
  convergence, improved time, 137
  EIGRP, 232–233, 250
    automatic, 229
    bounding queries, 224
    improved convergence time, 137
    manual, 230–231
  flat WANs, 28
  hierarchical WANs, IP, 35–36
  IP addresses, 114–115
    bit boundaries, 120–121
    over-summarization, 117
    stringency in summarization, 117
    summary masks, 118–119
  longest prefix rule, 139
  network stability, 136
  OSPF, 153, 173, 198–199
    external, 202
    inter-area, 199–201
  sub-optimal routing, 139

routed backbone, LANs, 350–354
router hops, minimizing, hierarchical WAN
      costs, 38
router IDs, DR election process, OSPF, 167
router links, OSPF, 156
router overhead, dynamic routing over Frame
      Relay WANs, 73
routers
  increased overhead, flat WANs, 26
  memory problems, BGP, 263
  OSPF
    ABRs, 181–182
    ASBRs, 183–184
    backbone, 181
    internal, 181
routes, floating static. *See* floating static routes.
routing
  BGP
    asymmetrical, 289
    policy based, 282–283
    scalable AS, 290
  dynamic. *See* dynamic routes.
  EIGRP
    filtering, 239
    path determination, 239
    policy based, 226
  LANs
    segmentation, 321–324
  OSPF, external costs, 186
  static. *See* static routes.
routing loops, 130
  distance vector routing protocols, 127
  EIGRP, 239
  prevention, 129
routing metrics
  best path determination, 133
  limitations, 134
  OSPF, 161
routing policies, hierarchical WANs, 42
routing protocols
  classful, 124
  classless, 123
  convergence, 131
  distance vector, 122
  IP, 122–123
  link state, 123
  performance parameters, 125–127
  security, 142

routing tables
    Internet, BGP route optimization, 289
    IP. *See* IP routing tables.
    OSPF
        best paths, 155
        building, 155
        calculating, 161
        recalculating via SPF algorithm, 154
RSVP (Resource Reservation Protocol),
        VoIP/video, 103
RTP Reserve (Real Time Protocol),
        VoIP/video, 103

S

SAR (Segmentation And Reassembly), ATM
        WANs, 91
scalability
    AS routing, BGP, 290
    distance vector routing protocols, flat WANs, 26
    intermediate layer, hierarchical LANs, 342–343
    LANs, 309
        backbone, 347
    network design, 5
    OSPF, 152, 173, 249
        areas, 179
        link state database issues, 172
    routing protocols, 126
        hierarchical WANs, reduction in
                neighbors, 35
SCR (Sustainable Cell Rate), ATM WANs, 93
SecureID, 456
security, 142
    accounting, 457
    authentication, 457
    authorization, 457
    availability of data, 438
    confidentiality, 437
    device hardening, 476–477
    DKE, 451–452
    encryption, 449
        VPNs, 453
    external threats, 439
    firewalls, 461–462
        components, 464
        operations, 461
        policies, 467

impediment to data access, 436
integrity of data, 437
internal threats, 439
intrusion detection, IDSs, 454–455
IP address spoofing, 480
IPSec, 458–460
IPv6, 458
ISDN, 479
multi-channel protocols, 446–447
network design, 7
networks
    fiberoptics, 479
    malicious attacks, 478
    routing data, 478
packet filtering, 442–446
passwords, 456
policy development, 440
PSTNs, 479
RADIUS servers, 457
risk/vulnerability assessments, 438
SKE, 451
SNMP, 481
stateful packet filtering, 447
    random/changing port numbers, 448–449
static routes, 144
SYN flooding, 480
TACACS servers, 457
TCP three way handshakes, 444
Teardrop attacks, 481
security policies, hierarchical WANs, 42
segmentation
    LAN routing, 321–324
    LAN switching, 325–329
sequencing data, Multilink PPP WANs, 87
serial links, WANs, 60–62
    compression, 62–63
    IP Unnumbered feature, 63
    load balancing, 62
    redundancy, 61
serialization, VoIP, 102
server mirroring, LANs, 305
server-client traffic flow, LANs, 310
servers
    LANs
        centralization, 318–319
        locating, 316–318
    RADIUS, 457
    TACACS, 457
services, disabling, firewall policies, 471–472

sessions, BGP, resetting, 264
SIA (stuck in active), EIGRP, 220
simplicity of design, flat WANs, 23
site selection, hierarchical WANs, 45
SKE (single key encryption), 449–451
SNMP, security, 481
soft reconfiguration, BGP, 265
SPF algorithm,OSPF
    calculating routing table, 161
    recalculating routing table, 154
spf-delay time, OSPF, 163
split horizon
    Frame Relay WANs
        disabling, 65
        dynamic routing, 75
    routing protocols, 129
spoofing IP addresses, 480
stability, routing protocols, 127
stabilizing networks, route summarization, 136
STAC compression, PPP WANs, 86
stateful inspection, security packet filtering, 446
stateful packet filtering
    random/changing port numbers, 448–449
    security, 447
stateless inspection, packet filtering, 443
states, neighbor formation, OSPF, 160
static routes
    advantages, 143–144
    dialup connections, 144
    EIGRP, VLSM subnets, 227
    hierarchical WANs, 41
    ISDN WANs, 79
    security, 144
    stub networks, 143
    VLSM, 144
stub areas, OSPF, 188–189
stub networks, static routes, 143
sub-optimal routing
    EIGRP, adjusting administrative distances, 241
    route summarization, 139
subinterfaces
    ATM WANs, 89
    Frame Relay WANs, 65
subnet addresses, discontiguous networks, 135
subnet masks, IP addresses, 110–113
subnets
    flat WANs, fewer needed, 24
    IP addresses, 109–110

successors, EIGRP, 215
summary LSAs, OSPF, 157
summary masks, IP addresses, 118–119
summary routes, EIGRP, 240
supernetting, BGP, 290
support costs, network design, 8
suppress limits, BGP, 264
switched backbone, LANs, 350–354
switching
    LANs
        Ethernet, 311–312
        layer 3, 331–333
        layer 4, 334
        segmentation, 325–329
    Layer 3, hierarchical WANs, 40
SYN flooding, 480
synchronization, BGP, 261–262
synchronous serial links, WAN design, 60–62

T

TACACS servers (Terminal Access Controller
    Access Control System), 457
TCP (Transmission Control Protocol), three way
    handshakes, security, 444
tech support, hierarchical WANs, 45
telecom carriers, WAN design, cost issues, 53
three way handshakes, TCP security, 444
throttling, Frame Relay traffic shaping, 77
throughput, LAN backbone, 344
Tier-1
    ATM MAN site connections, 49
    hierarchical WANs, 31, 47–49
        bandwidth, 51
        minimizing overhead, 50
        policies, 51
        resilience, 52
Tier-2, hierarchical WANs, 31
    designing, 46
    functions, 44
    leased line aggregation, 33–34
    local users, 45
    resources, 45
    site selection, 45
    tect support, 45
    Tier-3 network connectivity resilience, 47

Tier-3 site support, 46
Tier-3 to Tier-1 resilience, 47
traffic capacity planning, 46
Tier-3, hierarchical WANs, 31
  networking functions and policies, 41
  preventing Tier-4 sites, 43
  route filtering, 42
  routing policies, 42
  security policies, 42
  static routes, 41
  Tier-1 resilience, 47
  Tier-2 network connectivity resilience, 47
  Tier-2 site support, 46
topologies
  Frame Relay WANs, 69
  LANs, 358, 360
topology table, EIGRP, 214-215
total burst rate. *See* EIR.
Totally Stubby Areas, OSPF, 190
traffic capacity planning, hierarchical WANs, 46
traffic management, Frame Relay WANs, 76
traffic prioritization, VoIP/video, 102
traffic shaping, Frame Relay WANs, 76
transitive attributes, BGP, 271
triggered updates, 129
troubleshooting ATM WANs, 93
types of LSAs, OSPF, 156–157

U

UBR (Unspecified Bit Rate), ATM WANs, 95
UDP (User Datagram Protocol), 445
unequal cost load balancing, 142, 225–226
update mechanisms, convergence, 131
updates
  BGP, 255
  EIGRP, 210
  routing protocol performance, 126
usage guidelines
  OSPF areas, 174–176
  OSPF stub areas, 188
utilization of bandwidth, hierachical WANs, 33

V

VBR (Variable Bit Rate), ATM WANs, 95
VCIs (Virtual Channel Identifiers), ATM WAN
      VCs, 90
VCs (Virtual Circuits), ATM WANs, 89
video
  ATM WANs, 100–101
  dial plans, 103–105
  QoS, 101–102
  queuing, 102
  serialization, 102
  traffic prioritization, 102
virtual links, OSPF, 193–194
  discontiguous areas, 196
  redudancy, 195
VLSM (Variable Length Subnet Masking), 135
  EIGRP, 227
    migration issues, 245
    static routes, 227
  flat WANs, 24
  OSPF, 197
  IP addresses, 111–113
  static routes, 144
VoIP (Voice over IP), 99
  ATM WANs, 100
  dial plans, 103–105
  Frame Relay WANs, 99
  QoS, 101–102
  queuing, 102
  serialization, 102
  traffic prioritization, 102
VPIs (Virtual Path Identifiers), ATM WAN
      VCs, 90
VPNs (Virtual Private Networks), 453
vulnerability assessments, security policy
      development, 438

W

WANs (Wide Area Networks)
  ATM
    ABR (Available Bit Rate), 95
    bandwidth, 89
    broadcasts, 90

CBR (Constant Bit Rate), 94
CDV (Cell Delay Variation), 94
cell tax, 91
CLR (Cell Loss Ratio), 94
CTD (Cell Transfer Delay), 94
dedundancy, 92
increased hop counts, 92
latency in hop counts, 92
OAM, 93
overhead, 91
PCR (Peak Cell Rate), 93
private, 97–98
PVCs, 90
QoS, 94–96
SAR (Segmentation And Reassembly), 91
SCR (Sustainable Cell Rate), 93
subinterfaces, 89
UBR (Unspecified Bit Rate), 95
VBR (Variable Bit Rate), 95
VCs, 89
designing, 18
bandwidth, 53–54
cost issues, 52
latency, 54
redundancy, 55–57
resilience, 55–57
serial links, 60–62
telecom carrier costs, 53
flat, 18–20
collapsed back to central site, 23
dual homing, 22
enterprise services, 20
factors behind leased line costs, 24
fewer PVCs, 24
fewer subnets, 24
minimal router hops, 23
resilient connections, 22
simplicity of design, 23
VLSM (Variable Length Subnet Masking), 24
Frame Relay
BECNs, 76
broadcast queuing, 78
broadcast replication, 64
CIR (Committed Information Rate), 76
Discard Eligible packets, 76–77
dual partial mesh, 69
dynamic routing, 72–75
EIR (Enhanced Information Rate), 76

FECNs, 76
full mesh, 71
hub and spoke, 68
meshing PVCs, 68
multipoint PVCs, 68
partial mesh, 69
point-to-point PVCs, 67
private implementations, 78
QoS, 77
queuing, 77
subinterfaces, 65
traffic management, 76
hierarchical, 20
broadcast control, 37
cost issues, 37
disaster recovery, 37
IP route summarization, 35–36
Layer 3 switching, 40
leased line aggregation, 32–34
leased linedistance reduction, 34
minimizing router hops, 38
NAT (Network Address Translation), 44
PVC aggregation, 33–34
reduced leased line distance, 34
reduction in core router ports, 35
scalable routing protocols and reduction in
neighbors, 35
Tier-1 sites, 31
Tier-2, 31, 44–45
Tier-3 sites, 31
ISDN, 79
bandwidth top-up, 62
dial backup, 83
distance vector routing protocols, 81
dynamic routes, 80
floating static routes, 82
Frame Relay backup redundancy, 82
interesting traffic, 82
line state changes, 84
link state routing protocols, 81
static routes, 79
Multilink PPP, 87
PPP, 86
serial links, 61–63
VoIP, 99, 101–102
Weight attribute, BGP, 273
well known attributes, BGP, 270
wiring closets, LANs, 308

INTERNATIONAL CONTACT INFORMATION

AUSTRALIA
McGraw-Hill Book Company Australia Pty. Ltd.
TEL +61-2-9417-9899
FAX +61-2-9417-5687
http://www.mcgraw-hill.com.au
books-it_sydney@mcgraw-hill.com

CANADA
McGraw-Hill Ryerson Ltd.
TEL +905-430-5000
FAX +905-430-5020
http://www.mcgrawhill.ca

GREECE, MIDDLE EAST,
NORTHERN AFRICA
McGraw-Hill Hellas
TEL +30-1-656-0990-3-4
FAX +30-1-654-5525

MEXICO (Also serving Latin America)
McGraw-Hill Interamericana Editores S.A. de C.V.
TEL +525-117-1583
FAX +525-117-1589
http://www.mcgraw-hill.com.mx
fernando_castellanos@mcgraw-hill.com

SINGAPORE (Serving Asia)
McGraw-Hill Book Company
TEL +65-863-1580
FAX +65-862-3354
http://www.mcgraw-hill.com.sg
mghasia@mcgraw-hill.com

SOUTH AFRICA
McGraw-Hill South Africa
TEL +27-11-622-7512
FAX +27-11-622-9045
robyn_swanepoel@mcgraw-hill.com

UNITED KINGDOM & EUROPE
(Excluding Southern Europe)
McGraw-Hill Publishing Company
TEL +44-1-628-502500
FAX +44-1-628-770224
http://www.mcgraw-hill.co.uk
computing_neurope@mcgraw-hill.com

ALL OTHER INQUIRIES Contact:
Osborne/McGraw-Hill
TEL +1-510-549-6600
FAX +1-510-883-7600
http://www.osborne.com
omg_international@mcgraw-hill.com